Understanding Capitalism

Understanding Capitalism

Competition, Command, and Change in the U.S. Economy

Samuel Bowles
Richard Edwards
University of Massachusetts, Amherst

HARPER & ROW, PUBLISHERS, New York
Cambridge, Philadelphia, San Francisco,
London, Mexico City, São Paulo, Singapore, Sydney

Sponsoring Editor: David Forgione
Project Editor: Ronni Strell
Text Design Adaptation: Michel Craig
Original Text Design: Frances Torbert Tilley
Cover Design: CATED Associates/Graphic Designers
Cover: Mondrian, "Composition avec rouge, jaune et bleu, 1930."
Private Collection, Zurich. Giraudon/Art Resource. Courtesy,
SPADEM.
Text Art: Vantage Art, Inc.
Production: Debi Forrest Bochner
Compositor: Ruttle, Shaw & Wetherill, Inc.
Printer and Binder: R. R. Donnelley & Sons Company

Understanding Capitalism: Competition, Command, and Change in the U.S. Economy

Library of Congress Cataloging in Publication Data

Bowles, Samuel.
   Understanding capitalism.

   Includes index.
   1. Economics. 2. Capitalism. 3. United States—
Economic conditions. I. Edwards, Richard, 1944–
II. Title.
HB171.5.B6937 1985   330.12′2   84-21729
ISBN 0-06-040897-9

85 86 87 88 9 8 7 6 5 4 3 2 1

CONTENTS

PREFACE

Understanding Capitalism is an introductory text designed for use in either microeconomics, macroeconomics, or single-semester micro- and macroeconomics courses. It may also be used as a supplement or as a contrasting text in courses using neoclassical approaches to economics, or in interdisciplinary courses in the social sciences.

Understanding Capitalism introduces what we call "three-dimensional economics," a new view of economics and of the U.S. economy. Our subtitle, *Competition, Command, and Change in the U.S. Economy* indicates the tri-partite focus of this approach:

competition and choice through market interactions

command and the exercise of power in markets, within firms, and in the society as a whole

change in the basic institutions that govern economic life, viewed both theoretically and historically as an ongoing process.

Part One, "Competition, Command, and Change," introduces three-dimensional economics and explains its relationship to other approaches. Its roots in the Keynesian, Schumpeterian, and Marxian traditions are described.

Part Two, "Capitalism and Class," develops the concepts and introduces the facts necessary for the study of the capitalist economy.

Part Three, "Microeconomics: Markets and Power," develops the theory of the firm and of markets, including the labor market, and analyzes technological change. The approach adopts a Schumpeterian model of dynamic monopolistic and oligopolistic competition. Most important, it develops an analysis of profits and the profit rate that is used throughout the remainder of the book, providing the integrating principle of three-dimensional economics, and the link between the microeconomic and the macroeconomic analysis. Those using the text for a primarily macroeconomic approach might wish to pass over Chapters 7 through 10. However, a careful reading of Chapter 6 (on the profit rate) is essential.

Part Four, "Macroeconomics: Instability and Growth," develops an aggregate model of an open international economy in which unemployment is a more-or-less permanent feature of labor markets and plays an important regulatory role of the macroeconomy. A chapter on the government and the economy is included, as well as an analysis of the past three decades of boom and stagflation in the U.S. economy. Those using the text for a primarily microeconomic approach may want to eliminate Part Four, although Chapter 14, on the postwar U.S. economy, may be read without difficulty by those who have not studied the preceding macroeconomic chapters and may be of general interest.

Part Five, "American Capitalism: Promise and Performance," introduces the reader to the evaluation of the performance of the U.S. economy along the dimensions of three values: fairness, efficiency, and democracy.

Each of the three major sections (Two, Three, and Four) concludes with a chapter using the concepts developed in the preceding chapters to analyze the historical evolution of the basic structures of the U.S. economy.

The list of variables used, the glossary, the definitions of terms placed in the text margins, and the clear descriptions that accompany each figure in the text will assist readers in mastering the basic language and analytical tools of economics. The boxes in the text raise many issues and present facts that are ideal for classroom discussion materials.

The index (prepared by Marc Kitchell, of the University of Massachusetts) will assist the reader in locating key concepts and other material. An instructor's manual (written by Manuel Pastor, of Occidental College) offers model lesson plans, theoretical elaboration, additional readings, test and discussion questions, and teaching tips based on extensive classroom experience with the material presented in the text.

Understanding Capitalism presents an approach to teaching about economics and the economy that we have developed over the past decade in our introductory economics courses at the University of Massachusetts. To the thousands of students and dozens of teaching assistants whose criticism, suggestions, enthusiasm, and, sometimes, indifference have guided us, we owe special thanks.

Our most profound debt is to James Crotty, our colleague at the University of Massachusetts, with whom we began writing this book some years ago. His acceptance of the time-consuming responsibility of chair of our department made it impossible for him to continue as a coauthor, but his contributions are present in all aspects of the book, from the overall conception to the treatment of particulars.

Others, at universities throughout the country and beyond its borders, have read drafts and given the kind of advice that only outstanding teachers and researchers can offer. Thomas Weisskopf, of the University of Michigan, gave us exceptionally detailed comments on the entire text, resulting in many improvements; Robert Buchele, of Smith College, Gerald Epstein, of the New School for Social Research, and Andrew Glyn, of Oxford University also read the entire text and commented extensively.

Others offered their expertise on particular sections: Eileen Appelbaum, of Temple University; Peter Dorman, of the University of Massachusetts; Jack Edwards, of the College of William and Mary; Alfred Eichner, of Rutgers University; David M. Gordon, of the New School for Social Research; Carol Heim, of the University of Massachusetts; Jeanne Hahn, of Evergreen State College; Robert Haveman, of the University of Wisconsin; E. K. Hunt, of the University of Utah; Laurence Kahn, of the University of Illinois; David Kotz, of the University of Massachusetts; Frances Moore Lappé, of the Institute for Food and Development Policy; Arthur MacEwan, of the University of Massachusetts (Boston); Leonard Rapping, of the University of Massachusetts; Thomas Riddell, of Smith College; Michael Reich, of the University of California; Juliet Schor, of Harvard University; William Shepherd, of the University of Michigan; Charles Wilber, of Notre Dame University; and Robert Sutcliffe, of the London Polytechnic University.

Peter Alexander, Suzanne Bergeron, Jenny Cashman, Lisa Kroeber, Isobel Taylor, and Meg Worcester provided invaluable assistance in preparing the manuscript.

Our editors at Harper & Row, David Forgione, Jack Greenman, and Ronnie Strell advised and guided us with skill and insight.

We owe special thanks to all of those—too numerous to mention and cumbersome to footnote in an introductory text—whose research and insight have guided us.

Samuel Bowles
Richard Edwards

PART ONE

COMPETITION, COMMAND, AND CHANGE

CHAPTER 1

CAPITALISM SHAKES THE WORLD

The capitalist age is like no other. During the relatively short life of capitalism—short, historically speaking—the world has changed more quickly, more constantly, and more profoundly than during any period before. Moreover, the pace of change appears to be quickening, so we can expect further dramatic change in our lifetimes.

Capitalism, as we will see in detail later, is an economic system in which employers hire workers to produce goods and services with the intention of making a profit.

Where this economic system has taken root, it has left no aspect of society unchanged: there have been revolutionary improvements in our consumption standards, changes in our family life, technological breakthroughs, realignments of power, redistributions of wealth, and changes in our ideals and beliefs.

Since we have lived with such changes all our lives, we tend to think of the changes, and even the very process of change, as being natural, normal, and mostly beneficial. Yet from historical comparison we can see that this rapid and unremitting alteration of our social and physical world is anything but typical. Inertia, not change, has been the byword of most earlier economic systems. And we shall see that rapid social change brings progress, but it also imposes great costs.

The *capitalist epoch* began around A.D. 1500, when capitalist organization of work first appeared in parts of England, the Low Countries, and Italy. Initially capitalism affected few people, even

Capitalism is the prevailing economic system in the United States, Western Europe, Japan, and some eighty other countries.

The **capitalist epoch** began in some parts of Europe around A.D. 1500 when capitalist organization of labor processes first appeared. It continues to the present in much of the world.

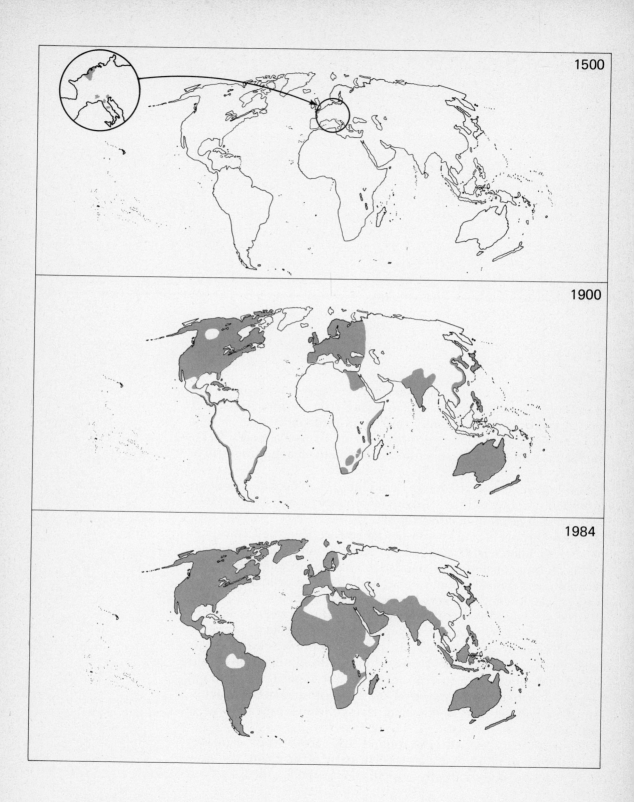

1500

1900

1984

FIGURE 1.1 Capitalism spreads across the world. The shaded portions in the three maps show areas in which capitalism had come to be the dominant economic system by 1500, 1900, and the present. The growth from 1500 to 1900 covered the globe (most of it occurred between 1800 and 1900). Since 1900 capitalism has ceased to be the dominant economic system in China, the Soviet Union, Eastern Europe, Cuba, and other areas.

in the countries where it first appeared, but as capitalist organization spread and became stronger, its impact likewise grew. It would eventually revolutionize the world.

The development of capitalism, and the social changes which it brought, occurred at different times in different places, and its impact was highly uneven. In some places development occurred quickly, in other places very slowly. Capitalism had become the dominant economic system in Britain by the beginning of the nineteenth century. In the United States, capitalism triumphed by the middle of that century, a victory confirmed by the destruction of the slaveholders' power in the Civil War. In some regions of the world, capitalism is only now replacing precapitalist economic systems. In other countries—Russia and China for example—capitalism had gained a foothold only in the big cities, and it was subsequently replaced by another economic system. Figure 1.1 shows the spread of capitalism around the world, from its beginnings to its high point prior to World War I to the present.

Consider for a moment what life was like at the dawn of the capitalist age, say in the year 1500. Through most of the world, in Asia, Africa, and the Americas as well as in Europe, most people lived in humble circumstances. They had short lifespans; they had virtually no experience with places or people further than the nearby village or town; and they depended almost entirely on food and other goods they grew or made themselves or obtained locally in exchange for other things which they grew or made. They lived in societies in which little had changed since the time of their parents, their grandparents—indeed, since the time of earlier generations now gone and long forgotten. Although around the world these people demonstrated remarkable diversity in how they organized their societies, most were only dimly aware of this diversity, for they lived out their lives in their own small localities.

The dynamism unleashed by the growth of capitalism in Europe has everywhere disrupted the world that existed in 1500. Europeans explored the other continents, "discovering" the New World. Traders and colonists, mainly financed by investors seeking easy and fabulous riches, quickly began encroaching upon the indigenous peoples in Virginia and Peru and South Africa and China.

Perhaps the greatest change is the world population explosion. As Figure 1.2 shows, the number of people in the world changed very slowly from 8000 B.C. until the eighteenth century or so. But since then, the curve changes as population shoots up. From A.D. 1 to 1750, the population grew at a slow rate (0.56 per thousand annual growth); at that rate it took 1200 years for the population to double. Between 1750 and 1950, it grew at a faster rate (about 5.7 per thousand), one that doubled the population every 120 years. After 1950, the population grew so quickly (about 17.1 per thousand) that it doubles roughly every 40 years. As Figure 1.2 shows, this population boom is simply without precedent in human history. Such rapid population growth is a new social phenomenon, characteristic only of the capitalist epoch. While in recent years population growth has slowed down in the United States and some other countries, it continues to accelerate in other countries.

This population boom can be seen in the data for Great Britain, the first capitalist country. Britain's population growth (unlike that of the United States) was fueled mainly by internal growth rather than by migration. As we see in Figure 1.3, Britain's population, despite ups and downs, remained relatively small and constant for centuries, until the dawn of capitalism. Population began growing after about 1500, but the huge, spectacular increases occurred after 1800—when capitalism became the dominant economic system. Between 1800 and 1980 the population increased sixfold. Only recently has the population again stabilized.

And while new populations were being created, whole other populations were being destroyed; still others were transported long distances. The Indian populations of North America were

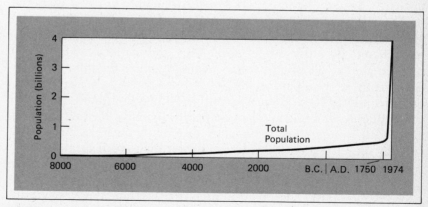

FIGURE 1.2 World population growth. The total population of the world grew very slowly for most of the past 10,000 years. Population started growing rapidly in a few countries a couple of centuries ago, but the *world* population explosion began in the present century. The growth of world population continues, but since the 1970s at a slightly reduced pace (not shown in figure).

Source: "Human Population, a Symposium," *Scientific American* 231, Sept. 1974, pp. 30–62.

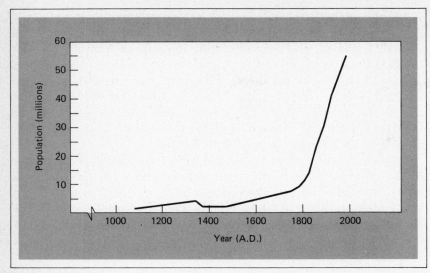

FIGURE 1.3 Population of Britain, the world's first capitalist country. The population of Britain did not grow much until the beginnings of capitalism in the sixteenth century. The decline in population between 1300 and 1450 was due in large part to bubonic plague. Since the sixteenth century, population has grown very rapidly, only leveling off in recent years.

Source: *Cambridge Economic History of Europe, Volume VII*, and Brian Murphy, *A History of the British Economy, 1086–1970.*

virtually eliminated, the remnants driven to remote territories. Millions of Africans—conservative estimates suggest at least 10 million, others say perhaps 100 million—were transported in chains from their own communities across the seas to slavery (or, for as many as half who did not survive the crossing, to a watery grave). Chinese and (Asian) Indians, conscripted under conditions little different from slavery, were shipped to faraway places—the Chinese to build railroads in North America, the Indians to build railroads in East and South Africa.

Other populations "voluntarily" chose to migrate long distances, often because they found their traditional livelihoods destroyed by the changes at home. Irish who had been excluded from productive farming land; Germans escaping from political repression, the decline of agriculture, or the demise of their craft occupations at the hands of new capitalist factories; Poles, Italians, Greeks, Jews, Hungarians, Russians—all found need to move. It matters little whether we say that they moved because of the "pull" of new opportunities that awaited them or whether they were "pushed" by circumstances at home so desperate that they were no longer tolerable. What is important is that vast, almost unimaginable change entered their lives: disruption, new possibilities, destruction of the known and opening of the unknown.

These changes have accelerated and spread in more recent times. A glance at occupations, to take but one dimension, makes the change apparent. The overwhelming majority of Americans living in 1800 were food producers of one sort or another: independent farmers, food-producing slaves, fishermen, and so forth. Today, by contrast, in the United States about 2 percent of the population farms, and another 12 to 14 percent work in food processing industries, producing enough food for the other 85 percent of the people (with a large surplus left to export).

As people left or were forced out of farming, another dimension of the change became apparent: *urbanization,* or the growth of cities. Instead of being scattered around the countryside, with only a tiny fraction living in cities, people were drawn into urban areas. In 1800, only 6 percent of Americans lived in towns or cities with more than 2500 people. Today, 74 percent live in such urban areas. London's population, only 70,000 in 1500, grew to 600,000 by 1700 and approached three-quarters of a million in 1800, making it the biggest English-speaking city in the world. Philadelphia, the second largest in 1800, had 60,000 people. Today, London has a population of 8 million, while metropolitan New York has nearly 10 million, and metropolitan Mexico City has 15 million.

This period also witnessed a series of scientific and technological revolutions. In 1500, goods were made almost entirely by hand, using simple tools; power machinery was limited to the water wheel that turned the miller's grinding stone. People's understanding of how the physical world worked was rudimentary: Good harvests and bad, births and deaths were often understood in terms of magic, superstition, or "God's will." As late as 1800, traditional craft production, using ancient skills handed down from generation to generation, prevailed in virtually all lines of work. But the new era brought new ideas, new discoveries, new methods, and new machines in every field of science and technology, making old ideas and old tools obsolete. And the new ways were in turn made obsolete by yet newer ones.

Developments in the field of transportation are perhaps as dramatic and revealing as any. In the year 1500, moving either people or freight overland was arduous, costly, slow, and highly uncertain; transport was by walking or wagon, the latter pulled by people or occasionally by livestock. For all but the most wealthy, travel beyond a few miles from home was virtually impossible, and freight was so expensive that it did not pay to send anything other than the most valuable and lightweight goods, such as spices and silks. Water transport on rivers or along the coasts was better, but ships were small, slow, and unsafe. Few advances had been made over what was available to the Romans 1000 years earlier.

Within a century, sea transport was greatly improved. Ships regularly crossed the Atlantic or negotiated the Cape of Good Hope on the East Indies route. Within three centuries, by 1800, clipper ships raced from China to London in 80 days, from New York to San Francisco in 22 days, and the Atlantic crossing had become almost routine. Within four centuries steam power replaced sails, and the construction of the Suez Canal (and soon thereafter the Panama Canal) greatly shortened world trade routes. Before the end of capitalism's fifth century, oil tankers, each carrying 2500 times the cargo of Columbus's ship, clogged the shipping arteries of the world and outgrew all but the largest and deepest natural harbors. Today those who can pay the price of a Concorde ticket now jet from Paris to New York, overtaking the sun and arriving "earlier" than they left.

Land transport was revolutionized as well. First, inland canals were dug, chopping the costs of overland haulage. Then in the mid-1800s came the railroads, further cutting the time and cost of moving goods or people. By 1900 tracks crisscrossed all the world's great industrial areas and even penetrated the vast Russian steppes, the Chinese hinterland, the East African highlands, the Canadian Rockies, and the North Indian plain. Yet all this was but prelude to the great twentieth-century land transport revolution based on automobiles and trucks, which in turn eclipsed the railroads.

These enormous advances in transportation were matched by developments in communications, in the manufacture of steel or textiles, in medicine, in hybrid varieties of corn and rice, in insecticides, in the discovery and production of toxic chemicals, and in the improvement of weaponry to the point where it is quite possible to destroy humanity itself. In all these areas, technical and productive advances have occurred so quickly and so profoundly that there is simply no precedent in human history.

These vast technical changes were accompanied by parallel changes for people. People's incomes and consumption levels rose; they did not always rise steadily, but over long periods the growth was substantial. Between 1800 and 1950, for instance, the buying power of the average income in the United States probably increased fifteenfold. Diets changed, meats assuming a larger place on the dinner table. Housing also changed as people moved to cities and ideas of privacy altered.

The way people earned their livelihoods changed as well. At the dawn of the capitalist era, most families consumed what they produced or what they obtained by exchanging their produce. With the rise of capitalism, people increasingly became dependent upon employment; that is, on getting a job working for someone else. They likewise became subject to the dangers and hardships of unemployment. Unemployment, when there were no alternative employments available, left families and even whole regions destitute and desperate. It became a capitalist form of plague, potentially hitting at anyone who was not independently wealthy, and therefore threatening and creating insecurity for almost everyone.

Similarly, such rapid change made even the most skilled workers vulnerable, as technological changes steadily rendered their skills obsolete. Workers might have spent arduous years learning their skills, but new production processes could make them useless almost overnight. Iron makers in the nineteenth century, for instance, progressed through long apprenticeships, learning exactly how much to heat the iron and how to process it; when steel making rather abruptly replaced iron manufacture, the skilled iron makers were obsolete, their distress part of the "social costs" to be paid for technological progress.

The changes also transformed working conditions. Increasingly workers found employment in the huge factories and mills, in circumstances where dangerous machinery, poor lighting and intense heat, long hours, and the pressure to produce quickly combined to make such jobs hazardous and exhausting. The ranks of the wounded from industrial accidents mounted like the casualties on a battlefield.

Nothing was untouched by this dynamic economic system: Time itself changed. Precapitalist lives tended to follow natural time, marked by the passing of the seasons or the movement of the sun across the sky. Individual work tasks could be performed irregularly, when the person doing the work wanted to, with periods of high work effort and periods of rest. The work pattern could follow the natural rhythms of the worker, or it might be dictated by the harsh natural rhythms of the weather. But in capitalist employment, labor was paid for by the hour and work tasks were defined in terms of milliseconds by time and motion studies. Starting and stopping time, lunch breaks, even coffee breaks and "toilet time" came to be measured in minutes. Clock time supplanted natural time. Clocks appeared on public buildings, in schoolrooms, at factory gates, and even on people's wrists. "Time is money," Benjamin Franklin said 200 years ago, previewing what was to come. A machine pace, steady and unremitting, became the ideal for work, and workers, having escaped the rigors of nature, were increasingly pressured to accommodate their rhythms to the machine.

Social and family life have also been transformed in the capitalist era. The household as a social and productive unit has been reshaped, emptied of its functions, and nearly eliminated. Previously a family of three generations and several married couples might live within a stone's throw of each other or even under the same roof, often sharing tasks and meals. By the mid-twentieth century the typical household had been reduced to a nuclear family (married couple with their children), with grandparents living in a nursing or retirement home, and brothers and sisters scattered throughout the country. In the late twentieth century, divorce, improved birth control, abortion, increasing numbers of couples who choose not to get married, greater longevity, and other factors have changed the nuclear family, further moving people away from the traditional household. Households are much smaller now, averaging fewer than three people. By 1981, American "households" composed of one or more single persons were quite common. There was one such "nonfamily household" for every 2.2 married couples. Thirty years earlier there had been over seven married couples for every "nonfamily household."

At the same time, many of the customary functions of the family have been removed from the family's domain and been replaced by goods or services purchased in the market or provided by government. Production activities like making clothes and preparing and preserving food are now done in factories and elsewhere. The people now doing these jobs outside the home are often the very women (or their grandchildren) who once worked in the kitchens or at the home loom. Rearing children, providing education and medical care to family members, and other tasks also have been entrusted to the care of outside professionals.

Finally, the family finds itself in a greatly changed social network. Once, families tended to live in one community from generation to generation, with skills and occupations being passed from parents to children and each family having an acknowledged and often hierarchically ordered place in that community. Today few families remain in one spot from generation to generation. Many are forced to move in search of work. Indeed, it is common for families to move several times even within one generation, thereby further diminishing the remaining bonds of community. Over a five-year period, about half of the people in the United States move. As a result, families cannot draw as much upon their neighborhood communities for support or assistance. This further contributes to their use of purchased services and government assistance. The day-care center and the babysitter have taken over for grandmother or older children.

As population and production for profit soared, so too has the use and destruction of our natural environment. The strains placed on basic ecological systems like water, air, soil, and weather are vastly beyond any in prior human experience. For instance, in 1983 the U.S. government warned that pollutants now being added to the atmosphere are creating a global "greenhouse" effect; the world is, as a result, being warmed up, with incalculable consequences: possible melting of the polar ice caps, rising sea levels that may put large coastal areas under water, changing climates and rain patterns that may destroy the world's prime food-growing areas. It is speculated that by the year 2100 New York City may have the climate now experienced by Daytona Beach, Florida—if, that is, rising sea levels do not obliterate the city.

The list of fundamental environmental changes seems endless. The atmosphere's ozone layer, which protects us from the cancer-causing ultraviolet rays of the sun, is being depleted. Acid rain is destroying forests and killing life in lakes. Nuclear wastes, which must be stored "safely" for hundreds of thousands of years, are routinely produced. The tropical jungles, which are the earth's main way of keeping the balance between oxygen and carbon dioxide in the atmosphere, are being cut down. Virtually all of the earth's major rivers are being polluted. The oceans themselves, through oil spills, the dumping of toxic or radioactive chemicals, and routine discharges from tankers and industrial plants, are being spoiled. Toxic chemicals are leaking into the earth's groundwater, the last major source of pure drinking water. Increasing numbers of animal and plant species are being rendered extinct. Insecticides and herbicides are poisoning prime farming soils, and vast areas of farmland are destroyed through urban development. And on and on and on. These changes in our physical world, when considered individually and especially when taken all together, promise a scale of destruction simply unknown and unknowable.

Government and people's relation to government have also been altered. In 1500 most of what was to become the capitalist world was ruled by some type of despotic ruler, with kings or emperors basing the claim to rule on God's will or hereditary right. Moreover, typically there were few ways in which ordinary people could protect themselves from the arbitrary powers of such rulers.

Hereditary rulers were challenged by the British revolutions of the seventeenth century and the great American and French revolutions of the eighteenth century. These revolutions established the vital precedent of "consent of the governed," although it was usually only property-owning white males who could vote. But these revolutions placed important limitations on absolute rulers. They were followed by written constitutions, widespread white male suffrage, elimination of property qualifications for voting, and extension of the franchise to females and minorities. In the nineteenth and twentieth centuries, largely as a result of intense, lengthy struggles by workers, women's suffragists, antislavery groups, and others, all the major capitalist countries participated in the growth of democratic government.

But while government in some countries has become more democratically accountable, everywhere it has also become more intrusive. In the twentieth century, great centralized bureaucracies have assumed enormous power. Governments have attained greater power to invade the privacy and influence the sentiments of the citizenry. Governments have assumed major responsibility for the rearing and schooling of children. The modern citizen is more influenced by centralized government policy than were the humble subjects of even the great Sun King, Louis XIV of France two-and-a-half centuries ago.

In all these ways and more, then, the capitalist epoch has been a time of enormous, unprecedented social change. The world and the world's people have been remade, as virtually all the old patterns of life and livelihood were disrupted and reconstructed. No aspect of life has been untouched by this great rolling force of change.

☐ Suggested Readings

Carlo Cipolla, *Economic History of World Population* (Baltimore: Penguin Books, 1964).

Maurice Dobb, *Studies in the Development of Capitalism* (New York: International Publishers, 1947).

David Landes, *Revolution in Time: Clocks and the Making of the Modern World* (Cambridge, Mass.: Harvard University Press, 1983).

Barrington Moore, *The Social Origins of Dictatorship and Democracy* (Boston: Beacon Press, 1966).

Eric Wolf, *Europe and the People Without History* (Berkeley, Calif.: University of California Press, 1982).

CHAPTER 2

A THREE-DIMENSIONAL APPROACH TO ECONOMICS

Understanding capitalism has become essential for anyone who reads the newspaper, watches the nightly news, listens to political candidates, or simply wonders why it's so hard to find a good job or pay one's bills. Since capitalism is an economic system, understanding capitalism requires that you understand economics. But what *kind* of economics should you understand?

This question would have seemed surprising a decade ago. Until quite recently economics was presented as a science, a unified body of knowledge on which, minor disagreements aside, virtually all economists agreed. Experts (economists) *knew* it, you had to *learn* it. But now economists disagree. There exist many different approaches to economics, and these different approaches come to differing, often directly opposite conclusions.

This book presents one way of thinking about economics, what is generally termed *political economy* or what we call the "three-dimensional approach to economics." Political economists believe that the approach presented here makes more sense, is a more useful way of understanding our economy than its chief competitor, the *neoclassical,* or "conventional," approach to economics found in many introductory textbooks. But ultimately you must judge whether this approach or some other kind of economics makes the most sense to you.

What is certain is that you should not accept one kind of economics because that is what some experts believe. You must choose for yourself. You must ask: "Does this make sense to me?" "Does this help me understand things I have experienced or believe to be true?"

This is not to say that any opinion about economics is equally valid. A useful approach to economics, whether it be political economy or any other kind of economics, must be logical, internally consistent, and in accord with what we know about economic reality ("the facts").

This chapter explains the principal elements of the three-dimensional approach to economics.

The main idea of this chapter is that political economy considers all three dimensions of economic life: competition, command, and change.

This main idea is expressed in four main points:

1. Capitalism is an *economic* system.
2. Every economic system can be analyzed in terms of three dimensions: a horizontal dimension (*competition*); a vertical dimension (*command*); and a time dimension (*change*).
3. Political economy, like all social theories, incorporates certain values; in the case of political economy, these values are *efficiency, fairness,* and *democracy.*
4. Political economy is a theoretical approach to economics based on ideas contributed by many economists; among the most important contributors were *Karl Marx, Joseph Schumpeter,* and *John Maynard Keynes.*

Each of the concepts introduced in this chapter reappears throughout the analysis developed in later chapters. In Chapters 3 through 14, we investigate *how* capitalism works; in Chapter 15 we evaluate *how well* it works.

□ Economic Systems and Capitalism

Human societies have developed a number of different economic systems: slavery, self-sufficient households, capitalism, tribal commonwealths, state socialism, feudalism, and many others.

What all these systems have in common—what makes them *economic* systems—is that they are ways of organizing the human labor which in all societies is needed to produce the goods and services which support life. Economic systems organize *how* work is done, *what* work is done, and *how the resulting products are used.*

Economic systems are fundamentally *relationships among people.* These relationships may be direct, face-to-face relationships, such as when you buy an orange from a small grocer; they may be relationships extending around the globe, as when an Iowa farmer produces grain that will later appear as bread on a table in Egypt; they may also be institutional relationships, expressed through laws, customs and beliefs, politics, corporations, and even the

An **economic system** is a set of relationships among people that organize labor processes that all societies need to sustain life.

language we use. These relationships are affected by the physical things and by the types of technologies used in production. They are shaped by a wide variety of other influences, including geography, custom, religion, and whether production is agricultural or industrial. Still, the *social* relationships among economic actors—employer and worker, consumer and seller—are what an economic system is all about.

How human work is organized differs from one economic system to another. To understand how work is organized in any particular society we must investigate its economic system. In this book we mainly consider the predominant economic system of the United States—capitalism.

We will not define capitalism as yet—we will do that in Chapter 3—but it is familiar enough. It is the economic system not only of the United States but also of Great Britain, Japan, Chile, France, Brazil, West Germany, South Africa, and, in one form or another, of about 80 other countries. Thus, we need not study capitalism at second hand, because we experience it every day.

In a capitalist economic system, most goods and services are produced at the direction of employers (called businessmen, capitalists, or entrepreneurs) who seek to make *profits* by selling the goods and services on markets. Most people in capitalist economies work for someone else (their employers) and receive a *wage* or *salary* in return. So *work* is organized for profit; the capitalist or his appointed manager, not the workers, is the boss at the work place; and goods, services, and people's time (labor) are exchanged through *markets*.

To understand capitalism, we must learn answers to the following questions: How is work organized? How do markets work? What determines how much goes to profits and how much to wages? What determines which technologies will be in use? Why do some workers get paid more than others?

Neoclassical or **conventional economics** is a theory of capitalism emphasizing the horizontal dimension of markets and voluntary exchange.

One view of capitalism, that of neoclassical or "conventional" economics, is that capitalism is like a machine. The main parts of the machine are markets. Individuals—consumers buying goods, businessmen selling goods, employers buying labor services, workers selling labor time, and so on—come together in these markets and trade. Economics, according to the conventional view, is thus essentially a story about how markets work, and how a market system (the machine) works.

Two aspects of this conventional approach are particularly important. First, exchanges on markets are presumed to be *voluntary;* no one is forced to buy or sell anything unless he or she *chooses* to do so. In the conventional view, then, concepts such as command, deprivation, domination, power, coercion, authority, and force have no place in a theory of the market system (except as lapses from the market ideal). Competition is not only a central theme, it is almost the only theme of the conventional view.

Second, the machine continues to work without any change in its basic design. It may need repair or replacement parts from time to time, but basically the machine (capitalism) remains unaffected by its own operation: it is relatively trouble free and not very accident prone. The remaining few bugs in its operation are fairly easily programmed out of existence. Moreover, the machine does not change itself; if it changes, it does so because of something outside of itself.

This is a very limited view of capitalism. It is one-dimensional, focusing on competition and voluntary exchange in markets, and it leaves out two other basic dimensions: command and change. The analysis of capitalism presented in this book is called "political economy" or "three-dimensional economics."

☐ Three-Dimensional Economics

The relationships making up any economic system may be analyzed in terms of three dimensions: competition, command, and change.

Competition. The first or horizontal dimension is called *competition,* and it refers to that aspect of economic relationships in which voluntary exchange plays the most important part. In capitalism, competition occurs primarily through the mechanism of markets (and elections—more on that later). For instance, when a motorist chooses to buy gasoline at one rather than other gas stations, he or she is exercising what we can all recognize as choice among competing suppliers.

This dimension is called "horizontal" because competition tends to be created when a relative equality of power exists among those offering the choices. In the gas station example above, the sellers of gasoline must compete with each other to entice the motorist; gas dealers are formally equal, and none can dictate to the others (or to the motorist) where the motorist will buy the gasoline.

Political economy shares with conventional economics an emphasis on the competition dimension as essential to understanding our economy. When, as in capitalism, much of economic life is organized through markets—as opposed, say, to simply following traditional patterns, or being planned by a central bureaucracy—choice through competition is necessarily given wide scope.

Command. The second dimension is called *command,* and it refers to that aspect of economic relationships in which power, coercion, hierarchy, and being a subordinate or superior come into play. For person *A* to command person *B, A* must have power over

Political economy is a theory that analyzes capitalism in terms of the three dimensions of competition, command, and change.
Competition, or the horizontal dimension in economics, refers to aspects of economic relationships in which voluntary exchange and choice play the predominant role.

Command, or the vertical dimension in economics, refers to aspects of economic relationships in which power plays the predominant role.

B in some way. In capitalist societies, command is a central aspect of the workplace, of the household, of the government, and of relations among different groups in society, especially among classes, among races, between men and women, and among nations.

The command dimension is called "vertical" because it necessarily involves people or groups who are unequal, one being "higher up" than the other. One person or group is "on top"; the other is "subordinate." The opposite of command is choice.

Distinguishing choice from command is not always easy. Suppose a thief points a gun at your head and demands, "Your money or your life!" This is *literally* a choice. You could presumably choose either to surrender your life or your money. Yet we all recognize this as *in fact* a command to hand over your money. Similarly, when a boss orders a worker to do *X*, we can recognize his order as a command, for the alternative to carrying out the order may be getting fired.

In most cases, as we see in later chapters, choice and command are combined. Usually we cannot say an economic relationship is entirely one of choice or one of command.

The most common pattern is one in which someone uses power (the essential ingredient of command) to influence or shape the conditions under which another person will be making a choice. The thief with the gun obviously has used his power (possessing the gun) to create a situation in which the other person's "choice" is almost automatic.

Corporations do something similar (though with a vast difference in the degree of direct coercion) when they advertise their products: They seek to use their financial resources (power) to alter the conditions under which consumers will be making choices. If, for instance, an aspirin producer's TV commercials can convince consumers that its product is "stronger," works "faster," or is "recommended by most doctors," then when consumers reach the aspirin counter, they will tend to choose this product more frequently. Power (command) has been used to shape or condition choice.

Change, or the time dimension in economics, refers to the historical evolution of economic systems.

Change. The third dimension of economic systems is called *change.* It refers to the way in which the operation of an economic system changes the system itself. In capitalism, change occurs because big profits can be made by changing the way things are: building new and better machines, designing novel products to meet needs that we may not even have been aware of, expanding production, building factories in distant corners of the world. Central to the changefulness of capitalism is the system of investment for profit which creates a tendency for capitalism to expand. By expanding, capitalism alters its environment. Expansion may also transform the way capitalism itself works.

Change is called the "time" dimension because change is a process that occurs through time. It necessarily involves thinking in terms of "before" and "after" or "early" and "late."

More generally, emphasizing the change dimension of economics forces us to remember that each economic system works differently at different points in time. Each has a history, and the way that that system functions at any particular time depends in part on its

Economics, Politics, and History

Economics is the study of how people interact with one another and with their natural surroundings to produce their livelihoods. As the three-dimensional approach to economics stresses, these interactions are not limited to the process of competition and market exchange that forms the central focus of conventional economics.

The vertical dimension—command—brings in the question of power. Conventional economists would like to banish power from economic models and leave it for political scientists to study. Abba Lerner, a prominent conventional economist, once commented that economics had become the "queen" of the social sciences by focusing on those political problems that had already been solved. When the political problems have already been solved, the ensuing relations are expressed in contracts and market exchange. Three-dimensional economics is not limited to "solved political problems." Using command as one of its central relationships, political economy sees the economy as the terrain of an endless and often bitter struggle in which power plays a decisive role—between workers and their employers, between buyers and sellers, and among giant corporations. This is one of the reasons why three-dimensional economics is also called political economy.

The time dimension of three-dimensional economics—change— suggests that studying economics also means studying history. The process of change in society cannot be understood without considering the past and how it changed, eventually reaching the present. Change in political economy may be contrasted with the static approach of conventional economics which freezes time at a moment. Economic reality, according to political economy, is better represented as a process of change rather than a frozen state of affairs: It is a movie compared to the neoclassical snapshot.

In political economy, the usual distinctions between different disciplines in the social sciences—history, political science, economics, as well as others, particularly sociology, anthropology and psychology—appear to be quite arbitrary. They divide up social reality into parcels which reflect the traditional boundaries between university departments, but they obscure our understanding of how the economy works.

history. American capitalism works differently in the twentieth century from how it worked in the nineteenth century, and although it is still capitalism, our analysis of how it works today must be informed by the way it has changed.

Our economic system will undergo further change in the future. The present and even the future will become the past: What is, will not be. Indeed, as we have seen in Chapter 1, capitalism is one of the most dynamic—or change-ful—economic systems ever.

We are most interested here in how economic and social change comes about through the normal, everyday functioning of the economic system. Of course, many things may cause change: wars, new discoveries, plagues, drastic weather changes, science and technology, religious upheavals, and so on. To take one example, a major nuclear war would surely cause enormous, abrupt, devastating change. In part our economic analysis may help explain why these events occur. But mainly our focus is on change not as it is created by sudden catastrophe or good luck, but rather as it emerges from the routine and persistent operation of the economic system.

☐ Values in Political Economy

Most people are interested not only in how our economy works (or doesn't work) but also in what is good and what is bad about it. The economy is the subject of much controversy and debate. It used to be said that if you wanted to avoid an argument, stay away from politics or religion. Today, better advice might be: Don't mention economics.

Debate about economics involves not only *what is* but *what should be*. The latter statement (what should be) is a matter of values.

Often economists (and economics textbooks) avoid values, saying that economics involves analyzing what is, not what should be. But this is misleading, since every approach to economics incorporates values, and these values have a big influence on what each approach chooses to focus on. For example, conventional economics focuses almost entirely on the horizontal dimension (competition). Accompanying this focus are usually three (implicit or explicit) assumptions: (1) a capitalist economy can be adequately described in terms of voluntary exchange or choice through competition; (2) command plays an unimportant role in a capitalist economy; and (3) fundamental change in how an economic system works is either impossible or undesirable.

All of these assumptions, as later chapters show, involve values:

What is an "adequate" description? What if it leaves out the power of employers over workers, or racial or sexual discrimination, or destruction of the environment, or other important aspects of the economy? Who decided that it was "adequate" even if it left out something important? How do we know that fundamental change should be ruled out?

Economics is thus not value neutral, no matter how much individual economists may wish to separate economics from values.

Economics inevitably involves values. This is as it should be. The values a theory begins with provide the basis for judging whether we think an economic system is good or bad, or, less grandiosely, what processes or outcomes of an economic system are better or worse.

What, then, are the values in political economy which we use to judge the merits of an economic system? There are three general values:

Efficiency. One criterion in evaluating economic systems is the degree to which it promotes efficient use of our labor and other available resources, rather than wasting those resources. *Efficiency* means that, when using a given amount of inputs—whether those inputs be our own effort, intelligence, and creativity; our natural surroundings; or other inputs—the maximum amount of useful goods and services is produced. An economic system that uses its resources more efficiently than another is—according to this criterion—a better economic system.

Efficiency means that for a given amount of productive inputs used in an economic system, the maximum output of useful goods and services is produced.

Efficiency refers to the production of *useful* goods and services. The production of goods and services that are not useful should be left out of the efficiency calculation. For instance, the production of advertising (beyond the extent to which it simply informs the consumer) is highly profitable—that is why it is produced—but not useful. The same may be said of some forms of military goods production.

Similarly, all inputs used in production, whether paid for or not, must be counted in the efficiency calculation. One input that is usually forgotten is our natural environment. A technologically advanced factory that dumps out toxic wastes may be less efficient or even inefficient when all resources are considered, since in addition to the inputs it pays for, the factory is also using (consuming or destroying) the natural environment.

Another input that is often overlooked in conventional economics is the effort and health of the worker (as distinct from the worker's time). An assembly line that speeds up production may increase profits, but it may not be efficient if its increased output is made possible only by an even larger increase in the employees' work effort.

Still another input that is frequently ignored is household labor.

When we consider all inputs and all outputs of an economic system, we must include work in the home as well as production organized in factories and elsewhere.

Fairness means that people in an economic system suffer the burdens and enjoy the benefits of that economic system equitably.

Fairness. A second major criterion for evaluating economic systems is the fair distribution of the system's burdens and benefits. *Burden* refers primarily to the work necessary to produce; *benefits* refer primarily to the use of what is produced. Who does how much work? And who consumes the fruits of the work that is done? Just as in evaluating efficiency, all costs and gains from production should be included. *Fairness* here means that people within the economic system should suffer the burdens and enjoy the benefits of the economic system equitably. An economic system that distributes its burdens and benefits more fairly than another is a better economic system, according to the fairness criterion.

We might wish to specify the criterion of fairness further by saying that there should be a presumption of equality; equal outcomes to be modified only by the extent to which differences of circumstances require, or democratic decisions determine, that people should be treated differently. For instance, large households may need more income than smaller households, older people may deserve more income than younger people. But in the absence of circumstances or democratic decisions to the contrary, fairness implies equality.

Even an economic process that produces equal outcomes may be unfair, however. Racial discrimination, regardless of the outcomes produced, violates the criterion of fairness. Even if racially segregated, "separate-but-equal" facilities really did allow equal outcomes, enforcing segregation in such facilities would be unfair as a process. Similarly, unequal treatment of people because of their sex violates the fairness criterion.

Democracy is a process with three characteristics: power is accountable to those affected; guarantees of civil rights and personal liberties exist; and citizens have relatively equal access to political resources and influences.

Democracy. The third major criterion for assessing an economic system is the extent to which that system promotes *democracy*—does the economic system support or inhibit democratic control over the major decisions in the society? One important part of this criterion is the extent to which the economic system promotes or hinders the democratic functioning of the government. Another part is the extent to which it promotes democratic control over other aspects of society, including, in particular, democratic control over the economy. An economic system that promotes democracy in all these areas is better than one that does not, according to the democracy criterion.

By "democratic control" or "democracy" we mean a process with three characteristics: the accountability of power; civil liberties; and political equality. First, decision makers (whether in the government or elsewhere) must be accountable to the people affected by their decisions through periodic review and possible replacement; generally we think of elections as the appropriate mechanism for democratic accountability. Second, there must exist guarantees for the exercise of those various civil rights and personal liberties associated with democratic citizenship. The rights to free speech and assembly, for instance, are necessary to democratic decision making. Third, the citizens in a democratic system must have relatively equal resources with which to participate in the democratic process and therefore relatively equal influence over that process.

Democratic control does not imply that all decisions should be made through voting. The individual should be free to make any decision when the consequences of that decison are entirely or mainly felt by the individual himself or herself. For example, the choice of which food to consume for dinner is, almost always, a decision affecting only the eater or the eater's family. In this respect, political economy, like conventional economics, values individual choice.

When a decision affects more than one person, however, democratic rule implies that individual choice must give way to collective (and democratic) decision. For example, the decision of whether to close down or modernize an old factory clearly affects many people: it affects the investors, current or potential workers, people who live near the plant who may consume the good being produced or be bothered by noise or pollution from the plant, the community that may depend upon the plant's taxes, and so forth. In this case, the democracy criterion implies that individual choice—for instance, the plant owner's right to choose whether to close his plant or not—is inappropriate because it is undemocratic. All those affected by the decision must have a say in making the decision.

Democracy and command are not necessarily inconsistent. A command can certainly be undemocratic; for instance, an order given by a dictator or an employer may be undemocratic if the people affected by the decision have no influence on the decision maker. But equally, a command may be a means of carrying out a democratic decision. Take, for example, an environmental protection law that was democratically voted upon and passed; to enforce this law, it may be necessary for a federal court to command polluters to stop polluting. Or consider the command given to a worker by an elected manager in a worker owned and worker run cooperative. In these cases, implementing or enforcing democratic decisions requires commands.

Economic systems should be judged according to how well they meet three standards: efficiency, fairness, and democracy. It is possible that some systems perform some of these tasks better, while other systems perform other tasks better. Slavery, in some of its forms, was efficient but unfair and undemocratic, whereas production by independent producers (for example, independent farmers who owned their own land, as in colonial New England) may have been less efficient but fairer and more democratic. Moreover, systems may change over time in terms of their performance on these three criteria. Necessarily, then, our judgments must be more complex than simply "better" or "worse."

□ The Lineage of Political Economy

The political economy or "three-dimensional" approach to economics is, like neoclassical economics, partly new and partly old. Many of the research findings and applications reported later in this book are the products of studies completed in the past ten or so years. Yet many of the ideas can be traced back a century or more in the tradition of economics writing.

Many great economists contributed to this approach. We could focus on the so-called "classical" economists, Adam Smith, David Ricardo, and John Stuart Mill, who laid the foundation for both political economy and neoclassical economics. The American "institutionalist" economists—Thorstein Veblen, John R. Commons, and John Kenneth Galbraith—are less well known but their contributions are important nonetheless. We could also mention the Marxists Paul Sweezy, Michel Kalecki, and Eric Hobsbawm, and the great Cambridge University economists Piero Sraffa and Joan Robinson. Here, however, we focus on the three who were perhaps the most important.

Karl Marx. The first is the ninteenth-century economist and philosopher Karl Marx. Marx's contribution was to reformulate the classical economists' theories in such a way as to give us what we label the three-dimensional approach. He thus provided an early version of the overall framework for our analysis.

Marx recognized that in the real history of capitalism (as opposed to theoretical models in the heads of Adam Smith and the other classical economists) there were three elements that needed to be added to or emphasized in the classical models:

(1) Conflict as well as harmony of economic interests exists. When two individuals trade together under the terms of voluntary exchange, each can benefit (otherwise, why would each trade?); this is the lesson of neoclassical economics, which defines economics exclusively in terms of exchange (or competition). But all parties do not benefit equally from exchange. Marx noted that the conditions under which people make trades (remember the thief's

A Great Radical Economist: Karl Marx (1818–1883)

Few scholars have been as revered and as hated as Karl Marx. Most intellectuals suffer the indifference of their contemporaries and are little remembered after their death. Not so with Marx. His works—primarily his major book, *Capital*—are widely read and hotly debated to this day.

Though he was born in Germany and began his career as a journalist there, he spent a good part of his early years on the run. His newspaper *Rheinische Zeitung* was closed by the government because it advocated freedom of the press and other democratic rights unpopular with the autocratic rulers of the day. Seeking a more tolerant environment, he moved to Paris but was soon expelled for writing articles exposing poverty and economic injustice and advocating radical solutions to these problems. In 1848, he moved to London with his wife and family—often barely making a living by writing articles for such newspapers as the *New York Daily Tribune*. (His mother once commented, "Karl, I wish you would *make* some capital instead of just writing about it.") He remained in England, writing *Capital* and working with his friend Friedrich Engels, until his death in 1883.

Marx devoted most of the latter half of his life to a study of the capitalist economy. He first mastered the theories of the classical economists—Adam Smith, David Ricardo, and others—and then developed a criticism of their ideas and an alternative way of looking at capitalism. The classical economists writing at the time of the birth of capitalism a generation or two before Marx had explained how the emerging capitalist economy would work for the benefit of all. But Marx and Engels had seen enough of the real history of capitalism to have a different view. They saw the immense productivity of modern industry juxtaposed with the grinding poverty and economic insecurity of the new industrial towns.

Capitalism, according to Marx, is an economic system that constantly expands the *potential* to harness science and human labor so as rationally to meet the needs of all people. In *The Communist Manifesto*—probably the most widely read pamphlet in human history—Marx and Engels wrote: "The bourgeoisie, during its rule of scarce one hundred years, has created more massive and more colossal productive forces than have all preceding generations together."

At the same time, capitalism is itself an obstacle to tapping society's productive potential. This is partly because under capitalism production is motivated by the prospect of private economic gain rather than meeting human needs. Moreover, because capitalist societies are characterized by glaring inequalities between workers and the owners of the capital goods used in production, the use of human energy and human intelligence will be systematically diverted toward making profits and away from meeting human needs.

Marx also thought that an alternative to capitalism—what he called socialism or communism—could continue the development of the productive potential of society but at the same time make better use of its potential.

Most countries that have taken up Marx's writings as their official ideology—such as the Soviet Union—have made quite significant economic progress. But they have also imposed forms of dictatorship far more oppressive than those that Marx criticized as a young journalist.

Source: "The Communist Manifesto," in Robert Tucker, ed., *The Marx-Engels Reader* (New York: Norton, 1978).

terms: "Your money or your life!") affect the outcome of those trades, and that power, coercion, and force (what we call "command") are crucial elements in how the economy works also. Most importantly, in capitalism some people (employers) own income-earning property such as land, factories, office buildings, and the like, while most people (workers) do not, and this discrepancy shapes the economic relationships between them.

(2) Groups as well as individuals act to defend and advance their interests. Conventional economic theory focuses on competitive market relations and on individual economic actors or agents. But Marx noted that people often acted in groups, and that a theory based just on individual behavior would miss this important aspect. Of course, there exist many different groups, and these groups may be of different size, may have overlapping memberships, may be loosely or tightly organized, may have different purposes—steel manufacturers, people in the Northeast, blacks, Catholics, Yankee fans, and so on. Marx emphasized in particular the importance of economic classes such as workers and employers.

(3) Economic systems change over time, especially in response to their own operations. Rather than thinking of an economic system as a fixed set of relations (for example, competitive markets and voluntary exchange), Marx insisted that the operation of an economic system itself tended to change the conditions within which that system operated. Marx emphasized in particular that in capitalism, the accumulation of capital—a process we investigate in detail later—would fuel economic change, leading to the growth of cities, increased material abundance, worldwide migrations, changes in family life, and the like.

Joseph Schumpeter. A second contributor to political economy is Joseph Schumpeter. Schumpeter added to the analysis at two points.

First, Schumpeter deepened Marx's argument that capitalism

creates change: "Capitalism is by nature a form or method of economic change and not only never is, but never can be stationary."[*] He applied this perspective to market competition and technological innovation.

His idea was simple. What is important about competition, he argued, was not the niggling price competition, in static and unchanging surroundings, that is depicted in the standard introductory textbook—the kind of equilibrium analysis of one tiny supplier offering a fractionally lower price until all, like bb's in a barrel, come to rest at equilibrium. Schumpeter explained competition less in terms of physical mechanics and more in terms of military strategy and counterstrategy. What is economically important about competition, according to Schumpeter, is the incentive for firms to achieve monopolies and new breakthroughs, based on great bursts of innovation and profit. It is these bursts that break up old ways of doing business and cause the economy to leap ahead.

Second, Schumpeter looked at the broad history of capitalism and detected what have come to be called "long waves" or "long swings" in economic activity. A long swing is an extended period of prosperity or boom (lasting perhaps for 20 or 30 years), followed by a lengthy period of stagnation or economic hard times. We will return to this insight in Chapter 14.

John Maynard Keynes. The third important contributor was John Maynard Keynes, economist, adviser to the British exchequer, and member of the House of Lords. He influenced both neoclassical economics and political economy. However, what has come down to us in the conventional textbooks (what Keynes's collaborator Joan Robinson called "bastard Keynesianism") is quite different from what Keynes contributed to political economy.

Keynes's main contribution to political economy was to provide a model of the whole economy (the macroeconomy) with one unique feature: there will generally be unemployed people looking for work and not finding jobs. According to Keynes, capitalism will produce chronic umemployment, unless the government does something to alter its basic workings.

By contrast, in the world of neoclassical economics, where voluntary exchange is the general form of economic relationships, involuntary unemployment is not possible. According to neoclassical economics, unemployment must mean that workers are refusing to accept jobs at lower wages, since the "price" (in this case the wage) must equate supply and demand in the labor market as in other markets. And if labor supply equals labor demand, everyone who wants to work (offers to supply labor) can find work.

---

[*] Joseph Schumpeter, *Capitalism, Socialism, and Democracy* (New York: Harper & Row, 1942), p. 82.

A Great Conservative Economist: Joseph Schumpeter (1883–1950)

The aristocratic and the modern were inextricably combined in Joseph Schumpeter. The paradoxes of this great economist—who served as Minister of Finance in the government of Austria and Professor of Economics at Harvard University—are suggested by the fact that at his first teaching post, he fought a duel with the university librarian so students could have freer access to books.

Joseph Schumpeter tackled the big problems in economics. The title of his most famous book—*Capitalism, Socialism, and Democracy*—indicates the range of his intellect and interests.

Perhaps Schumpeter was attracted to the big issues because he himself witnessed such drastic changes in society. He was raised in pre–World War I Vienna—a city dominated by a glittering aristocracy made rich by the immense wealth of triumphant late nineteenth-century capitalism. The city was a center of splendorous art, music, opera, palaces, and balls. Yet there was an air of impending doom in Viennese high society. The propertied classes were imbued with a sense that this privileged and beautiful life could not last. Poor working people crowded the industrial districts of the city, and the whole Austrian empire, of which Vienna was the capital, tottered. Bourgeois life seemed like an overripe fruit, ready to drop as soon as the tree was shaken.

Schumpeter identified with the aristocracy and valued its culture. Yet he could see that capitalism was an enormously dynamic system that continually changed society and threatened to disrupt established (and cherished) institutions.

For Schumpeter, change—our time dimension—was central to any economic theory. Among his many novel ideas, the most powerful are his notions of innovation and "creative destruction." For Schumpeter, innovation was not just technological change but organizational and social change as well. Innovation was central to his idea of the process of capitalism because it destroyed equilibrium. Capitalist innovation "incessantly revolutionizes the economic structure from within, incessantly destroying the old one, incessantly creating a new one." For progress to occur, the old methods of doing business must be disrupted in a creative burst. Hence the idea of creative destruction: old ways must be destroyed to create the basis for new leaps forward.

This view of innovation and creative destruction brought Schumpeter to see monopoly in an entirely different light from conventional economists. Where they saw monopoly as a source of inefficiency and misallocation of resources, Schumpeter argued that monopoly makes possible the concentration of resources necessary for making big innovative jumps. Where mainstream economists focused on the static problems produced by monopoly, Schumpeter perceived the dynamic potentialities associated with these concentrations of power.

Schumpeter had a gloomy view of capitalism's future. Just after World War II and a year before his death, he warned the American Economic Association of what he termed "the march into socialism." He believed that capitalism would solve the production problems of society and that its success would sow the seeds of its own demise. In particular, large organizations would destroy the climate for innovation and the intellectual classes in society would turn against the system, destroying its cultural or ideological legitimacy. "I do not advocate socialism," he began his remarks to his economics colleagues. And echoing the gloom of prewar Vienna, he went on:

> Capitalism does not merely mean that the housewife may influence production by her choice between peas and beans; or that the youngster may choose whether he wants to work in a factory or on a farm; ... it means a scheme of values, an attitude toward life, a civilization—the civilization of inequality and of the family fortune. This civilization is rapidly passing away.

Unlike so much of what Schumpeter wrote, this assessment has not been borne out, or at least not yet. The decades following Schumpeter's warning were in many ways a golden age for the capitalist economy.

Source: Joseph Schumpeter, *Capitalism, Socialism, and Democracy* (New York: Harper & Row, 1942), pp. 83, 416, 419.

Yet Keynes's model showed that capitalism had no tendency to eliminate involuntary unemployment—that is, unemployment in excess of the voluntary unemployment caused by people who have quit one job and are simply searching for a better one. Keynes's book, *The General Theory of Employment, Interest, and Money,* published at the height of the Great Depression in 1936, thus undermined the prior idea of the economy as a self-adjusting mechanism and supported the idea that to avoid large-scale unemployment and economic instability the government would have to regulate the economy in some way.

Marx, Schumpeter, and Keynes have all contributed to political economy or what we call the three-dimensional approach to economics. In the following chapters we do not label each idea Marxian, Schumpeterian, or Keynesian, in part because modern-day political economy builds upon, integrates, and changes many of the ideas of these earlier economists in light of current realities. But you will no doubt recognize the general themes that these economists emphasized.

A Great Liberal Economist: John Maynard Keynes (1883–1946)

John Maynard Keynes was born the year Karl Marx died; but the man who was to revolutionize twentieth-century economics was himself no revolutionary. Keynes led the fashionable life of a Cambridge University professor and a leading member of English intellectual and cultural circles. Lord Keynes, Baron of Tilton, was also a director of the Bank of England and the financial adviser of Kings College at Cambridge University (where his speculations multiplied the value of the College's assets tenfold).

Neither was he modest. In the mid-1930s he wrote to his friend George Bernard Shaw: ". . . I believe myself to be writing a book on economic theory which will largely revolutionize . . . the way the world thinks about economic problems. . . . I cannot expect you or anyone else to believe this at the present stage. But for myself . . . I'm quite sure."

He was right. *The General Theory of Employment, Interest, and Money,* written at the height of the Great Depression, took the economics profession by storm. Unlike the reigning economic theory of the day, it explained why there generally would be unemployment in a capitalist economy.

Keynes explained that the process of investment and growth in a capitalist economy depends on a precarious balance between what are now called the cost conditions affecting investment and the demand conditions affecting investment. Operating on its own, he argued, there is no reason to expect the capitalist economy to achieve this balance in such a way as to provide jobs for all who seek them. He therefore advocated government policies—particularly expanding government demand for goods and services—in order to maintain a level of total demand sufficient to ensure full employment and adequate profits.

Because he supported the idea of more government involvement in the economy, Keynes's theories were initially regarded as "dangerously radical" by some business groups. But what came to be known as Keynesian economics gradually became the accepted basis of government policy. John F. Kennedy is often considered to have been the first Keynesian president. Partly as a result of the adoption of Keynes's ideas, major depressions have been avoided in the post–World War II era and unemployment rates have generally been lower than before the war.

Because Keynesian policies prevented a second Great Depression, Keynes is often credited with having saved capitalism. If so, it was not out of love that he did it. In 1933 he wrote: "The decadent international but individualistic capitalism in the hands of which we found ourselves after the (First World) War is not a success. It is not intelligent, it is not beautiful, it is not just, it is not virtuous—and it does not deliver the goods. In short, we dislike it and we are beginning to despise it. But when we wonder what to put in its place we are extremely perplexed."

Though he favored more economic planning, he did not count himself as a socialist or as an ally of the working class: "When it comes to the class struggle as such," he wrote, "my own personal patriotisms . . . are attached to my own surroundings. The class war will find me on the side of the educated bourgeoisie."

Sources: John Maynard Keynes, "National Self Sufficiency" *The New Statesman and Nation*, July 15, 1933; John Maynard Keynes, "Am I a Liberal?" in *Essays in Persuasion* (New York: Norton, 1963); and Robert Heilbroner, *The Worldly Philosophers* (New York: Simon & Schuster, 1972).

☐ Suggested Readings

Robert Heilbroner, *The Worldly Philosophers* (New York: Simon & Schuster, 1972).

E. K. Hunt, *Property and Prophets: The Evolution of Economic Institutions and Ideologies* (New York: Harper & Row, 1972).

John Maynard Keynes, *Essays in Persuasion* (London: Macmillan, 1933).

Joseph Schumpeter, *Capitalism, Socialism, and Democracy* (New York: Harper & Row, 1942).

Robert Tucker, *The Marx-Engels Reader* (New York: Norton, 1978).

PART TWO

CAPITALISM AND CLASS

CHAPTER 3

THE SURPLUS PRODUCT AND SURPLUS LABOR TIME

Walk into almost any travel agency and you will see posters that tell a very interesting economic story. You may see a poster of India, showing the Taj Mahal. Beside it may be a picture of Egypt and the pyramids. Another poster invites you to visit Rome and see the ancient Colosseum or the fabulous treasures of St. Peter's. Then on to France to view the delicate opulence of the chateaux, including the splendor of the Sun King's Versailles Palace. Far-off China beckons, with the attraction of the Great Wall. Closer to home, you can take a tour of the U. S. South, visiting the great plantation houses of the former slaveholders.

What story do these posters tell? What do the Taj Mahal, the pyramids, the Great Wall, and the slaveholders' mansions have in common? Simply this: Even today, these great edifices inspire awe (and attract tourists) not only because of their beauty, but also because of the almost inconceivable amounts of human labor that were required to build them. Thousands upon thousands of workers spent years, decades, even centuries making such fabulous constructions. One can imagine whole generations of workmen, and their sons and grandsons, working to build Versailles or cut the marble for St. Peter's.

Yet these posters raise a number of troubling questions as well. How was it possible, in poor societies such as ancient Egypt or medieval France, for the society to feed and clothe these thousands of workers? After all, while they were building mansions and tombs, the workers could not feed and clothe themselves. Where did the kings and bishops and emperors and slaveholders obtain such great wealth? And a final question: 500 years from now, when tourists want to visit the monuments of our present society, what will they go to see? And what questions will they ask?

The answers to these questions, and the common element in all the posters, lies in one of the central ideas of this book: the surplus product. The *surplus product* is simply that part of the total output in excess of what is needed for reproducing and replenishing the labor, tools, materials, and other inputs used or used up in production. The surplus product may take the form of luxury goods, increased education, the construction of more or better machinery used in production, cathedrals, palaces, military hardware, and a host of other things.

The main idea of this chapter is that economic systems provide both a horizontal organization of labor processes (exchange) and a vertical arrangement (use and control of the surplus product).

This main idea is expressed in three main points:

1. An economy is a collection of *labor processes*. Each labor process is made up of a *technology* (a relation between inputs and outputs) and a *social organization of production* (a relation among those doing the labor and between them and those who own the tools, land, and other production inputs). Each labor process produces one or more useful (or thought to be useful) outputs.
2. Economic specialization creates the need for some kind of *exchange* among the producers of distinct products (through markets, gift, barter, or some other means). *Market exchanges* are governed by *supply* and *demand*. Exchange is the main aspect of the horizontal or competition dimension of the economy.
3. A *surplus* is produced whenever the labor processes in an economy produce more than is needed to maintain the producers at the standard of living to which they are accustomed and to replace the materials used and machines used up in production. The production and control of the surplus is the main vertical or command dimension of the economy.

☐ The Labor Process and Economic Specialization

In all societies, people are economically interdependent. The story of Robinson Crusoe, who was self-sufficient, growing his own food and making the things he needed for his own existence, provokes our fantasies exactly because it is so different from what we experience. But in all real societies, each person depends on the products of other people's labors. Even Crusoe had his slave, Friday.

The basis of economic interdependence is economic specialization. The people who make up any economic system produce different things; some make shoes, others generate electricity, others cook meals. No one produces all the things that he or she needs. Most people produce, or help to produce, more of some good than that person alone can or chooses to consume. The things produced must then be distributed to others through some method of exchange.

The first step is production. Producing something useful necessarily involves human labor. A *labor process* is a transformation of our natural surroundings with the intention of producing something useful (or thought to be useful). A labor process thus involves both inputs (such as work itself, raw materials, and machines) and outputs (such as a ton of steel, a haircut, or whatever). First let us consider the process of transforming nature, then we will describe different kinds of inputs and outputs.

A **labor process** is a transformation of our natural surroundings using human labor with the intention of producing something useful.

Think about making something, say, pancakes. If you made a list of all the things needed and how much of each, including the various activities necessary to mix the batter, turn on the stove, flip the pancakes and so on, you would have a very complete recipe for pancakes, more detailed than that in a cookbook. This recipe describes the labor process for making pancakes; similar lists of inputs and activities could describe the labor process for making the flour used in making the pancakes, for the gas burned, for making the stove itself, and for the other inputs.

Technology is the relationship between inputs and outputs in a labor process.

This recipe or any other relationship between inputs and outputs in a labor process is called a *technology. Technical change* refers to a change in one of these input-output relations; a way to make pancakes with a different kind of flour that does not need to be sifted, for example. *Technical progress* is a technical change allowing the same amount to be produced with less labor, or less of some other input.

Technical progress is a change in the relationship between inputs and outputs which permits the same output to be produced with less of one or more of the inputs.

An *economy* is a collection of labor processes. Of course, countless numbers of different things are produced in an economy, and an economy uses countless different inputs, including different kinds of labor. Simply to discuss them it is necessary to group these distinct inputs and outputs in some way; how we group them depends on what we want to find out.

An **economy** is a collection of labor processes.

We may begin by noting that every economy produces two types of outputs. The first kind of output is all the goods and services that we consume or that businesses use. We are quite familiar with products of this kind, for they correspond to the normal everyday meaning of *production*. The second type of output is different, and we usually do not think of it as "produced" at all: It consists of the people themselves.

Production is a labor process whose output is a good or a service.

People are produced by labor processes, mainly labor processes in the home, which involve not only biological reproduction but also the feeding, caring for, training, and other tasks of child rearing and family care. Not only children, but adults as well are fed and cared for: When we prepare a meal, eat, and relax after a day's work we are, among other things, replenishing our energy and maintaining our ability to function.

To distinguish these two types of outputs, the first (production of goods and services) is called *production* and the second (production of people) is called *reproduction*. This book focuses on production, especially capitalist production, although labor processes in reproduction are also very important, even in capitalist societies.

Figure 3.1 is a picture of an economy; it shows one of the ways that the different labor processes, inputs, and outputs are linked together. Labor processes producing things (goods or services) are shown in Figure 3.1 in the center at the top; labor processes reproducing people are shown in the center at the bottom.

The outputs of a labor process producing things may be materials or machines intended for use in a subsequent production process, or consumer goods to be consumed by people, or outputs not used in any labor process. Materials or machines, as we see in Figure 3.1, later become inputs into the labor processes producing things. Consumer goods (including what are sometimes called "consumer durable goods" like stoves or blenders) become the inputs into the labor processes reproducing people.

Similarly, some of the people reproduced by the labor processes in the lower part of Figure 3.1, people who become producers of shoes or steel, for example, find employment in the production of things. Others, parents who care for children, for example, work in the labor processes reproducing people. And some people, "people of leisure," do no labor at all.

Of course many people divide their labor time between production and reproduction; women employed outside the home, in particular, often have two "jobs," one at "work" and another after they get home.

Next, we can ask about the inputs to each labor process (starting with the labor processes producing things): Is the input itself a thing, or is it people (that is, labor)? Things that are used in the production of things are either materials or machines. The word *machines* refers to all durable production equipment and structures (including buildings) used in production; an alternative name for machines is *capital goods*. *Materials* differ from capital goods in that they are *used up* in the production process: Think of cotton, which ends up as part of the shirt being made, or fuel, which is burned up. Capital goods—the machines, buildings, and all other long-lasting things needed in production—are used, and will experience wear and tear, but will only be used *up* over the course of years. *Labor* is any activity performed by people that is needed for production or reproduction.

These terms may be illustrated by a labor process producing

Reproduction is a labor process whose output is people; it includes not only biological reproduction but also such activities as child rearing, training, feeding, and care giving.

Materials are goods needed in production and used up during the process of production.
Machines or **capital goods** are goods which are needed in production, but which are durable, and will be used up only over the course of years.
Labor is any activity performed by people that is needed for production or reproduction.

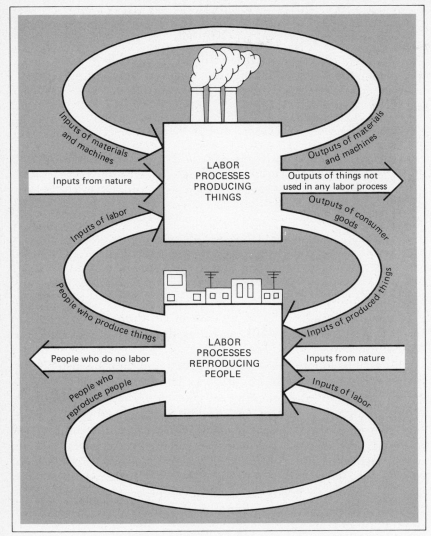

FIGURE 3.1 The production-reproduction cloverleaf. The economy is composed of interdependent labor processes including the production of goods and services (things) and the reproduction of people. The arrows represent the movement of goods or people from one labor process to other parts of the economy. Each labor process uses three different types of input: inputs produced elsewhere in the economy, inputs produced in that labor process itself, and natural inputs. Each also produces three different types of output: outputs used in the labor process itself, outputs used as inputs elsewhere in the economy, and outputs not used as inputs anywhere in the economy.

pancakes at a fast food restaurant. This is an example of a labor process producing a consumer good directly consumed by people. Other labor processes have as their outputs materials or capital goods. Still other labor processes reproduce people, including such

> **The House of Pancakes Pancake Technology**
>
> *Inputs*
>
> | | |
> |---|---|
> | Materials used | Flour |
> | | Gas or electricity |
> | | Eggs, etc. |
> | Capital Goods ("machines") used up | Wear and tear on the stove |
> | | Wear and tear on the bowls, mixing spoons, and other utensils |
> | | Mixing batter |
> | Labor | Turning the pancakes over, and so on |
> | | Waiting on customers |
>
> *Output*
>
> | | |
> |---|---|
> | Consumer good | Pancakes |

activities as giving birth, taking care of children, training people in the necessary labor skills, and providing the support and care needed for family life.

The various labor processes are distinct, but they are also closely connected, as we see in Figure 3.1. Their connection, which is called economic interdependence, takes many forms. Some of the outputs of some processes are used as inputs in other processes. Coal is used to make steel. But some of the machinery used in coal mining is itself made out of steel. We have seen this already in the case of materials and machines, which enter into the production of other goods. The various parts depend on each other in other ways as well. Consumer goods are used in the process of the reproduction of people, just as machines and materials are used in the production of things.

The production of materials and machines can be thought of as replacing or expanding the supply of the machinery, raw materials, buildings, and other things used up in labor processes. The reproduction of people and the production of consumer goods likewise can be thought of as reproducing or expanding the supply of producers, meaning the replacement of the workers who leave the labor force through death or retirement and the replenishment of the energy which is daily used up by workers as they work.

There are two kinds of outputs in Figure 3.1 that are special, in that they do not end up being used in any labor process. First, there are things produced, like luxury goods, monuments, cathedrals, and military equipment, that do not enter into any labor process. They are not used to produce anything else, however important they may be to the culture or safety of the society in question. They often appear on posters in travel agencies.

Second, there are people who are reproduced but who do not themselves produce anything (see Figure 3.1). These include the kings, slaveowners, and warriors of past times, and those today who live on what others have produced.

Just as there are some outputs that are not used as inputs in any labor process, so there are some inputs that are not produced. These may be called natural inputs; they refer to our physical environment in its broadest sense: air, water, arable land, the minerals in the earth's substratum, the sun, and so on. These inputs are presented in Figure 3.1 by arrows entering the two types of labor processes from "outside" the system. To say they are provided by the environment does not mean they cannot be used up. Many natural inputs are nonrenewable and can be used up. A few, like the sun, can be used quite extensively (to grow crops, to warm houses) without being used up.

The economy, then, is a collection of labor proceses that are specialized in the production of distinct outputs and that are connected by a circular relationship called economic interdependence.

It will be useful to look at the economy from two vantage points, one that will emphasize its horizontal dimension, and the other that will illuminate its vertical dimension. The crucial concept for understanding the horizontal dimension is market exchange; the crucial concept for understanding the vertical dimension is the surplus. We turn to these two dimensions in our next two sections.

☐ Market Exchange: Supply and Demand

Our "reproduction cloverleaf" (Figure 3.1) is something like an aerial photograph of the economy. It represents the horizontal dimensions of the economy as a circulation of goods and services (things) and of people (producers). Goods produced in one location end up being used in another. People born and raised in the home leave and take up employment in factories, offices, or sometimes in their own homes. This is called the horizontal dimension because from this perspective goods and people are not moving "up" or "down" in the economy, but rather "across," that is, from place to place.

Understanding the horizontal dimension of the economy means explaining the movements of goods and people from one place to another, or being able to answer questions such as: Why do some people work at some jobs and some at others? What determines who and how many will raise children, pour concrete, or make shoes? Why do the resulting products move from one labor process to the other? Why do the children go to work when they grow up? How do the shoes get from the shoe worker to the shoe wearer?

In various societies throughout the course of human history, and across the world today, these questions have been answered in very different ways. We will begin with a self-sufficient family farm on the American frontier in the early nineteenth century. Here most of the various labor processes and movements of products listed in Figure 3.1 took place within a single household. (That is what self-sufficient means.) Reproducing labor and producing the materials and capital goods needed for production took place under one roof. Tools were made and repaired, draft animals were tended, a new fence was put up. Food was prepared, firewood was collected, children were born and raised, clothing was made. What goods were produced and how they were used was coordinated by a combination of custom, necessity, and patriarchal authority. Tasks were assigned according to age and sex. Though not common today, this is one distinct way of determining who will do what labor and how the resulting products will be used.

If each family does not produce everything its members use, if the family unit is not self-sufficient—that is, as in almost all of the modern world—the situation is more complicated. Specialization exists between as well as within families, and families must engage in trade or what we call "exchange." Various social arrangements determine how labor will be specialized, and how outputs will be distributed. In some parts of India, for example, people are born into occupational groups (castes), so that who does what is determined by birth. The goods produced are then exchanged according to customary rules. In the Soviet Union, both who does what labor and how the resulting goods are used are organized by the government according to a very detailed economic plan. In some societies, theft or tribute has played a significant role in determining who produces what and how the resulting products are circulated; in other societies, these outcomes are determined almost entirely by an elaborate process of gift giving.

Caste, custom, plan, gift, theft, and tribute are all ways of determining what goods will be produced, and by whom. All of these play some part in the United States today. But far more important than any of these is market exchange.

A *market exchange* occurs when the owner of a good or service sells that item to someone else. Usually, the item is exchanged for money: The seller transfers ownership of the item to the buyer, and receives money in return; the buyer pays out money to acquire ownership of the good or service. The seller may then take the money and use it to buy something else. (Direct exchange—trading one product for another—is called *barter.*)

The term *market* refers to the buying and selling activities of all

A **market** refers to all the buying and selling activities of those persons wishing to trade a good or service; a market consists of suppliers wanting to sell and demanders wanting to buy.

those who want to trade (buy or sell) a particular good or service. For example, the beer market refers to all the buying and selling activities of those who want to buy or sell beer.

Market activities are sometimes but not always concentrated in one location. Examples of markets with specific locations are the New York Stock Exchange and the Boston fish market; in these cases, you can actually go to see the buying and selling of stocks or fish in one location. For other markets, however, there is no specific place where you can "see" the market; for example, the Chicago labor market includes buyers and sellers of labor time, who may meet and make market trades anyplace in the Chicago area. Markets, then, are not places but rather a set of activities.

Markets work to determine two basic economic outcomes: the *price* at which a good or service is exchanged and the *quantity* of it which will be bought and sold. Every market consists of two parts: *demanders,* or those wishing to buy the good or service and *suppliers,* or those wishing to sell the good or service.

We can understand how a market works by looking at the interaction of demanders and suppliers. Let us consider the market for a particular item, say, beer in Iowa City, Iowa.

The *demand curve* represents the buyers' side of the market. It depicts the buyers' willingness to purchase beer, depending on what the price of beer is. Imagine that we asked every person in Iowa City (and all those who might travel to Iowa City to buy beer), "How many bottles of beer will you buy today if the price is $2 per bottle?" We would then add up all the answers; suppose the total came to 520 bottles. This exercise would yield one point on the demand curve: At price = $2, buyers will demand 520 bottles of beer.

We might then repeat the survey, asking buyers how much they would buy, first, if the price were $1 and, second, if it were $0.50 per bottle. Suppose we obtained answers of 1268 bottles at price = $1, and 2043 bottles at price = $0.50. We now have two additional points on the demand curve.

In Figure 3.2a, the demand curve *DD* depicts the buyers' demands for beer at all the possible prices. We see that at price = $2, demanders will buy 520 bottles, at price = $1 they will buy 1268 bottles, and so on.

Demand curves are almost always thought of as sloping downward to the right (having a negative slope, as *DD* in Figure 3.2a). If the price is high, say $2 per bottle, then consumers will tend to buy relatively few bottles of beer; if the price is low, say $0.50 per bottle, demanders will tend to buy a relatively large number of bottles. The lower the price, the more of the good buyers will want to buy.

Notice that the demand curve does not necessarily represent

A **demand curve** indicates, for each possible price, how much of the good or service demanders are willing and able to buy.

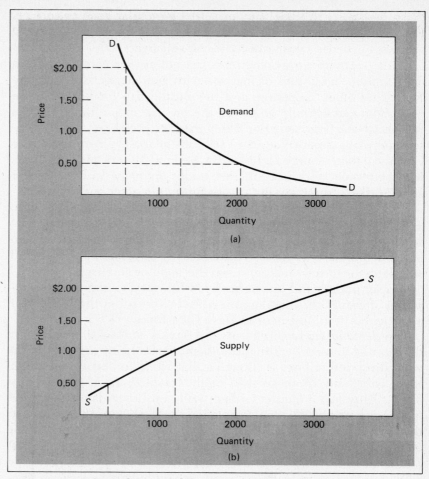

FIGURE 3.2 The demand curve and the supply curve. The demand curve *DD* provides the following information. If the price of beer per bottle is *p* dollars, the amount demanded by consumers will be *q* bottles a day. For example, if the price is $2 a bottle, consumers will buy 520 bottles a day.

The supply curve *SS* provides similar information about what producers will offer on the market. If the price is *p* dollars per bottle, suppliers will offer *q* bottles per day on the market. For example, if the price is $2 a bottle, beer suppliers will want to sell 3200 bottles a day.

what buyers *need*, only what they are *willing and able to purchase*. "Demand" means nothing more than a want backed up by dollars. We cannot tell from *DD* whether the buyers of beer are desperately thirsty after performing arduous labor or whether they have already had more beers than they should have had. Indeed, if there are some people in Iowa City who desperately need beer but have no money to buy it, their needs will not be expressed in *DD* at all, since the demand curve only expresses what people are willing and able to buy. All the demand curve tells us is how much beer consumers will buy at any given price.

How much beer people are willing to buy will almost certainly depend on other considerations besides the price. For example, it may depend on the buyers' incomes: If everybody suddenly got a pay raise, people might want to buy more of many things, including beer. If new people came to town, they would tend to increase the demand for beer. Similarly, demanders might want to buy more beer on a hot summer day than on a frigid winter one. And so on.

A demand curve, then, expresses how much the buyers are willing and able to buy, at the various possible prices, *assuming* that nothing else affecting their demand changes.

If nothing else changes, the demand curve allows us to say how a price change will change the quantity demanded. For instance, in Figure 3.2a, we see that if the price changes from $2 per bottle to $0.50 per bottle, *and if nothing else changes*, the quantity demanded will rise from 520 to 2043 bottles.

The supply curve represents the sellers' side of the market. It depicts the sellers' willingness to sell beer, depending on what the price of beer is. In Figure 3.2b, the supply curve SS shows what quantity of beer sellers will supply to the market at the various prices. For instance, if the price were $2, suppliers would try to sell 3200 bottles; if price = $0.50, suppliers would try to sell 384 bottles. And so on.

A **supply curve** indicates, for each possible price, how much of the good or service suppliers wish to sell.

Supply curves are almost always thought of as sloping upward to the right (having a positive slope, as SS in Figure 3.2b). When prices are high, suppliers will want to sell a lot of beer compared to when the price is low. The high price may attract new suppliers from nearby cities where sellers are not able to get such a high price. When the price is low, some suppliers in Iowa City may try to find other cities in which to sell their beer, or even look to other lines of work. The higher the price, the more beer suppliers will want to sell.

Other factors besides price will usually influence how much of a product suppliers want to sell. For example, the cost of producing beer and the rewards one could achieve from selling other items may affect suppliers' willingness to sell beer.

A supply curve, then, represents the quantities that sellers are willing and able to supply to the market, at the various possible prices, *assuming* that nothing else affecting their supply changes.

If nothing else changes, the supply curve tells us how the quantity of the good supplied will change when the price changes. For example, in Figure 3.2b, we see that if the price rises from $0.50 to $2 per bottle, suppliers will want to increase the amount they sell from 384 to 3200 bottles.

Supply and demand together determine both the amount traded

and the price at which the good will be sold. Figure 3.3 combines in one graph the supply and demand curves for beer in Iowa City.

The first point to notice is that competition in the market tends to produce a uniform or marketwide price for a product. Beer in Iowa City of the same quality will tend to be sold at the same price. If the price of beer is higher in one store than the price of the same beer in another store, consumers will tend to switch to the lower-priced store. If higher-priced stores can find all the customers they want, stores with lower prices will be tempted to raise their prices. The result will be that only one price tends to prevail in the market at one time.

This price—the "going" or market price—will be determined by the interaction of supply and demand, and in particular by competition among sellers and among buyers. Let us suppose that the beer price in Iowa City is $2 per bottle; what will happen?

At the current price ($2), suppliers will wish to sell 3200 bottles (from the supply curve SS), whereas demanders will want to buy only 520 bottles. The difference, 2680 bottles, is an *excess supply*. While those suppliers who can find buyers at this (relatively) high price will be happy, others who cannot find buyers will be dissatisfied. Those without buyers will offer slightly lower prices (say $1.75 or $1.50 per bottle) to attract customers.

So long as any excess supply persists, some suppliers will try to cut prices and thereby gain customers. When the prevailing price falls to $1 per bottle, the quantity that suppliers wish to sell (1268 bottles) just equals the quantity demanders wish to buy (1268), and no excess supply exists. Price cutting by suppliers will therefore stop at this price.

Similarly, if the initial price in the market had been $0.50 per bottle, an *excess demand* would exist. (Excess demand equals 136 bottles of beer at price = $0.50.) Demanders would not be able to find suppliers for all the beer they want to buy at this price, and those unable to buy would tend to bid up the price. Excess demand would be eliminated when the market price reached $1.

Competition in the market for goods tends to produce a "market-clearing" price—the price at which sellers want to sell exactly the quantity that demanders want to buy. Excess supply and excess demand have been eliminated, and the market is said to "clear." In Figure 3.3, price = $1 is the market-clearing price.

So far we have been considering how the quantity demanded and the quantity supplied change when the price changes. Now let us consider what happens if something else, not the price, changes. For instance, suppose that demand curve DD represents the demand for beer on graduation day at the University of Iowa; when the term is over and the students leave campus, however,

Excess supply exists when at a particular price more of some good or service is supplied than is demanded.

Excess demand exists when at a particular price more of some good or service is demanded than is supplied.

Market clearing occurs when, at the given price, buyers want to purchase exactly the quantity that sellers want to sell.

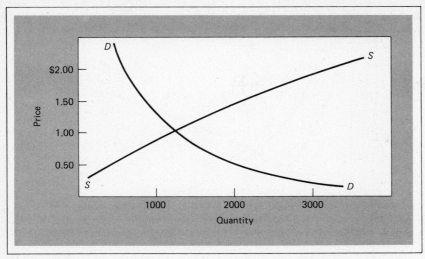

FIGURE 3.3 The beer market in Iowa City (hypothetical). Markets bring together buyers and sellers wanting to make an exchange. A market—such as the market for beer in Iowa City—can be represented graphically by putting together the two parts of Figure 3.2: demand (the buyers) and supply (the sellers). When the price is high, suppliers will want to sell more than demanders will want to purchase— excess supply will exist. A low price leads to the opposite result—an excess demand. When the price results in an amount demanded that is exactly equal to the amount supplied, neither an excess supply nor an excess demand exists. This result is called *market clearing*. The price at which this happens is called the *market-clearing price*. The amount of beer bought and sold is the *market-clearing quantity*.

less beer will be demanded in Iowa City at every given price. This change is represented by a *shift* of the whole demand curve from DD to D*D*. This new, postgraduation demand curve for beer shows how, in the new situation, the quantity demanded will change when the price changes.

A change in the price therefore produces a *movement along* the demand curve; a change in something affecting demand other than the price produces a *shift* in the demand curve. As we see in Figure 3.4a, the shift in the demand curve from DD to D*D* has changed the market-clearing price from $1 to $0.80 per bottle.

Similarly, the supply curve will shift if there is a change in something affecting supply other than the price of beer. Suppose, for instance, that the cost of the grain used to make beer increases. This additional cost may induce some suppliers to depart from the beer market and cause others to reduce their operations. These changes would shift the whole supply curve from SS (in Figure 3.4b) to S*S*. This shift in the supply curve, with DD unchanged, causes the market-clearing price to rise to $1.20 per bottle.

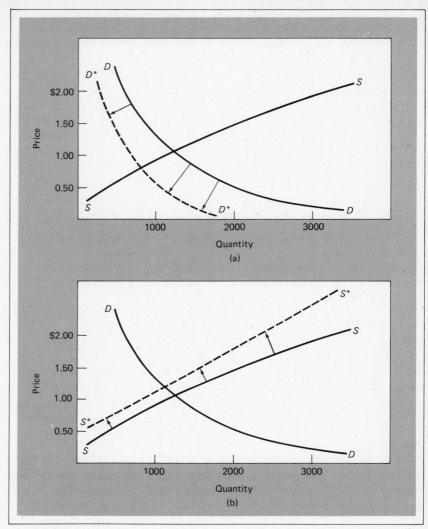

FIGURE 3.4 Shifts in demand and supply. A higher price will lead consumers to demand less and suppliers to supply more. These changes are termed *movements along the demand curve and supply curve*. But changes in the amount supplied or demanded may take place for reasons other than a change in the price. When something other than price causes a change, the demand curve or the supply curve has *shifted*.

The top panel shows a *shift in the demand curve* from DD to D*D*; at every price, the amount demanded after the shift will be less than before. The bottom panel shows a *shift in the supply curve* from SS to S*S*; it indicates that at any given price, less beer will be offered.

In these cases, the curves shifted to the left, indicating less supply or less demand at the same price. Shifts to the right, increasing the amount supplied or the amount demanded at a given price, also take place.

As with the demand curve, so for the supply curve a change in the price of the good creates a movement along the supply curve, whereas a change in something else affecting supply causes a shift in the whole supply curve.

Markets, then, provide a way of coordinating the specialization of labor through buying and selling, or market exchange. Competition among buyers and among sellers tends to produce a market-clearing price at which the quantity demanded equals the quantity supplied. Market interactions thereby determine both the price of the good and the quantity which will be bought and sold.

The horizontal aspect of the economy—who does what labor and how these labors are coordinated—is only one aspect of economic systems. There is a second, vertical, aspect: Who lives off the labor of whom, and who controls the labor process? Who is "on top"? To analyze this aspect of economic systems we will need to introduce another key concept: the surplus.

☐ The Surplus Product and Surplus Labor Time

What did the splendorous kings and queens of the past live on? And the legendary warriors and otherworldly saints: Who produced what they ate, and why? What made possible the glittering Versailles Palace, the mammoth Chinese Wall, the imposing Jefferson Memorial, and the war machine of Adolf Hitler? And how was metal working transformed from the blacksmith's shop to the great mills of Pittsburgh, Kobe, and Dortmund? To answer these questions we need to investigate the surplus product and surplus labor time.

The *surplus product* is defined as follows. A society's economy produces a certain amount of goods and services during a year; call that amount the *total product*. This total product is divisible into two parts: the necessary product and the surplus product. Therefore:

$$\text{total product} = \text{necessary product} + \text{suplus product}$$

The *surplus product* is that part left over out of the total product after necessary product has been deleted.

The *necessary product* also includes two parts. First, the producers of the total product consume some of the product themselves; the output to provide for their consumption, at the "customary" or "traditional" standard of living, constitutes the first part of necessary product.

The **surplus product** is what remains out of the total product after the necessary product has been deleted.

The **total product** is the total amount of goods and services produced in an economy during a year.

The **necessary product** is the amount of goods and services needed to maintain the inputs in the labor process—both workers and tools—at a given level.

necessary product	=	consumption of producers at customary standard of living	+	replacement of capital goods used up in producing total product

Second, some capital goods (tools, machines, and so on) used in producing the total product will need to be repaired or replaced; the output needed to restore capital goods to their condition at the beginning of the year is the second part of necessary product. It is sometimes called depreciation.

Total product is not a very useful measure of the output of an economy, because it includes some outputs that must be set aside to replace the machinery and materials used up in the production process. A preferable measure of output is *net product*, or total product minus the amount of goods and services that must be used to replace used up materials and machinery.

Surplus labor time is just that part of the year's total work time that was devoted to producing the surplus product. Some work time each year is devoted to producing the necessary product; the rest is surplus labor time.

How then does the concept of society's surplus product help us understand who produced what, and why? Let us start with a society that has no surplus product. Imagine a society in which all adults work; they produce just enough each year to provide for the food, clothing, and other aspects of the producers' customary standard of living and to repair or replace any tools, equipment, draft animals, or other things used to produce output. Using the terms introduced above, the amount of this society's total product is thus just enough to provide for the reproduction of the producers at their customary standard of living and to replace the capital goods used up in production. At the end of each year, this community is exactly where it started: The population is as healthy, well fed, and numerous as before, and it has on hand neither more nor fewer capital goods with which to begin production again. This is a no-surplus economy.

This is not necessarily a poor or a subsistence society. The customary standard of living may be high or low. This standard or level is simply the amount of goods sufficient to restore the workers' energies at the end of the workday, to reproduce new workers to replace those who retire, and to maintain all of them—future workers, present workers, and former workers—at some given or customary level of living. (We will devote considerable attention to what determines the living standards of workers, but it would be getting ahead of our story to say more than this: It is *not* primarily a matter of biological survival.) Moreover, the normal work-

Net product is the total product minus materials and capital goods used up in the course of producing the total product.
Surplus labor time is that part of the year's total work time which was devoted to producing the surplus product.

day among the producers in this society may be eight hours, or it may be five hours, or some other amount.

The word *necessary* thus refers to what is required continually to maintain the inputs into the labor process—both workers and tools—at some given level. It is the maintenance of society at a given level which is the basic idea behind *necessary product*, not the adequacy of that society's living standards, the level of its technology, or the diligence of its workers.

Now return to our example of the no-surplus society. Imagine that some group of people have equipped themselves militarily and have gained control over the rest of the community. They order people to work harder or for longer hours. If the new rulers are successful, the total product of the community will now exceed that which reproduces the producers at the customary standard of living and also replaces the capital goods used up in this process. The society will now be producing a surplus product. The producers will be performing surplus labor time.

One way to apreciate the importance of surplus product and surplus labor time is to ask yourself how much of the total product could remain unused (locked in a warehouse, or shot off into space) while still having enough goods both to maintain the producers and their families at the normal living standards *and* to repair or replace all wear and tear on the capital goods used in production. Surplus labor time is similar. It is the amount of reduction in the total hours of work which could take place in a year while still producing enough product to maintain both the producers and the capital goods as they were at the outset.

Without a surplus product, it would be impossible for any group in the society to avoid doing productive work more or less permanently. (Children and old people often do not work, but we are here talking of people who may engage in leisure, knightly conflict, religious meditation, land speculation, buying and selling stocks, or other nonproductive activities over an entire lifetime.) But with a surplus product, nonproducers have a new opportunity: They can force the producers to let them (the nonproducers) consume the surplus product (or use it in other ways).

Depending on the type of economic system in question, this surplus product will take the form of rents and feudal dues paid by serfs to feudal lords, or the income of slave plantation owners, or a portion of the harvest paid by sharecroppers to landlords, or profits received by the owners of today's business corporations.

The surplus product is important for other reasons as well, for it potentially makes possible economic change and growth. When a surplus is produced it may be used to improve or expand the stock of capital goods, allowing for even more production or for less work

Total Product and Surplus Product

In the Old South, slave plantations mainly grew cotton. The cotton was then sold to cotton mills in Britain or New England, and the slaveholder used the money he received to buy food, clothing, provisions for the slaves, tools, and luxury items for himself and his family.

Imagine a slaveholder watching the harvest come in from the fields. First he directs his slaves to put all the bales of cotton together in one big pile; this is his total product.

Then he orders the slaves to put the bales of cotton into one of these piles:

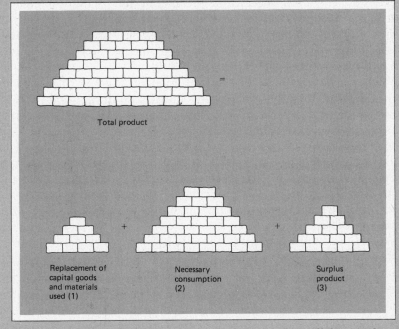

Total product

=

+ Replacement of capital goods and materials used (1)

+ Necessary consumption (2)

+ Surplus product (3)

The money received from the sale of pile (1) will be used to repair or replace the capital goods used in production: to buy new tools and livestock, repair buildings, seed and so forth. The money obtained when the second pile is sold will be used for feeding and clothing the slaves. The money from the third pile is reserved for the slaveholder's own consumption or the purchase of more slaves or other inputs to expand production; it is the surplus product.

The *necessary product* is made up of the first and second piles together.

The *net product* is made up of the second and third piles added together.

The total product of an entire economic system can be thought of as being divided into the same three piles.

in the future. When the surplus is used in this way it is called *investment*.

Alternatively the surplus could allow for population growth, so that rather than simply reproducing the same number of producers, more people could live at the customary standard of living. The surplus could even allow people to work less hard or for fewer hours without lowering their living standards, assuming, of course, that they were allowed to choose how much work they would do.

For all these reasons, the size of the surplus product, how and why it is produced, and who controls it are crucial questions for understanding any economic system.

The idea of the surplus product is so important that we should make it considerably more precise. We will do this by means of a simple example—a model—that is designed to bring out the most important points, while ignoring what is unessential.

The point of our model is to clarify the relationships among the terms introduced earlier in this chapter: specialization, technology, technical change, and the replacement of the capital goods used, the reproduction of the producers, surplus product, and surplus labor time.

To make matters simple, we will consider the labor processes of a single family which is part of a society made up of families similar

Investment is any use of the surplus product which is intended to increase the stocks of materials or capital goods available for use in future production processes.

Economic Models

Economic models, like any scientific models, are attempts to simplify a problem so that we can understand it better. The point of a model is to represent what is important for the purposes at hand, not to represent every detail of the problem. Thus the airplane models used in wind tunnels do not have seats in them, though great care is taken with every detail concerning the shape of the wing. Similarly architects models focus upon the visual and spatial aspects of a proposed building; the fact that the models are made of wood and plastic rather than the concrete and steel that will go into the resulting construction is considered to be unimportant. Models are frequently used in economics, the most common being the familiar supply and demand curves explaining prices under conditions of perfect competition.

Models allow us to think about complex problems in simple ways. Economic models which successfully highlight what is important without ignoring essential aspects of a problem are as necessary a tool of economic reasoning as the modern telescope is to the astronomer's craft. However, models can be very misleading when they are based on unrealistic assumptions, or when they oversimplify things to such an extent that essential aspects are left out.

in the respects emphasized by our model. In this family there are two labor processes, childrearing and grain growing. Childrearing reproduces people. Grain growing produces a consumer good—grain—used in the reproduction of people: people eat the grain. Grain growing also produces capital goods, for the grain is also used to feed the oxen or other draft animals so that they may continue working and reproducing other draft animals for future crops. Grain is also one of the materials used in the production process, because grain itself must be used as seed for the next crop. Thus the grain technology can be represented as follows:

The Grain Technology

1. Inputs
   a. Labor   Planting, harvesting
   b. Materials   Grain (seed)
   c. Capital goods   Grain (used for maintaining and
                                   reproducing draft animals)
   d. Nonreproducible inputs   Land, rainfall
2. Output
   a. Consumer goods   Grain to be eaten
   b. Capital goods   Grain to be used as food for draft
                                   animals
   c. Materials   Grain to be used as seeds

The way the grain technology is presented here it is easy to distinguish between total product and net product: *Total product* is all the corn that is produced, while *net product* is gross product minus the output required to replace anything used up in production (in this case seed for next year's crop and feed for the draft animals). Net product is the more important concept, because we really care about how much is produced above and beyond how much was used up in the process.

We can represent the grain technology in another way as well, one which indicates how much of the inputs are required for each bushel of grain in net product. In Figure 3.5 the total hours of grain-producing labor are measured (from right to left) on the horizontal axis and the bushels of gross and net product are measured on the vertical axis. The line *Oa* describes the relationship between hours of labor and total product; the line *Ob* describes the relationship between hours of labor and net product. Thus if the family members work 10 hours daily over the relevant growing season, they will produce 4 bushels of total product. One bushel of this output will be required to replace the capital goods for next year's crop (set aside seeds or perhaps to feed any draft animals they use). The resulting net product is 3 bushels.

Figure 3.5 indicates, also, that more or less than ten hours of daily labor will produce more or less net product. For instance,

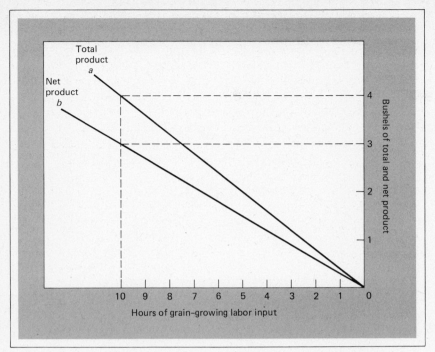

FIGURE 3.5 A grain-growing technology: Labor inputs, total output, and net output. If 10 hours of labor are devoted to grain growing, 4 bushels of total output (3 bushels of net output) can be produced. Lesser amounts of labor yield lesser amounts of grain, as the two lines in the figure show. The output is measured vertically. The input is measured horizontally—points farther to the *left* represent *more* labor input. The distance between the net-output and total-output lines represents the amount of grain that must be set aside as seed and feed for the draft animals so that the same amount of total and net outputs can be produced the next season.

with seven hours of grain-growing labor, less than 3 bushels of net product are produced.

We can use a similar diagram (Figure 3.6) to show the effect of technical change. Figure 3.6a traces the effect of an increase in the efficiency of labor. For example, suppose the producers discover an easier (less time-consuming) way to irrigate the grain. The result will be that for every hour of labor put into grain growing, more grain will be produced. The line showing initial gross product (Oa) rotates upward to show gross product after the technical progress (Oa'); similarly the net product line rotates from Ob to Ob'. This is termed *labor-saving technical progress* because each bushel of gross product requires less labor to produce.

Another type of technical progress is shown in Figure 3.6b. Consider, for example, an improvement in animal breeding that greatly improves the disease resistance of draft animals. This change

Labor-saving technical progress is an increase in the efficiency of labor, permitting producers to produce more output for every hour of labor input without working any harder.

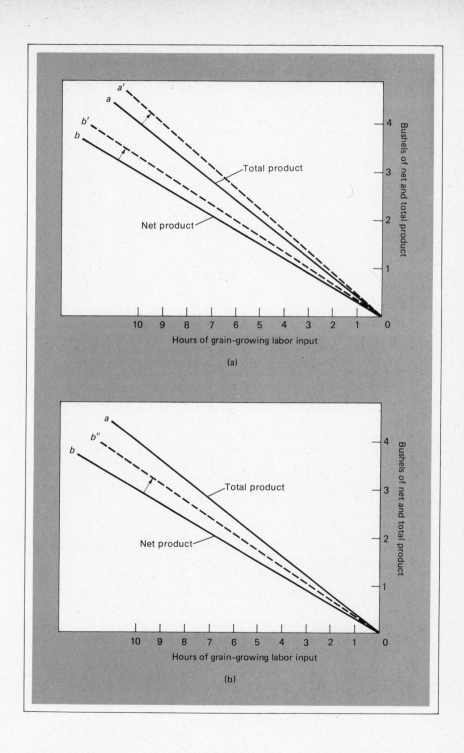

Bushels of net and total product

a'
a
b'
b

Total product

Net product

10 9 8 7 6 5 4 3 2 1 0

Hours of grain-growing labor input

(a)

Bushels of net and total product

a
b"
b

Total product

Net product

10 9 8 7 6 5 4 3 2 1 0

Hours of grain-growing labor input

(b)

FIGURE 3.6 **Technical progress in grain growing.** A labor-saving technical change is illustrated in the top panel. This type of change moves both the net and total output lines upward, from the solid to the dashed lines. The same amount of labor time devoted to grain growing produces more total output. And because the amount of seed and animal feed that must be set aside has not changed, the net output increases as well.

A capital-goods-saving technical change shifts only the net-output line upward. There is no change in how much total output will be produced by any given amount of labor. But because this type of change reduces the amount of capital goods (seed and animal feed) needed to produce the total output, any given amount of labor produces more net output.

would reduce the number of draft animals that must be fed and maintained to plow the fields and to reproduce the stock of animals. This does not change the total product line Oa, because a given amount of labor will still produce the same amount of total output; but it does result in the net product line rotating upward, toward the total product line, from Ob to Ob''. This is termed *capital-goods-saving technical progress* because each bushel of gross product requires fewer capital goods (grain to maintain the stock of draft animals) to produce.

Capital-goods-saving technical progress is a reduction in the gap between gross and net product, permitting producers to obtain the same net output using fewer capital goods.

Each family engages in childrearing as well as grain growing. We can now put the two labor processes—childrearing and grain growing—together. In Figure 3.7 we measure the total working hours along the horizontal axis. Let us assume that, taken as a whole—including the hours of all who work—the family does 16 hours of labor per day, and that whatever time is not spent on childrearing will go toward grain growing. The division of the 16 hours between these two activities is indicated by a point along the horizontal axis of the figure. As shown in Figure 3.7, point L indicates that the family has allocated 10 hours of its labor to grain growing and 6 hours to childrearing. The total hours of work may be divided up in other ways: Points farther to the left along the horizontal axis (for example point Q) indicate more grain-growing labor and less childrearing, points farther to the right (like point R) indicate less time devoted to grain and more to childrearing.

The net product of grain, line bb in Figure 3.7, is the same as the Ob line in the previous graphs. The graph can be read as follows: With 6 hours being spent on childrearing and 10 hours on grain growing, (point L), 3 bushels of net product are being produced. The line bb shows all of the possible combinations of hours of childrearing time and (net) bushels of grain per family that are possible, given the existing technology, the number of hours of work, and at the normal level of work effort.

Line bb is called *production possibility frontier*. It indicates that, as long as the technology does not change and the amount and intensity of work remains the same, the only way the family can

A **production possibility frontier** shows all the possible combinations of outputs available using a given technology and a fixed amount of inputs.

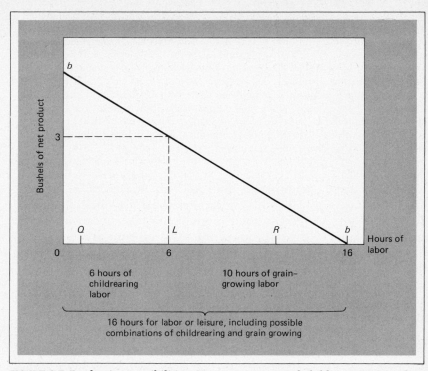

FIGURE 3.7 Production possibilities: Net grain output and childrearing time. This graph shows the possibilities for grain growing and childrearing together. The line *bb* is the net-output line from Figure 3.5. As before, it indicates (measuring from right to left) that when 10 hours of labor are devoted to grain growing, 3 bushels of net grain output can be produced. If the total labor time is 16 hours, 6 hours are left for childrearing. Point *L* thus represents one possibility: 3 bushels of grain and 6 hours of childrearing. Any point farther to the right, such as *R*, on the horizontal (hours of labor) axis indicates more childrearing labor and less grain-growing labor; the result will be less net-grain output and more attention being given to children. Any point to the left, such as *Q*, indicates more grain output and less childrearing time.

increase its output of grain is to transfer some of its labor time from childrearing to grain growing. Conversely, the only way to spend more time on childrearing is to reduce its output of grain.

Only if the family is producing grain less efficiently than is possible with the existing technology could it obtain more grain without reducing childrearing time. It could do so simply by producing more efficiently.

If we know what the customary standard of living is, we can determine if this society is producing a surplus product. In the example above, let us assume that this family is an average or representative family; its customary standard of living is simply the number of bushels of grain consumed by all the family members in a year plus the number of hours of childrearing per day normally devoted to children. Let us say that 3 bushels of grain per year and 6 hours of child care daily are required for the reproduction of the producers at the customary standard of living. Given this customary standard of living, this society is not producing a surplus: Net product is exactly equal to the grain required to support the producers at their customary level, and no more (net) product can be produced without cutting into the normal level of child-care activities.

How might such a society come to produce a surplus? One obvious way would be for the customary standard of living to be reduced. If people could be persuaded (or more likely forced) to accept a permanent reduction in the amount of grain they live on, while continuing to work as hard as before, for as many hours, and as productively as before, necessary product would fall. But the total amount produced would remain the same, and hence a surplus product would arise.

We illustrate this change in Figure 3.8. The grain devoted to reproducing the producers has, in Figure 3.8, now fallen to 2 bushels; total work time remains 16 hours daily, of which 6 hours are devoted to childrearing. Net product is unchanged at 3 bushels, because 10 hours are still devoted to grain labor (it takes 3.3 hours to produce one bushel of net output). The surplus product is 1 bushel per family. Surplus labor time is the time it takes to produce this surplus of 1 bushel per family, or 3.3 hours.

Are there yet other ways that a grain surplus might be produced? Yes, the producers can work harder, or more effectively, with no corresponding increase in their standard of living. If they work harder, more is produced for a given hour of work through an intensification of labor.

A change in the technology—the discovery of better kinds of tools, for example—would allow workers to work more effectively, thus increasing the productivity of a given amount of work. This case may seem similar to "working harder," but it is really quite different: In the "working harder" case there was no increase in productivity, only an increase in effort; in the "working more effectively" case, workers did not work harder, yet they still produced more.

Last, the family could work longer, spending, say, 18 hours a day rather than 16 on childrearing and grain growing combined. Here the productivity of work and its intensity are unchanged, but the amount of grain-growing labor has increased, and, as long as the living standard of the workers has not risen, a surplus will be produced.

We are not very interested in how a nonsurplus-producing society turns into a surplus-producing society, because, as we will soon

How is the surplus product produced? ?

↳ mechanics

The **intensity of labor** is how much work effort producers must expend per hour of work.

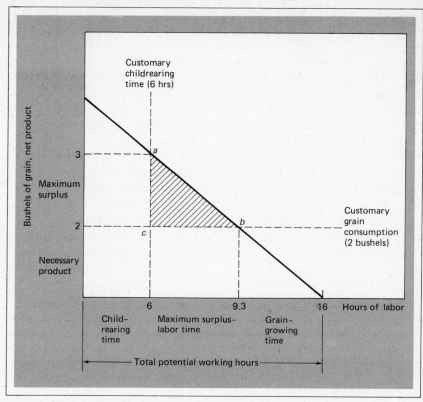

FIGURE 3.8 Specialization, surplus labor, and surplus product. If the customary standard of living of the family is 2 bushels of grain per year, the necessary product can be produced by devoting 6.7 hours daily to grain growing (this is shown as the distance between the total of 16 hours of labor and 9.3 hours); 6.7 hours is necessary labor time. If the customary standard of living also includes 6 hours of childrearing time per day, the maximum surplus labor time is 3.3 hours. When workers work a full 10 hours at grain growing, they produce a surplus product of 1 bushel. If they work only 6.7 hours, they have free time instead of working surplus labor time.

see, our society is, and for a long time has been, a surplus-producing society. But our model will help us understand something very important: What determines the amount of the surplus and therefore what will raise and lower it. We can summarize what the model can tell us about this.

The following changes, if they come about without altering any of the other facts of the situation, will raise the amount of the surplus: (1) An increase in the hours worked on the production of goods and services; (2) a reduction in the customary standard of living of the workers; (3) an increase in the intensity of labor of the workers; (4) an increase in the productivity of a given amount of labor, working at a given level of intensity (labor saving technical progress); and (5) a decrease in the amount of output required to replace the materials or machines used in production, reducing the difference between total and net product (capital-goods-saving technical progress).

The model also indicates some of the possible uses of the surplus. Figure 3.8 indicates that the society could consume a 1-bushel-per-family surplus while devoting 10 hours to grain growing and 6 hours to raising children (point *a*). Alternatively it could have no surplus product and 3.3 more hours of free time (point *b*). Or, the workers could continue working 10 hours at grain growing but work only two-thirds as hard, producing only 2 bushels of net output (point *c*). In fact any combination in the shaded area of Figure 3.8 is possible. Other possibilities include *investment*, such as setting aside from the 1 bushel surplus more than the minimum seed for next year's crop or raising draft animals and thus increasing output or lightening the work load next year. Or, as has often been the case in actual societies, the surplus might be controlled by an elite class, who use it for their own enjoyment (luxury consumption) or with the intention of further enhancing their power or prestige (using the grain to maintain an army or to feed workers employed to build monuments).

This model illustrates the relationship among our concepts almost as an architect's drawing illustrates the spatial relationships among parts of a building. But it does not do much more than that, for it does not tell us *why* the technology is what it is, or *why* the workers work a total of 16 hours, or *why* they work as hard as they do, or *how* the "customary" standard of living is determined. All of these important questions will be taken up in the chapters that follow. The model does not even say *who* gets the surplus if there is one, and what is done with it. To begin to address these questions we will turn in the next chapter to the idea of class and how class relationships define economic systems.

☐ Suggested Readings

Paul Baran, *The Political Economy of Growth* (New York: Monthly Review Press, 1957).

Samuel Bowles, David Gordon, and Thomas Weisskopf, *Beyond the Waste Land: A Democratic Alternative to Economic Decline* (New York: Doubleday, 1983).

E. J. Hobsbawm, *Industry and Empire: The Making of Modern English Society* (London: Penguin Books, 1968).

Karl Polanyi, Conrad Aronsberg, and Harry Pearson, eds., *Trade and Market in the Early Empires* (New York: Free Press, 1957).

Charles Tilly, ed., *The Formation of Nation-States in Western Europe* (Princeton, N.J.: Princeton University Press, 1975).

CHAPTER 4

CAPITALISM AND OTHER ECONOMIC SYSTEMS

Cambridge, England, sits at the edge of a low plain stretching north and east to the sea. Here the earth itself reveals how capitalism has transformed society.

In feudal times this marshy, swampy ground (called the "fens") had poor drainage, and in the winter rains much of it lay flooded and unusable. The town of Ely grew up on a small hill, the "isle of Ely," that usually escaped the flooding.

Over a thousand years ago Ely became the focus of church building—an important feudal use of the surplus product. An abbey was established in the ninth century, burned down, and was rebuilt. Soon after the Normans conquered England in the eleventh century, workers under their command began building the great cathedral that stands upon the site even today. Massive and elegant, the cathedral consumed the labors of thousands of artisans and required 110 years to build. But it was never really finished: New chapels were built, more elaborate furnishings added, the tower heightened. Its west tower now soars 200 feet above the surrounding floodplain (and so would its east tower, if it hadn't collapsed in the fourteenth century). For centuries it stood as a dry monument to the religous use of the surplus, while all about it the waterlogged fens frustrated cultivation.

In the seventeenth century, the fens were transformed by the capitalist use of the surplus. The Duke of Bedford, owner of some 20,000 acres in the area, sensed the possibility for profits and organized an investment company to drain the fens. Engineers were hired, and workers dug two huge ditches, 100 feet wide and 30 miles long, to carry the excess water to the sea. Many additional miles of feeder ditches and channels drained into the main ditches. This colossal construction project transformed the marsh into rich and well-drained agricultural land (and made the duke a very rich man).

The modern visitor to Ely can see both marvels, the cathedral and the ditches. Feudalism, with its cathedral, magnificent and dominating the landscape, actually drained the region's surplus product and left the economy unchanged and stagnant. Capitalism invested the surplus product and drained the fens, repaying the investors many times over. More important, the fens ditches, humble and easy to overlook, revolutionized the entire system of production in the area.

In this chapter we investigate what or who determines what each society does with its surplus product, and who benefits from how the surplus product is used.

Often people who did not produce the surplus product nonetheless control it. This was the case, for instance, in ancient Athens and the pre–Civil War U.S. South, when slaveowners lived off the fruits of their slaves' labor. The relationship between those who produce the product, including the surplus product, and those who control the use of the surplus product is called a *class relationship.* Class relationships exist between different *classes,* or groups of people who share a common position in the economy. The producers are one class; the controllers of the surplus product are another class.

An economic system in which the producers do not control the use of the surplus is called a *class society.* Capitalism is a class society. Though very different from U.S. capitalism, the economic system of the Soviet Union today—often called state socialism—is also a class society. In both the Soviet Union and the United States the surplus product is produced by the work of tens of millions of workers of all descriptions. But in both countries it is controlled by a relatively small group of people. The way these two economic systems work is, of course, very different, which is why they bear different names.

The main idea of this chapter is that how the surplus is controlled and used defines economic classes; and classes and the surplus product are the keys to understanding how each economic system works.

This main idea is expressed in four main points:

1. *Classes* exist in all societies with a surplus product; they reflect the division of people into those who *produce* the whole product, including the surplus product, and those who *control* the surplus product. Class is the principal aspect of the vertical or command dimension of the economy.

2. *Economic systems* represent different ways of organizing and controlling labor processes based on different property systems or other ways of determining how the surplus will be used. Each economic system has a distinct set of classes associated with it.
3. *Capitalism* is a particular economic system in which *commodities are produced for profit* using *privately owned capital goods* and *wage labor*. There are two main classes in capitalism—workers and employers; other classes (the "middle" classes) also are important in capitalism.
4. In capitalism, the surplus appears as *profits* received by those who own the capital goods used in production; people who receive profits control the surplus product by using their profits to buy the commodities that make up the surplus product.

At Ely the different uses of the surplus product left visible reminders for us to see of the differences between feudalism and capitalism. The cathedral is hard to miss; the ditches, by contrast, are not so obvious unless we know where to look and what we are looking for. Similarly, while it is reasonably easy to see how the feudal economic system worked, understanding capitalism is much more difficult, unless we know where to look and what to look for: classes and the surplus product.

☐ Class and Class Relationships

Like other words, *class* is used in many different ways. If a ball player has class it means that he or she plays with style. If people are middle class it may mean that they have a certain lifestyle, perhaps owning a house with a swimming pool in the backyard. The upper class is rich. And so on. In political economy, the word has a different and very precise meaning.

A *class* is a group of people who share a common position in the economy; specifically, a common position with respect to the production and control of the surplus product.

A *class relationship* exists when one group of people, or a class, produces the total product, including the surplus product, whereas another group—another class—is able to command the use of the surplus product. Both groups—the producers of the surplus product and those who control its use—are classes. Slaves were one class, slaveowners another; the serfs who worked the land in medieval Europe constituted a class, their feudal lords were a different class.

Three aspects of this definition of a class are important. First, every class is defined in terms of a relationship. It is like the word cousin, which refers to someone, but which is meaningless unless there is another person who is also a cousin: You cannot be your own cousin, you cannot be a cousin by yourself, you can only be

A **class** is a group of people who share a common position in the economy with respect to the production and control of the surplus product.

A **class relationship** exists between the producers of the total product, including the surplus product, and those who command the use of the surplus product.

your cousin's cousin. A class cannot exist by itself, it can only exist in relationship to some other class.

Second, a class relationship refers to a labor process: classes are defined by the particular positions that they occupy with respect to the labor process. A class is not defined by its status or by the social esteem which others have for its members. A class is not defined by the income of its members: the rich and the poor are not classes, though it may well be that most of the rich are in one class and most of the poor in another. A status group such as "the well educated" or an income group—those receiving less than $10,000 a year, for example—is a collection of people, defined by some characteristic. They are not defined by their relationship to another group in the labor process. For this reason they are not classes.

Members of a class may be very different, one from another. They may live in different parts of the country or the world, they may be more or less well off, they may have different lifestyles, and if they are workers, they may have very different jobs. They may be in competition with one another—to find jobs, to sell products, or for any other reason. What makes the members of a class alike is their relationship to the other classes. (This is again analogous to cousins; the only thing we *know* they have in common is their relationship to one another.)

A number of social groups very important to economic analysis are not classes. Nations are not classes, nor are races, nor are sexes, for none of these groups is defined by its relation to a labor process. Females and males, for example, are defined biologically, and though men and women often do different kinds of work, it is not their position in the labor process that defines them. (To define women as those who produce children and men as all others would classify women without children as men!)

Third, class relations are hierarchical, or vertical; they refer to a group on top and a group on the bottom. What is vertical about the relationship? Why can we call it hierarchical? The group on top is not necessarily happier; nor are they better, nor more productive (they may not be productive at all: Consider the slaveowners). They are said to be on top because they control the labor of others and its products. The slaveowner employed the overseer who controlled the work of slaves. What they produced was the property of the slaveowner.

The feudal lord's bailiff overseer directed the work of the serfs on the lord's land. What the serfs grew on the lord's land belonged to the lord.

The owner of a company selects the management that directs the employees in their work. The commodities they produce are owned by the owner.

In each case, of course, the producers consume something, either a part of what they have produced or goods produced by other workers. Slaves and serfs grew food on their "own" plots which made up a major part of their diet. Workers today are paid wages and salaries, with which they buy most of what they consume. What is important is that in each case the producers—slaves, serfs, or workers—produce more than they get. Correspondingly, the class on top gets something that it did not produce.

There are usually more than two classes in a society. So usually there are class relationships more complex than just the relationship between producers and controllers. For instance, in the nineteenth century in the United States, an important relationship existed between the (northern) working class and the (southern) slaves. The relationship between these two classes was not vertical—the slaves did not live on the surplus product of the workers nor vice versa. Their relationship was partly characterized by class interdependence, since slaves grew the cotton needed in the mills where (some) workers found jobs; conversely, the mills' demand for cotton provided the revenues that kept the slave plantations going. The textiles produced in the mills became the slaves' clothing. Political relations also existed between these two classes, as when workers volunteered in the northern armies to fight for the emancipation of the slaves. However complex the slave-worker relationship was, both classes were defined with respect to a simple vertical relationship: workers to employers; slaves to slaveholders.

☐ Classes and Economic Systems

What is an economic system? We have already named several different economic systems: slavery, self-sufficient households, capitalism, state socialism, feudalism, and so on. We also know that what they have in *common,* what makes the *economic* systems, is that they organize the human labor by which all societies live. But what makes them *different* from each other?

Each economic system has a distinct set of class relationships. Associated with each class relationship is a distinctive way of organizing and controlling its labor processes. For instance, we call one system "slavery" because its constituent classes are slaves and slaveowners. Inherent in the very definition of "slaves" and "slaveowners" is a particular method for organizing labor processes, namely, that the human input to production is itself owned as a piece of property. Every economic system has distinct class relationships, and every class relationship implies a distinct method of organizing labor processes and controlling the surplus product.

This combination of class relationships and associated methods for controlling labor processes is usually expressed legally in a set of *property rights*. To continue our previous example, the slaveowner is a slaveowner because of his ownership of a particular piece of property (slaves), and his ownership conferred certain rights on the owner: the right to direct the slaves' labor, the right to own the product of the slaves' labor, the right to own any children the slaves might bear, and so on.

Economic systems differ, then, because they have different class relationships with different associated ways of controlling their labor processes and different sets of property rights.

Let us consider, as an example, feudalism, the dominant economic system of Europe in the Middle Ages. Feudalism contained two principal classes, the lords (either church officials or secular, nonchurch nobles) and serfs. Other classes in feudal Europe included artisans; bailiffs and other members of a lord's retinue; and merchants. The serfs produced the total product (except for goods made by artisans), some part of which, the necessary consumption, they retained for their own use. But the lords obtained part of the output, the surplus product, to support themselves, to build their castles and cathedrals, to finance their Crusades, and otherwise lead their noble life-styles.

How did they obtain the surplus product? Why did the serfs turn over part of their output to the lords? First, how: serfs usually owed rents to their lords; in addition, they generally owed labor duties—they were obligated to work on the lord's land for a certain number of days a year, and the lord owned what was produced on this land. Sometimes serfs were obligated to pay other fees, for example, for milling grain at the lord's gristmill, even, in one case, to support the lord's dancing bear, a fee that continued even after the bear died.

In feudalism, then, the surplus product was paid by the serfs in rents, labor duties, and fees owed to the lords. But why did the serfs pay? They were legally obligated to make these payments, and feudal courts enforced the lords' property rights to them. The lords generally had the military power to punish anyone who refused to pay, although escape to cities or to open lands or even to competing lords was sometimes possible. The lords thereby controlled the use of the surplus product.

In slavery, as it existed in the American South, there were again two principal classes, the slaves and the slaveholders. Other classes in the South included nonslaveowning farmers, overseers, urban craftspeople, free blacks, and merchants. The slaveowner owned *all* of the inputs to the slave labor process, including even the laborers themselves. The slaves produced the total product, all of which was owned by the slaveowner. Part of this output—either foodstuffs grown on the plantation itself or supplies purchased with

Property rights are a legal expression for the combination of class relationships and associated arrangements for using and controlling the surplus product.

Feudalism was the dominant economic system in europe in the Middle Ages; lords obtained the surplus product through rents and other customary obligations owed by the serfs.

Slavery was the dominant economic system in the U.S. South before the Civil War; slaveholders obtained the surplus product by owning all of the inputs (including slaves) and the output of slave production.

the revenues from the sale of the tobacco or cotton crop—was used to provision the slaves; this portion represented the customary consumption. Part of the output had to be set aside to feed mules, replace wornout tools, and otherwise replenish the capital goods used up in producing the output. And what remained—the surplus product—was left for the slaveholder to use, for personal consumption, for the purchase of more slaves, for the construction of beautiful mansions, for education of the slaveowner's children, for foreign travel, or whatever.

Whether slavery, feudalism, capitalism, or something else, each economic system has a distinct class relationship. It has an associated way of organizing the labor process and an attached system of property rights that together govern the control and use of the surplus product. These relationships may be thought of as a set of rules governing economic life.

Economic systems may be thus understood in terms of an analogy to games. What defines any game is the rules by which it is played. Thus what makes baseball different from basketball is not who plays it, or where it is played, or when, or anything other than the rules by which each game is played.

The same is true of economic systems. Each economic system has a distinct set of "rules of the game," that is, the distinctive way that classes interact with respect to the surplus product. Economic systems are *not* defined according to *what* is produced—grain, haircuts, or cars; *where* it is produced—in urban areas or the country, in the United States or Africa; or *who* makes up the economic system. As in sports, it is the rules of the game that distinguish one economic system from another.

Class relations, or the "rules of the game," are very easy to see in the slave and feudal economic systems. The basic class relationship of capitalism is less obvious, but it exists as well. We turn now to the capitalist class relationship and to the definition of the capitalist economic system.

□ Capitalism

Capitalism is an economic system in which commodities are produced for profit using privately owned capital goods and wage labor; capitalists obtain the surplus product in the form of profits.

Capitalism is an economic system in which commodities are produced for profit using privately owned capital goods and wage labor.

The relationship between capitalists and workers is defined by three characteristics of the labor process. First, the labor process produces commodities. Second, the capital goods used in production are privately owned. And third, the labor employed is primarily wage labor. We will explain each of these three aspects—commodity production, private ownership of the capital goods used in production, and wage labor—in turn.

Commodities

A *commodity* is anything—a good or service, whether intended for people to consume or for businesses to use as a production input—that is produced with the intention of selling it in order to make money.

To clarify the idea of a commodity, think about pancake making. In the previous chapter we focused on the recipe, on the pancake technology. Now we turn to the social organization of pancake making. To do this we will have to say where the pancakes are being made and why they are made. The labor process for making pancakes at home on a Sunday morning is organized in a very different way from the labor process for making pancakes at the House of Pancakes, or some other restaurant.

Let us start with the House of Pancakes case. What explains who is doing what tasks in producing pancakes? What explains how the pancake eater gets the pancake? The answer to these questions is—markets. The labor market determines the first question, and the pancake market (and others) determines the second.

A **commodity** is any good or service that is produced with the intention of selling it in order to make a profit.

Commodities—Two Views

—From an advertisement:

"Many aspire to owing an S. T. Dupont lighter. Few know how to use one properly.

As a weapon: An S. T. Dupont lighter can be a psychological club. A glimpse of an S. T. Dupont lighter can upend an opponent.

As visual musk: An S. T. Dupont lighter is a symbol of your ability to get what you want. And power is, baldly stated, an aphrodisiac.

As an appliance: An S. T. Dupont lighter does a fine job of producing fire. So does a book of matches.

Suggested retail prices range from $100 to $3,000, depending on the model."

—From a mother:

"I will never give up my oven for a new one. It has been here forty years and is an old friend. I would stop baking bread if it gave out. My sons once offered to buy me an electric range . . . and I broke down. It was a terrible thing to do. The boys felt bad. . . . Later my husband said they all agreed I was in the right; the stove had been so good to us and there is nothing wrong—the bread is as tasty as ever, I believe.

I watch my son Domingo and his son Domingo; they both have plans: next year we buy this, and the year after, that. Such plans are sad to hear. Those are the moments I feel suddenly old, the only time I do."

Dolores Garcia, quoted in Robert Coles, *The Old Ones of New Mexico* (Albuquerque, New Mexico: University of New Mexico Press, 1973).

The pancake eater gets the pancake by paying for it. He or she gives up something—some money—to acquire the ownership of the pancake. A market is one particular way of exchanging the ownership of things. How much money is required? The price is determined by the competitive strategies of buyers and sellers, whose interactions were described in the demand and supply curves of the previous chapter.

How the pancake eater gets the pancake also explains why the pancake is made. It is made to be sold in exchange for money.

It is not made because the workers at the Pancake House particularly like making pancakes instead of something else or because they want their customers to be well fed. They make the pancakes because they are paid to do it. If they did not get paid they would quit. If they could make more money making hamburgers, they would probably be at McDonald's.

The pancake is not made because the owner of the Pancake House enjoys presiding over pancake making. He may live in another town or even another country. He may never have seen the Pancake House. In any case, if he could make more money putting his money into steel making or sheep raising, he would probably not be the owner of the Pancake House.

The point is making money, not making pancakes.

The pancake at the Pancake House is called a *commodity*. The point of producing commodities is to sell them. The likes and dislikes of the producers or the owners and their concern (or lack of it) for the nutrition or other enjoyment of the buyer may be very important to the people involved, but it does not determine what commodities will be produced and who will get them. What commodities are produced and who gets them are determined strictly by the prices at which the goods can be sold and the costs of producing them. For this reason commodity exchanges are anonymous; anybody coming into the Pancake House and putting down the right price gets a stack of pancakes. It does not matter who the buyer is; only the price matters.

It is not like this around the Sunday morning breakfast table. If a stranger walked in, he might be asked to come back later, or never; or he might be invited to sit down and have some pancakes. But he would not get them just by putting down $2.50 on the kitchen table.

Pancakes made at home are not commodities. The recipe may be exactly the same as in the House of Pancakes, but this does not make them commodities. It is not the technology that determines what is a commodity; it is why it is produced, how its production is organized, and how it is distributed.

Pancakes made in the kitchen of an army base are not commodities either. They are made because someone in authority ordered

Money Talks (and Eats)

During the early 1970s over 100,000 people in West Africa died of hunger and hunger-related causes during one of the worst famines in recent history. Starvation was not the result of scarcity, however: The United Nations Food and Agriculture Organization documented that even during the drought that brought on the famine, the area produced enough grain to feed its population. Mali, a country at the center of the region, continued the export of highly nutritious peanuts throughout the famine. During the famine planes took off regularly from Dakar, the capital of famine-stricken Senegal, carrying asparagus bound for the elegant restaurants of Paris.

A couple of years later, *New York Times* food columnist Craig Claiborne described a sumptuous meal he and a friend enjoyed in one of these Parisian restaurants: "The foods were elegant to look at, but the overall display was undistinguished, if not to say shabby. ... The food itself was generally exemplary, although there were regrettable lapses there too." But overall: "We feel that we could not have made a better choice, given the circumstance of time and place." The tab? $4,000. (In 1984 prices, about $7000)

Considering the world's population as a whole, the World Bank estimates that a quarter of us are seriously malnourished. According to the United Nations Food and Agriculture Organization, 40,000 children die of hunger every day. Yet the world produces enough grain alone to provide everyone with ample protein and more than 3500 calories a day, above the average for Americans. But it is more profitable to feed grain to livestock to be sold later to those who have the money to pay for it as beef and other meats. Livestock consume about as much grain as the entire human population of the world. And the livestock are rapidly overtaking the people: a decade and a half ago only about one-third of the world grain output was fed to livestock.

Food is a commodity. It is produced to make money, not to fill empty stomachs.

Sources: Frances Moore Lappé and Joseph Collins, *Food First: Beyond the Myth of Scarcity* (New York: Ballantine Books, 1979); Francis Moore Lappé and Joseph Collins *World Hunger: 10 Myths* (San Francisco, Calif.: Institute for Food and Development Policy, 1982); *new York Times*, November 14, 1975; *Le Monde,* May 1981.

---

them to be made, and those making them do so because they have been so ordered. No price is charged for the pancakes: To get a pancake one must simply be part of one of the units at the base.

Commodities are the most prevalent form taken by the products of labor in the United States today. But as we have already seen, they are not the only form. Some products are rarely, if ever, commodities. Schooling is primarily not a commodity, though special-

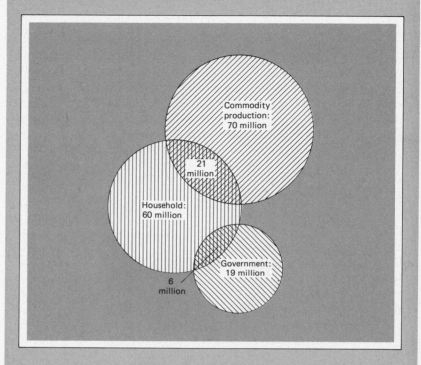

United States Workers Engaged in Commodity Production as Compared to Other Labor Processes, 1983

Commodity production: 70 million

21 million

Household: 60 million

Government: 19 million

6 million

If we divide all labor processes into those that go on within the family, those in the government, and those that produce commodities, we can see from the figure above that commodity production involves considerably more workers (full-time equivalents) than the other two. The size of each circle indicates the number of full-time equivalent workers. The shaded overlapping areas of each circle indicate people who work in more than one kind of production; for example, the overlapping area of family production and commodity production represents the fact that many house workers also hold jobs as commodity producers, and almost all commodity producers do at least some housework.

Source: The estimates above are based on data presented in *Statistical Abstract of the United States, 1984* (Washington, D.C.: Government Printing Office, 1984).

ized training often is. People are not produced as commodities, even though the labor that people do is often determined by markets. (People were "produced" as commodities on American slave-breeding plantations prior to the Civil War.) In many societies, both today and in the past, commodities are much less important. In some societies, market exchanges in food were forbidden: It was simply thought to be too important to be left up to the buying and selling of each individual. The price of food even today in the United States, and in every other country, is directly determined in some part by government policy rather than by anonymous commodity exchange.

Commodity production is very different from other ways of organizing production and distributing its results—other ways such as parental relations in the family, or military command at an army base, or the democratic processes of a town meeting; it is one of the keys to understanding the economy of the United States today.

By itself, commodity production does not define capitalism; commodity production occurs in other economic systems as well as in capitalism. For instance, slave plantations in the American South produced tobacco or cotton, which was then sold.

For commodity production also to be called capitalist production, there must be employers and workers. The relationship between employers and workers is defined by two further characteristics of the labor process. First, the capital goods—the tools, raw materials, factories, offices, and other goods used in production—must be privately owned. And second, the labor employed must be primarily wage labor.

Privately owned capital goods

The second defining aspect of capitalism is private property in capital goods. By the private ownership of property we usually mean that the thing in question may be sold or used by the owner or those designated by him at his discretion, and that others may be excluded from its use. That is what a "Private Property" sign means.

The idea of private ownership of the capital goods needed in production, while not unique to capitalism, is nonetheless far from universal. For instance, many Native American peoples did not have such a concept, which made it impossible for them to sell anything in the sense that the European settlers understood as a sale or purchase. The derogatory expression "Indian giver," referring to someone who gives you something and then wants it back, illustrates this point. The phrase arises from the Europeans' (and most present-day Americans') inability to understand that among Native Americans, some things such as land were neither mine nor yours, but ours or no one's. Other societies have also had very complex notions of property.

How could capital goods *not* be privately owned? They might be owned by a government body, like a municipal electricity com-

Privately owned capital goods are machines, buildings, offices, tools, and other durable things needed in production and whose owner, because of a property right, determines how the property will be used.

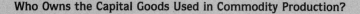

Who Owns the Capital Goods Used in Commodity Production?

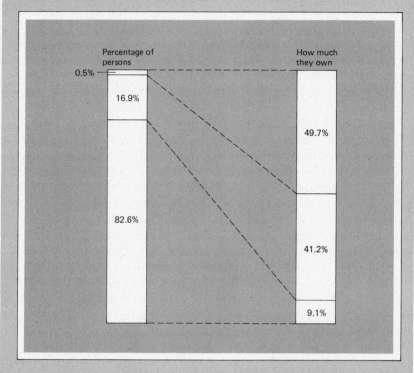

The left column shows the percentge of all persons, the right column shows how much they own of the capital goods used in production. The richest 0.5 percent of the population own about as much (49.7 percent) of all the capital goods as do the entire remaining 99.5 percent of the population (50.3 percent). On the average, the richest 0.5 percent own $1,018,186 (in 1983 dollars) in capital goods used in production. Their total wealth was much greater since they typically also own real estate and other assets not counted here.

Of course, many people own *some* corporate assets; for instance, about 25 percent own some corporate stock. But the stock and other corporate assets owned by the bottom 82.6 percent, when added together, amount to less than 10 percent of all corporate assets held by Americans.

The average person in the least wealthy 82.6 percent of the population owned $1,166 in corporate stocks and bonds. Suppose people receive an average after-tax return of 10 percent on their assets. The poorest 82.6 percent of the population would then receive $116 a year from their ownership of capital goods. By contrast, a 10 percent after-tax rate of return would yield the average person in the richest 0.5 percent an annual income of $101,818, enough to live on without working.

pany. Or they could be not owned at all, or at least not in the sense that we usually mean when we talk about private property.

Today private-property rights in the capital goods used in production generally imply the right to exclude others and the right to sell. The right to exclude others implies the right to fire workers, since that is nothing other than excluding workers from the workplace; the related right, the right to determine who is included, is the right to hire. So the power to hire and fire is an aspect of the property rights of capitalists.

The right to use one's property at one's own discretion is considerably limited by zoning laws, union contracts, public health codes, occupational health and safety regulations, pollution controls, and the like. However, even with these restrictions, the idea of private property in capital goods expresses a basic aspect of the capitalist class relationship.

Wage labor

The third charcteristic of a capitalist economic system is wage labor. Wage workers are simply people who live on the wages or salaries they receive in return for working for an employer; their work is called *wage labor*. Everyone who "earns a living" (that is, obtains the things necessary for life) as an employee is a worker.

What other kind of work is there? As we shall see, 200 years ago most people in the United States did not work as wage workers; they were independent farmers or other self-employed persons or slaves. Some producers in the United States today are still not wage workers. These are the people who work for themselves, or in partnerships, or cooperatively owned establishments. Some work at their own family farms or shops.

Wage labor is fundamentally different. If you work for yourself, you make your living either by producing what you yourself consume or by selling a commodity. If you work for wages you make your living by selling yourself, or more precisely, your time. Your wage or salary is what you live on. You depend on employment to obtain your wage. In exchange for the wage, you work under someone else's direction, producing something that you will not own.

Wage labor is work performed under the direction of an employer in return for a wage or salary.

Wage Labor

"The village blacksmith shop was abandoned, the roadside shoe shop was deserted, the tailor left his bench, and all together these mechanics [workers] turned away from their country homes and wended their way to the cities wherein the large factories had been erected. The gates were unlocked in the morning to allow them to enter, and after their daily task was done the gates were closed after them in the evening.

Silently and thoughtfully, these men went to their homes. They no longer carried the keys of the workshop, for workshop, tools, and keys belonged not to them, but to their master. Thrown together in this way, in these large hives of industry, men became acquainted with each other, and frequently discussed the question of labor's rights and wrongs."*

"The proprietors of . . . establishments and their operatives do not stand upon an equality, their interests are, to a certain extent, conflicting. The former naturally desire to obtain as much labor as possible from their employees, while the latter are often induced by the fear of discharge to conform to regulations which their judgment, fairly exercised, would pronounce to be detrimental. . . . In other words, the proprietors lay down the rules and the laborers are practically constrained to obey them."†

* Terrance Powderly, Grand Master Workman, Knights of Labor, *Thirty Years of Labor 1859–1889* (Columbus, Ohio: Excelsior Pub. House, 1889).
† U.S. Supreme Court, Holden v. Hardy, 1898, cited in Michael Reich, *Racial Inequality* (Princeton, N.J.: Princeton University Press. 1980).

If everyone owned a farm, a small shop, or the tools necessary to go into business on one's own, many would not need to work for someone else for wages (or salary). For this reason, the concentration of ownership of capital goods in the hands of relatively few people and the existence of wage labor are closely related. On the one hand, only people who own a substantial amount of property can live on their property income. On the other hand, those people who own few or no capital goods—the 82.6 percent of the families shown in the box on page 74 who own but 9.1 percent of income-producing assets, for instance—usually must have a job to survive. Concentration of ownership in one part of the population implies the need for wage work among most of the rest.

☐ Capitalism, Profits, and the Surplus Product

We can now see the link between the basic class relationship of capitalism and the surplus product. Employers—capitalists—hire

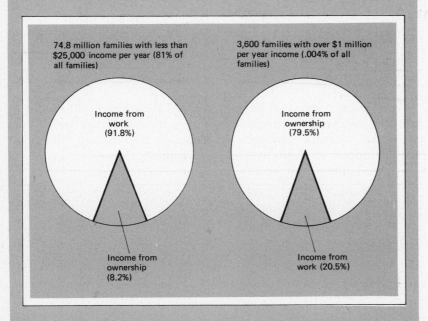

Income from Work and Income from Ownership

74.8 million families with less than $25,000 income per year (81% of all families)

Income from work (91.8%)

Income from ownership (8.2%)

3,600 families with over $1 million per year income (.004% of all families)

Income from ownership (79.5%)

Income from work (20.5%)

How can we see the class relationships in capitalism? One way is to ask how the big owners and employers in the United States make their money. Do they work? Yes, most of them do (paying themselves salaries as high as several million a year, according to *Business Week*). Is this how they make their money? No, as the chart above shows; they make their money—most of it—not through their work, but through their ownership of property. The income they receive from ownership—profits, rent, and interest on money loaned out or invested—does not depend on any work they do; they receive it no matter what they do, even if they do nothing. The chart also indicates that the great majority of people earn most of their living from salaries and wages, that is, from work.

Source: Internal Revenue Service, *Statistics of Income, 1979: Industrial Income Tax Returns* (Washington, D.C.: Government Printing Office, 1982).

workers to produce the output (the total product), which the capitalists then own. The capitalists then sell their products. Assume that, out of their sales revenues, they pay each worker a wage sufficient to provide workers with the customary standard of living. Assume also that capitalists set aside from their revenues the amount needed to replace the materials used and the tools, machines, and other capital goods used up in producing the total

Profits are the form of the surplus product in a capitalist economic system; they are what is left over, out of sales revenues, after wages, the costs of materials used up, and wear and tear on machines have been paid.

product. Then the remainder is the surplus. In a capitalist economic system the surplus product is the capitalists' *profit*.

In the simple example of the previous chapter the surplus was a certain quantity of grain, or an amount of labor time. In actual capitalist economies, the surplus is not only a quantity of goods, or labor time, but it is also a quantity of money—called *profits*. Profit is the capitalists' form of income, and it is obtained as a result of their ownership of capital goods and their control over the labor processes.

The capitalist may not be able to keep all of the profit resulting from the capitalist labor process. For instance, part of profit may go to pay interest payments to banks or individuals who have loaned money to capitalists. Such payments, however, are really

---

Three Hundred Billion Dollars is Missing!

A holdup at Fort Knox? No. Federal Reserve Chairman Paul Volcker hit the delete key on his computer by mistake? Wrong again.

The daring daylight heist was pulled by a cast of millions.

The amount of income that people report to the Census Bureau and the Internal Revenue Service for tax purposes may be hundreds of billions short of what they actually received, according to a Commerce Department study.

When people are asked how much money they make, they often misreport their income. Some simply cannot remember. Others, believing that consistency is a virtue even when honesty is not, report the often greatly understated figure they reported to the Internal Revenue Service for tax purposes.

In 1974 the Census Bureau attempted to estimate how much underreporting there was. It compared the figures given to the census takers with overall economic data based on the total output of the economy and other information. Wages and salaries were underreported by 2 percent. Property income was underreported by 55 percent.

Of course, it is a lot harder to misrepresent your income if it is wages or salary, because your employer reports this figure directly to the I.R.S. on your W-2 tax form. Profits—or what the Commerce Department calls income from property—are much easier to hide.

If the Commerce Department estimate is correct, and if people understated their property income as much on their tax forms as they did in responding to the census taker, $203 billion escaped notice (and taxation) in 1972. If the same underreporting continued to the present, $303 billion was missing in 1983.

Source: M. Sawyer, *Income Distribution in O.E.C.D. Countries* (Paris: O.E.C.D. Occasional Study, July, 1976).

---

just a different form of profits, since they are paid to those who *indirectly* own the capital goods used in production. (Instead of directly owning the capital goods, the bank loans money to the firm, obtaining in return a promissory note from the firm. So although the bank does not own capital goods, it has obtained an indirect claim, through the firm, on the profits.) A somewhat different case is taxes on profits, which may take part of the surplus for government to use; we investigate the role of taxes in Chapter 13.

Capitalists (or banks and others who receive interest payments) spend the profits to buy commodities: new machinery for the factory (above and beyond that needed to replace the capital goods worn out in producing the profits), luxury housing, research and development services, or other things.

The surplus product is all of these things that are bought with profits. They make up a very diverse collection of goods and services. What all these surplus products have in common is that none is needed to keep the basic productive apparatus of the economy— its workers and its capital goods—intact. As before, the time it took to produce all of these goods is surplus labor time.

The capitalist surplus (profits) and the associated class relationship are illustrated in the following example. During the year 1979 American coal miners dug an average of about 15 tons of bituminous coal daily. For this they were paid $105 in wages. The coal they dug was sold by the coal companies for an average of $23 per ton, or a total of $350 per miner. The miners' wages were paid from the proceeds of the sale of the coal. But what of the $245 left over? Some of it, about $180, was used to purchase other necessary inputs such as electricity and to replace structures, machinery, and other equipment as they wore out. About $36 of it was spent on the salaries and wages of employees such as managers, supervisors, and secretaries, who are not miners.

And what of the $29 remaining? It went to the owners of the mining company in the form of profits. Some of the profits then went to pay interest and rents. (Some of the owners may also have received salaries as managers.)

The box "Class Relationships in Coal Mining, 1979" summarizes these calculations. The relationship between the coal miners and the owners of the coal companies is a class relationship. The $29 profits is the amount of surplus received by the owners of the mines for each day of a miner's labor. Whatever the coal operators and their bankers spent the $29 on is the surplus product. The coal miners are workers; the owners are capitalists.

To summarize, capitalism is a way of organizing labor processes characterized by commodity production, private ownership of capital goods used in production, and wage labor. Capitalists gain control and use of the surplus product in the form of profits.

The *capitalist class* owns the capital goods used in the production of commodities and controls not only their own work, if they do any, but also the labor of others, that is, of wage workers; capitalists

---

Class Relationships in Coal Mining, 1979

	(1)	(2)	(3)
To begin with the worker, each miner each working day dug on the average	15.2 tons		
which was sold by the coal company for a per ton price of	$ 23.50		
Some of this price was accounted for by indirect business taxes ($.50), so the coal company received per ton a price of	$ 23.00		
giving the coal company a total return per miner's work day of			$350.00
The average miner was paid per hour	$ 10.26		
The miner also received daily wage supplements amounting to	$ 22.56		
or a total daily pay (for an eight-hour day) of about		$105.00	
Of course, the miner kept only part of this, paying in income taxes about	$ 14.00		
The coal company also had to pay for some other inputs:		$216.00	
to suppliers for inputs such as transportation, power, and so on	$141.00		
to replace worn out machinery and structures	$ 39.00		
to managers, supervisors, secretaries, and other nonproduction workers	$ 36.00		
The remainder was profits		$ 29.00	
a part of which they had to share with their banker in the form of net interest	$ 5.00		

The items in column 2 add up to the total in column 3.

Source: All data are from the Statistical Abstract of the United States, the Handbook of Labor Statistics (Bureau of Labor Statistics), and unpublished data from the Bureau of Economic Analysis of the U.S. Department of Commerce (detailed national income and product data for coal mining).

Private Property among the Arapesh of New Guinea

A typical Arapesh man [lives] for at least part of the time on land which does not belong to him. Around the house are pigs which his wife is feeding, but which belong either to one of her relatives or to one of his. Beside the house are coconut and betel palms which belong to still other people, and the fruit of which he will never touch without the permission of the owner.

He hunts on the bushland belonging to a brother-in-law or a cousin at least part of his hunting time, and the rest of the time he is joined by others on his bush, if he has some. He works his sago in others' sago clumps as well as in his own.

Of the personal property in his house, that which is of any permanent value, like large pots, well carved plates, good spears, has already been assigned to his sons, even though they are only toddling children. His own pig or pigs are far away in other hamlets; his palm trees are scattered three miles in one direction, two in another; his sago palms are still further scattered, and his garden patches lie here and there, mostly on the lands of others.

If there is meat on his smoking rack over the fire, it is either meat which was killed by another—a brother, a brother-in-law, a sister's son, etc.—and has been given to him, in which case he and his family may eat it, or it is meat which he himself killed and which he is smoking to give away to someone else, for to eat one's own kill, even though it be only a small bird, is a crime to which only the morally, which usually means with the Arapesh mentally, deficient would stoop.

If the house is nominally his, it will have been constructed in part at least from the posts and planks of other people's houses, which have been dismantled or temporarily deserted, and from which he has borrowed timber. He will not cut his rafters to fit his house, if they are too long, because they may be needed later for someone else's house which is of a different shape or size. . . . This then is the picture of a man's ordinary economic affiliations.

Source: Margaret Mead, *Cooperation and Competition among Primitive Peoples* (Boston: Beacon Press, 1961), p. 31.

---

obtain their income as profits. The *working class* consists of those people who do not own the capital goods used in the production of commodities and who work under the control of others; workers receive their income in the form of wages and salaries. Workers typically do own cars, homes, and other personal property, but these are not the capital goods used in production.

The definition of capitalism stresses the social organization of the labor process: Nothing is said about its technology or about what is produced. A capitalist system may produce factory goods

The **working class** or **workers** are those who perform wage labor; they neither own the capital goods used in their labor processes nor command control over the labor of others.

Who Are the Richest American Capitalists?

The capitalist class comprises about 2 percent of all families, or roughly 1.5 million families.

The top 400 families and/or individuals taken together owned over $118 billion in assets in 1983. Nelson Bunker Hunt of Dallas, who is worth $1.4 billion commented: "We're not as smart as other people, so we need every advantage."

The wealthiest families (including members not shown below) appear to be:

duPont family	over $10 billion
Hunt family	$6–7 billion
Rockefeller family	$3–5 billion
Bass family	$2 billion
Cullen family	$2 billion

The wealthiest individuals are listed in the table below.

Name	Residence	1982 Net worth billions of dollars	Original family source of wealth
Anschutz, Philip	Denver	1.0	Oil
Davis, Marvin	Denver	1.0	Oil
Getty, Gordon	San Francisco	2.2	Oil
Hill, Margaret (Hunt)	Dallas	1.0	Oil
Hunt, Nelson	Dallas	1.4	Oil
Hunt, William	Dallas	1.0	Oil
Ludwig, Daniel	N.Y.C.	2.0	Shipping
Mars, Forest	Las Vegas	1.0	Candy
Mitchell, George	Houston	1.0	Oil, Real Estate
Packard, David	Los Altos Hills, Calif.	1.8	Hewlett-Packard
Perot, Ross	Dallas	1.0	Computer Services
Rockefeller, David	N.Y.C.	1.0	Oil, Real Estate
Schoellkopf, Caroline (Hunt)	Dallas	1.3	Oil
Sam Warton	Bentonville, Ark.	2.1	Marketing
An Wang	Lincoln, Mass.	1.6	Computers

Source: *Forbes*. Fall, 1983, pp. 71-159

or farm goods, tanks or love beads. What is capitalist about it is how it is organized.

The definition of capitalism says nothing about the form of government: Capitalism may coexist with democratic governmental institutions as in the United States, with fascism as in Hitler's Germany, or with other forms of dictatorship, as in many capitalist countries of Africa, Asia, and Latin America. Moreover, democratic government may exist alongside other economic systems besides capitalism; for instance, as we see in the next chapter, during the early days of American democracy, capitalist organization hardly existed at all.

Capitalism provides one set of "rules to the game," one set of procedures and class relationships that determine how social decisions are made. Democracy and dictatorship provide other sets of rules, rules to other games; that is, other methods for making social decisions. In families, the authority of adults, particularly household heads, as well as custom and tradition, provide still a different way of determining how things are done. This book is mainly about the capitalist rules to the game.

In the next chapter we will see how capitalism—and particularly the way the surplus is used—has transformed both the United States and capitalism itself.

☐ Suggested Readings

Michel Beaud, *A History of Capitalism, 1500–1980* (New York: Monthly Review Press, 1983).

Richard Edwards, Michael Reich, and Thomas Weisskopf, *The Capitalist System* (Englewood Cliffs, N.J.: Prentice-Hall, 1985).

Eugene Genovese, *Roll, Jordan, Roll: The World the Slaves Made* (New York: Random House, 1972).

Jurgen Kuczynski, *The Rise of the Working Class* (New York: McGraw-Hill, 1967).

M. M. Postan, *The Medieval Economy and Society* (Berkeley: University of California Press, 1973).

CHAPTER 5

AMERICAN CAPITALISM: ACCUMULATION AND CHANGE

Life in these United States isn't like it used to be.

When the first American factories opened, at the beginning of the nineteenth century, employers had to worry about finding enough workers. Who, they wondered, could they get to take the jobs in the mills? It was not just a question of wages; in fact, wages were quite good. Rather, it was a question of status: most adult males considered it humiliating, perhaps even un-American, to work for somebody else. Those who did, in the language of the day, were called servants, whether they worked in people's homes, in factories, or in mines.

Having a boss (instead of being your own boss) was thought to destroy one's independence and put oneself in a position little better than slavery. Wage labor, declared some Baltimore mechanics in 1833, would "bring [workers] to a state of servitude less enviable than that of the vassals of the feudal lords and princes— because they may hold the name but lose the rights of freemen."* Lynn, Massachusetts, shoemakers protested industrial employment, writing, in 1844, "Let us prove that we are not menials or the humble subjects of a foreign despot, but free, American citizens."† Later, just before the Civil War, the shoemakers, now wage workers, complained that while once they had made their living selling shoes, they now were reduced to selling themselves: their pay was no longer a price; it was a wage.

---

* Baltimore *Republican and Commercial Advertiser,* September 12, 1833.
† *The Awl,* July 17, 1844.

Recognizing how difficult it was to find men willing to do wage work, Alexander Hamilton had recommended hiring women and children. In his famous "Report on Manufactures," written in 1791, Hamilton noted that with industrial jobs "women and children are rendered more useful, and the latter more early useful." Indeed, not only would the employers find workers, but also "the husbandman himself experiences a new source of profit and support from the increased industry of his wife and daughters. . . ." Even so, mill owners had trouble finding workers. General Humphreys, when he opened his woolen mill in Connecticut in 1803, nearly went bankrup before he made the "innovation" of hiring mainly children. So was Samuel Slater forced to hire mostly children at his Rhode Island spinning mill. And the famous Lowell, Massachusetts, mills were staffed by young women and girls from Yankee farms recruited from as far away as Maine. Newspapers like the *Massachusetts Spy* were filled with advertisements seeking "families of five or six children each" to work in the mills; and recruiters were driven farther and farther afield to lure new workers.

More recent news suggests that the employers' problems in finding workers are less serious now. In March 1981, for example, when the Johnson Controls Company of Toledo, Ohio, announced it had 90 job vacancies, over 5000 people turned up to apply; some waited up to 18 hours in a line that stretched for blocks. When, in June 1981, Procter and Gamble sought to fill 8 jobs on its St. Louis, Missouri, production line, at least 3000 job seekers turned out. The Marriott Company built a new hotel in Hempstead, New York; in September 1982, when the company took applications for its 296 job openings, 4508 would-be workers filled out the papers. A month later, in Austin, Texas, 2817 people turned up to apply for 187 jobs. When 200 new public service jobs in the Buffalo, New York, area were announced in April 1983, over 15,000 residents showed up to get the application forms. At any one time during 1983, 8 million or more Americans were looking for work but could not find jobs.

What has caused such a great change in the attitude toward wage work? What has caused such a great transformation of our society that so many people are looking for work (and not finding it)?

This chapter considers that time dimension, or the *change* aspects, of capitalist organization of production. We look particularly at changes in American capitalism. We have already seen, in Chapter 1, some of the enormous social, political, and economic changes that have occurred during the capitalist period of history. How and why does capitalism cause change? And how has American capitalism itself been changed by its own historical development?

The main idea of this chapter is that in capitalism, competition forces capitalists to invest most of the surplus product; and this investment process generates continual economic, social, and political change, including, as we see in American history, the transformation of the class structure and major changes in the capitalist economy itself.

This main idea is expressed in three main points:

1. *Accumulation,* or the reinvestment of the surplus product, is the most fundamental source of change. In capitalism, competition for profits among capitalists forces them to invest most of the surplus product, leading to continual change.

2. In this process of change, *capitalism has become the dominant economic system* in the U.S. economy. Capitalism, which initially accounted for only a minor portion of American labor processes, has replaced other economic systems that formerly were more important. In this process, the American class structure has been transformed.

3. The process of change has also affected capitalism itself; American capitalism has been characterized by several distinct institutional settings for the accumulation process, or *social structures of accumulation.* These social structures of accumulation define the phases or stages of American capitalism, including *competitive* capitalism, *monopolistically competitive* capitalism, and *contemporary* capitalism.

Not only does the struggle over the surplus product tell us much about how an economic system works at any particular point in time; it also tells us much about the historical development of that society.

☐ Accumulation as the Source of Change

What in the operation of capitalism unleashes such powerful forces for change? The most basic answer is accumulation.

Accumulation is the process of mobilizing, transforming, and exploiting the inputs used in capitalist production and then selling the output. The basic driving force in capitalist accumulation is profit making and investment; these actions are themselves shaped by competition among capitalists, as capitalists vie with each other for profit opportunities. Profit making and investment inevitably transform labor processes, generate new supplies of labor, increase the stock of capital goods, and mobilize or transform other resources to make them available for use in commodity production. Accumulation refers to this whole complex of related activities.

Profits are both the lever and the lure of change: They are the lever, because profits, when invested, create change; and they are the lure, because capitalists repeatedly change the world in order to make more profits.

To see the link between accumulation and change, we must consider how profit making works over some period of time.

In the process of profit making—as in other economic pro-

Accumulation is the process of mobilizing, transforming, and exploiting the inputs required in capitalist production and then selling the output; profit making and investment lie at the heart of the capitalist accumulation process.

[handwritten margin note: competitive cap. monop. comp. contemporary]

cesses—*the past affects the present.* Day 3 is not identical to Day 2, because whatever change or development occurred during Day 2 obviously does not exist at the beginning of Day 2, but it does become the starting point for Day 3; and both Days 2 and 3 affect Day 4. Likewise, the latter part of an historical epoch is different from the earlier part, because the change or development that occurred in the earlier part influences the latter part (but not vice versa).

Let us think about how the introduction of political economy's third dimension, time or history, sheds light upon the process of profit making.

Suppose a particular capitalist has made a successful investment in T-shirt production in Period 1. His investment was made at the beginning of the period, when he purchased the machines, materials, and labor necessary for production of T-shirts; the T-shirts were then produced and sold at a profit. Even after repairing the wear and tear on the machinery and paying for the materials used and labor hired, the capitalist has a larger amount of money than he began with. What will he do with this profit?

The capitalist might choose to use the profit to buy goods for his own consumption. Because the machinery had been restored but not increased, the business would remain unchanged.

But factors outside the firm may have changed. Even if the capitalist tried simply to repeat in Period 2 what had been done in Period 1, he might find that it was impossible to do so. For example, the prices paid for input commodities might have changed, so now the original investment might purchase less than it did in Period 1. Or perhaps customers have changed their preferences, and they no longer demand the kind of T-shirts he is producing. Possibly some other capitalist has noticed the substantial profits to be made in T-shirt making and is now entering the field as a competitor. In these cases, if the first capitalist tried to reproduce in Period 2 just what he had done in Period 1, he would be frustrated.

Note how the situation would be different if the output were not a commodity, intended for sale, and instead the producer intended to use the product himself. In the self-sufficient household (or on the feudal manor), there was little uncertainty about input prices or the preferences of customers changing from period to period. The household or manor provided its own inputs and itself consumed the products of its labors. If the family head or feudal lord chose to carry on its production in the same way year after year or generation after generation, so it would be. But the capitalist, who produces a commodity for exchange, cannot stand still without falling behind.

Not only does a capitalist face uncertainty from unknown events, he faces the certainty of competition in the market. He knows that other capitalists, also fearing uncertainty and wanting higher profits, will attempt to increase their profits; they will also try to make changes that raise their profit rates. Hence we see that the capitalist *knows that all other capitalists are actively trying to change the situation.* This makes the probability of change much greater.

Competition for profits is the scramble among capitalists and firms seeking new ways of doing business, new markets, new products, and other possibilities for profitable investment.

Competition for profits drives all capitalists constantly to seek improvements or changes in their operations. Those who fail to do so will be left behind, with higher priced inputs, more costly methods of production, and obsolete (that is to say, nonsalable) outputs. The capitalist who tries to maintain things as they are by making no changes from period to period will in fact sink further and further behind. Only those capitalists who continually revolutionize their operations have a chance, and of those, only the ones who make the right changes succeed.

Those capitalists who succeed (and survive) in one period are like runners who are ahead half-way through a race; the leaders maintain the lead only by continuing to run, and those who stop see the race go by. There are, however, two peculiar features to this capitalist "race." The first is that new competitors keep jumping into the race from the sidelines as the race progresses. So even as some firms fall behind or drop out of the race, new firms enter afresh, and even the leaders must worry about this potential competition. The second peculiar feature is that there is no end to the race: for capitalists, it goes on forever.

Firms must continually compete for profits in order to survive. This is true even if the owners and managers of the firms do not personally care about profits, for the survival of firms (and the ability of their owners and managers to remain owners and managers) depends on profits. A firm grows by investing, that is, by using its profits to increase its ownership of capital goods. The owners can do this either by ordering the building of new factories and offices or by buying existing ones. If the owners use all of the profits for investment, the increase in the firm's capital goods will be exactly equal to the amount of profits.

Thus if a firm is not making profits it cannot grow; zero profits will, in general, mean zero growth. But if it does not grow it will soon be overshadowed by those firms that do grow. Survival requires growth; growth requires profits. This is the market's law of the survival of the fittest; it is analogous to Charles Darwin's principle of evolution of species through natural selection.

Comparing capitalism with other economic systems reveals the strength of capitalism's inherent impulse toward accumulation and change. Earlier economic systems (such as feudalism or slavery) tended to promote consumption of the surplus product by an economic elite; although capitalism has also created an elite with lavish consumption levels, it tends to promote investment of a large part of the surplus product.

In feudal society the lords had little incentive and few opportunities to invest the surplus to enhance productive capacities, and more important, their positions as lords were strengthened if they consumed the surplus product. Secular nobles spent their portion of the surplus product on maintaining a large retinue (subordinate knights and others), building castles, going on crusades, and other activities that made them powerful. The high clergy, including those at Ely, spent their portion of the surplus product in similar ways but also built cathedrals, supported the Church hierarchy, and so forth. Whatever other consequences these uses of the surplus had, they tended to leave the productive system stagnant and unchanging. Old methods of producing were continued or were modified only gradually; few resources were available either for new methods or for expanding old ones.

The capitalist use of the surplus product is quite different. However much capitalists might like to consume all of their profits, the competition for profits forces individual capitalists to reinvest much of one period's profits in order to keep up with their competitors in the next period. The overall result is that the capitalist surplus product is largely invested in and continually changes the productive process. In contrast to feudalism, where few resources were invested in new methods, the capitalist arrangement makes huge quantities of resources available for investment on a regular and continuing basis. (Indeed, as we shall see in Chapter 12, there is often a problem in capitalism of providing profitable investment opportunities for all the resources that capitalists have to invest.) This continual plowing back of the surplus creates the pressure for continual change and the revolutionizing of production.

Indeed, capitalism is the first system to have a dominant class whose members *must* invest the surplus and revolutionize production (that is, create change) in order to survive and continue as members of the dominant class. A feudal lord whose fields were very unproductive was just a shabby noble; by contrast, the capitalist whose factories turn out high-cost products may soon be an ex-capitalist.

Capitalism's normal functioning produces tremendous pressures for change; it creates both the incentive (competition for profits) for individual capitalists to introduce change and the means (profits or the surplus) for implementing change.

☐ **Capitalism Becomes the Dominant Economic System in the United States**

The American economy did not begin as a capitalist economy. Rather, over the past two centuries capitalism has grown from a relatively small part of the economy to the dominant economic system.

If we look at how labor processes were organized in, say, 1780, around the time of the Declaration of Independence (1776) and the U.S. Constitution (1787), we see that capitalist production involved a very small part of society. Figure 5.1 shows that in 1780 several different economic systems coexisted. However, those persons involved in capitalist relations (capitalists and workers together) represented no more than about 6 percent of the people participating in the economy.

Two other economic systems accounted for over 90 percent of the producers in the early American economy. One was slavery. Considering slaves and slaveowners together, the slave system accounted for about a third of early American society. The slaves, of course, greatly outnumbered the slaveowners.

Independent production of commodities is an economic system in which the producers own the capital goods needed in production and use (primarily) their own labor.

The other important economic system in the early American economy was *independent production of commodities*. Independent or self-employed producers of commodities—farmers, craftsmen, self-employed artisans, and other producers—constituted approximately 60 percent of the people in production. Independent producers of commodities owned the capital goods needed for their own particular labor processes; for instance, farmers owned the land they farmed as well as the tools, livestock, barns, and other capital goods needed in farming. They used mainly their own labor (together with that of other family members) and only rarely or in small degree depended upon the labor of slaves or wage workers.

Independent producers of commodities typically produced some or many items for their own consumption (food, for instance) as well as some output for sale through the market. Who did what

		Private property in capital goods?	
		Yes	No
Wage Labor?	Yes	Capitalism (6%)	Government arsenals
	No	Slavery (32%) Home production and commodity production by independent producers (60%)	Native American communal/kinship production (2%)

FIGURE 5.1: Economic systems in the U.S. 1780. Economic systems can be categorized according to the presence or absence of two charcteristics: (1) wage labor as the main form of labor and (2) private ownership of the capital goods used in production. Each box indicates one of four possible combinations. The percentages in each box indicate, of all persons engaged in production, the approximate percentage accounted for by each economic system in 1780. Those engaged in reproduction—childrearing and related tasks—are not included.

work in independent commodity production was determined in part by markets and in part by the assignment of tasks within the family, the latter often dominated by the father. The hallmark of independent producers of commodities was that they were self-employed—they were their own bosses.

Early capitalism appeared, then, in an economy mainly composed of independent commodity production and slavery. Soon competition emerged, competition in particular between the independent producers of commodities and capitalists. (Slave production concentrated mainly on tobacco, rice, and cotton planting; it was never much displaced by capitalist plantations.) Independent shoemakers, as we have seen, found their products brought increasingly into competition with the shoes manufactured under capitalists' direction by wage workers. Self-employed blacksmiths, weavers, spinners, harness makers, and others found themselves increasingly drawn into a competitive struggle, as emergent capitalists invaded these markets to sell their output.

The intensifying competition between independent producers of commodities and capitalists subjected the independent producers to the same logic of market competition as capitalists (described in the previous section). Soon they were faced with the choice of using cheaper methods of production—accumulating profits and reinvesting them and, in fact, becoming capitalists themselves to survive—or falling behind, seeing their incomes decline and facing eventual ruin as independent producers. The status of the independent producer was being undercut, and independent producers had to jump one way or another.

Many independent producers attempted to hire workers, expand production, and become capitalists themselves. Some succeeded: many more failed in the effort.

Others, those with less wealth or ability or luck and those who failed at becoming capitalists, saw their position eroded and their ability to support their families decline. Many found that the only practical alternative was taking a wage job.

It is remarkable how strenuously they objected to this and what hardships they were prepared to endure to avoid wage labor. Running away to sea, prospecting in the gold fields, and homesteading in the West provided many people with a last-ditch chance to escape the dreaded wage jobs. Yet while their efforts delayed the eventual capitulation to wage employment, over the longer sweep of history it did not change the end result.

At the same time, the influx of large numbers of immigrants also contributed to the creation of a supply of wage workers. Many of the immigrants possessed virtually no wealth or other property, and so, lacking alternative ways of earning a living, a very high percentage of them entered wage employment directly.

The outcome of these processes and of the abolition of slavery

| | Owns capital goods used in production? | |
	Yes	No
Controls the labor of others? Yes	(1) Capitalist Class (1%) Slave Owning Class (3%)	(3) New Middle Class (1%)
No	(2) Old Middle Class (60%)	(4) Working Class (5%) Slave Class (30%)

FIGURE 5.2 The U.S. class structure, 1780. Classes can be categorized according to two characteristics: (1) whether or not its members control the labor of others and (2) whether or not its members own the capital goods used in production. Each box indicates one of the four possible combinations. The two main class relationships in 1780 were between box 1 and box 4—between the capitalist class (yes/yes) and the working class (no/no) and between the slaveowning class (yes/yes) and the slave class (no/no). The numbers in parentheses indicate the percentage of the labor force who are members of the class indicated. The labor of those involved in childrearing and other aspects of reproduction does not appear in this or the next figure as it is not directly part of the class structure.
Sources: Estimates based on data in Gary B. Nash, *Class and Society in Early America* (Englewood Cliffs: Prentice-Hall, 1970); and Jackson T. Main, *The Social Structure of Revolutionary America* (Princeton: Princeton University Press, 1965).

is evident if we compare Figure 5.2 with Figure 5.3. Figure 5.2 depicts the U.S. class structure in 1780; Figure 5.3 depicts the class structure in 1982.

In box 1 of each figure are listed the classes—capitalists and slaveowners—that own capital goods and control the labor of others. In 1780, these groups constituted about 4 percent of people active in labor processes; by 1982, the capitalist class had grown from 1 to 2 percent, but of course the slaveowning class had been destroyed, so the total in box 1 declined to roughly 2 percent.

In box 4 of Figures 5.2 and 5.3 are listed the classes that own no capital goods and do not control the labor of others—wage workers and slaves. In 1780, slaves represented about 30 percent of those participating in production, and, of course, there were no slaves in 1982. *Wage workers*, however, *grew from only 5 percent to fully 80 percent of the population.* Here we see the transformation of four-fifths of American society; wage work, which once had been a detested and despised status, believed to be destructive of one's independence and to be avoided if at all possible, has now become the common condition for the overwhelming part of the labor force.

| | | Owns capital goods used in production? | |
		Yes	No
Controls the labor of others?	**Yes**	(1) Capitalist Class (2%)	(3) New Middle Class (10%)
	No	(2) Old Middle Class (8%)	(4) Working Class (80%)

FIGURE 5.3 The U.S. class structure, 1982. The main class relationship today is between the capitalist class (box 1) and the working class (box 4). Comparing this figure with Figure 5.2, a number of basic changes are apparent. There is only one main class relationship today. The slaveowning class and the slave class disappeared with the Emancipation Proclamation Act in 1863. The old middle class is much smaller, and the new middle class has assumed a larger place in the class structure.
Sources: Calculated from *Handbook of Labor Statistics* (Washington: G.P.O., 1983), Tables 3 and 17; and *Statistical Abstract of the United States, 1982–3* (Washington: G.P.O., 1982), p. 385.

And what of boxes 2 and 3? Recall that Chapter 4 defined the capitalist class and the working class in terms of two features of commodity production: Capitalists both owned the capital goods used in commodity production *and* controlled the wage labor of others, whereas workers neither owned capital goods nor controlled the wage labor of others. But what about those who have one but not the other of these features?

The *middle classes* are defined as those groups that possess *one* but *not both* of the defining characteristics of the capitalist class. The term "middle classes" (plural) is used because there are obviously two quite different groups of people, with two quite different relationships to other classes and to the labor process.

The *old middle class* (box 2 in the figures) is composed of those who *do not* regularly employ and control the labor of others but who *do* own the tools of their trade or whatever capital goods they need to work with. It includes self-employed persons and independent commodity producers such as self-employed doctors, carpenters, artists, family farmers, mom and pop storekeepers, and so on. They do not sell their time as wage workers; they sell a commodity, whether it be their crops or medical advice. The old middle class is not really part of the capitalist labor process, although it is related to it through buying and selling. It is called the old middle class because it existed before capitalism developed.

The *new middle class* (box 3 in the figures), on the other hand, is composed of those who *do* control the labor of others but who

Middle classes in capitalist society possess one but not both of the attributes of capitalists; they therefore stand between capitalists and workers.

The **old middle class** consists of those who do own the capital goods used in their own labor processes but who do not regularly control the labor of others; they are self-employed.

The **new middle class** consists of those who do not own the capital goods used in their own labor processes but who do regularly control the labor of others; it includes managers and supervisors.

do not own the capital goods used in production. Managers and supervisors make up most of this category. They usually receive a salary; they sell their time, not their services or products; and they can be fired. While controlling others is a large part of their jobs, they are also controlled by the owners or top executives of the places where they work. They are truly a middle class, because they are in the middle between employers and workers.

Let us now return to Figure 5.2. We see that the old middle class was the biggest category in 1780, representing, as we noted before, about 60 percent of people in production. But as capitalism has grown, the old middle class has shrunk. Independent commodity production, the economic system of the old middle class, is practically irrelevant today; Figure 5.3 shows that the old middle class today amounts to only about 8 percent of the labor force. Still, the reality of the early American economy, when a majority were "their own bosses," lives on in people's hopes and memories. There are not many Americans who at some time in their lives have not dreamed of getting out from under the boss and going to work for themselves.

☐ The Stages of Capitalism

The capitalist accumulation process has not only destroyed earlier economic systems, transformed the class structure, and unleashed a whole series of social changes, it has also changed capitalism itself. Capitalism has undergone its own historical transformation.

The basic "rules of the game" of capitalism remain unchanged; that is, its historical transformation has not altered the fact that the economy continues to be a capitalist economy. Indeed, the changes described so far—the demise of the old middle class, the abolition of slavery, the growing proportion of wage workers—all are reflections of the extension of capitalism.

Yet *within* the capitalist economy virtually everything has changed—the types of products made, the technologies used, the geographical location of production, the hours of work, and so on. The most important changes are the changes in the institutional setting within which accumulation takes place.

Social structures of accumulation

A **social structure of accumulation** provides an institutional setting within which profit making and accumulation occur; it structures relations among capitalists, between capitalists and workers, among workers, and between government and the economy.

The *social structure of accumulation* refers to the set of laws, institutions, and social customs that provides the institutional environment for accumulation. Accumulation—the making and reinvesting of profits by individual capitalists or firms—occurs within this "social structure" or institutional setting and is shaped by it.

Accumulation can occur within different social structures of accumulation. While the goal—profits—remains the same, the conditions under which capitalists try to make profits change. For example, in the nineteenth century there were few large firms, whereas today there are many; a firm today, no less than its nineteenth-century predecessor, seeks to make profits, but what strategy it chooses to use may well be different because it must consider how to compete with large corporations.

Each social structure of accumulation can be described in terms of several important relationships: relations among capitalists; between capitalists and workers; among workers; between government and the economy. In each social structure of accumulation, a variety of institutions both domestic and international gives a particular form of these key relationships. Some, perhaps all, of these relationships are different in different social structures.

Each social structure of accumulation is a long-lived but not permanent feature of capitalism. Typically each social structure lasts for several decades. As we will see below, the U.S. economy has passed through three social structures of accumulation in roughly 150 years. Each social structure lasts a long time because it is rooted in highly durable social relationships: sets of laws, institutions, class relationships, organization of political parties, and customary ways of producing and consuming. Each of these arrangements, once established, works to the advantage of particular groups in the society, who become this accumulation structure's natural defender. Unless these groups are weak or divided, the social structure of accumulation thus typically takes a long time to change.

Though long-lived, the social structure of accumulation is not immortal, and there are different phases in its life. If the existing structure is highly favorable to capitalists, it will establish a context in which their profit rates are high and they have confident expectations for the future. Accumulation will tend to be quite rapid, and the economy will seem to work well. This phase is called the "period of consolidation."

The period of consolidation is followed by a "period of decay," during which the social structure becomes less and less capable of providing such a favorable environment for accumulation. Economic problems multiply, and people's expectations, especially investors' expectations for the future, become more modest and pessimistic. Accumulation occurs at a slower rate.

This alternation between consolidation and decay can be seen in *long swings* in how the economy performs. Consolidation is reflected in a lengthy period of good economic times, or boom, whereas decay is indicated by a long period of hard times. For example, in the U.S. economy in this century, we see the following pattern:

1890s	hard times
1899 through 1929	boom
1929 through 1941	hard times (Great Depression)
1941 through 1973	boom
1973 to present	hard times (inflation, unemployment)

The periods of consolidation (1899 through 1929 and 1941 through 1973) were economic booms, whereas the decay periods (1929 through 1941 and after 1973) were economic hard times. This alternating pattern of good times and hard times can be found in nineteenth-century American economic performance as well.

Why cannot the boom last forever? What tips a social structure of accumulation from consolidation into decay? This question cannot be answered in general. The very success of the accumulation process may erode the favorable conditions that the social structure had initially established; this was partly the case in the 1920s and 1960s. The requirements for continued accumulation may become more inconsistent or self-contradictory as accumulation proceeds; this too occurred in the 1920s and 1960s. And there may be other causes.

The most that can be said in general is that, whereas the social structure of accumulation tends to change slowly, the accumulation process organized within it changes very rapidly. When a tension develops between the (slowly changing or "sticky") institutions and the (rapidly changing) profit-making process, the old social structure no longer provides such a favorable climate for accumulation. The particular causes forcing consolidation to give way to decay are the result of specific historical forces existing at that moment; they are likely to be different for each social structure of accumulation. We shall look into such a process of consolidation and decay in the post-World War II U.S. economy in Chapter 14.

The period of decay may create a "crisis," during which large numbers of people become disaffected and social conflict is heightened. Employers are forced to speed up their efforts at innovation, especially organizational innovation, and workers are likely to demand a "new deal." Some of the erstwhile defenders of the old social structure of accumulation find they are getting less and less out of it. New ways of organizing the economy are proposed.

As a result, the old alignments may change, and new electoral coalitions emerge, sometimes reforming the dominant political party from within, sometimes establishing a new dominant party. Electoral realignments took place at the height of the last two crisis periods, around what political scientists call the critical election years, 1896 and 1934–1936.

Out of this period of crisis, decay, conflict, and change may come the construction of a new set of social relationships—a new social structure of accumulation. Such reconstruction is by no means inevitable, since it depends on the outcome of many specific conflicts and deals. Nonetheless, the crisis creates a situation in which the inadequacies of the old social structure of accumulation become visible, the problems more pressing, and the demand for action urgent. Thus the conditions have been laid for overcoming the inertia of the old institutions and implementing a new set of relationships.

We will investigate, in the following chapters, the most important dimensions of the current social structure of accumulation. We will be able to see how it works and why it changes.

The stages of American capitalism

The U.S. economy has passed through three social structures of accumulation in roughly 150 years. Each social structure of accumulation defines a stage of American capitalism. Figure 5-4 illustrates these stages and some of the key social structure relationships within each stage.

Competitive capitalism. The first stage, competitive capitalism, marked the growth in the United States of capitalist labor processes from a small to a large proportion of the economy. More significant, capitalism was established as the economic system that would clearly become dominant in the future. Slavery was destroyed, and the competition between capitalism and independent producers of commodities turned decisively in favor of the former.

American capitalism during this stage was characterized by small businesses, which competed with each other in the widening markets mainly by price cutting. The prices of most goods fell. Workers, many of whom retained the skills they had acquired in independent commodity production, now found themselves working for a wage under capitalist supervision; in many cases they also retained their associations ("brotherhoods" or trade unions) to bargain over wages and working conditions. The government played a crucial role in enforcing the capitalist rules of the game (for example, in enforcing contracts and in breaking strikes), but otherwise it had a minor effect on the economy.

It was during this stage that capitalism became the dominant economic system, having such a great effect on the evolution of society that it was the overwhelming economic determinant of the society's development.

The **stages of American capitalism** are distinct phases in the development of U.S. capitalism; each is defined by a separate social structure of accumulation.

Competitive capitalism was the first stage of American capitalism, from the 1840s through the 1890s.

Key relations in the social structure of accumulation	Social structure of accumulation I: Competitive capitalism (1840–1890)	Social structure of accumulation II: Monopolistically competitive capitalism (1890–1940)	Social structure of accumulation III: Contemporary capitalism (1940–present)
Capital-capital relations	Small business, local, competitive capitalism	National monopolistic competition, large corporations (trusts)	Monopolistic competition on a world scale, U.S. corporations dominant
Capital-labor relations	Strong craft-based unions in some industries, extensive workplace control exercised by skilled workers	Capitalists are dominant, unions weak, not recognized	Labor accord, unions recognized with legal rights
Labor-labor relations	Craft-based distinctions between skilled and unskilled workers	Homogenized labor, semiskilled factory, operatives become important	Segmented labor markets, unions among mass production workers
Government-economy relations	Limited government	Limited government (some regulation, e.g., Federal Reserve)	Keynesian regulation of macroeconomy, United States as world policeman for capitalism

FIGURE 5-4 **Stages of American capitalism.** American capitalism has passed through three stages: competitive capitalism, monopolistically competitive capitalism, and contemporary capitalism. Each stage is defined by a distinct social structure of accumulation. Key aspects of the social structure of accumulation concern relationships among owners of the capital goods used in production, between them and the workers, among workers, and between all economic actors and the government.

Monopolistically competitive capitalism was the second stage of American capitalism, from the 1900s through the 1930s.

Monopolistically competitive capitalism. The second stage of American capitalism was inaugurated by the rise of many large corporations (then called "trusts") around the turn of the twentieth century. This stage lasted until the 1940s.

Monopolistically competitive capitalism was characterized, in the leading industries, by large firms with substantial market power engaged in competition with one another. Employers opposed labor unions, and workers who had attempted to organize and defend unions suffered such serious defeats (until the very end of the period) that unions enjoyed little influence during these years. The government, although slightly more involved in the economy than during competitive capitalism, retained its basically limited role in the economy.

Contemporary capitalism is the current stage of American capitalism, from the 1940s to the present.

Contemporary capitalism. The present stage of American capitalism dates from World War II and its aftermath. (Some economists have speculated that we are now beginning the transition to a fourth stage.)

Contemporary capitalism is characterized by monopolistic competition on a world scale; increasingly, large American corporations must compete not only with one another but with similarly large firms from the other advanced capitalist countries—Japan, Germany, and elsewhere. For most of this period workers in labor unions were powerful enough to force employers to recognize and bargain with them, producing a compromise arrangement called a *labor accord*. And during this stage government played a major role in the economy. Among other things, it attempted to regulate the overall level of unemployment and economic growth; it redistributed income through taxes and transfers; and it maintained a large military force, extended over much of the globe.

In the remainder of this book we will be most concerned with contemporary capitalism, with how it works and what its problems and prospects are. We will study each of its various aspects in more detail, to see how competition, command, and change operate in today's economy.

☐ SUGGESTED READINGS

Alan Dawley, *Class and Community: The Industrial Revolution in Lynn* (Cambridge, Mass.: Harvard University Press, 1976).

David Gordon, Richard Edwards, and Michael Reich, *Segmented Work, Divided Workers* (New York: Cambridge University Press, 1982).

Morton J. Horwitz, *The Transformation of American Law, 1780–1860* (Cambridge, Mass.: Harvard University Press, 1977).

Grant McConnell, *The Decline of Agrarian Democracy* (Berkeley, Calif.: University of California Press, 1953).

Norman Ware, *The Industrial Worker, 1840–1860* (Boston: Houghton Mifflin, 1924).

PART THREE

MICROECONOMICS: MARKETS AND POWER

CHAPTER 6

CAPITALIST PRODUCTION AND PROFITS

Capitalism is sometimes said to be a system of profit and loss. And so it is for individual firms: Chrysler Corporation, for example, made a $118 million profit in the fourth quarter (October–December) of 1983; but in the fourth quarter of 1982 the company reported a loss of $96 million.

Yet for capitalists as a group, every year brings profits, not losses. In fact, capitalists have made profits in every year of this century. (Only in 1932 and 1933, in the two worst years of the greatest depression in history, did businesses as a whole report losses. Even then, other payments to owners of capital goods, such as interest, exceeded reported losses.) Despite the misfortunes of particular companies, capitalists as a whole have made profits every year.

And the amount of profits has been pretty substantial. In 1983, for instance, profits and other property income payments were $551 billion, an amount equal to about $5,500 for each person working in the economy.

In 1983, the richest 400 people in the United States, whose income came almost entirely from profits, increased their wealth by $26 billion—an average of $65 million each. For these people, even a bad year for the economy as a whole is unlikely to be too uncomfortable—their average increase in wealth in 1983 was 3000 times the income of the average American family.

Why, in a system of profits and losses, does the capitalist class as a whole virtually always make profits instead of losses? And what determines how big their profits will be? This chapter investigates these questions.

Some people believe that profits exist either as a reward for capitalists who take risks or because machines (and other capital goods) are productive. It is of course true that capitalists take risks—so do workers—but risk taking does not explain why profits exist. If you could buy lottery tickets or play the slot machines and be assured of never having a losing year, you wouldn't consider that a risk—bettors would call that a lead-pipe cinch, practically a license to steal! At most, risk taking may explain why some capitalists make higher profits than others.

Likewise, it is certainly true that machinery is productive, but the ability of machinery to assist the production process does not explain why profits flow to the owner of the machine, who may never even have seen the machine and who most likely would not know how to operate it. (Recall that profits are the money made after subtracting the wear and tear on machinery.)

Profits are simply a deduction from society's net product that is made possible by the power of employers. But how is it possible for employers to exercise power in a system where there are no laws requiring anyone to work for anyone else? The class structure exists and is perpetuated, but there is no law that says that a worker cannot become a capitalist or vice versa. The owners of large companies receive huge incomes, which represent the fruits of the labor of their workers, but any one of these workers is free to quit if he or she does not like it.

People in capitalism are free to sell or use their property as they choose and to use the proceeds to buy other property. Workers are free to move, change jobs, and decide for themselves how much to work. Capitalists must compete with one another; most forms of overt collusion—fixing prices, for example—are, in the United States at least, illegal. The formal legal rights of citizens, whether workers, capitalists, or whatever, are equal. The law does not recognize privilege.

Capitalism is easy to misunderstand. Some people, struck by the lack of any general plan for the coordination of the economy, come to the conclusion that there is no logic to it at all. Others, impressed by the fact that the dominant class does not take control of the surplus product at the point of a gun, believe that therefore there is no dominant class.

But behind the chaos of competition there is a very distinct capitalist logic to how the economy works. And this logic provides the means for the dominant class, capitalists, to control the surplus product. The key to understanding how all this happens is profits.

The main idea of this chapter is that the profit rate is the basic tool for analyzing how capitalism works. The profit rate helps us to see how capitalism organizes production and distributes its products, and it illuminates the dynamics of competition, the control of the surplus product, and how the class system is perpetuated. It is the concept that best brings together the horizontal, vertical, and time dimensions—competition, command, and change—of economic life.

This main idea is expressed in four main points:

1. *Profit* is the remainder or surplus left for capitalists after their output commodities have been sold and the inputs (materials used, wear and tear on machines, and labor employed) have been paid. The *profit rate* is defined as the amount of profit divided by the value of the capital goods invested.
2. Profits are only possible at all if capitalists have a certain degree of *power over workers*. This power is usually based upon the existence of unemployment in capitalist society.
3. The level of the profit rate—how high the profit rate is—is set by a series of factors called the *determinants of the profit rate*. Competition among capitalists and much of the conflict between classes in capitalism concerns the determinants of the profit rate (and hence ultimately the level of the profit rate itself).
4. Capitalists' *search for profits* is the basis for the allocation and reallocation of labor and other inputs to the different labor processes in the capitalist economy. Higher profit rates in an industry attract capitalists (and the labor they hire), whereas lower profit rates cause capitalists to move to another sector, reduce their operations, or go out of business.

This chapter focuses on the interaction of the horizontal relations—relations of workers to workers, of capitalists to capitalists, and in markets generally—with the vertical relations—relations between capitalists and workers in producing profits. We concentrate on the operations of the capitalist economy and do not here consider the role of government. In later chapters we will reintroduce the third dimension—time—to trace the evolution of both the vertical and the horizontal aspects of the U.S. economy, and we will investigate how government affects the economic process.

☐ Profits and the Profit Rate

The profit rate and the search for profits are the key to understanding how capitalism works. But what exactly are profits and the profit rate?

There are two basic ways to make a profit, and they are quite different. One is far more important than the other, and it is that type of profit making we will focus on here.

The less important way to make a profit is to "buy cheap and sell dear." The profits that result from buying cheap and selling dear are called *commercial profits.* Buying cheap and selling dear

Commercial profits result from selling something for more than it cost to purchase ("buying cheap and selling dear"); no labor process is involved.

works because the price at which you buy something is less than the price at which you can sell the very same thing, even if you have not improved or in any other way changed the thing. Ticket scalping for World Series games or rock concerts is an example. Buying gold in the hope that the price will go up—called speculating—is another.

The distinguishing characteristic of commercial profits is that these profits do not result from a labor process. Because nothing is produced, there must be losers as well as winners in the buying-cheap-and-selling-dear game. In fact it is called a "zero-sum game" because the sum of the gains and losses is zero, one person's gain being exactly offset by another person's loss. If you buy a concert seat for $25 from the scalper at the last minute, your loss is, say, $15 over what it would have cost if you had bought it at the box office a week earlier; this loss exactly matches the scalper's gain of $15 over what he *did* pay a week earlier.

Capitalist profits are profits that result (directly or indirectly) from a labor process. They do not depend on markets failing to equalize prices. Gains are not necessarily matched by losses. Something is produced. Production for profit works because the price of the resulting commodity is greater than the cost of the labor time and other inputs used in the labor process that produced it.

Capitalist profit is a remainder or residual, the amount by which the output price exceeds the cost of producing the output. Capitalist profit includes all forms of income received as a result of the ownership of capital goods used in a capitalist production process. Capitalist profit thus includes not only what corporations and small businesses report as profits, but also the rents, interest, and dividends they pay to others for the use of the capital goods owned by the people who receive these payments.

Profit does not include wages, salaries, or other income received as a result of labor. Labor may be considered private, but it is not private *property* unless it can be sold, which would be true only if the worker were a slave. At the end of a particular time—the period of the wage contract—the ownership of the labor remains with the worker rather than with the employer. (Only baseball teams can sell "their" workers to other employers.) There are some other forms of personal income—gifts, rents on housing paid by families rather than by businesses, and thefts—which we will not be concerned with. Another form of income—welfare payments, subsidies to business, and other transfers from the government—will be discussed when we have introduced taxes and government spending in Chapter 13.

We often refer to the *rate of profit* rather than simply the amount of profits. We know that a large firm will typically make a big profit, while a small firm makes a smaller profit. But the profit rate tells

Capitalist profits are profits that result from a labor process.

The **rate of profit** is the amount of profit divided by the value of the capital goods invested.

us how well each did per dollar of capital goods owned. The rate of profit is defined as the amount of profits divided by the value of the capital goods invested.

$$r = \frac{K}{R} \qquad\qquad (6\text{-}1)$$

where   r = rate of profit
         R = amount of total profit (in dollars)
         K = value of capital goods owned (in dollars)

So the profit rate is an indicator of the degree of success in the profit-making process, because it measures how much profit was made *compared to* how much money was invested to make the profit.

Total profits includes several different types of payments made to the owners of the capital goods used in production: dividends (paid to owners of stock), interest (paid to bankers and others who have lent money to the firm), rents, and "retained earnings" (that part of profits kept by the corporation for investment and other purposes). Total profits (R) is thus the sum of all these claims by the owners of any private property used in production.*

Equation 6.1 defines the rate of profit for an individual firm. To take a concrete example, in 1983 the General Motors Corporation owned $19.5 billion worth of buildings, machinery, and other capital goods used in production. It made profits totaling $5.5 billion in that year, thus achieving a profit rate of 28 percent. (For details, see p. 117.)

Similarly, equation 6.1 can be used to define the profit rate (r) for the economy as a whole. In this case R is the total amount of profits in the whole economy divided by the economy's capital stock (K). The overwhelming proportion of business is conducted by corporations, so let us focus on all U.S. corporations (except banks) taken together. From Figure 6.1 we see that in 1979 all corporations made profits of $512 billion, yielding an average profit rate of 9 percent. Of course this percentage is an average, and some corporations did much better and others did a lot worse.

☐ Profits and the Power of Employers over Workers

Why do profits exist at all? How are capitalists, by exercising their rights to private property in capital goods, able to capture the surplus product (in the form of profits)?

There is no reason why there must be a surplus product at all; and no surplus product means no profits. As we have seen in Chapter 3, if customary consumption plus the replacement of capital goods used up in production exceed total output, there will be no surplus product. Whether a suplus is produced or not will depend upon:

---

* Total profits *before taxes* equals the surplus product; the roles of taxes and government are examined in Chapter 10.

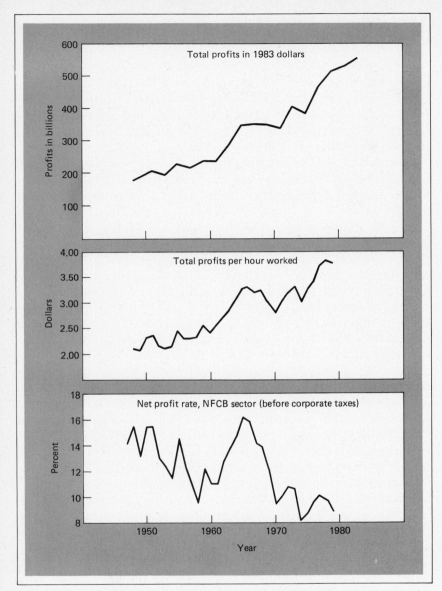

FIGURE 6.1 Profits in the United States, 1948–1983. Total profits have risen as the economy as a whole has grown over the post–World War II period. *Total profits (R)* is the real value (corrected for inflation) before taxes of all the income received as a result of ownership of the capital goods used in production (the sum of corporate profits, net interest, rents, and the income from ownership of the capital goods used in production in noncorporate business).

Total profit per hour of labor employed in the economy as a whole has also risen, as the figure indicates.

The *profit rate (r)* is a better measure of profitability from the standpoint of business. It has fluctuated, attaining high levels in the 1960s and low levels since. The profit-rate line indicates the ratio of before-tax profits to the stock of capital goods owned by nonfinancial corporations. (Profits received by U.S. businesses in their foreign operations are not included.)

Sources: Calculated from *Economic Report of the President, 1984* (Washington, D.C.: G.P.O.); and U.S. Department of Commerce, *National Income and Product Accounts* (Washington, D.C.: G.P.O.).

how productive are the technologies used in production

how much work is done per hour

how high are the wages paid to workers

how large is the fraction of the total product needed to replace used up materials and capital goods

Workers would like higher wages and work that is not excessively hard. If they succeed in getting them, the surplus—and profits—will fall. Therefore there is a conflict of interest between workers and the capitalists who employ them.

In order for profits to exist, the conflict between workers and capitalists must be resolved in a way favorable enough to capitalists so that a surplus product will exist. How can the capitalist class achieve this?

Historically there have been three answers to this question: *fascism, social democracy,* and *unemployment.* Fascism is the direct use of dictatorial governmental power by capitalists to limit workers' demands. Workers may be forbidden from joining real unions, going on strike, or taking other actions that threaten profits. Fascism existed in Italy (1922–1943), Germany (1933–1945), Spain (1939–1975), Portugal (1940–1974), and Japan (1931–1945). Something similar to fascism appears today in many of the authoritarian governments in Asia, Africa, and Latin America.

Social democracy relies on a democratically determined government intervention to obtain an agreement between capitalists and at least the most important groups of workers (such as national labor unions). The government works out an economic program, or "social contract," which may set prices, wages, taxes, and other important economic variables. Capitalists and workers therefore bargain through the government, and the success of each depends in part on how much electoral and other political strength each has. Social democracy has existed in Norway, Sweden, and Denmark since the 1940s (with a few interruptions), in Austria since the 1950s, and off and on in Great Britain during the 1960s and 1970s.

The third way to resolve the conflict between workers and capitalists on terms favorable to capitalists is unemployment. The threat of unemployment weakens workers' bargaining position. This is the most general and common reason why capitalists make profits rather than losses. The first two possibilities rely on government intervention in the economy; unemployment does not rely on the government, although, as we will see in Chapter 13, government may intervene to encourage unemployment and thereby try to raise the profit rate. Unemployment may function independently of government policy to maintain profits, or it may reinforce the repressive measures of fascist governments or the democratically determined social contracts of social-democratic governments.

Fascism is a form of government intervention in the economy in which an authoritarian government uses its power to limit workers' demands.

Social democracy is a form of government intervention in the economy in which a democratic government obtains agreement between at least the most powerful groups of employers and workers on a "social contract."

Unemployment has been the main guarantor of profits throughout most of the capitalist era, including almost the entire history of capitalism in the United States.

Unemployment explains how capitalists, even without direct governmental intervention, are able to control the surplus product (maintain a positive rate of profit). It is the threat of losing one's job that keeps workers working hard enough and at low enough wages so that the capitalist profit-making process continues to make profits. Like all simple answers, this one is more complicated than it looks.

It is fairly obvious why workers do not want to be laid off. Losing your job means a significant loss of income. How big a loss depends on how long it takes to find another job, on the coverage of unemployment insurance, and on how soon the unemployment insurance benefits run out. It may force drastic changes in how you live, or where you live, or in your own or your family members' educational plans and career prospects. It almost always causes worry and strains among family and friends, often a loss of self-respect.

The basic reason why unemployment is such a threat for workers is quite simple. Unlike the independent producer, who owns the tools of the trade, a worker cannot make a living in the long run except by selling labor time to an employer. Unemployment means

---

Unemployment Hurts

People who are out of work have to deal with a lot more than the loss of a job; often one's sense of self, one's self-respect, and even one's feeling of being a part of society depends on having a job. Some indication of the social distress caused by unemployment is the fact that as unemployment increases during business-cycle recessions, more people commit suicide. A recent statistical study estimates that an increase in the unemployment rate from 5 percent to 9 percent—roughly that which occurred between 1979 and 1982—would lead to 1270 more suicides.

Another study estimates that a 1 percent increase in unemployment has the following effects:

death from heart disease up 1.9 percent
murder up 5.7 percent
admissions to state mental institutions up 3.4 percent
admissions to state prisons up 4.0 percent

Source: Morton Schapiro and Dennis Ahlburg, "The Ultimate Cost of Unemployment," *Journal of Post Keynesian Economics*, 1983; and Harvey Brenner, "Influence of the Social Environment on Psychopathology: The Historical Perspective," in James E. Barrett et al. (eds.), *Stress and Mental Disorder* (New York: 1979).

not being able to sell one's labor time. Therefore being unemployed means not being able to make a living. If a person could maintain his or her standard of living without selling labor time (as can, for example, many highly paid executives who are also substantial owners of capital goods), then this person is simply not a worker. Nor is he or she very likely to be laid off!

But are not capitalists faced with similar problems? When business is bad are they not threatened with lost income? Certainly, hard times can be hard for capitalists as well as workers. But capitalists can usually make ends meet, even if they cannot find customers for their output commodities, because they typically own substantial amounts of property (their capital goods) which they can sell. Of course both capitalists and workers may have personal property (cars and houses, for instance) which they can sell, but capitalists usually are in a better position because they have more property (personal goods plus capital goods) and because selling the *type* of property they own (capital goods) is less disruptive to one's life than selling personal goods. Moreover, if the capitalist did have to reduce his or her consumption, there would probably be quite a few frills that could be cut before the family homestead would have to be sold, or the children pulled out of college, or necessary medical attention cut back. For these reasons, the worker who loses his or her job is likely to suffer much more than the capitalist who has trouble selling all the commodities he or she owns.

It is often said that capitalism is a system based on the pursuit of private gain. We should add, "and the fear of economic insecurity." There is a connection between the two. Those who make the greatest gains are those who have the best protection against economic insecurity—ownership of capital goods. By contrast, the insecurity that workers experience—that if they cannot find a job they cannot support themselves and their family—is a double burden. Not only must workers bear the personal and psychological costs of the insecurity itself, but they are also as a result put in a weak bargaining position with their employers, and for this reason they receive less pay.

The asymmetry between employers and workers would not exist if every time a worker was laid off, he or she could walk across the street and find another job at the same or better pay. But as we shall see in later chapters, unemployment—not enough jobs to go around—is a permanent feature of U.S. capitalism. Full employment—enough jobs to go around—has occurred only rarely in U.S. history, most recently, in 1942–1945, 1952–1953, and 1964–1968, that is, during World War II, the Korean War, and the Vietnam War. In Chapters 11 to 14 we will explain why unemployment exists,

Unemployment occurs when there are not enough jobs for all those who want jobs (an excess supply in the labor market).

and how sometimes it is actually increased through government policy as part of a strategy by employers to increase their power over workers.

The relationship between workers and employers is partly a market or exchange relationship and partly something else. Of course workers and employers meet in markets. In commodity markets, workers (as consumers) are the chief customers for capitalists when they try to sell their goods; and in labor markets, workers sell the labor time that employers need to make production go. These are market relationships.

But employers and workers also meet in a nonmarket situation, in the workplace. Here the relationship of employers to labor is not one of exchange settled by a wage contract; instead, workers and employers face an unresolved conflict based on their opposing interests concerning the pace of work and its safety, boredom, and other aspects. The employer's power in this conflict is based on his ownership of the capital goods used, including the workplace itself, and the resulting right of exclusion (the power to hire and fire). This legal right is in practice an effective economic weapon, because it is almost always more difficult for a worker to find another job than for the capitalist to find another worker. Most important, the threat of unemployment and the control by employers over the labor process explains why wages remain low enough and workers hard working and productive enough for profits to be made by most, if not all capitalists.

Perhaps the best way to explain the nature of profits is to imagine a well-traveled road. Suppose that some individual or corporation has gained the right to construct a toll gate. The tolls collected could be said to be simply a cost of getting from one end of the road to the other. But they are quite unlike other costs, say the costs of the gas used or the wear and tear on your car. The tolls, like profits, exist only because of the power of the toll collectors to impose this cost on travelers.

The basis of profits (or control of the surplus product) is thus not risk or the productivity of capital goods, but rather the power that comes from ownership of the capital goods needed in production.

☐ The Determinants of the Profit Rate

What determines how high the profit rate will be?

If it is the power of capitalists over workers that makes profits possible at all, then does the *degree* of capitalists' power determine how high profits are? The answer to this question is yes; however, as we will see, there are many constraints on the capitalist exercise of power, and other influences on the rate of profit as well.

Understanding just what determines the rate of profit is important, because the profit rate summarizes the relationships between classes and among capitalists. It will thus be at the center of our attempt to learn about the kinds of strategies that capitalists are likely to adopt in attempting to increase their profits, a topic taken up in Chapter 7. It also reveals much about the conflict between employers and workers (Chapters 8 and 9) and about the relationship of business to government (Chapter 13).

Knowing what determines the profit rate will also be essential to understanding the overall growth of the economy. Capitalists will use their surplus product to expand production only if they

Capitalism Comes to Grain Growing

Suppose that a society produces only grain. The average producer works 10 hours per day growing grain, and he or she produces 4 bushels of grain per day. Some (1 bushel) must go to replace the seed, feed the draft animals and so forth, leaving a net output of 3 bushels per producer per day. (This is similar to the situation depicted in Figures 3.7 and 3.8.)

Now suppose that we learn that this is a capitalist society, and the producers are in fact workers hired by a capitalist. They are paid a wage of $2 per hour, and grain sells for $10 per bushel.

The capitalist owns the net output (3 bushels per worker); he sells 2 bushels to the worker and exports the third bushel to foreign customers. The capitalist has total sales revenue of $30, of which $20 must be paid to the worker, leaving a profit per worker of $10. With this $10 the capitalist imports luxury consumption goods from abroad.

Each day the average worker earns $20. With this wage he or she can purchase 2 bushels of grain.

These relationships can be expressed equivalently either in bushels or dollars.

In bushels		In dollars	
Gross output	4 bu.	Gross revenues (if all gross output is sold)	$40
Less materials used and wear and tear on capital goods	1	Less depreciation (feed and seed)	10
Net output	3 bu.	Net sales revenues (from sale of net output)	$30
Less necessary consumption	2	Less wages paid	20
Surplus product	1 bu.	Profit	$10

anticipate making at least as high a profit by so doing as they could make on other activities, such as building factories in other countries or playing the stock market or engaging in real estate speculation. For this reason, an answer to what determines the level of profits is also central to our treatment of booms and economic crises in Chapters 12 and 14. So the things that determine the profit rate appear prominently in much of the analysis to come.

The profit rate depends on (or is determined by) the *determinants of the profit rate*. When we know a value for each of the determinants of the profit rate, we can easily calculate the profit rate itself.

The **determinants of the profit rate** are the things upon which the profit rate depends; they determine how high the profit rate will be.

We already know some of the determinants of the profit rate from our analysis of the surplus product (see Chapter 3). When we introduced the example of grain producers and the grain surplus, we did not specify what kind of class structure or economic system it represented. Now let us take the same example (see page 54) and assume that the family sells its grain-growing labor time for wages to a capitalist. The capitalist also owns the land and owns the resulting commodity—grain—that the worker produces. The wage, we assume, is just enough to purchase the necessary product. (In the example, the income from labor—wages—is 2 bushels and the income from ownership of the land—profits—is 1 bushel.)

Because profits are simply the surplus product measured in money terms (rather than bushels), the amount of profit is determined by the same four things that determine the size of the surplus product: how much work people do per hour; how productive their work is; how much workers are paid per hour; and the quantity of materials used and machines used up in production.

The *profit rate* in a capitalist economy differs from the amount of surplus product in our simplified grain example in two ways. First the capitalist economy, like most economies, produces a variety of different outputs, not simply grain, and workers are not paid in grain. This means that we will not be able to measure all our outputs and inputs in bushels. We will measure them in terms of money or market values. Thus profits are measured in *money*.

Second, the profit rate is not the amount of profit, but the *ratio* of the amount of profit to the amount of capital goods owned by the capitalist or capitalists. As in our earlier example we will leave taxes and government subsidies out of the picture until we get to Chapter 13.

To see exactly how these determinants affect the profit rate and to discover what other determinants might exist as well, we need to derive the precise relationship between the profit rate and its determinants. We begin with the definition of the profit rate as before:

$$\text{profit rate } (r) = \frac{R}{K} \qquad (6.1)$$

where r = profit rate
          R = total profits (in dollars per year)
          K = value of capital goods owned (in dollars)

  and

$$\text{total profit } (R) = S - M - W \qquad (6.2)$$

where S = total value of sales
          M = value of materials used and machines used up
          W = total wages and salaries

Net output (Y) is the value of total sales minus the value of materials used and wear and tear on machines.

$$Y = S - M \qquad (6.3)$$

where Y = value of net output

Using equations 6.2 and 6.3 we can rearrange the terms as follows:

$$R = Y - W \qquad (6.4)$$

or alternatively

$$Y = R + W \qquad (6.5)$$

This expression, equation 6.5, states that net output is divided between profits and wages.

Let us now use equation 6.4 to rewrite the basic profit rate equation 6.1:

$$r = \frac{Y - W}{K} = \frac{\text{value of net output} - \text{total wages}}{\text{value of capital goods owned}} \qquad (6.6)$$

We can express each of the variables on the right-hand side of equation 6.6 in a different way—let us express each *per hour of labor*. For example, "value of net output" becomes "value of net output per hour of labor." To rewrite the variables this way, we divide each one by total labor hours used in production:

$$r = \frac{(Y/Labor) = (K/Labor)}{(K/Labor)}$$

where   *Labor* = total labor hours used in production per year

The **value of net output per hour of labor** is the dollar value of the total output minus materials and machine costs divided by the total number of hours worked.

To illustrate this change, suppose B-E Company employs 2 workers for 8 hours each; they produce a net output worth $160. The "value of net output" (Y) would be $160; the "value of net output per labor hour" (y) would be $160 divided by 16 labor hours or $10 worth of net output produced *per hour worked*.

General Motors' Profits

General Motors is the world's largest producer of cars and trucks. In 1983 GM employed 677,000 people around the world, 380,000 of them production workers in the United States. These workers produced 7.8 million cars and trucks in 1983, or about a fifth of all cars and trucks produced in the world.

The average price per unit, Pz, was \$9,564, so GM's worldwide total value of sales, S, was \$74.6 billion.

GM paid a total wage bill (including management salaries), W, of \$19.5 billion.

Five billion dollars went to replace the wear and tear on machinery and other capital goods used in production (depreciation) in 1983, and another \$44.6 billion was spent buying materials used as inputs into the cars produced. Thus M was \$49.6 billion.

GM's profit from producing automobiles, R (GM refers to this as "operating profit") was

$$R = S - M - W = \$74.6 - \$49.6 - \$19.5 = \$5.5 \; billion$$

The total value of the capital goods used in production owned by GM was \$19.5 billion (coincidentally, the same as the wage bill).

Thus the profit rate, r, was

$$r = R/K = \$5.5/\$19.5 = 28 \; percent$$

For every dollar of capital goods owned by GM, 28 cents in profit was made in 1983.

GM's profits amounted to \$8,124 per employee during the year.

GM also had nonautomobile investments. Counting all of its profits (automobile production profits plus other income), the company made \$6.5 billion. GM paid \$2.2 billion of this in taxes, leaving total profits (R) of \$4.3 billion. Out of these profits, \$600 million was paid in interest to indirect owners of the capital goods used in production (banks), leaving \$3.7 billion for the direct owners (stockholders) of GM.

Source: General Motors operating statements and *Wall Street Journal*, February 21, 1984.

Now we can rewrite equation 6.6 as

$$\text{profit rate} = \frac{\text{value of net output per hour of labor } (y) - \text{hourly wage } (w)}{\text{value of capital goods owned per hour of labor } (k)}$$

where y = value of net output per hour of labor
  w = wage rate per hour of labor
  k = value of capital goods owned per hour of labor

Using lowercase letters to remind ourselves of this change to per-labor-hour variables, we can now write the profit equation as

$$r = \frac{y - w}{k} \qquad (6.7)$$

The Fist, the Handshake, and the Invisible Hand

For capitalism to exist, profits must exist. Using equation 6.7, we see that for profits to exist the value of net output per hour (y) must be greater than the wage rate (w). Some method must be found to manage the capital-labor conflict in such a way that workers do not end up getting paid as much as their net product. Three quite different arrangements (parts of three distinct social structures of accumulation) have achieved this result in the twentieth century—the Fist, the Handshake, and the Invisible Hand.

The fist: fascism

Repressive and authoritarian governments ensure that y is greater than w by using force to limit workers' demands. Chile in the 1970s and early 1980s is an example. When the military dictatorship overthrew the elected government of Salvatore Allende, it also imprisoned or killed those trade unionists who opposed it. The political parties that had represented Chilean workers were destroyed or driven underground. Both real wages and the share of wages in total output (w/y) fell by about 40 percent in the next two years.

Under these circumstances, profits may be very high—y may exceed w by a wide margin—because the government uses its power for capitalists against workers.

Fascism does not need to resort to unemployment to put workers on the defensive. During the 1930s, while the other capitalist nations experienced record-setting levels of unemployment, Germany under Hitler almost entirely avoided unemployment. German workers who considered resisting their boss's commands did not fear for their jobs; they feared for their lives.

The handshake: social democracy

Social-democratic governments may keep y larger than w by getting major employers and national unions to agree on a social contract. In Sweden, for example, 90 percent of the work force belongs to labor unions, which together bargain with the Employers' Association to settle on an agreement for almost the entire economy. Under social-democratic governments, workers may be able to obtain quite high wages and other benefits (government services, unemployment protection, and so on) because they are able to use their bargaining power effectively. Moreover, they may not have to worry much about unemployment because the economic system does not rely so much on unemployment to regulate relations between employers and workers. In Sweden, for instance, unemployment between 1963 and 1983 averaged only 2 percent. Swedish workers and employers negotiated a significant reduction in the hours of work, from over 40 per week to less than 30. Rapid growth in wages did not eliminate profits because the productivity of labor—net output per hour employed—also grew very rapidly.

The expression in equation 6.7 is the basic equation for the profit rate used in succeeding chapters. Although we will see that the terms y and k can themselves be broken up into more specific variables, the simple expression in equation 6.7 summarizes the basic profit relationship.

The denominator of this expression (k) measures the value of the machinery, tools, and buildings owned by the capitalist divided by the number of labor hours used to work the machinery. This ratio would be quite high in such industries as petrochemicals processing, where few workers work with many (or costly) machines; it would be quite low in some others, such as garment making or fast foods, where many workers work with few (or low-cost) machines.

The **value of capital goods owned per hour of labor** is the employer's total investment divided by the total number of hours worked by employees.

The numerator ($y - w$) measures, for every hour that someone worked, the money left over for the capitalist. But note that this amount ($y - w$) is that which is left only after the resulting commodities have been sold, after the goods used to produce these commodities and to replace the worn-out or used-up machines and tools have been paid for, and after the wage has been paid to the workers. It is the capitalist's profit per hour of the worker's labor.

If workers were paid the value of the net output of their work, that is, if the hourly wage were equal to the value of what the worker produced in an hour, $y - w$ would be zero. There would then be no profits, and the profit rate would be zero.

To understand more fully what determines the profit rate let us investigate more closely the three variables in equation 6.7: y, w, and k.

Perhaps the easiest to understand is w (the wage rate). This term is just the amount of money paid to the worker per hour worked; for instance, B-E Company's wage rate might be $6 per hour.

The **wage rate** is the amount paid on average to a worker for each hour worked.

The other variable in the numerator, y, is the value of net output per hour of labor. We have already seen that B-E Company's 2 workers, each working 8 hours, produced $160 worth of net output, and y was $10 per hour. Of course, for net output to be $10 per hour, the *gross* or total output must be more than $10 per hour; to obtain its net output, B-E Company must deduct enough money to pay for the materials used and the wear and tear on machines.

The value of net output per hour of labor (y) is the amount left over, out of the value of gross output per hour, after a deduction has been made for the cost of materials used and wear and tear on machines. Imagine that each of the B-E Company's workers produces 3 units of output every hour; that is, $z = 3$.

$$\begin{array}{l}\text{value of net out-} \\ \text{put per hour } (y)\end{array} = \begin{array}{l}\text{value of gross} \\ \text{output per hour} \\ (Pz)\ (z)\end{array} - \begin{array}{l}\text{cost of materials} \\ \text{used and wear} \\ \text{and tear on ma-} \\ \text{chines per hour} \\ (Pm)\ (m)\end{array} \quad (6.8)$$

where Pz = price at which output is sold
  z = amount of gross output produced per labor hour
  Pm = price at which new materials and machines can be purchased to replace those used or used up
  m = amount of materials used up and wear and tear on machines per labor hour

If this output sells at a price (Pz) of $4 per unit, then the value of gross output is:

$$\begin{array}{l}\text{value of gross} \\ \text{output per} \\ \text{labor hour}\end{array} = (Pz)\ (z) = (\$4 \text{ per unit}) (3 \text{ units}) = \$12$$

Let us imagine that in producing this output, 4 pieces of materials (or machines) are used, and the price of each (Pm) is $0.50. Then the cost of materials used and wear and tear on machines per hour is

$$\begin{array}{l}\text{cost of materials} \\ \text{used and wear and} \\ \text{tear on machines} \\ \text{per labor hour}\end{array} = (Pm)\ (m) = (\$0.50 \text{ per piece}) (4 \text{ pieces}) = \$2$$

so now we know the value of net output per labor hour (using equation 6.8) is

$$y = (P_z)\ (z) - (Pm)\ (m) = \$12 - \$2 = \$10$$

From this example we can see that the value of net output per labor hour (y) depends upon

  Pz = price of output (if Pz rises, y will rise)
  z = amount of gross output per labor hour (if z rises, y will rise)

Pm = price of materials used and wear and tear on machines (if Pm rises, y will fall)

m = amount of materials used and wear and tear on machines per labor hour (if m rises, y will fall)

We can go one step further to see what z depends on. The amount of gross output actually produced per labor hour depends on both how efficiently the worker's work activities are used and how hard the worker works in that hour.

$$z = ed \qquad (6.9)$$

where e = "efficiency" or the amount of gross output per unit of work done

d = "work done" or how hard the worker works per hour

The **efficiency of labor** or **amount of gross output per unit of work done** is the total amount produced for a specified or given amount of work effort (intensity of work). **Work done** is the amount of work effort expended per hour of labor.

For example, if each unit of work done produces one unit of output (so $e = 1$) and workers work at the rate of 3 units of work done per hour (so $d = 3$), then

$$z = (1)(3) = 3 \text{ units of gross output per hour}$$

So we can see that the value of net output per hour further depends upon

e = efficiency of work done (if e rises, y will rise)

d = amount of work done per labor hour (if d rises, y will rise)

The last term in the definition of the profit rate, the denominator of equation 6.7, is the value of the capital goods owned by the capitalist per hour of labor employed (k). This term simply measures the size of the capitalist's investment per hour of labor.

$$\begin{matrix} \text{value of capital} \\ \text{goods owned per} \\ \text{hour of labor } (k) \end{matrix} = \begin{matrix} \text{price of} \\ \text{capital} \\ \text{goods } (Pc) \end{matrix} \times \begin{matrix} \text{amount of capital} \\ \text{goods owned per} \\ \text{labor hour } (CG/Labor) \end{matrix} \qquad (6.10)$$

where Pc = price of capital goods

CG = amount of capital goods owned (number of machines)

$Labor$ = labor hours employed

To understand the term k remember that B-E Company's investment includes all machinery, buildings, and other capital goods that it owns, and its profit rate must be calculated on this total investment. Yet frequently there are some machines or facilities that B-E is not actually using in production, perhaps because the level of demand for the product is low. This idle investment, or *idle capacity*, cannot actually generate any profits, of course, since it is idle.

Let us then define:

CG *in use* = the amount of capital goods actually in use

The **price of capital goods** is the average price of a machine or capital good.

Idle capacity consists of machines and other capital goods that are currently not being used in production.

And since $\left(\dfrac{CG\ in\ use}{CG\ in\ use}\right) = 1$, we may rewrite equation 6.10 as

$$k = Pc\left(\frac{CG}{Labor}\right) = (Pc)\left(\frac{CG}{Labor}\right)\left(\frac{CG\ in\ use}{CG\ in\ use}\right)$$

or rearranging terms:

$$k = Pc\left(\frac{CG}{CG\ in\ use}\right)\left(\frac{CG\ in\ use}{Labor}\right) \qquad (6.11)$$

The middle term, $\left(\dfrac{CG}{CG\ in\ use}\right)$, is more easily understood if we turn it upside down:

The **capacity utilization ratio** measures the percentage of all capital goods that are currently being used in production.

$$cu = \frac{\text{capacity utilization ratio (or percentage of owned capital actually in use)}}{} = \frac{CG\ in\ use}{CG}$$

The middle term in equation 6.11 is thus just reciprocal of the percentage of owned capital actually in use, or $\left(\dfrac{1}{cu}\right)$

The last term in equation 6.11 is the amount of capital goods in use per hour of labor. Using the lowercase letters to signify per-labor-hour variables, we can write

The **amount of capital goods in use per hour of labor** is the number of machines actually used in production divided by the total number of hours worked.

$$cg\ in\ use = \frac{CG\ in\ use}{Labor}$$

So equation 6.11 becomes

$$k = (Pc)\left(\frac{1}{cu}\right)(cg\ in\ use) \qquad (6.12)$$

For example, suppose B-E owns five machines. We know that B-E employs two workers, and suppose each worker tends two machines. Thus, even though B-E owns five machines, only four are currently in use. Suppose further that each machine costs $10,000, and that the two workers work 1000 hours each during the year. Then k—the value of the capital goods invested per labor hour—can be calculated as follows:

$Pc = \$10{,}000$
$CG = 5$ machines
$CG\ in\ use = 4$ machines
$Labor = 2000$ hours

The Profits Determinants: A Short Form and a Long Form

There is a short way and a long way of writing the determinants of the profit rate. The short way (equation 6.7) is:

$$r = \frac{y - w}{k}$$

where
- r = profit rate
- y = value of net output per hour of labor
- w = wage rate per hour of labor*
- k = value of capital goods owned per hour of labor

The long way results from rewriting y and k in terms of their components.

(a) The value of net output per hour of labor (y) is (combining equations 6.8 and 6.9):

$$y = (Pz)(e)(d) - (Pm)(m)$$

where
- Pz = price of output*
- e = amount of gross output produced per unit of work done*
- d = work done per hour*
- Pm = price of materials used and wear and tear on machines*
- m = amount of materials used and wear and tear on machines per hour of labor*

(b) The value of the capital goods owned per hour of labor hired (k) is (from equation 6.12):

$$k = Pc \left(\frac{1}{cu}\right) \left(cg \text{ in use}\right)$$

where
- Pc = price of capital goods*
- cu = capacity utilization ratio or the percentage of owned capital goods actually in use*
- cg in use = amount of capital goods in use per labor hour*

so the long way to write the profits determinants equation, listing all the determinants is

$$r = \frac{Pz\,ed - Pm\,m - w}{Pc\left(\dfrac{1}{cu}\right)(cg \text{ in use})} = \frac{\begin{array}{c}\text{value of} \\ \text{gross output} \\ \text{per labor} \\ \text{hour}\end{array} - \begin{array}{c}\text{cost of materials} \\ \text{used and wear} \\ \text{and tear on} \\ \text{machines per} \\ \text{labor hour}\end{array} - \begin{array}{c}\text{wage} \\ \text{per} \\ \text{hour}\end{array}}{\begin{array}{c}\text{value of capital goods owned per} \\ \text{labor hour}\end{array}}$$

* Each of these terms is listed in Figure 6.2. Note that one determinant—taxes—is not considered until Chapter 13.

From these data we see that

$$cu = \frac{4 \text{ machines in use}}{5 \text{ machines owned}} = .80 = 80 \text{ percent}$$

and

$$cg \text{ in use} = \frac{CG \text{ in use}}{Labor} = \frac{4 \text{ machines in use}}{2000 \text{ hours}}$$

Using equation 6.12,

$$k = (Pc) \left(\frac{1}{cu}\right) (cg \text{ in use})$$

$$k = \$10,000 \left(\frac{5 \text{ machines owned}}{4 \text{ machines in use}}\right)\left(\frac{4 \text{ machines used}}{2000 \text{ total labor hours}}\right)$$

$$k = \$25 \text{ worth of capital goods per labor hour}$$

From this example we can see that the value of the capital goods owned per labor hour (k) depends on:

Pc = price of machines and other capital goods (if Pc rises, k will rise)
cu = capacity utilization ratio (if cu rises, k will fall)
cg *in use* = amount of capital goods in use per labor hour (if *cg in use* rises, k will rise)

We now have enough information to make a complete list of the determinants of the profit rate; this list appears in Figure 6.2. We can use the list to identify possible ways for capitalists to raise the profit rate—either as the owner of a single company or as a member of a whole class. The only determinant of the profit rate which is missing from Figure 6.2 is taxes, which we will consider in Chapter 13. You may wish to think of other examples of strategies to raise the profit rate than those listed in Figure 6.2.

Notice that some strategies may be inconsistent with one another, even for an individual capitalist. For example, a way of finding additional markets so as to put idle factories to use (strategy number 9 in Figure 6.2) would be to *lower* the price of output (contrary to number 1). Similarly, many technological improvements that might raise the amount of gross output per unit of work done (number 2) will require an *increase* in the amount of machinery in use per labor hour employed (contrary to number 8).

Moreover, the efforts by some capitalists to increase *their* rates of profit may work to reduce the profits of *other* capitalists. For instance, suppose one capitalist sells a material (for example, oil) needed in the production processes of other capitalists. If the first capitalist raises his output price, his profit rate will increase, other things constant, via strategy number 1; but the profit rates of the

Determinants of the Profit Rate	Possible Ways for an Individual Capitalist to Raise the Profit Rate
1. Price of output (Pz)	Gain monopoly power so that prices can be raised
2. Efficiency, or gross output per unit of work done (e)	Improve technology
3. Amount of work done per hour of labor (d)	Speed up the production line or hire more supervisors to control the pace of work
4. Amount of materials used and machines used up per labor hour (m)	Develop production methods that reduce amount of wasted materials or broken tools
5. Price of materials used and machines used up (Pm)	Find new supplier with lower prices
6. Hourly wages (w)	Locate a source of cheaper labor; decertify unions
7. Price of the capital goods used in production (Pc)	Find a cheaper supplier of the machines used in production
8. Capital goods in use per hour of labor employed (*cg in use*)	Develop production methods that use less equipment, for example, use production methods that pollute rather than installing waste-treatment equipment
9. Capacity utilization ratio, or percentage of owned capital actually in use (*cu*)	Find markets for additional outputs so that idle factories or machines can be put to use

FIGURE 6.2 The determinants of the profit rate. The profit rate depends on (is determined by) the terms listed in the first column. A capitalist may attempt to increase the profit rate by changing any of the profit-rate determinants in a favorable direction, for example, raising Pz or lowering w. Some of the possible strategies for doing this appear in the second column. Chapters 7–9 consider these and other strategies. In order to be successful, a capitalist must understand how the determinants of the profit rate are *themselves* determined and find a way to change them. Others (consumers and workers, for example) may oppose these strategies to raise profits; consumers and workers may want lower (not higher) Pz and higher (not lower) w.

other capitalists will fall (for them, the oil price rise is an increase in Pm, contrary to strategy number 5). Similarly, suppose all capitalists successfully cut their wage rates (number 6); but workers (as consumers) provide much of the market demand for capitalists' output, so many capitalists would find that, contrary to strategy number 9, they could no longer find customers for as much of their

B-E Company Profit Rate

We can calculate B-E Company's profit rate since we know enough information (given in the text).

Let us start with:

$$r = \frac{y - w}{k}$$

We know that

w = \$6 per hour (by assumption)

and

y = \$10 per hour (because B-E's two workers produce \$160 when each is working eight hours)

k = \$25 per hour (see text)

So then

$$r = \frac{\$10 - \$6}{\$25} = \frac{4}{25} = 16 \text{ percent} = \text{profit rate}$$

output. Capacity utilization (cu) would fall, and their profit rates would decline. These aggregate or macroeconomic effects are investigated in Chapters 11 and 14.

We could now calculate the profit rate itself if we knew the values for each of the determinants of the profit rate listed in Figure 6.2. In the following chapters we will investigate how each of these determinants is itself determined: for instance, what determines d, the average amount of work done per hour? or cu, the percentage of capital goods actually employed in production?

☐ Suggested Readings

Geoff Hodgson, *Capitalism, Value, and Exploitation* (London: Martin Robertson, 1983).

Michael Howard, *Profits in Economic Theory* (New York: St. Martin's Press, 1983).

Franz Neumann, *Behemoth: The Structure and Practice of National Socialism, 1933–1944* (New York: Harper & Row, 1944).

Andrew Shonfield, *Modern Capitalism: The Changing Balance of Public and Private Power* (New York: Oxford University Press, 1969).

Paul Sweezy, *The Theory of Capitalist Development* (London: Dennis Dobson, 1942).

CHAPTER 7

COMPETITION AND CONCENTRATION

Ford Motor Company, after four years of preparation, brought a new compact car to market in 1983. The car was sold in two versions, the Ford Tempo and the Mercury Topaz. But as the *Wall Street Journal* observed, ". . . in fact, the only differences are minor styling changes." (*Wall Street Journal*, May 4, 1983).

When advertising its one-car/two-versions product, Ford made them seem anything but similar. The Tempo was supposed to be speedy, sporty, and sexy. In the initial commercials for Tempo, a sexy young woman whizzed along in a Tempo, inviting viewers to "pick up the Tempo of your life." The car sped past letters 40 feet high spelling TEMPO, then did a loop-the-loop around the *O*. Male viewers could hardly be blamed for coming away with the impression that buying the car would bring them success with the young woman.

Topaz, by contrast, was advertised as the right car for intelligent, low-key, sophisticated buyers. No reckless loop-the-loop here; rather, the Topaz was depicted as "tasteful," almost like a Mercedes, and the backgrounds in commercials were expensive country houses. The Topaz slogan—"A car as advanced as those who will own it"—flattered the intelligence of anyone gullible enough to believe it.

Why does Ford go to the trouble of producing two versions of the same car, with only minor styling differences between them, and then spend millions of dollars to advertise the differences? The answer, as we all know, is that they are competing for customers and profits. And with this in mind, the Ford Motor Company is in the business of producing tastes and needs as well as producing cars.

Capitalists invest money in order to make more money—profits. But in their search for profits, they quickly discover that other capitalists have the same idea. The quest for profits, then, necessarily brings capitalists into *competition*.

The prospect of profits spurs capitalists to action, but competition channels their activity. Competition limits what any one capitalist can do. It also shapes what all capitalists (considered as a group) are driven to do. This chapter examines how competition among capitalists occurs and how the process of competition generates constant change in the economy.

Neoclassical or conventional economics depicts competition as producing "equilibrium" rather than change. It asks you to imagine a marketplace—say an open-air fruit market—where there are many sellers and many buyers. In this simple supply-and-demand situation, market equilibrium is achieved when competition drives the price of fruit to a level where suppliers want to sell exactly the quantity that demanders wish to buy. Supply and demand determine the price and quantities of fruit to be exchanged, and the market "clears." The next day dawns, the sellers return with a new supply of fruit to be sold, the buyers bring a new demand for fruit, and the competitive process is repeated. Equilibrium is achieved every day, and competition itself provides little impetus for change.

This conventional view of relations among capitalists is not wrong, but it is quite limited and misleading. It is one-dimensional; it considers the horizontal (competition) dimension, but it fails to consider either the vertical (command) or time (change) dimensions of competition. Once equilibrium is achieved in the neoclassical model, nothing can change until something from the outside, an "exogenous" factor, intervenes.

This chapter presents a three-dimensional view of competition. It supplements the conventional, one-dimensional analysis by showing how power and command relations enter into competition and how the process of competition itself leads to change and development.

The main idea of this chapter is that, as capitalists search for profits, competition drives them to change their operations almost continuously. This competitive scramble limits what any one capitalist can do, shapes what all capitalists are driven to do, and produces an enormous pressure for continual change in the capitalist economy as a whole.

This main idea is expressed in six main points:

1. Capitalists must *compete for profits,* and they do so by attempting to

improve the determinants of their own profit rates. They are severely limited in what they can do, however, by the discipline of competition.

2. Competition among capitalists takes three principal forms: efforts to achieve a price advantage (*price competition*); efforts to create new situations in which potential competitors are at least temporarily left behind (*breakthroughs*); and efforts to eliminate competition (*monopoly power*).

3. For all three types of competition, firms must *invest to compete*. Investment is the primary way that firms achieve price advantages, breakthroughs, and monopoly power.

4. Because firms must invest to compete, competition is *inherently dynamic*. The process of competition among capitalists contains within itself powerful forces for change. This internal dynamic insistently changes every market situation even as competition occurs, and it imparts a powerful dynamic tendency to the economy as a whole.

5. The competitive scramble both continually generates new and divergent profit rates among firms and tends to equalize existing rates. Whether there is any overall *equalization of profit rates* depends on the balance between these opposing forces.

6. Competitive dynamics also lead to both economic concentration (large firms increasing their role in the economy) and the erosion of established positions of market power. Whether there is any continuing *tendency toward economic concentration* depends on the balance between these opposing forces.

Competition among capitalists leads to identifiable, predictable changes in competition itself. This is a case where "history matters," that is, where political economy's third dimension (change or time) must be considered. Competition thus both causes change and changes itself.

☐ Competition for Profits

Capitalists seek profits; for this purpose they invest. But how can they tell which projects will be most profitable? And, having invested, what can they do to ensure high profits?

Most investments are risky—that is, there is no way for capitalists to be sure what the (future) profit rate will be. Still, they can know what to look for. In Chapter 6 (see Figure 6.2 for summary), we learned that a firm's rate of profit is

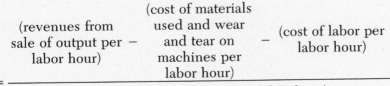

$$r = \frac{\begin{pmatrix}\text{revenues from}\\ \text{sale of output per}\\ \text{labor hour}\end{pmatrix} - \begin{pmatrix}\text{cost of materials}\\ \text{used and wear}\\ \text{and tear on}\\ \text{machines per}\\ \text{labor hour}\end{pmatrix} - \begin{pmatrix}\text{cost of labor per}\\ \text{labor hour}\end{pmatrix}}{(\text{value of capital invested per labor hour})}$$

An individual company's profits will be increased, other things being unchanged, when its revenues from outputs per labor hour rise, its costs of labor or materials used per labor hour decline, or its investment per hour worked is less. More specifically, the profit rate will be higher:

The Larger Is:	and/or	*The Smaller Is:*
Pz, the price of the output		m, the amount of materials used and wear and tear on machines per labor hour
e, the efficiency of the work done		Pm, the price of materials used and wear and tear on machines
d, the amount of work done per hour		w, the hourly wage
cu, the capacity utilization ratio		Pc, the price of the capital goods used in production
		cg in use, the amount of capital goods in use per hour of labor employed

As each capitalist searches for ways to influence and improve these determinants of his profit rate, he will be brought into competition with other capitalists and competition will limit what he can do. Thus, for instance, a capitalist may not be able to increase his profits simply by raising the price he charges. Why? Because if he puts his price up higher than the price charged by other suppliers of the same product, some or all of his customers will switch to the other firms and buy their products. The result will be a fall in sales, and some of his output will go unsold.

Similarly, the capitalist usually cannot simply lower the prices he pays for materials, labor, or capital goods. Again, the reason is competition; sellers of these inputs will choose to sell to other firms that pay them higher prices.

For some of the profit determinants, the capitalist is limited by the present state of knowledge or technology. It may be impossible to raise efficiency (e) or reduce the amount of materials used and wear and tear on machines (m) until new technologies are developed.

The amount of work done per hour (d) can be increased only if employees can be induced or compelled to work more quickly or intensively. The employer's attempts to speed up production are likely to be met by opposition from the employees.

In all these ways, the capitalist is limited by competition. Moreover, one capitalist's profits are often another's misery. The quadrupling of oil prices after 1973 poured billions of dollars of profits into the accounts of oil companies, but it reduced the profits of energy-using sectors of the economy (such as the steel industry) and of those sectors that depend on cheap gas or cheap energy to sell their products (such as the automobile industry).

At the same time that competition limits what any one capitalist can do to improve his profit determinants, it is already eroding those conditions that make possible his current or existing profits. Every successful investment, and the high profit rate produced by it, attracts competitors. Other firms seek to share the high profits, and so current success means more intense competition in the future.

Notice that the winners in competition are those firms that are most *profitable*. Profitability is sometimes confused with efficiency, but what is essential for a firm is that it be profitable. Efficiency will usually contribute to profitability (by, for instance, raising e), but other factors (all the other profit-rate determinants) also contribute to profitability. Hence, the most efficient firm may not always be the most profitable firm—if its greater efficiency is more than offset by more disadvantageous levels of the other determinants. As we will see in Chapter 8, efficiency is not the same thing as profitability, and competition only rewards the profitable.

Profit making is a never-ending struggle by each firm to break out of the limits set by competition. The ensuing warfare among the combatants determines who the winners, and the losers, will be.

Competition is rarely "stable" or "static" or "in equilibrium." If ever an "equilibrium" is established, the competitive pressure to reinvest disrupts and overturns the very conditions of that "equilibrium." A static equilibrium is as unimaginable as a bicycle that can remain upright even when it is brought to a stop. The internal dynamic of competition changes competition itself. We need not wait until some external force disrupts the market—competition incessantly does that itself.

Moreover, this dynamic of competition continues *without an end or limit*. After all, the end of one period of competition is but the beginning of the next period. Those firms that fail to take advantage of every chance for growth will be outcompeted by other firms that will. There is no rest for the weary, nor even for the victors!

☐ The Forms of Competition

There are three principal forms of or strategies for competition. Each one offers the possibility for staying even with or ahead of one's competitors.

Price competition occurs when firms attempt to attract customers by offering them products equivalent to those offered by other firms but at a lower price. Firms following a price-competitive

Price competition is a form of or strategy for competition in which firms attempt to attract customers primarily by offering lower prices.

strategy continue to pursue the activities they have followed in the past, making small improvements here and there as opportunities appear. Price competition may lead employers to try to cut wages, speed up the pace of work, eliminate waste in production, and otherwise attempt to cut costs wherever possible, in order that they can also cut their prices and still earn profits. Many competitors may be doing approximately similar things, and success goes to those firms that are best able to squeeze profits out of routine operations.

Breakthroughs occur when firms discover or develop something totally new: a new source of inputs, a new method of organizing production, or a new product or market. In this case firms can earn profits, often big profits, not because they are the best at the old game but rather because they are the first player in an entirely new game.

If a firm with a breakthrough has developed a new product, it may have little competition at all. If, on the other hand, its breakthrough creates a large cost advantage in producing a product that is already made by other firms, the breakthrough firm may be able to cut the price of its product *and* still make exceptional profits.

A firm that consistently achieves breakthroughs is likely to have better access to credit and better chances to grow, to reduce costs, to attract skilled personnel, and to develop production know-how. Being first gives the firm a temporary relief from competition, which lasts until other firms enter the market. Big profits, however, are sooner or later likely to attract competitors who want to capture some of these profits themselves.

Monopoly power exists when firms are able to exercise significant power over the market by excluding some or most competitors. Firms can rarely exclude all other firms ("pure monopoly"), but often three or four or more firms ("oligopoly" or "shared monopoly") can effectively exclude all others or limit their sales to a small part of the market. For monopoly to last any significant time, the monopoly firms must have some economic advantage or other basis for preventing the other firms from competing. In this case firms are able to charge higher prices for their output, pay lower prices for their inputs, or have sole access to superior technologies or methods of organization.

Competition for profits creates an enormous pressure for firms to discover new ways of doing business, innovations great or small that will give them an advantage over competitors. Breakthroughs and monopoly power *do not end* competition; rather, for the firm, they are strategies for waging competition more effectively. They provide a possibility for competing by means other than price cutting.

A **breakthrough** occurs when a firm discovers or develops a new method of doing business such as a new way of organizing work, a new product, or a new market.

Monopoly power is the ability of one or a few firms in an industry to exercise substantial control over the market price and other aspects of competition, usually by excluding other firms.

Oligopoly or **shared monopoly** is a market situation in which several firms together, but no one firm by itself, can exercise substantial monopoly power.

Price competition

Price competition confronts each firm with a dilemma: The firm attracts customers with a *low* price, but, other things equal, its profits will be higher the *higher* is its price. It cannot both cut its price and raise its price.

The reason for this dilemma becomes clear if we rewrite the profits determinants equation (see box) to read:

$$r = (ru)(cu) \tag{7.1}$$

where ru = profit rate on capital goods in use

         cu = percentage of owned capital goods actually in use

In equation 7.1 we see that the overall rate of profit is equal to the rate of profit on those capital goods in use (ru) times the capacity utilization ratio (cu).

In 1982, for instance, the average American manufacturing firm utilized about 70 percent of its capacity. The average profit rate (return on total depreciable assets for nonfinancial corporations)

The Rate of Profit on Capital Goods in Use

The overall rate of profit (r) may be divided into two parts, the rate of profit on those capital goods (machines) actually used (ru) and the percentage of all owned capital goods actually in use.

From equation 6.13 we have

$$r = \frac{Pz\,e\,d - Pm\,m - w}{Pc\,(cg\ in\ use)\,(1/cu)}$$

$$= \underbrace{\frac{Pz\,e\,d - Pm\,m - w}{Pc\,(cg\ in\ use)}}_{\substack{\text{profit rate on capital} \\ \text{goods in use}}} \underbrace{(cu)}_{\substack{\text{percentage} \\ \text{of owned} \\ \text{capital goods} \\ \text{in use}}}$$

If we let ru = profit rate on capital goods in use, then

$$r = (ru)\,(cu)$$

For example, suppose a company owns five machines but is using only four of them. If the profit rate on the machines in use (ru) is 20%, then

$$r = (20\%)(4/5) = 16\%$$

before taxes was 9.5 percent. The profit rate on *capital goods in use* was 13.6 percent.

$$r = (ru)(cu)$$

$$9.5\% = (13.6\%)(70\%)$$

If the typical firm could have used its full capacity and nothing else changed, it would have increased its profits by nearly 40 percent (from 9.5 to 13.6).

A change in the firm's price will generally have opposite effects on ru and cu. From Figure 7.1 we see that if the firm raises its price (Pz) from $P1$ to $P2$, the quantity sold will drop from $Z1$ to $Z2$. The price rise itself will tend to raise ru, as we know from the box on page 133. On the other hand, if the firm does not want unsold goods piling up on its shelves, it must adjust to the lower quantity sold by cutting back on production, thereby lowering cu. Similarly, a price reduction from $P1$ to $P3$ will tend to lower ru but raise cu.

The overall effect of a price change on the profit rate (r) is uncertain. We cannot tell, unless we have more information, whether the rise (or fall) in ru will be bigger or smaller or the same size as

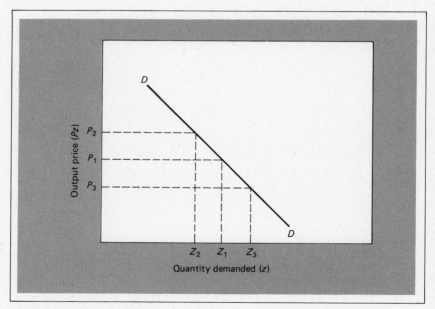

FIGURE 7.1 The demand curve limits a firm's choice of price and output. The demand for a firm's product is represented by the line *DD*. Higher prices mean fewer units of output will be demanded and sold. The demand curve shows how competition among producers limits what profit-raising strategies the firm will be able to carry out.

Price Competition and the Profit Rate

When a firm raises the price of its output (Pz), it can expect two effects on its profit rate. The higher price means that it will receive more revenue for each unit of output sold, raising the profit rate on utilized capacity (ru) and thus tending to *raise* the profit rate itself. A higher price will also, however, attract fewer customers, lower the capacity utilization rate (cu), and thereby tend to *reduce* the profit rate. Remember: the profit rate, r, is simply ru times cu.

To see how the firm will balance these opposing effects, we begin with the demand curve for the firm's output. Instead of measuring quantity in units of output, however, we can measure it in percent of the firm's capacity utilized. For instance, suppose the firm's capacity is 200 units of output per year. Where on a standard demand curve would be marked quantity = 200, in graph (a) we mark instead cu = 100%; where quantity = 100, we mark instead cu = 50 %; and so on. This new demand curve indicates which combinations of Pz and cu are possible, given the demand for the firm's output. The higher the price, the lower the capacity utilization. At $P1$, the firm finds enough customers to use 40 percent of capacity; at $P2$, the firm uses 80 percent of its capacity.

We can draw a second curve based on what effect changing Pz and cu will have on the profit rate (r). Every profit rate (for instance, r = 15%) can be produced by many combinations of Pz and cu, assuming that none of the other things that influence the profit rate changes. Graph (b) shows the various combinations of Pz and cu that

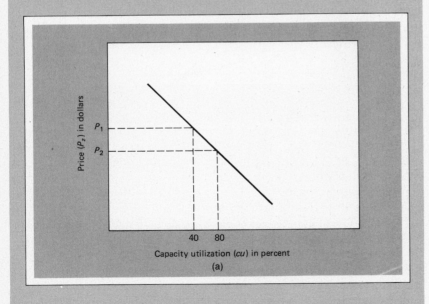

(a)

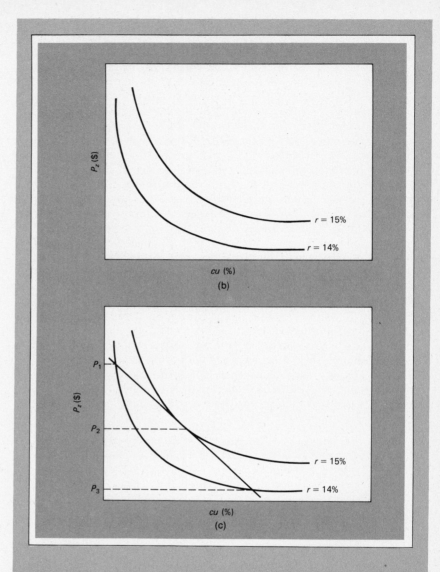

(b)

(c)

would result in a 14 percent profit rate and those that would result in a 15 percent rate.

If we put the first two graphs together, we see that the firm could achieve a 14 percent rate of profit if it sets its price at either $P1$ or $P3$, but if it sets the price at $P2$ it can attain a 15 percent profit rate. Any price higher or lower than $P2$ reduces the profit rate.

If the demand curve shifted to the right, then the firm would have new opportunities and could earn an even higher profit rate.

the fall (or rise) in *cu*, and so we cannot know how *r* is affected. Nonetheless, the dilemma of price competition is evident: Cutting prices likely improves *cu* but lowers *ru*; raising prices likely raises *ru* but reduces *cu*.

Market competition sharply limits a firm's profits in a price-competitive market to the amount needed to cover the costs of materials and labor inputs plus an average or normal profit for the seller—and no more. The price that will tend to be established in such a market is a *markup* over costs:

$$
\underbrace{\text{price of output}}_{\substack{\text{sales} \\ \text{revenue} = \\ \text{per unit}}} = \underbrace{\text{materials cost and wear and tear on machines per unit of output} + \text{labor costs per unit of output}}_{\substack{\text{cost of production} \\ \text{per unit}}} + \underbrace{\text{profits per unit of output}}_{\substack{\text{markup for} \\ \text{profit per unit}}}
$$

The details of the markup are presented in the accompanying box. What is important here, however, is that in this price-competitive market an output price will be established by supply and demand. If that price is so low that firms earn less than they could earn elsewhere, then some firms will be driven out of production or forced to produce some other, more profitable item. If that price is so high that it permits above-normal profits, new producers will be attracted to the field.

The average profit rate may be high or low, satisfactory or disappointing. (In Chapters 11 through 14 we investigate how this aggregate or average profit rate is established.) Market competition tends to limit the profits firms can make, pushing them toward the average level.

To achieve even the average profit rate, firms must constantly struggle. Nothing is guaranteed. Every method of reducing costs must be pursued; every profitable innovation introduced by competitors must be faithfully copied or improved upon if possible.

Breakthroughs

Price competition, even for the winners, usually promises small profits compared to the much larger profits available from breakthroughs and monopoly power. To see this, note that a firm achieving a breakthrough or monopoly power could always act like a price-competitive firm; thus, at worst, its profits would be at the price-competitive level. But the breakthrough or monopoly power

The Components of Output Prices

We can use the expression for the profit rate in equation 6.13 to see how the market will set the price of output (Pz). We start with

$$r = \frac{(Pz \cdot z) - (Pm \cdot m) - (w)}{k}$$

Then multiply by k, divide by z, and rearrange terms to get

$$Pz = \frac{Pm \cdot m}{z} + \frac{w}{z} + \frac{rk}{z}$$

The first term, $\frac{Pm \cdot m}{z}$, is the cost of materials used and wear and tear on machines per unit of output. The second term, $\frac{w}{z}$, is the cost of labor per unit of output. The final term, $\frac{rk}{z}$, is profits per unit of output. So our new expression tells us that

price of output = unit materials + unit labor cost + unit profit cost

The price is sometimes said to be a "markup" over costs, because sellers first calculate the unit costs of producing their output and then add a markup for profit.

For instance, suppose the (materials, machine wear and tear, and labor) cost of producing an IBM personal computer is $2000 and IBM's markup is 50 percent. Then the price would be

price of computer = (unit costs) (1 + markup) = ($2000) (1 + .5)
= $3000

This would yield IBM a per-unit profit of $1000.

At the price of $3000 per computer, IBM may find that it has too few or too many customers. If it has too few, it will have to cut back on production, lowering its capacity utilization (cu). If it has more customers than it has computers to sell, it may be able to raise its markup. Supply and demand therefore govern the size of the markup and/or the rate of capacity utilization.

by definition permits it to do better, that is, achieve bigger profits.

We are not concerned here with the question of justice, the question of whether from society's perspective the profit rate is too high or too low, fair or unfair. That is a separate question. Moreover, the average profit level will fluctuate, being high in some periods and lower in others (see Chapters 11 through 14). Rather, the point here is that each capitalist sees that, whatever the average level of profits, higher profits can be achieved through breakthroughs and monopoly power.

Firms want to break out of the limits of price competition. For that purpose they search for breakthroughs and monopoly power, both of which introduce elements of command (or power) in the relations among capitalists and between them and others.

A breakthrough is something new—a new product, a new way of recruiting labor, a new technology, or anything innovative that gives one firm an advantage over its rivals. A breakthrough changes the terrain on which the competitive struggle is fought. If price competition is like trench warfare, breakthroughs are like tank warfare.

A breakthrough creates a competitive advantage because the firm with the breakthrough is first. Other firms may try to follow it, but until they catch up, the breakthrough firm can achieve a higher profit rate.

A breakthrough may involve any of the determinants of the profit rate. For instance, a firm may discover a new market for its output. This may allow it to charge a higher price (Pz) or use more labor with its capital goods (reducing *cg in use*), for example, by running two shifts per day in its factories. Atari achieved a breakthrough by creating a new market in video games. Or a breakthrough may involve any of the other profit determinants.

A breakthrough raises the profit rate for a firm because it releases the firm, at least temporarily, from the limits set by competition. For instance, when Atari opened the video games market, it could charge prices high enough to produce much higher than normal profits. It was protected from price competition because other firms were not yet able to make video games. (Only later, when new firms entered the market, did prices come down; then the profit rate tumbled toward the average level.)

Similarly, a breakthrough affecting one of the other profit determinants permits the firm to escape the limits on that determinant set by competition. For instance, new airline companies (for example, Air West) use nonunion labor, paying their employees substantially less than the older, more established firms such as American or Eastern. As a result, at least some of the new airline companies have been able to attain high profit rates.

Breakthroughs, then, raise a firm's sales revenues or reduce its costs sufficiently to produce a higher than normal profit rate. This competitive advantage lasts only until other firms catch up, yet this temporary relief from competition may produce substantial profits. And while other firms catch up and the advantage is being eroded, the breakthrough firm can already be searching for a new breakthrough. This is the attraction of breakthroughs.

Competition also induces a fear of being left behind, and this too spurs firms to seek out breakthroughs. Even a capitalist content with the current rate of profit must fear somebody else's breakthrough: the subsequent unequal competition could well destroy his or her own profits in the future. So here as always, competition provides both the carrot and the stick; it attracts the greedy and spurs the lazy.

In the marketplace, notions of "competitive equilibrium" are left far behind. Like Alice in Wonderland, the capitalist must keep running just to stay in the same place.

Monopoly power

Capitalists can also achieve higher profits by creating monopoly power, that is, by escaping competition or insulating themselves from its effects. If competition is eroded or eliminated, then the firms with monopoly power can unilaterally change the profit rate determinants and thereby raise their profits.

Notice that the term "monopoly power" refers both to the situation of a single firm (perfect monopoly) and to that of a small group of firms (oligopoly or shared monopoly); in either case, if some firm or firms can exclude others, monopoly power exists.

Breakthroughs and monopoly power are very similar. Both create a higher profit rate for the breakthrough or monopoly firm by excluding other firms. Indeed, the economist Joseph Schumpeter understood breakthroughs as creating "temporary monopolies." And Schumpeter's insight points to the main difference between them: breakthroughs are temporary, until other firms catch up; monopoly power is longer lasting, based on some economic or legal or institutional obstacle that excludes other firms. These obstacles are often called "barriers to entry."

Barriers to entry are obstacles that make it more difficult or costly for new firms to enter a market; examples include technical secrets, initial investments that are very large, and exclusive marketing arrangements.

Just as with breakthroughs, monopoly power may be exercised with respect to any of the determinants of the profit rate. But although we can find examples of monopoly power for all the profit rate determinants, one is of much greater economic importance than all the rest: monopoly power over the output price (Pz).

Firms establish monopoly power in output markets in three ways: (1) by being the only seller of a particular product; (2) by conspiring or colluding with other producers of the product not to compete against one another; or, most commonly, (3) by establishing informal and tacit relations with other companies to avoid competition.

An example of the only-seller case is the electric power company. If you want electricity service in your home, you have little choice. You must buy it from your local power company.

The second method is collusion. A dramatic example of collusion occurred in the decades before 1960 when General Electric, Westinghouse, and other companies fixed the prices of electrical equipment, involving sales of millions of dollars each year.

The third case, that of shared monopoly, is both the most common and the most complicated. In the breakfast cereal, steel, or tobacco industry, for example, a few firms have dominated the industry for many years. These firms "share" monopoly power in the following sense. Without direct conspiracy or collusion, they have developed ways of behaving that permit them largely to avoid price competition and to share the higher profits associated with monopoly power. Each of the shared-monopoly firms has learned to live within certain rules or ways of doing business that all of the shared-monopoly partners accept. Competition tends to be governed by these rules.

Shared monopoly is thus like an uneasy coalition among potential enemies. It holds together so long as each partner sees the agreement as being in its own self-interest. Higher potential profits create a real benefit to be gained from cooperation. And the most powerful firm or firms, by threatening retaliation on those firms that do not agree, may, of course, make noncooperation very costly for a firm. So shared monopoly operates on the basis of a set of tacit or informal rules to which all firms agree.

What are these rules? We will investigate them in more detail in Chapter 10, but here we may note the two most important: (1) shared monopoly firms develop ways to avoid price competition; and (2) firms continue to compete by nonprice methods, particularly by an intensive sales effort.

Price competition is avoided because shared monopolists develop informal, tacit, and indirect methods to establish prices. Such methods for avoiding price competition differ from industry to industry, with each industry's system being shaped by the peculiar circumstances of its historical evolution. Most commonly, these methods reflect the long experience each firm has had in dealing with the others.

But if price competition is avoided, other forms of competition attain a new intensity. The industry demand curve still limits what producers can sell. Thus, a battle for *market shares* ensues, and each shared-monopoly firm tries to get the biggest market share it can. If the industry's price is set by tacit agreement and a firm has constant or declining average costs when output expands, the corporation's profits will increase directly with sales. It becomes profitable, then, to compete by intensifying its efforts to sell its products—its *sales effort*.

A **market share** is one firm's sales as a percentage of the total sales in an industry.

The sales effort includes anything that firms do to persuade customers to buy their products. Corporations recruit armies of sales agents, hire public relations firms, and spend billions on advertising. They continually repackage their products ("the all-new Tide"). They expend enormous sums on celebrity endorsements. They have been convicted of bribing foreign governments. They sponsor sports events. They contribute to charities or public television. All is aimed at increasing their market shares.

The **sales effort** consists of all those activities by a firm that relate to the selling of the firm's product.

Monopoly power, like a breakthrough, makes possible a higher than normal rate of profit. It eases the limitations that competition imposes by eliminating some of the competition. Firms compete to see who can first or most effectively escape competition.

☐ **Investing to Compete**

One aspect common to all three forms of competition is *investment*. Price competition, breakthroughs, and monopoly power all require that firms invest (or reinvest) to achieve the benefits. To compete, firms must invest.

More important, a firm can reinvest its profits from one year to achieve a competitive advantage in the next year. Profits already earned (or other funds borrowed) provide the resources with which to attempt to get ahead or stay ahead of rivals.

All of the profit determinants listed in Figure 6.2 become potential targets for reinvestment. If the firm can discover a way to reinvest its profits so as to improve one or more of these determinants, then it will have achieved a higher profit rate. It will have broken out of the limits of static, conventional competition (with its average rate of profit) and positioned itself to capture higher, dynamic profits. The real world of competition is a never-ending (and never totally successful) attempt to break out of the limits set by competition. Some firms will be successful and achieve high profits with which to compete in the future; others will fail and be driven from business.

A firm will only reinvest profits if it expects to earn more profits; it would not make sense to risk some of the profits if only the same amount of profit or less would be returned. So every firm must compare the *cost* of investment with its *expected return* from investment.

Let us assume that a firm is considering a certain investment, say purchasing a new machine. To make the example simple, we will assume that the machine will have a working life of one year, after which it will have to be replaced. Suppose further that the firm must pay I dollars to the machine maker to buy the machine. How can the firm determine whether this investment will be profitable or not?

The profit that the firm earns on its investment is the amount of income received over and above the investment itself. For instance, when an individual puts $100 in a savings account, the gain to the individual is the amount of money received over and above the original $100. Similarly, we can think of the total return derived from the investment as consisting of two parts: the repayment of the investment (I) and the profit (R).

$$\text{total return from investment} = I + R \qquad (7.2)$$

The profit rate (r) on this investment is

$$r = \frac{R}{I} \qquad (7.3)$$

or the dollars of profit received per year (R) divided by the dollars invested (I). We can rewrite equation 7.3 above as $R = r(I)$, so equation 7.2 becomes

$$\text{total return from investment} = I + r(I). \qquad (7.4)$$

The **total return from an investment** consists of two parts, the repayment of the investment and the profit (or loss) earned.

Let us now consider the costs of the investment. There is, first, I dollars, the cost of the project itself.

In addition, however, there is the cost of money used to make the investment. What is this cost? Let us assume that a firm can either borrow funds (get a loan) at the prevailing *interest rate* (i), or, if it has excess funds, it can itself loan out its excess funds at this same rate (i). A corporation, for example, may obtain loans from banks or other lenders if it wishes to borrow funds, or it can lend money to other companies if it wishes to loan out funds.

The **interest rate** is the cost of renting money; for a firm that borrows money, it is the percentage of the amount borrowed that must be repaid in addition to the amount borrowed.

An **opportunity cost** is the value of the best opportunity given up (foregone) in order that whatever was chosen could be undertaken.

The interest rate (i) measures the cost of each dollar used in investment. If the firm must borrow to invest, it must pay interest (to banks or bondholders) at the rate i. And if the firm uses its own profits to invest, it gives up the interest (i) it *could* have earned if it had loaned the funds out rather than used them for investment. The second type of cost is called an *opportunity cost* because it is the cost of the opportunity lost when, instead of using the money to make a loan, it was used to buy the machine. The cost of the money used to undertake the investment is iI, the cost per dollar (i) times the number of dollars invested (I). Thus

$$\text{cost of investment} = I + iI \qquad (7.5)$$

The **total cost of investment** consists of two parts, the cost of the capital goods purchased and the opportunity cost of the money used to purchase them.

To determine the profits from the investment, we subtract the costs (equation 7.5) from the returns (equation 7.4).

$$\begin{pmatrix}\text{profits from} \\ \text{investment}\end{pmatrix} = \begin{pmatrix}\text{returns from} \\ \text{investment}\end{pmatrix} - \begin{pmatrix}\text{costs of} \\ \text{investment}\end{pmatrix}$$
$$= (I + rI) - (I + iI)$$
$$= rI - iI$$
$$= (r - i)\,I \qquad (7.6)$$

In equation 7.6, the number of dollars invested, I, is always a positive number. But what about $(r - i)$? It could be either positive or negative, depending on which is bigger, r or i.

If r is greater than i, the term $(r - i)$ will be positive and the firm will receive sufficient profits from investing so that even after paying interest to the bank (which becomes the bank's profits), it will have some left over. But if r is less than i, the term $(r - i)$ will be negative, and the investment will make a loss to the firm, even if the profit rate (r) is positive. This is because the firm will have to pay more interest to the bank, or it could have earned more interest itself by loaning out its money, than it is making in profits. So the firm must compare r and i to see if the investment is a good idea.

Unfortunately for the firm, it cannot compare r and i directly. When a firm undertakes an investment, it cannot know for sure how the investment will work out; all investments are risky. It usually does know how much the investment will cost (I) and what the interest rate (i) is, but it cannot know with certainty what the (future) profit rate (r) will be. Hence, in evaluating an investment, it must compare the *expected* profit rate (*expected r*) with the interest rate (i). The expected profit rate is that rate that the firm thinks or expects it will achieve; it may or may not turn out (later) to actually have been achieved.

So the firm will choose to invest only when

$$\begin{matrix} \text{expected} & & \text{interest} \\ \text{profit rate} & > & \text{rate} \\ (expected\ r) & & (i) \end{matrix}$$

The **expected profit rate on investment** is a firm's estimate of the future profit rate that it thinks will be earned on its investment.

If the *expected r* is higher than i, we can see from equation 7.6 that firms will expect to make profits and will therefore want to invest. If the *expected r* is less than i, then firms will refuse to invest and will instead try to loan out any excess funds.

Whether firms invest, then, depends in large part on investors' optimism or pessimism about the future. If they are optimistic and are confident of good or better conditions in the future, they will tend to evaluate investment projects more favorably, seeing the positive possibilities and down-playing the dangers; the *expected r* will tend to be high. If, on the other hand, investors are pessimistic, expecting difficult times ahead, they will be more wary, worrying about the chances that investments will not pay off; the *expected r* will tend to be low. Their optimism or pessimism will lead, therefore, to more or less investment.

Of course each investor will view the future somewhat differently, and some will have expectations that turn out to be more correct than others. (In Chapter 11 we will see that some economy-wide forces contribute to building or eroding investor confidence; the expectations of most or many investors will be influenced by these general economic conditions.)

The level of investment also depends on the interest rate. A low interest rate will tend to stimulate investment, whereas a high interest rate will discourage investment.

The amount of investment a firm will make will also depend on whether it has idle capacity (*cu* less than 1). For unless the new machines are a big improvement over the older machines, it obviously does not make a lot of sense to buy new machines when the firm is not using all the ones it already has.

☐ The Dynamics of Competition

We can now see the close connection between investment and competition. Investment is the firm's way of carrying on competi-

COMPETITION AND CONCENTRATION 145

tion in the future. And competition, because it forces firms to invest, is inherently dynamic.

Suppose that we are considering the beer industry and that initially many firms of approximately equal size populate the industry. Each firm attempts to make as big a profit as possible, but price competition limits most firms to the average rate of profit.

What will these firms do with their profits? They can reinvest profits to improve their competitive prospects in the years ahead. For example, one possibility is to invest in things (research, new machinery, more effective supervision of workers) that reduce the cost of production. In this case we would observe that situation depicted in Figure 7.2. We can see that all firms start out in year 1 with costs of $C1$ per barrel. But whereas the firms that do not reinvest (panel a) continue to have costs of $C1$, those firms that do reinvest (panel b) see their costs fall as time goes on—to $C2$ in the second period, $C3$ in the third period, and so on. With lower costs, they will have higher profit rates or lower prices than the higher-cost (panel a) firms.

Firms that reinvest may also expand their scale of output. While it is theoretically possible for reinvesting firms to undertake only cost-reducing investments and never try to expand their output, it is unlikely that they will do so. The reason for this is simple. It is precisely the ability of lower-cost firms to undercut their higher-cost rivals that permits them to capture larger sales. Thus the lower-cost firms usually have an investment opportunity that the higher-cost firms do not: they can profitably invest in expansion of output; that is, it is profitable for them to grow larger.

Notice that it is profitable for the dynamic, reinvesting, lower-cost firms to grow even if they do not achieve decreasing costs. These firms may choose to expand by building an additional factory that simply replicates their existing (already lower-cost) facilities. In this case, doubling output may not lead to further reduction in per unit costs but will simply reproduce the advantages (and higher profit rates) of the existing operations. Of course, if decreasing costs are also present, then it will be even more advantageous for these firms to grow.

This dynamic competition will tend to produce very uneven results, with winners and losers. If all firms in an industry reinvested in the same way and in the same proportions and with the same results, the reinvestments would not confer an advantage on any firm.

But even in this situation, substantially higher profits may be earned by those firms that invest *first*, even if others eventually follow. In the time between when the leader reinvests and when other firms finally catch up, the lower costs of the leader will generate a higher profit rate. Moreover, when the other firms do

Decreasing costs refers to a situation in which the average cost of producing something declines as the volume (scale) of production increases.

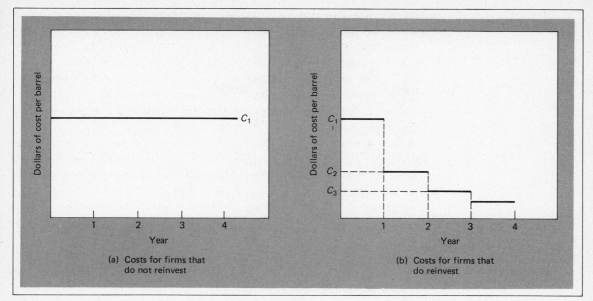

FIGURE 7.2 Dynamic cost advantage. Assuming that the prices of inputs (including the wage) do not change from one period to the next, firms that do not reinvest will find their unit costs remaining constant. Firms that successfully reinvest (in better equipment, for example) will be able to lower their unit costs from one period to the next. Lower costs allow the firm to achieve either higher unit profits or price reductions. Either higher unit profits or lower prices will give the firm a competitive advantage against the firms that failed to reinvest.

finally reinvest, the first firms may already be using their higher profits to reinvest again; they may still stay a jump or two ahead.

More realistically, there is no reason to expect that all firms will reinvest in the same way, in the same amounts, and with the same results. Instead, some firms will reinvest in one thing expected to raise the profit rate, other firms in other things; some firms will not reinvest at all. Firms that do reinvest will reinvest different proportions of their profits. Some firms will be highly effective or lucky, investing in ways that pay off; others will be unsuccessful or unlucky and never see their hoped-for higher profits materialize. Thus, the competitive scramble for profits is likely to produce very uneven results, with some firms coming up big winners and others being big losers.

Moreover, not all firms will be equally well situated. Some firms may have better access to needed raw materials (for example, mountain water) or be closer to big markets, or simply have better management or luckier owners or whatever. The well-situated firms will have higher profit rates than the poorly situated ones.

Firms that achieve high profits in one period have more to reinvest in the next period. The higher the profit rate, the more that can be reinvested; unsuccessful capitalists have low profit rates and hence little to reinvest.

Investment, then, is the firm's way of competing in the future. And investment necessarily produces change. The result of any investment is that something has been altered: a new market invaded, costs reduced, new machinery introduced, output expanded, or some other alteration of the circumstances that existed before the investment.

Since firms must invest to compete, the competitive process is inherently dynamic. No "equilibrium" can be established, because there are forces already operating in the marketplace that will disrupt and alter it. We need not wait for "outside" events to change matters; competition itself will do so. Competition may produce market clearing, but it does not produce equilibrium.

What are the consequences of this constantly changing, dynamic, disruptive pursuit of profits? On the grandest level, it is this process by which capitalism transforms society (see Chapter 1). More immediately for the operation of firms, competition has consequences for how equal profit rates are and for the degree of economic concentration.

☐ Toward Equal Profit Rates?

At any particular time many different profit rates exist in the economy. Some firms will have low profit rates, others high rates. Competition both produces these diverse rates and tends, over time, to bring them closer together.

Equalization of profit rates refers to the process by which competitive pressures on firms in different industries, different geographical regions, or different markets push their profit rates toward a common or average level.

The profit rate (r) achieved by each firm during a given year depends on the profit rate determinants for the particular firm. How effectively each firm manages its materials and machines input (m), how much work it extracts from its workers per hour (d), and how well it organizes its other operations determine that firm's profit rate. Since some firms do these well or are lucky, whereas others do more poorly, there exists a diversity of profit rates, some low, some slightly higher, some much higher, and so on.

The dynamics of competition, by forcing firms to invest in new and risky projects, continually generates a new diversity or variation in profit rates. Breakthroughs and monopoly power, for instance, make possible exceptionally good profit opportunities. Relative to other firms, firms with breakthroughs and monopoly power will have high profit rates. Firms that must compete with the breakthrough or monopoly-power firms, however, will likely have low profit rates. The advantage enjoyed by firms with breakthrough or monopoly power is precisely a *disadvantage* for the firms they compete with.

In contrast to these ways in which it produces divergent profit rates, competition also contains processes that tend to equalize profit rates. Price competition contributes to equalizing profit rates. As many firms try to squeeze out small cost or marketing advantages, their profit rates will be limited by competition from other firms and all firms' profit rates will be compressed toward the average rate. In addition, when firms invest, they will leave low-profit areas of the economy and enter high-profit areas. This movement tends to bring about more equal rates.

Consider the opportunities facing a firm that wants to undertake an investment. It must compare the cost of each dollar invested (i) with the returns (*expected r*) available from each potential investment project. Investments in areas of the economy—in industries, geographical regions, or whatever—currently achieving high profit rates will be likely to have a much higher *expected r* than areas currently with low profit rates, and so the high-profit areas will attract many more new investments than the low-profit areas.

The movement of firms and investments from low-profit areas to high-profit areas will have two effects, both of which tend to make profit rates more equal. First, the exit of firms and investments from low-profit areas will shift to the left the supply curve in that industry. In Figure 7.3 this is depicted as a shift in the industry supply curve from S1 to S2. This shift in the supply curve will raise the price (Pz) from P1 to P2. However, since some firms have left the industry, this higher price will not reduce the capacity utilization (cu) of the firms remaining, and so the higher price will have the effect of raising their profit rates.

Second, as new firms enter the high-profit industry, they will shift the market supply curve outward (from Sa to Sb in Figure 7.3). This will cause the market to establish a new lower price (in Figure 7.3, the price changes from Pa to Pb) for the output. And although this lower price will attract new customers, these new customers must be shared with the newly entered firms, and hence the lower output price will simply produce lower profit rates.

The movement of firms and investments therefore tends to make profit rates more equal. Exits raise the profit rates in low-profit industries; entries reduce the profit rates in high-profit industries. If this process continued long enough, and if it were not offset by the creation of new profit rate differences, the average profit rate would be the same in each industry and area.

Whether competition tends to equalize profit rates or make them more unequal depends on which set of opposing forces is stronger—those forces (like breakthroughs and monopoly power) that create divergent profit rates or those pressures (like price competition and exit and entry) that equalize profit rates.

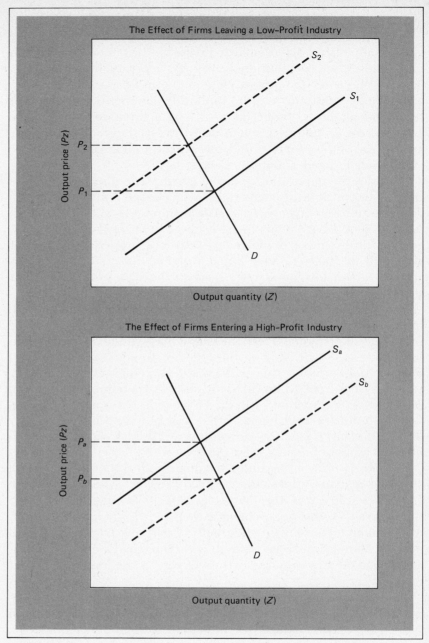

FIGURE 7.3 Entry and exit of firms tend to equalize profits. Low profits will drive some firms out of initially low-profit industry. Exits will lead the supply of output in that industry to be reduced, indicated by the leftward *shift* in the supply curve, from *S1* to *S2*. This shift will allow the remaining firms to raise their price from *P1* to *P2*, thus increasing their profits.

Exactly the opposite happens in initially high-profit industry. High profits attract new entries; and as the new firms start up production, the supply curve *shifts* to the right (increasing supply at each price). Entry of firms forces all producers to sell at lower prices and lowers the profit rate in that industry.

☐ Toward Economic Concentration?

Economic concentration refers to how much of an industry or of the whole economy is organized in very large firms. Consider, for instance, two industries of equal size. In one industry there are 100 firms, all about the same size, whereas in the other industry there are only 4 firms. The second industry is said to be more concentrated than the first. Similarly, for the whole economy, the greater is the role of big firms, the more concentrated the economy is.

Dynamic competition affects the degree of economic concentration because, like its effect on the equalization of profit rates, competition both generates and erodes economic concentration.

Competition generates concentration because greater size almost always enhances a firm's ability to achieve a higher profit rate, and so bigger firms usually can outcompete smaller firms. The business of big firms grows at the expense of smaller firms.

Let us consider why greater size almost always enhances a firm's ability to earn higher profit rates. Three factors are at work: (a) greater size permits greater exploitation of decreasing costs; (b) greater size increases the firm's ability to achieve breakthroughs and monopoly owner; and (c) greater size expands the firm's political and bargaining power with respect to labor, finance, suppliers, and the government.

As we have seen, the term "decreasing costs" refers to a situation in which the average cost of production falls as the volume of production gets larger. For instance, in the first decade of this century, over 200 small companies produced cars. Compare a small backyard shop producing automobiles with a large assembly-line factory. Not only will the big factory produce more cars, the cost of production for each car will likely be lower than in the backyard shop. Obviously, wherever decreasing costs are possible, bigger firms will be able to achieve lower costs than smaller firms. Decreasing costs may increase the profits determinant e (output produced per unit of work effort) and/or reduce m (materials used and wear and tear on machines used in production) or k (value of capital goods invested per worker hour). Increasing e or reducing m or k will raise the profit rate (r).

A second way in which greater size raises the profit rate is that it better equips the firms to achieve breakthroughs and monopoly power. With monopoly power the association is obvious. To be the only seller of a product the firm must be as big as the whole market for that product. More common, monopoly power is shared by a few firms who tacitly operate together; and shared monopoly is more easily established and maintained if there are only a few (large) firms in the industry. If there are many firms in an industry,

Economic concentration is the extent to which the economic activity of an industry or the whole economy is conducted in the largest firms.

the task of establishing tacit cooperation is very difficult; this is similar to the difficulty in getting many people to agree on a decision. Hence, large size, and the corresponding reduction in number of firms in the industry, makes monopoly power easier to attain.

Size also enhances the firm's ability to achieve a breakthrough and, more importantly, to *profit from* a breakthrough. Take the case of a technological innovation. If larger firms have higher profit rates, they could spend more on research—not just more dollars, but a proportionately larger share of their revenues—to discover new innovations. Studies of corporate research budgets suggest, however, that big firms do not spend (proportionately) more; if anything, they spend less. A second possibility is that big firms are more efficient in research activities, that is, that there are decreasing costs in research. But the evidence seems to discount this possibility as well. Thus, small and middle-size companies seem to produce at least their share of innovation.

However, things are different when it comes time to exploit the profit potential of a breakthrough. Here the big firms dominate. To profit from a breakthrough (say, in personal computers), the new product must be produced in quantity, distributed widely, advertised and defended against would-be competitors. For instance, although Apple, Osborne, and other small companies pioneered the small computer, giant IBM seems likely to capture most of the profit. A small firm, even one with an important innovation and big marketing ideas, generally cannot do all these marketing activities successfully. As a small company, it has limited profits and will not have access to the large amounts of credit needed to bring the innovation to fruition. Indeed, sufficient credit may only be granted on the condition that the bank or other lender be given control of the project. The small firm typically has no existing distribution network, its name is not widely recognized, and it has no funds for large-scale advertising.

In this situation, many small firms choose to sell the innovation to a big firm. In other cases, a large firm may decide simply to buy the small company itself. Although the selling price may provide the small firm with a large profit (given its modest investment), the remaining profits from exploiting the breakthrough will be captured by the large firm.

The third way in which greater size may raise the profit rate is by expanding the political and bargaining power of the firm. Big corporations have more clout than small businesses. Political power may be translated into more access to government contracts, better treatment in tariff or export policy (such as subsidies through the Export-Import Bank), and favorable government loans. More bargaining power for the corporation may mean lower interest rates and easier access to credit when the firm borrows money from banks, easier entry into foreign markets, and so on.

In all these ways, large firms may be able to translate political power into higher profits. Perhaps the best example of this is the military-industrial complex, the relationship between giant corporations and the Pentagon, which keeps lucrative contracts flowing to General Dynamics, Boeing, and other military goods producers.

Notice that only when decreasing costs are present is it true that greater size *directly* translates into higher profits. In all other cases, bigness increases the firm's ability to do something else (such as gain monopoly power), which in turn raises the profit rate. In real life, firms may grow because all these factors are mixed together: growth based partly on decreasing costs may lead to the creation of monopoly power; breakthrough profits may finance the firm's attempt to grow and thereby capture the benefits of decreasing costs; and so forth.

If firms encounter substantial increasing costs—unit costs *rising* as production grows—then such costs will limit any particular firm's growth. With increasing costs, the larger a firm gets, the greater is its cost disadvantage. However, increasing costs are almost always experienced at the *plant* (not the firm) level, so increasing costs limit how big the lowest-cost plants (not firms) can be. For instance, very large firms like General Motors operate hundreds of plants rather than concentrating production in one enormous plant. But increasing costs in a *plant* do not limit the *firm's* size, because large firms can (and do) operate many plants. That is why General Motors operates so many automobile factories. Increasing costs appear to be a minor factor limiting the growth of firms.

Increasing costs refers to a situation in which the average cost of producing something increases as the volume (scale) of production increases.

Competition does, however, erode economic concentration in a different way. The high profit rates attained by big firms, like high rates anywhere in the economy, attract competitors. New firms, or old firms seeking new profit opportunities, attempt to enter these industries. And in the intensified competition, the high profits tend to be competed away.

Concentration within any particular industry may be eroded by the entry either of small firms or of large firms whose main business is in another industry. The latter case, for example, occurred when some large firms (Exxon, Xerox, ATT) entered the computer and word processing industry, previously dominated by IBM.

Concentration in the whole economy reflects the balance between small firms and big firms. To the extent that large firms are able to increase their share or proportion of the economy, concentration in the economy will increase.

The extent of concentration in each industry and in the economy as a whole depends, then, on which set of opposing forces is stronger—those forces (like the advantages of size) that tend to increase concentration or those forces (like the formation of new firms) that tend to erode concentration.

☐ Suggested Readings

Alfred Chandler, *The Visible Hand: The Managerial Revolution in American Business* (Cambridge, Mass.: Harvard University Press, 1977).

Jim Hightower, *Hard Tomatoes, Hard Times* (New York: Hippocrene Books, 1978).

David Kotz, *Bank Control of Large Corporations in the United States* (Berkeley, Calif.: University of California Press, 1978).

Joseph Schumpeter, *The Theory of Capitalist Development* (Cambridge, Mass.: Harvard University Press, 1934).

William G. Shepherd, *Market Power and Economic Welfare* (New York: Random House, 1970).

CHAPTER 8

WAGES AND WORK

Our society is often described as a consumer society, one in which people express their creativity and enjoy a sense of freedom by consuming. Whether it be the pleasure of window shopping or wearing the (just right) shirt that one has found and purchased, we are said to make choices and express who we are by consuming. Some people go on shopping sprees to fight off depression or boredom.

If consumption is the bright side of the capitalist economy, production must be its dark side. People rarely say, "I'm feeling a little down, I think I'll go down to the plant (or office) and put in a little work." Work, sadly, had a bad reputation. William Faulkner, the great American novelist, has a dim view of it: "You can't eat for eight hours a day nor drink for eight hours a day nor make love for eight hours a day—all you can do for eight hours a day is work. Which is the reason why man makes himself and everybody else so miserable and unhappy."*

Perhaps Faulkner had a point. For many people who are fortunate enough to have a job, their work is little more than a way of making the money necessary to be able to consume later. It is not the antidote to boredom; it is the source of boredom. It does not make the individual feel either creative or free. Instead, it engages the person in the repetition of the same limited tasks day after day, often under the close supervision of management, or even under the peering eye of a TV camera.

* Quoted in Studs Terkel, *Working* (New York: Pantheon Books, 1972), p. ix.

Jobs are hard to find. Good jobs are even harder. Why? Many people object to the fact that they have so little choice about what they do at work or how they do it. Why is the work process organized from the top down, with armies of foremen, managers, supervisors, and officials (over 13.5 million in 1981) to oversee the process? Is the top-down control of work and its fragmentation into repetitious tasks simply the result of modern technology, which gives us no other choice? Is the unpleasantness of work just a natural human reaction to exerting ourselves?

If one's job is often a problem, not having one is even worse. Joan Robinson, a British economist, once quipped that the only thing worse than being exploited by a capitalist is not being exploited by one! The loss of one's job is often not only a financial disaster but a personal calamity as well. Suicide rates, marital breakup, and mental illness are all quite closely correlated with the number of people who are looking for work but cannot find it. Why is finding work this important to us?

This chapter investigates these questions.

For the majority of people in the United States, work means being an employee of someone else (or of a corporation). This relationship between employers and workers is a class relationship—employers and workers constitute different classes. This relationship is therefore different from the relationship among capitalists (examined in the last chapter) or from the relationship among workers.

All economic relationships contain aspects of competition, command, and change; but competition is more important in some relationships and command more important in others. Because capitalists compete with other capitalists and workers compete with other workers, these within-class relationships primarily reflect competition or the horizontal dimension. In contrast, the between-class relationships—*between* employers and workers, for instance—reflect primarily the command or vertical dimension. The class relationship is based on supervisors and subordinates—people "higher up" and people "under" them.

The employer-worker relationship is largely overlooked in neoclassical economics. It is assumed that both workers and bosses agree on how much work should be done each hour and that workers, after they have agreed to a wage, willingly supply the necessary effort. Labor can therefore be treated as simply another input to the production process, with no special characteristics. Indeed, today's most famous neoclassical economist, Paul Samuelson, once said, "In the competitive model, it makes no difference whether capital hires labor or the other way around."* Yet we know

* Paul Samuelson, "Wage and Interest," *American Economic Review*, XLII, no. 6 (December 1957), p. 894.

that in reality capitalists almost invariably hire workers, not the other way around!

This chapter focuses on the relationship between workers and employers.

The main idea of this chapter is that employers and workers have fundamentally conflicting interests in the workplace and that employers organize work hierarchically from the top down to extract work from workers.

This main idea is expressed in five main points:

1. Producing things—*work*—is not naturally boring, oppressive, or limiting. Neither is it naturally exciting and liberating. It is not "naturally" anything. What work is like, and how we experience it and react to it, depends in important ways on how the labor process is organized, how the rest of the society is organized, and where we fit into the labor process.
2. The capitalist enterprise—the firm—is a *system of command*, in which power is exercised from the top down. Unlike the marketplace, in which people and firms interact primarily through voluntary offers, in the firm the main form of interaction is the exercise of authority by bosses over workers.
3. There exists a *conflict between what workers want and what their employers want* to get out of the labor process. This conflict is over wages and the pace of work, and it follows directly from the determinants of the profit rate. It is inherent in the process of profit making and places workers and their employers in opposing positions.
4. Employers are able to exercise power over workers because there is almost always *unemployment*—an excess supply in the labor market. The labor market does not operate like other markets, which tend to "clear" or eliminate excess supply; rather, excess supply—unemployment—is a chronic feature of labor markets.
5. Employers organize labor processes in such a way as to enhance their opportunitites to *extract work from their workers*. In general this implies that work is organized hierarchically, with command or top-down control.

In this chapter we investigate the organization of labor processes and conflict in the workplace. Why is work organized hierarchically? What exactly is the conflict and why does it exist? In the next chapter we explore how employers and workers respond to the conflict.

☐ Work, Sloth, and Social Organization

Some people live for weekends; others start living when they get off work in the afternoon. Some, including many economists, divide the day between the hours of "work" and the remaining hours, called "leisure." The first is a "bad"—something to be avoided, except for the fact that it is necessary to get the money to buy "goods" with. Thus, economists sometimes say that people derive utility from goods and disutility from work.

This view undoubtedly describes how many people feel about work. But it is incomplete in two ways. First, it presents work as *naturally* a bad, intrinsically a source of displeasure, and second, it ignores many aspects of work that make work an important and positive experience to people.

Work takes time, and there are only 24 hours in the day. Because of this, there is always an *opportunity cost* to work. If you are working, you cannot also be at the beach (unless you're a lifeguard). In this respect, of course, work is no worse or better than any other activity, including going to the beach, for whenever we spend time doing one thing, that is time we could have spent doing something else.

Why, then, should work be singled out for such disrepute? Some have suggested that we have a natural tendency toward sloth; we intrinsically dislike exerting ourselves. But this does not seem to be the case; people greatly enjoy exerting themselves in sports, for example. Perhaps people do not like work because they do not like accepting the authority of others. But the very same people who resent supervision on the job might be more than pleased to play in an orchestra under the discipline of a stern conductor or to accept the training regimen of a demanding football coach. Other aspects that people do not like about work—that it is often composed of limited and repetitious tasks, for example—are, as we will see, often not necessary aspects of work itself.

Most people, in fact, can think of occasions when they have worked very hard, often at demanding work, and have enjoyed it greatly. People building a new room on their house, for example, often put in long hours on weekends, working at a pace that would provoke resentment if it were in the office or at the plant. Parents engage in one of the most physically, intellectually, and emotionally demanding types of work—raising children—usually with considerable pleasure.

The problem it seems, is not that work is naturally unpleasant but that some types of work are objectionable. The above examples suggest that one of the things that contributes to work being objectionable is the way it is organized and, especially, for whom it is being done. Physical exertion, discipline, responsibility—whether in sports, homebuilding, music, or childrearing—are often gladly accepted, even welcomed, if the activity is something that the people have chosen, or believe in, or are benefiting from, or if the project is benefiting someone they care about.

The idea of work as a "bad" is wrong for a second reason. People derive satisfaction from being able to produce something, from having productive and potentially useful work skills, and from associating with others at their workplace. Respect, friendship, pride of accomplishment, and a sense of doing something useful are all at least potentially part of the process of working.

If work does not live up to its potential, much of the reason is in how work is organized—who controls it and how the benefits from it are distributed. In the United States today—indeed in any capitalist economy—most work is done in firms. Understanding work will require an understanding of the organization of firms.

☐ The Capitalist Firm as a Command Economy

The capitalist economy is composed of firms and markets. Markets, as we have seen, involve *exchanges* of money for commodities. The firm is different.

Inside the firm—behind the office door or inside the factory gates—people are not engaged in exchanges but in *command relations*—in giving and taking orders.

Picture the capitalist economy as a sea dotted with many islands. Each island (or firm) produces a particular product and trades it to other islands. Market relations determine the trades *between* islands; command relations determine how production is organized *within* each island (or firm).

For this reason many economists define the firm as a "command economy." Figure 8.1 summarizes, for a firm, the relationship between buying and selling (market exchanges) and production (command relations).

The organization of work is determined by the interaction of market relations and command. In this chapter we focus both on the relationships of command within the workplace (the production relation in Figure 8.1) and on the labor market (exchange 1 in Figure 8.1). Exchange 2 was the focus of the previous chapter.

To say that the firm is a command economy does not mean that all commands are obeyed willingly or even at all. The most important command relations of the workplace are between workers and employers; and, as we shall see, although employers generally have the upper hand, they do not always get exactly what they want.

☐ The Conflict between Workers and Employers

Workers and employers occupy different positions in the production process. Workers perform the work required to produce

Market exchanges are relationships between buyers and sellers in which each party exercises substantial voluntary agreement to the particular exchange.

Command relations are relationships between superiors and subordinates in which the superior exercises substantial power over the subordinate.

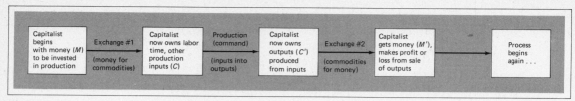

FIGURE 8.1 Exchange and command in the profit-making process. Profit making involves economic interactions of two kinds—exchange and command. In the first and third parts of the process, buyers and sellers exchange money for goods. First the capitalist exchanges money to purchase materials, machines, and labor time; and later the capitalist exchanges the finished, newly produced commodities for money. The production part of the profit-making process comes between the buying inputs and the selling outputs.

In the two buying and selling parts, economic actors come together in markets; their activities are regulated by supply, demand, competition, and other market conditions. In the production part, economic actors (employers and workers) come together in workplaces; their interactions are regulated by authority and command.

The buying and selling parts involve mainly the horizontal dimension of profit making. The production part is based on the vertical dimension of profit making.

something and are paid a wage for their labor time. Employers hire workers and take their output to sell.

This difference in position within production is why workers and capitalists constitute different classes. (Recall the discussion of classes in Chapter 4.) Because classes have different positions in production, they may have different and even conflicting interests in how production is organized and carried out. Indeed, in the case of workers and capitalists, there exists a direct conflict of interests. We can see this conflict by recalling the determinants of the profit rate discussed in Chapter 6.

Let us start with workers. What do workers want from their jobs? Workers usually want their jobs to be not too tiring and their wages to be as high as possible. Of course they may want lots of other things as well—interesting work, a safe workplace, flexible hours, more say in how the workplace is run, longer vacations, the right to stay home when children are sick, and so on. But to keep things simple and to explain the main point, we will start with how tiring the job is and how much it pays.

Why workers would want jobs that are not too tiring is obvious. An exhausting job is uncomfortable. It leaves each worker with less energy after work. Such jobs may be bad for the workers' health. Similarly, why workers want as high a wage as possible is also obvious: Higher wages make possible a higher level of consumption.

We may conclude that, in terms of the profit-rate determinants, workers want d (work effort per hour) to be low and w (wage per hour) to be high.

And what do capitalists want? Capitalists desire high profits.

Focusing only on those things that affect labor the most, from pages 120 or 125 we can see that profits will be higher:

the *higher* is
1. the workers' work effort per hour (d)
2. the output produced per unit of effort (e)

and the *lower* is
3. the wage (w).

We can see this same point in a different way. Let us consider a firm's *unit labor cost* (*ulc*)—the money that must be paid out by the employer to workers for each unit of output produced. Recall that unit labor cost is one of the components of output price (see page 137). We can define unit labor costs as follows:

Unit labor cost is the labor portion of the average cost of producing each unit of output.

$$ulc = \frac{(average\ wage\ cost}{per\ unit\ of\ output)} = \frac{wage\ per\ hour}{output\ per\ hour} = \frac{w}{z} = \frac{w}{ed} \qquad (8.1)$$

where w = hourly wage
z = output per hour
e = efficiency, or amount of output per unit of work done
d = work done per hour

This means that the unit labor cost is just the wages paid out per hour divided by how many units of the good were produced in that hour. For instance, if B-E Company paid wages of $6 per hour and the average worker produced 2 units of the good per hour, then:

$$ulc = \frac{\$6}{2} = \$3 \text{ in labor costs to produce each unit of the product}$$

Unless other things change, profits will be higher when *ulc* is lower; that is, as noted above, profits are higher (and unit labor costs lower) when e and d are higher and w is lower.

Capitalists, in their efforts to increase profits, will try to reduce w and increase e and d; or, said differently, they will try to reduce the labor cost in each unit of output (*ulc*).

For two of the elements in unit labor costs, workers and capitalists want exactly opposite things: workers want high w and low d, each capitalist wants low w and high d. (For the other component of *ulc*, e, workers may not have a personal stake directly contrary to their employer; we consider this point in the next chapter.)

With effort per hour and the wage, the conflict between a worker and his or her employer is direct and obvious. The more the employer is able to raise d, the harder the worker must work; the more the employer can reduce w, the less money the worker receives.

What determines the level of d and w? Both are determined in

> **Unit Labor Costs in Coal**
>
> From the example on page 80, we can derive the following:
>
> total pay (wages plus benefits) per hour   = $13.12
> output (tons of coal produced per labor hour)   =   1.9 tons
> ulc = unit
>
> labor cost = $\dfrac{\$13.12}{1.9}$ = $6.90 per ton

important measure by the relative bargaining strengths of workers—individually or in groups—and their employers.

Consider wages first. For four out of five employees, wage bargaining is mostly a matter between individual workers and the boss. For about one out of five workers, the bargaining takes place between employers and labor unions, through what is called *collective bargaining*. In the eastern coalfields, for instance, the United Mine Workers represents unionized workers and a council of mine owners bargains for employers.

Collective bargaining occurs when, in negotiating wages and other employment conditions, all workers in a firm or occupation are represented collectively by a union; employers may also be collectively represented by an employer's association.

What can be "won" in bargaining depends on a number of things that are largely beyond the control of either the workers or the capitalists. Employers cannot choose just any wage. If the employer's wage offer is too low, the firm will have difficulty attracting enough employees or in keeping them once they have been hired. Thus the state of the labor market—the level of wages in similar jobs and the level of unemployment in particular—has a major influence on the capitalists' wage offer.

Similarly, a union, no matter how strong, cannot demand and get just any wage. To take an extreme case, if the wage demanded would make the unit labor cost (ulc) higher than the price of the product, the employer could not make a profit from hiring labor, even if he had no other costs. So the profit-maximizing capitalist would hire no one at all in this case.

A wage bargain will be struck within the range set by the state of the labor market and the level of productivity and output prices. The wage will be toward the lower end of the range if the employer has the upper hand, and toward the higher end if the workers are stronger. Wage bargains are then formalized in contracts indicating the hourly rate of pay (w).

☐ The Extraction of Work from the Workers

The amount of effort—or work—that the workers do each hour is, like the wage, determined by a bargaining process. However, the results of this conflict are almost never settled in contracts.

Labor Costs at Lordstown

The conflicting interests of employers and workers can be illustrated using our concept of unit labor costs. For example, suppose a General Motors plant employed 1000 workers who worked 8 hours a day. If the assembly line moved at the rate of 1 car per minute (60 per hour), then these 1000 workers would produced 480 cars per day. Let us further suppose that the wage was $8 per hour. Then we can make the following calculations:

Cost of labor per day: 1000 workers for 8 hours at $8 per hour
$$= \$64,000$$

Cars produced per day: 60 cars per hour for 8 hours = 480 cars

$$ulc = \frac{\$64,000}{480 \text{ cars}} = \$133.33 \text{ per car}$$

Thus, under these arrangements, it would cost GM $133.33 in labor costs to assemble each car.

Suppose now that GM tries to increase the speed of the line, as it did in 1971 at its Lordstown, Ohio, plant. GM attempted to speed up the line to 1 car every 36 seconds, or 100 cars per hour. Wages did not change (they had been fixed in the contract already), so under the new regime we get:

Cost of labor per day: same

Cars produced per day: 100 cars per hour for 8 hours = 800 cars

$$ulc = \frac{\$64,000}{800 \text{ cars}} = \$80.00 \text{ per car}$$

GM would have been able to reduce its unit labor costs from $133 per car to $80 per car—almost a 40 percent cut—just by increasing the line speed! Workers would get paid the same wages but would have to work faster. The work effort per hour (d) would increase.

All did not go smoothly for GM in the Lordstown speedup case, however. Workers responded to the speedup with over 5000 grievances in a five-month period and eventually voted by a 97 percent majority to walk off the job, initiating a three-week strike.

The conflict over how much work will be done in an hour goes on every day. It is not something that comes up only when contracts are up for renewal. Why is this?

An employment contract specifies three conditions: (1) the wage rate; (2) the hours of work; and (3) the right of the boss to direct the workers' efforts during work hours. The first two conditions can be stated in advance with precision. Wage rates, for instance, are often specified down to the fraction of a penny for each job. The hours of work can be stated to the minute, with time out for coffee breaks, lunch, and even in some cases toilet time carefully specified.

The third condition, however, can usually not be defined precisely in advance. How hard must the workers work? With what precision must the workers obey the boss's commands? Only the broadest limits can be settled when workers are hired. At one extreme, workers could do everything the boss commanded with their full, 100 percent energies; at the other extreme, the workers could do nothing the boss commands except what was absolutely essential to keep from being fired. The actual outcome within this range cannot be specified in advance of the work itself.

The employer has purchased the right to *potential* labor services. Yet a moment's reflection will reveal that what the capitalist has purchased is hardly all that he needs for profit making. The capitalist needs actual human effort in production—real *work*—not just the *right* to direct the workers' time or *potential* labor services or control over the worker's *time*. Only real work, human productive activity, will produce commodities that the capitalist can sell to obtain a profit.

What the capitalist buys—potential labor services, what we may call *labor time*—is different from what he needs in production—the actual human activity of production, or work. To obtain profits, then, the capitalist must ensure that work results from the purchased labor time: he must extract work from the worker.

A simple example may illustrate the conflict between employer and worker over d, the amount of work done in an hour. Imagine a firm with a given work force and a given set of machines and other capital goods in use. The amount produced per hour of labor hired will depend on both d, the intensity of work, and e, the efficiency with which the work done is utilized. Figure 8.2 shows how the amount produced per hour of labor depends on the amount of work done per hour. The amount produced per hour is measured on the vertical axis in dollars; it is the quantity of output produced per hour (z, or, equivalently, ed) times the price per unit (Pz). Moving from left to right along the horizontal axis, the amount of work done per hour (d) increases and the amount of output at first increases. After a certain point, however, workers are working so hard that problems start to crop up, either through fatigue or through workers becoming resentful and deliberately sabotaging efficiency. As a result, e begins to fall and output per hour (de) levels off and then declines.

The conflict over the extraction of work from workers—over d, that is—arises because the employer would like the workers to work harder than the workers would choose to work. The employer would like to minimize unit labor costs. With a given hourly wage (w), the unit labor costs will be minimized by maximizing the amount produced per hour, or (in Figure 8.2) by maximizing the

Labor time measures the number of hours worked; it does not measure how much work gets done, since there are many different levels of work effort (intensities of work) possible.

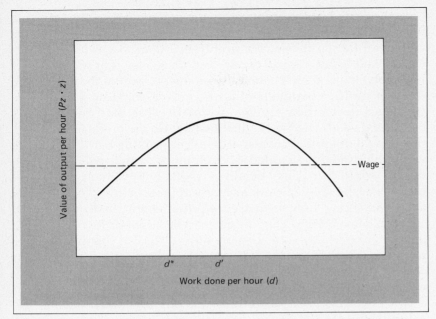

FIGURE 8.2 Output and the intensity of work. This graph shows the relationship between the intensity of work and the value of the output. As the work done per hour rises, the value of output per hour rises also (assuming that the price of the output remains unchanged). After some point, however, further increases in the intensity of work lead to a decline in efficiency (e) due to mistakes and perhaps even to workers deliberately sabotaging production. As a result, the value of output per hour may fall as d rises. Because the wage is paid for time, not for effort, the capitalist's profit-maximizing strategy is to make workers work at the intensity indicated by d'. The workers most likely prefer to work at a lesser intensity but fear losing their jobs. Depending on how effective the employer's strategies are and how effective the workers' counter-strategies are, a normal amount of work effort, say $d*$, will be determined.

distance between the output per hour curve and the wage line. This distance is simply the amount the employer has left over after paying the worker; some will be used to pay other costs and some will be kept as profits. This amount is maximized at the point d'.

The worker probably sees the problem from a different perspective. The worker will get the wage no matter how much work gets done, as long as he or she does not get fired by the employer. So depending on how much the worker likes the work, how resentful the worker is, how likely it is for the employer to find out if the worker is not working hard, and so on, the worker will choose to work at some level less than d'. This level of d is shown on Figure 8.2 as $d*$. There are ways the employer can get the worker to work harder, of course. We will consider some of these soon. But unless the worker wants to work as hard as d', there will be a conflict.

Part of the conflict arises because the worker is the one who does the work but the employer is the one who owns the resulting product. To see this, imagine that, instead of working for a capitalist employer, the producers referred to in Figure 8.2 work with machines and other capital goods that *they* own. These producers might be independent commodity producers (part of the old middle class) or perhaps members of a workers' co-op. How would these producers decide how much to work? Because they own not only the capital goods used in production but also the product produced, they would definitely have an interest in working hard. Hard work would be directly rewarded through more output, which the producers would own. They would be unlikely to work as hard as d', because as the level of work intensity approaches d', the additional output resulting from increased effort is quite small (the output curve is almost flat). They might choose to work less hard even than d^*, or perhaps harder; many have observed that people who work for themselves (and who therefore enjoy the fruits of their own labor) work harder than those who are simply paid an hourly wage.

However, the great majority of people who work outside the home in the United States today are not independent producers but wage workers, as we have seen in Chapter 4. For this reason the conflict between employers and employees over d is an essential aspect of our economy.

The process by which the capitalist obtains work from labor time is called *extraction* rather than *exchange* because it occurs under different circumstances from those existing in a market. There is a conflict between worker and employer over the pace of work, yet the results of the conflict do not usually take the form of a contract. Instead, the employer seeks to use some method of controlling the pace of work.

Employers organize work hierarchically, with bosses and those who work under bosses, to ensure the extraction of work from the workers. Management, including the various levels of bosses, foremen, and supervisors, is the central mechanism capitalists use to extract work from the labor time that has been purchased.

It is true, of course, that management does more than extract work from workers. Managers and executives determine how the output will be sold, decide when and where to invest, and coordinate other aspects of the firm's operations. Even with respect to labor processes, they do more than arrange for the extraction of work done. In labor processes where there is substantial specialization, some coordination of the different producers is necessary; in a shoe factory, for instance, the leather cutters must be told how much and what shapes of leather the stitchers need. Yet such coordination is often trivial or need not be done by those bosses (for instance, the stitchers could tell the cutters themselves).

With respect to labor, the principal function of bosses is to transform purchased labor time into work. Note that this situation only arises with respect to one input commodity, labor. When a ton of steel or a new machine is purchased, the capitalist need have no fears about translating these potential inputs into the production process. A ton of coal of a given type and quality yields more or less the same number of BTUs of heat in a given furnace. Steel and machines have no will of their own; when the boss commands, they cannot resist. There is no need to have a line of unemployed machines standing outside the factory gate to get the machines inside to work hard!

But labor comes only in the body of a worker and cannot be separated from the live human being who has needs, desires, and a will of his or her own. Human work only results when the boss is able to compel or induce the worker to cooperate. Thus labor, although it resembles other input commodities in some respects, is in fact unique.

In the old slogan, "a fair day's work for a fair day's pay," both parts are open for bargaining and conflict. The wage (the "fair day's pay"), of course, is bargained over when the worker is hired. What constitutes a "fair day's work," however, is established only in the actual work process.

A prevailing work speed may emerge—that is, a standard rate at which labor time will be translated into work. This prevailing rate (d) is the result of bargaining, conflict, dispute, and struggle in the workplace. It will be affected by political and legislative action, such as occupational safety and health regulations, the level of unemployment, the degree of unionization, or other factors that affect the relative strength of employers and workers. Thus the prevailing rate will be higher when employers are relatively more powerful (or in firms or regions where they are more powerful); it will be lower when workers are relatively stronger.

The conflict over the pace of work has no limit. (In the GM Lordstown speedup case, for example, the faster the assembly line moved, the lower were GM's costs and higher its profits.) Thus, employers generally have an interest in increasing d. No matter how high d is, a higher d will always bring bigger profits (as long as efficiency does not suffer). And no matter how fast the line moves today, tomorrow's costs will be lower if the line moves faster tomorrow.

If capitalists want to avoid the management problem, why don't they just pay for actual work performed rather than for potential work? Why don't they pay for work done rather than labor time? One method to do this would be for the capitalist to specify carefully in a contract all the tasks to be performed by the worker before hiring the worker; the worker's pay would then be withheld

A **contract specifying work done** is an agreement between an employer and a worker that specifies payment for actual work activities instead of for work time.

A **piece rate** is a form of wage payment in which the worker is paid for each unit of output produced instead of for work time.

until all the tasks were completed. This would be like hiring some-one to mow the lawn. If the lawn does not get mowed, the person does not get paid. Or alternatively, the capitalist could pay the worker a *piece rate*—that is, every time the worker produced one piece of work (sewed a collar on a shirt, for instance), the worker would receive a certain amount (for example, $0.50). In both meth-ods (and there are others), the capitalist would be paying for actual work, not potential work. Since the worker would only get paid for work actually done, there would be no need for command-type relations.

But each of these methods has real problems. The contract method is inflexible and costly. Imagine trying to write a contract specifying every activity that a worker might need to do in his or her job. Just listing all the duties would usually require a lengthy document. And even lengthy contracts cannot list all the things a worker must do to contribute to profits. It is no wonder that a very effective form of protest by workers is "working to the book," that is, following work rules and regulations exactly, often bringing production to a virtual halt.

A further problem is deciding if the work had been done or not. It is easy enough to see if the lawn has or has not been cut. But determining exactly how much work (and of what type and quality) each worker has done would be a costly process. And who is to decide? Both bosses and workers would have their own reasons to argue about it. Moreover, every time a new task needed doing or the worker needed to be reassigned, a new contract would have to be written.

The piece-rate system also is flawed for some of the same rea-sons. One problem is that it would not work in most jobs. If each worker is to get a piece rate, his or her output must be separate from the other workers' production; where many workers jointly produce the good (such as on an assembly line), piece rates cannot be applied. Another problem is that piece rates only work when the worker performs the same task over and over again; in more complicated jobs, there would have to be a rate for every task. Finally, although it might appear that the employer would be in-different to how fast a piece-rate worker worked (since the em-ployer only pays for output, not time), in fact this is not true. To the extent that the worker uses raw materials, tools, machines, or work space that the employer pays for, the boss still has an interest in making sure that the worker works quickly.

For these reasons and others, neither the contract method nor the piece-rate pay system is used much. The contract system (in the form of subcontracting) is sometimes used to hire electricians or plumbers, but otherwise its application is very limited. Piece rates have been more extensively employed, especially in manufacturing and in some agricultural jobs, but still their use is quite limited. In general, employers have found that other ways of organizing the labor process are more profitable. Employers attempt to speed the transformation of labor time into work; when they are successful, they achieve a reputation of efficiency or "being good managers."

Workers typically resist such efforts to make them work faster and faster. They may develop individual strategies of resistance, join together in informal work groups, or even openly resist through their unions. We will explore this conflict in the workplace in more detail in the next chapter.

☐ The Special Nature of the Labor Market

Employers hire workers and workers find jobs through the *labor market*. In this market, employers are the demanders of labor time, workers the suppliers of labor time. As in all markets, a degree of *voluntary exchange* exists; no one is obligated or forced to sign any contract unless he or she agrees to it. But in the workplace, employers must exercise some power over workers in order to be able to extract work from them. How, then, is it possible for employers to exercise command over workers in the workplace?

A **labor market** is a market in which workers sell their labor time (not work itself) in return for a wage; employers are the demanders and workers are the suppliers of labor time.

The government could intervene to establish relations between capitalists and workers. As Chapter 6 discussed, a fascist government may strengthen employers' hands by prohibiting workers from joining unions or engaging in other activities to defend their interests. Or a social-democratic government may use its power to establish an agreement between employers and workers.

But employers may exercise power over workers even in the absence of direct government intervention. The reason for this lies in the special nature of the labor market. The labor market does not work like other markets. Although it shares some features with other markets, it also differs in important ways.

The labor market shares with other markets the features of competition and conflict. As we saw in the previous chapter with commodity markets, so too in the labor market there is competition. There usually are many demanders for labor time, and there are almost always many suppliers. Perhaps more than other markets (certainly more than some commodity markets), the labor market is competitive.

And just as commodity markets are battlegrounds in which corporate giants fight it out for competitive advantage, so too the labor market is a battleground. Here, the conflict of interest between employers and workers—over wages, the intensity of work, safety conditions, and the like—is fought out.

Two features are special about the labor market. First, while commodity markets may clear, reaching and maintaining a situation of no excess supply or excess demand at the existing price, in the labor market a situation of market clearing or no excess supply (no unemployment) hardly ever occurs; and when it does, it does not persist. Second, while in commodity markets a reduction in price will usually increase the demand and reduce the supply (and hence reduce excess supply), in the labor market this may not be the case. A cut in wages may increase rather than decrease unemployment.

We will discuss the first peculiarity of labor markets in this chapter; we postpone discussion of the second until Chapter 11, when this point will be easier to understand in terms of the macroeconomic concepts developed there.

Let us first review some of the characteristics of a commodities market; then we can see how the labor market is different. In a commodity market characterized by price competition (or what is sometimes called "perfect competition"—many sellers, many buyers), the price and the amount bought and sold are determined by the interaction of supply and demand. If, at a particular price, the amount supplied exceeds the amount demanded—a situation of excess supply—the price will fall, increasing the amount demanded and decreasing the amount supplied. Price changes thus tend to eliminate excess supply (and by similar reasoning, excess demand), bringing the amount supplied into line with the amount demanded.

The result is called market clearing. At the going price, demanders want to buy exactly the amount that sellers want to sell; there is no excess supply and no excess demand. Until employers reinvest their profits, there are no internal reasons for change; none of the buyers or sellers has the incentive and the ability to change the resulting price or quantities bought or sold. The buyer who offers to buy at a lower price will not find any sellers; the seller who tries to charge a higher price will not find any buyers. In a commodity market characterized by price competition, the market clears.

Full employment is a situation in which there is no excess supply of labor time being offered in the labor market.

Frictional and search unemployment are voluntary forms of unemployment that result from people moving between or searching for jobs; even at full employment there will usually be some frictional and search unemployment.

But labor markets do not work like commodity markets. We should first note that even if there were "full employment," some people would be officially counted as "unemployed." A situation of *full employment* would still leave a few percent unemployed because some people are in transition between jobs or voluntarily unemployed while searching for new jobs. If you quit a job in New York to start a new job, two weeks later, in Los Angeles, you will be unemployed for two weeks; this is called *"frictional" unemployment*. If you quit a job today so you can more effectively search for a new job, you will be unemployed until you find the new job;

this is called *"search" unemployment*. Even if there were enough jobs available (full employment), there would still exist some frictional and search unemployment. We will ignore frictional and search unemployment in the following analysis. *Excess supply* or unemployment, then, is to be understood as unemployment over and above frictional and search unemployment.

With this qualification, let us return to the question: Do labor markets work like commodity markets? No, because labor markets do not clear. In the labor market, unemployment is a situation of excess supply. The amount of labor time supplied by workers is greater than the amount of labor time demanded by employers at a particular wage. Excess supply of labor—or *involuntary unemployment*—is a permanent feature of the labor market in a capitalist economy because, as we shall see, labor demand is determined in an almost entirely independent way from labor supply. When labor supply exceeds labor demand (unemployment), there is no tendency for labor markets to eliminate the excess supply.

Why is there no market clearing in the labor market? One way to answer this is to imagine what would happen if the labor market *did* clear, so that any worker looking for work at the going wage could readily find it. Could this situation persist? Or would there be forces tending to change the situation? One way to see that it could not persist is to recall the determinants of the profit rate. Employers buy labor time and then must find some way of getting the worker to actually work. An important determinant of the profit rate, as we have just seen, is the intensity of labor, or work done per hour (d). The profit-making process thus requires that employers have power over the workers in the conflict over the intensity or pace of work.

This power may be enforced by an authoritarian government, or the necessary condition for employers making profits may be established through a social contract by a social-democratic government. Otherwise, as in the United States, the power of employers over workers in the conflict over the pace of work is based on the right of employers to fire the workers. (Unlike earlier dominant classes, capitalists may neither beat nor imprison workers who resist the command of the boss.) The threat of firing is effective only if each worker would have difficulty finding another job. If the worker could readily find another job there would be no threat. If there were no threat, employers have no power over workers; the capitalist profit-making process would become unworkable, for workers would then be free to do what they please. This is why many businessmen see the value of occasional bouts of unemployment.

By itself, this argument does not answer the question, for to show

Involuntary unemployment results when there are not enough jobs for all of those who seek jobs (an excess supply of labor time exists).

that market clearing in the labor market would be unworkable does not yet prove that it cannot exist or explain how it might change. But what is unworkable for capitalists is unlikely to happen in a capitalist economy, and we can easily see why.

For capitalists the only point of production is to make profits. When capitalists do not expect to make a profit they withdraw from production. They stop investing and begin laying off workers, rather than hiring workers. But if capitalists lay off workers, they create unemployment, or excess supply of labor time, in labor markets. So if market clearing (no unemployment) did exist in the labor market, profits would fall, workers would be laid off, and unemployment would reappear. A clearing labor market would not and could not persist.

This special feature of labor markets results from the fact that labor is different from all other inputs to production (or outputs). While labor time can be bought, work done is not itself a commodity and hence cannot be bought. It must be extracted from workers. So work done is not itself available in the marketplace—it can only be obtained in production itself, and this is why profit making requires that employers have power over workers.

The fact that labor markets do not clear means that a situation of full employment (no excess supply in labor markets or no unemployment) is unlikely to come about in a capitalist economy. Moreover, if for whatever reason full employment did come about, there would be powerful forces set in motion to change the situation so as to restore unemployment. We will explore these forces in detail in later chapters.

☐ Suggested Readings

Jeremy Brecher, *Strike* (San Francisco: Straight Arrow Books, 1972).

Harry Braverman, *Labor and Monopoly Capital* (New York: Monthly Review Press, 1974).

Michael Burovoy, *Manufacturing Consent* (Chicago: University of Chicago Press, 1981).

Richard Edwards, *Contested Terrain: The Transformation of the Workplace in the 20th Century* (New York: Basic Books, 1979).

Andrew Zimbalist, *Case Studies on the Labor Process* (New York; Monthly Review Press, 1979).

CHAPTER 9

TECHNOLOGY, CONTROL, AND CONFLICT IN THE WORKPLACE

In 1979, coal miners dug an average of 1.9 tons of coal every work hour. For this work, they were paid $13.12 per hour, including benefits.

Digging 1.9 tons of coal every hour, 8 hours a day, 5 days a week, is a dangerous, dirty, and exhausting job. Understandably, miners would like their jobs to leave them less exhausted. Their wages, after taxes and other deductions, leave them about $455 per week to live on; they would like higher wages. And they would like safer jobs—more miners (coal and other) are killed on the job every year than police officers.

The coal companies, however, rightly see less exhausting work, higher wages, and safer mines as eating into their profits. With existing machinery, making work less exhausting would mean slowing the pace of work done. Paying higher wages would directly add to costs and delete from profits. And providing safer jobs would require slower work rates and increased investment in safety equipment. All these changes, other things constant, would reduce the companies' profit rates.

This fundamental clash of interests has turned the nation's mining regions into centers of intense, bitter, and continuing conflict. Indeed, the conflict has often turned violent. In the 1870s, for instance, the state of Pennsylvania hanged 19 "Molly Maguires"—militant miners seeking to form a then-illegal union. In 1914, the Colorado militia broke up a strike at a Rockefeller-owned coal mine; militiamen killed 21 people, including 11 children and 2 women, in what came to be called the Ludlow Massacre. In Kentucky, "Bloody Harlan" County has witnessed decades-long violence between coal companies and workers. Even today, union organizers face frequent harassment, intimidation, and threats of violence.

Violence is the most extreme but not the most common form of continuing conflict between employers and workers. Short of violence, how are the conflicting interest of workers and employers resolved? How do capitalists go about extracting work from workers' labor time? What do workers do to defend their interests? This chapter investigates these questions.

The main idea of this chapter is that every capitalist labor process necessarily combines both a social organization and a technology of production and that these two elements shape and are shaped by the conflict between workers and employers over wages and the intensity and conditions of work.

This main idea is expressed in six main points:

1. Capitalists organize workplaces in ways that they believe will maximize their profits; the *social organization of the labor process* derives from their search for profits and in particular from their effort to extract work from workers. Employers establish *systems of control* in the workplace to enhance their ability to extract work.
2. Known and available *technologies of production* impose certain constraints on how employers can organize production; however, which of the available technologies are actually used and what kinds of new technologies are developed are shaped by the conflict between workers and employers.
3. Employers and workers *struggle over the intensity and conditions of work and over wages* within this context of the social organization and technology of the labor process. Workers defend their interests in a variety of ways (for example, by attempting to organize themselves in unions), and employers likewise develop strategies for maintaining or improving their profit rates (for instance, by emphasizing racial and sexual differences among workers).
4. The outcomes—the actual pace of work (d) and level of wages (w)—will reflect, other things being equal, the *relative bargaining strengths* or *power of employers and workers*.
5. Employers seek to organize labor processes in the most *profitable* way, but this need not be the most *efficient* way. Efficiency is different from profitability, and where there is a conflict between the two, the ongoing competition among capitalists pushes them to seek out profitability, not efficiency.
6. *Markets* and *hierarchies* are mutually reinforcing elements in the capitalist profit-making process. Although sometimes thought of as alternate and opposing methods for organizing social relations, they are in fact both necessary for the capitalist firm.

As in previous chapters, the process of profit making is central to understanding the topics discussed here, for it is profit making that gives rise to the conflict between employers and workers. Sometimes this conflict appears to be a conflict between a single worker and his or her boss. In some cases, the conflict is evident in the bargaining or struggle between a firm's owner and groups of workers or even all the workers of that firm. In other cases, the conflict becomes a more general one between important groups in the working class and the capitalist class, or even between whole classes.

☐ The Social Organization of the Workplace

Capitalists try to organize workplaces in ways that will produce the highest profit rates. Their goal (profits) is no different here from what it is in their other activities. How capitalists organize the workplace and their immediate relations with their employees affect their profit rates most directly with respect to the intensity of work (d), the efficiency of work (e), and the wage rate (w). As we saw in previous chapters, if an employer can raise d or e and/or reduce w, other things remaining unchanged, his profit rate will increase.

Capitalists and their supervisors, managers, and foremen exercise power in the workplace, most fundamentally, because they have the right to hire and fire. Imagine what would happen to an individual worker (or even a group of workers) who did not obey the boss or who refused to work as hard as the employer thinks his or her potential replacement would work. The recalcitrant worker would likely be fired and a replacement hired. The replacement standing outside the plant gate thereby keeps the worker inside the factory working hard.

If all or most of the workers in a workplace do not perform up to the level demanded by the employer—for example, suppose they belong to a union and they resist speedup in their work—then the employer has a bigger problem but still retains the upper hand. At least two possibilities are open to him.

A **lockout** occurs when an employer locks the workers out of the workplace and closes down production in order to force workers to accept the employer's terms for wages, work pace, or other working conditions.

First, an employer can institute a *lockout* (or, the same thing, provoke the workers to strike). He closes down the plant, locks the gate, and waits for the workers to feel the financial pinch. He hopes the workers will be forced to work on his terms.

Alternatively, an employer can "run away" with his shop; he simply moves his plant to some place where workers will be more compliant. For instance, the legal and political climate of the U.S. South, New Hampshire, and the Rocky Mountain States have historically been much more hostile to unions than the industrial

Midwest and Northeast. Similarly, the repressive governments in South Korea, Brazil, Taiwan, and elsewhere have prevented workers in those countries from gaining many rights or benefits. Capitalists can run away because, since they own the capital goods, they are free to invest (build new plants) or disinvest (let existing plants run down) as they please and where they please. The *runaway shop* leaves the original workers without jobs; even the threat of running away may scare workers into accepting the employer's terms.

A **runaway shop** is a workplace that an employer has moved from an area where workers are strong to an area where workers are weak in order to escape having to meet workers' demands.

Making Steel: Three Views

Worker

"Somebody built the pyramids. . . . pyramids, Empire State Building—these things just don't happen. There's hard work behind it. I would like to see a building, say the Empire State, I would like to see on one side a foot wide strip from top to bottom with the name of every bricklayer, the name of every electrician, with all the names. So when a guy walked by, he could take his son and say, See, that's me over there on the forty-fifth floor. I put the steel beam in. Picasso can point to a painting. What can I point to? . . . Everybody should have something to point to.

We handle forty to fifty thousand pounds of steel a day. . . . You can't take pride anymore. Its hard to take pride in a bridge you're never gonna cross, in a door you're never gonna open. You're mass producing things and you never see the end result of it."

Mike Lefevre, steelworker, quoted in Studs Terkel, *Working* (New York: Pantheon Books, 1972).

Personnel Management Consultant

"I can say, without the slightest hestitation, that the science of handling pig iron is so great that the man who is fit to handle pig iron as his daily work cannot possibly understand that science. . . . The man who is fit to work at any particular trade is unable to understand the science of that trade without the help and cooperation of men of a totally different kind of education."

Frederick Winslow Taylor, the founder of "scientific management," to a Congressional committee in 1912, as reported in Frederick Winslow Taylor, *Scientific Management* (New York: 1947), p.49.

Capitalist

"The duty of management is to make money. Our primary objective is not to make steel."

David Roderick, Chairman of the Board, U.S. Steel (interview in the film *America's Business*).

Large corporations have developed a third strategy. Many corporations have opened *parallel plants*—plants located in different parts of the country or even the world but that make the same product. GE, for instance, makes clock motors in both Massachusetts and Hong Kong. With parallel plants, or what is sometimes called *coproduction*, the employer can tell workers in one plant that unless they agree to low wages and/or high work effort, the company will switch production to the other plant. Then it tells the same thing to the workers at the other plant. Unless the workers in these widely separated plants can somehow act jointly (a very difficult task), they will be left in a weak bargaining position.

These methods of maintaining the upper hand all derive from the employer's right to say who works and who does not work at his workplace. Private property, as we have seen, means the right to exclude others from its use, and private property in the capital goods used in production means the right to hire and fire. Of course, lockouts, runaway shops, and parallel plants impose costs on the capitalist as well, so the employer may choose not to push too hard on workers. Then too, each capitalist must offer jobs that allow him to fill the number of job slots he needs. If other capitalists offer workers a slower rate of work or better pay, this may limit what the employer can do unless there is a large pool of unemployed workers. Finally, some workplaces, especially those providing services, may not be movable (a Boston hotel owner with striking employees cannot move his hotel to Hong Kong and still service his Boston customers). These considerations constrain the employer's actions. Still, the right to say who works and who does not puts the capitalist in a powerful position.

These powers are further enhanced by the employer's *social organization of the workplace*—by the way in which jobs are defined and assigned and related to one another. Generally workplace organization is hierarchical. Hierarchy in the workplace builds on the right to hire and fire, but it allows more finely tuned control than the either-or choices offered by the simple power to hire and fire. Employers cannot effectively threaten to fire workers every day and every hour, for trivial or routine problems as well as important matters. Such threats, if used too often, no longer remain believable; and if, to make the threats believable, employers do frequently fire workers, the high turnover on the job may well disrupt work. Successful employers have developed a series of other incentives—rewards and penalties—to supplement and reinforce their ultimate power of dismissal.

When employers organize the workplace, they impose a whole social organization on the labor process. They define what will be the different jobs and responsibilities; they say what the work rules and worker rights will be; they establish the powers of supervisors and foremen; and they formulate the rewards for good work and penalties for the lack of it.

This social organization can be thought of as a *system of control*. It is the means by which the employer governs the workplace. The workplace is obviously not organized democratically; it is run from the top down. And since the reason the employer organizes work is to produce output commodities in order to make a profit, the system of control is designed to enhance the employer's ability to extract work from workers.

Employers have developed several different systems of control within the firm. Each one reflects a distinct strategy for extracting work or, what is the same thing, reducing unit labor costs, within the workplace. Following are the most important systems of control.

Simple control. One employer strategy for achieving low unit labor costs is to pay wages as low as possible and use supervisors and foremen to bully, charm, cajole, motivate, or drive workers to work hard. This strategy, simple control or the drive system, aims at keeping wages as low as possible while forcing workers to give high levels of effort (see equation 8.1).

A small textile mill or a McDonald's restaurant illustrates simple control. The firm pays wages very near to the legal minimum, and the wages by themselves provide little incentive for workers to do more than whatever minimal effort will keep them from being fired.

How do these employers get their workers to work hard? The employer (or his hired manager) personally directs the work, oversees workers and evaluates their work, and rewards or punishes the workers. For instance, the boss may reward a diligent worker

A **system of control** is an employer's strategy or method for governing the workplace to facilitate the extraction of work from the workers.

Simple control is a system of control that focuses on the supervisors' personal exercise of workplace rewards and sanctions to maintain the work pace.

Getting Back at the Boss?

According to a recent study financed by the U.S. Justice Department, more than two-thirds of workers knowingly engage in "counterproductive behavior" on the job, including excessively long lunches and breaks, slow and sloppy workmanship, sickleave abuse and use of alcohol or drugs on the job. One-third of the sample of 9175 randomly selected retail, manufacturing, and hospital workers admitted stealing from their employers. (The questionnaires were filled out anonymously.) In-depth interviews with a smaller sample of these workers revealed that a feeling of being exploited by the employer was a more important cause of their behavior than economic necessity.

Source: The *San Francisco Chronicle*, November 6, 1983.

by assigning him or her to a better shift or a more pleasant job; the boss may punish a worker by cutting back on his or her hours or giving the worker a dirty or unpleasant job to do. Unspoken, the threat of being fired is continually kept in the workers' minds.

Bosses may be petty and tyrannical or they may motivate the workers by charm and the force of their personalities. Either way, the result is to reduce unit labor costs by driving workers to higher work effort. Fast work and low wages imply low *ulc*.

Technical control is a system of control that incorporates a work pace designed into the machinery of production.

Technical control. An alternative strategy aims at achieving the same result as simple control but by different means. Once again the numerator of unit labor cost (*w*) is kept as low as possible by paying the lowest possible wages. Now, however, the work effort (*d*)—part of the denominator of *ulc*—is driven not by ever-present supervisors who urge the workers on but rather by the pace of the machinery of production. The machine itself urges the worker to work quickly. Equally important, the production process itself keeps tabs on who is not working up to par. Those who consistently fall behind are easily singled out and can be fired.

For example, on the General Motors assembly line, it is the flow of the line itself that sets the pace. If the line moves at the pace of 100 cars per hour, each worker must do his or her job in the 36 seconds before the next chassis comes by. Here the boss need not stand over the worker to instruct and exhort, since the line itself sets the pace.

Technical control does not eliminate the need for bosses. What happens if a worker refuses to "obey" the line? In assembly-line or other machine-paced factories, the bosses remain to evaluate the workers' performance and discipline those workers who fail to perform up to standard. Still, the pace of work is controlled, in the first instance, by the physical technology of production.

Technical control does not resolve the issue of who determines the pace of the line itself. Where workers are weak and not unionized, the boss may determine the line or machine speed without consulting workers. Where workers are highly organized, the pace of the line may be set by the bargaining of workers and employers. Even with a pace set by bargaining, however, the line enforces the collectively agreed upon speed on each individual worker.

Thus, the employer's control over the design and implementation of the physical technology provides an alternative form of command. The worker is harnessed to a line or machine that runs at a given pace, and the worker must respond to that pace.

Bureaucratic control is a system of control that uses job ladders, seniority rewards, and other organizational incentives in order to elicit work done.

Bureaucratic control. Bureaucratic control is still another strategy for achieving low unit costs. In a bureaucratic firm, the employer provides higher wages and, even more important, wages that systematically grow with the worker's seniority. Workers who remain employed by the firm can expect higher wages (and perhaps other benefits) in the future than are earned at present.

How do high and rising wages *reduce* unit labor costs? From equation 8.1, we see that high and rising wages will lower *ulc* only if there is an even greater increase in work effort. This is the "carrot" philosophy: workers will like their jobs enough and want to keep them enough, or they will feel committed enough to their employer, to volunteer a high level of work effort.

But there is a "stick" as well as a "carrot" in bureaucratic control. The only way workers can obtain the better jobs is by gaining seniority. And as a worker gets more seniority, the greater is his or her "investment" in the particular job and therefore the greater is the loss if fired; the longer the worker works, the bigger is the stick!

Usually firms employing this strategy establish elaborate work rules and procedures to organize these sophisticated incentives. Instead of being simply an employee, the worker is hired for a particular job, which has a job title and for which a formal *job description* exists. The duties and tasks of the job are outlined, and the worker's performance is measured against the prescribed duties.

The firm uses *job ladders* to set up its system of rising wages. Job ladders link together a series of jobs, each job being one "rung" on the ladder. For instance, the jobs of file clerk, general clerk typist, secretary, private secretary, and executive secretary may be linked together on one job ladder. The employer hires job applicants from outside the firm for the bottom rung (file clerk); workers are permitted to work their way into higher jobs on the ladder by superior performance in lower jobs. Thus the way a worker gets a better job is by working hard in his or her present job. Wages under this system will tend to grow with seniority. This is another carrot (positive incentive) for high *d*.

Job ladders link together a series of related jobs, in which a worker over the years climbs from one job to another and gains access to jobs higher on the ladder only by first succeeding in the lower job.

Merely having job descriptions and job ladders does not guarantee that they will be obeyed, and so bureaucratic control does not eliminate the need for bosses. Bosses still supervise work, direct workers, and assess and evaluate the workers' performances; and they determine who gets promoted or fired, who gets rewarded or disciplined. But in bureaucratically controlled firms, bosses rule by "applying company policy." They enforce the company rules, and thus the power relations are more hidden, embedded in the organizational structure of the firm.

These varieties of control—simple control, technical control, and bureaucratic control—represent different forms of command relations in the firm. (They are summarized in Figure 9.1.) Each workplace will have its own blend of these forms of control. Yet despite

| | Elements of Control | |
System of control	Wages	Supervision
Simple control	Low, with few rewards for long service	Direct observation by bosses
Technological control	Low, with few rewards for long service	Pace of work machine controlled: laggards machine detected Less direct supervision
Bureaucratic control	High, rising with longer service	Promotion and firing by a "rule of law" within the firm

FIGURE 9.1 Employers' systems of control. Because there is a conflict of interest between employer and employee, the employer's ability to make profits depends on an effective system of control over the labor process. The three different systems of control tend to be used in different sectors of the economy and have varied in importance over the years.

the varieties of control, they all exist to solve the same problem for the capitalist—to reduce unit labor costs.

☐ Technology and the Labor Process

Technology, as we defined it in Chapter 3 is the relation between inputs and outputs in a labor process. And *technical change* is a change in the relations btween inputs and outputs. Technical change—the introduction of new types of machinery, for example— will be carried out by capitalists whenever a new technology is available *and* capitalists believe that the new method of production will raise the profit rate.

Technical change can raise the profit rate in several ways. It may reduce the materials used or the wear and tear on machinery per labor hour (m); other things being constant, this would raise a firm's profit rate. Technical change may reduce the amount of capital goods in use per labor hour (*cg in use*); this also, unless other things change, would raise a firm's profit rate.

With respect to labor directly, technical change can raise the profit rate by reducing unit labor costs (*ulc*). In particular, technical change may raise the efficiency of labor (e) or make possible, as we will see, a greater intensity of work (d) or lower wages (w). Each of these would, other things being equal, reduce unit labor costs and raise the profit rate. Employers, then, are likely to see technical change as a potentially fruitful source of higher profits.

At any particular time, known and available technologies impose limits or constraints on what employers can do. For instance, existing technology may dictate that at least 3 tons of iron ore are needed to produce 1 ton of iron; no matter how much the capitalist desires to reduce the use of this input, the current technology will not permit it.

Similarly, existing technologies place limits on the social organization of the workplace. For instance, some production processes, an assembly line for example, may require many people to work together, whereas other jobs, such as those of telephone operators, may involve mostly individual tasks. And while some jobs may be done by workers with few skills and little experience, the current technology may dictate that other jobs require extensive skills and much experience. In these ways current technology limits how an employer can organize work.

The limits set by known and available technologies, however, are quite wide. The same product (for example, basic steel) is often produced by different firms using different systems of control, different proportions of skilled and unskilled workers, different relations between bosses and workers, and different wage structures. Some automobile factories are organized around highly fragmented jobs on assembly lines whereas others employ much more integrated, "teamwork" methods. Telephone operators' jobs may be lowly paid, insecure, with no promotion prospects, and subject to frequent supervisor scrutiny (simple control)—or they may be the entry level positions on a job ladder leading to more secure and highly paid positions (bureaucratic control).

So while technology places some limits on the organization of work, different ways of organizing the workplace are usually compatible with the existing technologies. And the existing technologies are constantly changing. The constraints imposed by any given technology are likely to become less important as time goes on because the employer's need to impose a system of control shapes the way technology develops.

Employers eager for technical change to raise their profit rates will naturally be more interested in some types of technical change than others. For instance, suppose that a capitalist is about to invest in research to develop a new technology. His research staff proposes two projects. The first project would develop a new technology that promises greatly to reduce input materials (m), but would simultaneously reduce the employer's ability to extract work (d) from the workers because it would require that workers work on their own, making supervision difficult. The second project promises to reduce m by somewhat less, but it does not reduce the employer's control of the work pace (d). The capitalist will be likely to fund the second project.

Here we see that social organization—the capitalist's need to extract work from workers—has shaped the direction of technical change. The process of technical change is "biased": employers, simply trying to maximize their profits, have encouraged some types of technological change (those consistent with the extraction of work) while discouraging others (those threatening the employers' power).

The technologies that are known and available at any particular time are just the products of past technical changes. So if the process of technical change is biased, the technologies existing at any particular time reflect, in part, this bias. Existing technology, as well as technical change, is shaped by the social organization of production and in particular by the power of employers and their search for profits.

☐ Conflict in the Workplace

As we have seen, employers and workers bargain over work pace (d), wages (w), and the other conditions of work. The workplace—this combination of social organization and technology—is a principal arena for their struggle. (They may also contest these matters elsewhere, for instance, by attempting to get the government to regulate the safety or other conditions of work.)

In this conflict, capitalists and workers use quite different means to defend and promote their interests, or, stated differently, they exercise quite different kinds of power. To start, the battle's terrain has been established by capitalists, for it is they who hire workers and organize production. While workers, individually or collectively, may decide to withdraw from this terrain (the workplace) by quitting their jobs or going on strike, they never or rarely have the opportunity to organize production themselves.

Because employers, not workers, organize production, employers have the power to initiate action or change circumstances. Workers, by contrast, are inherently placed in a defensive position, the position of defending their interests by reacting to the initiatives of employers. This difference in position is evident in such employer

---

Management Rights

The right to hire; promote; discharge or discipline for cause; and to maintain discipline and efficiency of employees, is the sole responsibility of the Corporation. . . . In addition, the products to be manufactured, the location of plants, the schedules of production, the methods, processes and the means of manufacturing are solely and exclusively the responsibility of the Corporation.

Source: The management rights clause of the contract between the United Auto Workers and General Motors.

strategies as running away or establishing a system of control. It is also evident in the way that technical change affects workplace conflict.

Technical change and conflict

Technical change may affect workers in two principal ways. First, it may raise the productivity of their labor without necessarily increasing their work load. In equation 8.1, e (output produced per unit of work effort) represents the technology currently in use; that is, e tells us how much output will be produced for a given amount of work. This first type of technical change lowers unit labor cost by raising e.

Let us consider an example. If a shoe stitcher working at an average pace ($d = 1$) can produce 2 shoes per hour, then $e = 2$. Now suppose the worker gets a computer controlled stitcher instead of a simple electrical machine. This technical change means that the way of making shoes has changed so that even when the worker works *no harder*, he or she is now able to make 3 shoes per hour. Technology (the way of making shoes) changed, raising e from 2 to 3.

Technical change that raises e can reduce unit labor costs without requiring that the worker get paid less or have to work harder. Hence there is no inherent conflict between workers and their employer concerning this type of technical change. (As we see in Chapter 14, rapid technical change of this kind was an important part of the post-1945 boom.)

Even here, however, e may be fought over by workers and capitalists. Workers realize, for instance, that one way of pressuring employers for a better contract on wages is for the workers intentionally to obstruct production—in effect, to reduce e. Although this results in no direct benefit for workers, it does impose costs on their employer; if these costs are greater than the workers' demands for higher wages, the tactic may force the employer to pay higher wages.

For example, workers on an auto assembly line, when they feel aggrieved, may put soda bottles in the doors of a few of the cars assembled during the day. Since this creates a rattle that must be corrected before delivery, other workers (more work) must be assigned to disassemble door panels and remove the bottles. This "sabotage" effectively reduces e, because it now takes more work to produce a given number of cars. Similarly, when workers "accidentally" spoil materials or break tools during production, this effectively slows down production. The Industrial Workers of the World, a militant union that organized unskilled workers between

1905 and 1920, expressed this point in a famous slogan: "Good Pay or Bum Work."

Technical change often affects the labor process in a second way. It frequently is a weapon used by employers to speed up work (raise d). The most obvious way for employers to use technology to control workers is in technical control and machine pacing or work. When auto companies introduced the assembly line, it immediately gave the employers a way to control and speed up the work. Equally important, it meant that no longer did the work remain stationary and the workers move around the plant (to get tools or parts or pass on finished work). Now the *work* moved and the *workers* were stationary. No longer did workers have much chance to get to know other workers in the plant, because all the workday was spent at one work station. Therefore, it became more difficult to plan joint resistance to speedup. Indeed, the enhanced control over both the pace of work and the workers' mobility in the plant constituted, in the employers' eyes, the assembly line's greatest merit. (Later employers found that the assembly line was a mixed blessing, as it was possible for a fairly small group of workers to bring the entire line to a halt. When they did so in the late 1930s, the famous "sit-down strikes" led to the formation and recognition of the United Auto Workers.)

Another way technical change may be used to control workers is through deskilling. *Deskilling* means changing production methods so as to require fewer skilled workers and rely more on unskilled workers.

Employers are interested in deskilling because the workers who are generally in the strongest position to resist speedup of work and are most able to bargain for high wages are skilled workers. Skilled workers are those who have some special training or knowledge or credential. (In some cases the credential itself is what is important, because some skilled workers have managed to limit access to their line of work to those who have obtained a license, even though the training needed to get the license may be irrelevant to the actual job.) Skilled workers tend to be in shorter supply than unskilled workers, since skilled workers can usually do unskilled work, whereas unskilled workers typically cannot or are not allowed to do skilled work. Because there are fewer skilled workers than unskilled workers, it is generally more difficult to replace skilled workers. So they are generally in a stronger position than unskilled workers. They can demand and get higher wages, more control over the pace of their work, and so on.

When employers seek to reduce their unit labor costs, their attention naturally turns first to the skilled workers; after all, these are likely to be the highest paid and most powerful. If the production process can be changed in such a way as no longer to require

Speedup is an effort by an employer to increase the pace of work.

Deskilling means changing a production process in such a way as to make it possible to employ workers with fewer skills.

skilled workers, then they can be replaced with unskilled workers, who will cost less and be less able to resist speedup. Deskilling makes it easier for an employer to fire currently employed workers and replace them with other workers, since replacements are more numerous for unskilled than for skilled workers.

Technical change may sometimes increase the skills required in production, but often it eliminates the need for skills. Technical change is an important means by which employers can deskill.

One important way that employers deskill work is to break up the overall labor process into many small tasks, then assign each person only one or a few tasks to do again and again. Since each worker now needs to know how to do only a few tasks, new workers can be trained quickly for these jobs.

One of the most common ways of fragmenting and deskilling jobs is called the *separation of conception from execution* in work. *Conception* means planning out the work, preparing in one's mind or in written plans how the output should be produced. *Execution* is carrying out the planned work according to the conception. Master craftspeople, for instance, needed both skills, and part of the enjoyment of doing a good job was planning the work and then seeing it materialize in one's own hands. Similarly, small farmers, surgeons, parents, and artists today continue to combine these skills, integrating conception and execution.

In contrast to this idea of craft work, most modern labor processes

The **separation of conception from execution** is one method for deskilling work in which the workers who plan production are different from those who carry it out.

increasingly separate conception from execution. Planning for production takes place in planning, drafting, and engineering departments; here, employees rarely produce anything except plans or designs. On the other hand, execution occurs in a factory where the workers who actually make the product do only the physical construction. They do not participate in planning or improving the product they are making. The result is that planning ("white-collar work") takes place in offices, while execution ("blue-collar work") takes place in factories, often located in an entirely different place or even in different countries.

A further refinement is that even white-collar work has been subjected to deskilling. Increasingly, such employees as clerical workers, draftsmen, record keepers, and sales personnel have seen their jobs computerized and deskilled; they too have become mainly operators of machines (video displays, office machines). They have become more like factory workers, and the possibility for exercising real mental skills in many of these jobs has declined.

Technological change is, in sum, a many-sided process. On the one hand, it is often introduced in such a way that it helps employers and does not damage workers' interests; indeed, it is common that the benefits of technological progress be shared by capitalists and workers (see Chapter 14).

On the other hand, technical change is often used by employers to introduce new controls on labor (to raise work effort levels) and to deskill work and thereby weaken workers. In this case employers will most likely try to hide the consequences of the new technology from their current workers, since the workers are more likely to resist the new work methods if they know that these methods are aimed at speeding up their work, eliminating the need for certain of their skills, and weakening their bargaining power.

Not surprisingly, the introduction of new technology frequently becomes a matter of contention, conflict, struggle, and bargaining between employers and workers. Where workers are weak and not unionized, they may not have much way of protesting; when the boss says he is introducing new technology, they simply must accept it and hope it does not result in layoffs, speedup, and deskilling. Where workers are stronger, for instance if they belong to a union, they may be able to bargain and prevent certain types of technical change.

But control over technical change is never equal. Whether workers are weak or strong, employers retain their fundamental power over investment. Technical change requires investment both for the research and development stage and for building and installing the new equipment. Only capitalists invest on a significant scale. So capitalists retain the power to initiate (or withhold) technical change. Workers, even in the best circumstances, can only hope to

shape or block technical change, and only rarely can they initiate
those changes that might be in their interests.

Unions

Workers organize and join unions to increase their strength in
bargaining with employers. The principle of unions is simple. If
each worker individually bargains with his or her employer, then
each worker competes with every other worker. The outcome will
necessarily be dictated by those workers who, for whatever reasons, are willing to accept the lowest wages, fastest work pace, and
least favorable other job conditions. The employer will simply
choose to make a deal with these workers and replace or not hire
anyone who holds out for better terms. If, however, all or most
workers can agree to bargain collectively through a union, the
union may be able to achieve for all or most workers better conditions than they could obtain otherwise.

A union, then, is a means for reducing the competition (the
horizontal dimension) among workers. If successful, it gives its
members monopoly power in the labor market. For exactly this
reason, employers have bitterly resisted the formation of unions.
The present union structure is the product of over a century of
harsh struggle, as workers fought for the legal right and the economic reality of unions and employers fought first to prevent the
formation of unions and later to make them as unthreatening to
profits as possible.

Unions today engage in two different types of activities. First,
they act as agents for their members in bargaining with employers.
For workers in a unionized workplace, the union negotiates a contract stipulating the wage rates and employment practices to be
observed during the period of the contract. Depending on the
industry and the strength of the union, the contract may attempt to
specify a general work effort level (the standard or rate) required
in each job, the procedures by which new technology is to be
introduced and new (different) jobs created, and the method used
to assign workers to different jobs. The contract also usually establishes a grievance procedure to decide cases when workers believe
the employer is not following the contract.

In all these ways the union contract shelters the worker from the
employer's unconstrained commands. Of course, whether the
union can provide an effective shelter depends on how strong the
union is—both at contract renewal time, in forcing the capitalist to
agree to a favorable contract, and during the life of the contract, in
forcing the employer to live up to the contract terms.

Through unions, workers are able to have some say in the social

A **union** is an organization of
workers established with the intention of providing a unified
and stronger voice on behalf of
the members' interests.

organization of the workplace. To the extent that the employer's system of control is modified or limited by union contracts or other forms of workers' power, it is also directly shaped by the fundamental workplace conflict. However, employers still have the power to initiate changes and workers, through union contracts or otherwise, the power only to limit or constrain such changes.

Unions undertake a second kind of activity as well. They promote general social changes that they expect will benefit workers as a whole, including but not limited to their own members. For instance, unions have often taken the lead in pressing the federal government to pass minimum wage legislation, workplace safety laws, social security benefits, civil rights and antidiscrimination laws, welfare and other social services programs, and so on.

Discrimination

Unions are a method for overcoming competition among workers. Discrimination, in contrast, tends to stimulate and reinforce divisions among workers. It also leads to systematic hardship for the victims of discrimination and, from the point of view of democracy, a deterioration of the overall quality of life for all.

Discrimination means treating someone differently simply because that person belongs to a particular group. The most important forms of discrimination today are discrimination against blacks and other people of color and discrimination against women. People with handicaps, homosexuals, and old people are also frequent targets of discrimination.

Discrimination stems from a variety of sources—historic, economic, religious, political, social, and psychological—which we will not investigate here. What is relevant to our discussion is that the capitalist profit-making process contains opposing tendencies for the perpetuation and the erosion of discrimination.

Capitalism affects discrimination in two ways—one way weakens it and the other strengthens it. Discrimination is weakened when firms compete with one another by attempting to minimize costs through hiring the best person at the lowest wage. Racial or sexual discrimination means that blacks and women who are qualified workers have limited opportunity for high-wage employment. If employers hire, among equally qualified workers, those who cost least, they will tend to hire women and blacks and thereby increase the demand for the labor of the discriminated group. There will be an improvement in the job opportunities for women and blacks, a reduction in their unemployment, and possibly an increase in their bargaining strength.

On the other hand, discrimination is perpetuated when capital-

Discrimination means treating someone differently simply because that person belongs to a certain group when membership in the group is irrelevant.

ists try to use discrimination in their conflict with workers over wages and the pace of work. Just as workers try to achieve greater bargaining strength for themselves through unions, so employers try to weaken the bargaining strength of workers by creating divisions and disunity among workers. To do this, they may attempt to foster and magnify whatever differences already exist. Racial and sexual divisions are (socially) the most prominent distinctions, so employers seize upon these dimensions to divide workers. Capitalists did not invent racism or sexism, but they have used preexisting prejudices or biases among workers to divide and weaken workers.

Indeed, an individual capitalist may personally be completely free of prejudice yet be forced by competition to discriminate to stay in business. This situation could occur if discrimination is profitable. Since higher-profit firms have a competitive advantage, the nondiscriminating firm may, over time, be forced out of business. If, on the other hand, the costs of discrimination outweigh the benefits, capitalists are likely to stop discriminating.

How can discrimination be profitable? Compare two firms. The first firm hires both black workers and white workers, and it treats all workers equally (for example, paying wages without regard to race). Suppose the workers, both black and white, join together to form a union, and the union then presses for higher wages, less strenuous work, and so on.

The second firm also hires both black and white workers, but it discriminates—it assigns blacks to lower paying jobs than whites. The workers of this firm try to form a union, but they have a more difficult time than the workers of the first firm. Not all workers in the second firm have the same interest. Black workers think the union should try to force the employer to eliminate the company's discrimination in job assignment and pay; white workers want more pay, but they also fear being paid "like blacks." Maybe white workers form their own union and exclude blacks so they can concentrate entirely on raising white wages. But now, when they start to negotiate with the boss, he threatens them by declaring his intention to hire more blacks and displace some white workers. Reluctantly, they accept lower wages, more speedup, and so on.

Comparing these two firms, we see that the first firm will face (black and white) workers who share a common interest in raising wages (w) and reducing the strain of work (d). To the extent that these workers are successful, the first firm's profits will decline. The second firm, by contrast, faces workers who are divided by racial conflict. These workers may have difficulty forming a union, and whenever black workers try to bargain with the boss, their position is weakened by the boss's threat to bring in more white workers (and similarly, white workers are weakened by the threat of more blacks). These workers will have little chance to bargain for higher wages or a reduced work pace.

The second firm will have increased its profits (relative to the first firm) by discriminating. Indeed, the first firm may be forced to begin discriminating if it wants to compete with the second.

Conventional economics argues that discrimination is costly, and hence competition for profits will eliminate discrimination. But this is just one side of the coin, the only side visible when the horizontal aspect of the economy—competition—is the focus of economics. But when the vertical or command relationships of the economy are included, a different picture emerges. When employers discriminate, it may be precisely because discrimination is profitable, and indeed, competition may drive (nonprejudiced) employers to discriminate.

Whether profit making tends to perpetuate or erode discrimination depends on which of its two opposing effects is stronger—employers' efforts to hire the lowest wage workers or their efforts to prevent worker solidarity.

☐ The Determination of Wages and Work Done

Workers and employers have directly opposing interests with respect to wages and the intensity of work. How these conflicts are resolved depends in large part on the relative bargaining strengths of the two groups.

The wage rate, as we saw in Chapter 8, is determined primarily through competition among workers trying to sell labor time and among employers trying to purchase labor services. This establishes a going or prevailing wage rate—actually an average of the differing wages for different types of labor. Although at this wage the market will typically not clear, leaving some people looking for jobs but not about to find them, it nonetheless does establish a prevailing wage.

The prevailing wage (w) will reflect in large part the bargaining strengths of workers and employers. During years when employers are relatively strong or in industries, occupations, or regions where employers are relatively strong, wages will tend to be lower. During other times or in other jobs or regions where workers are strong (for example, in unionized industries), wages will tend to be higher.

In a capitalist economic system, then, necessary consumption or the average standard of consumption of producers is determined in large part by the conflict over the wage rate. (Customary consumption is also affected by the level of benefits and services distributed by the government; see Chapter 13.) Just as in feudal or slave owning societies, this level is determined primarily by

"You Could Be Replaced!"

One way a boss can increase his strength in bargaining over both *d* and *w* is for him to make it easy to replace each worker with someone else. The ultimate power bosses have over workers is exactly the power to fire them. But is the boss's threat believable? That depends on how difficult it is to find a replacement worker. For example, imagine two situations.

The first is that of a skilled crane operator during a time of relatively low unemployment. The boss may bargain with this worker by threatening to find "somebody else to do the job who really wants to work." However, both the boss and the crane operator may know that there are few unemployed crane operators; that the union will protest the firing and may even get other workers to go out on strike; that it takes a long time for a new crane operator to learn the job routine (thus making the other workers on the job less productive while the new guy is learning); that cranes are expensive and accidents, more likely when someone is new on the job, are costly; and that in any case the crane operator can easily find another job at the same or better pay. In this case, the worker is in a strong bargaining position.

In contrast, the second situation is that of an unskilled factory worker during a time of high unemployment. Now when the boss threatens to fire the worker if he or she doesn't agree to low wages and faster work, the threat is entirely believable. There are many people looking for jobs who could, in fact, do this job. It doesn't take long to learn the job, and there is no union to protest if the worker gets fired. Here, the boss is in a very strong position.

Both bosses and workers realize that their bargaining strengths depend on how easily replaceable the workers are. The more easily the boss can replace the worker, the stronger the boss will be. Bosses try to make workers more replaceable; workers try to make themselves less replaceable.

conflict between the principal classes; in the case of capitalism, this conflict takes the form of bargaining between employers and workers over the wage.

The intensity of work (*d*) is determined primarily in the workplace itself, and it too reflects the bargaining strengths of employers and workers. Although in principle the intensity of work as well as the wage rate could be settled in advance in the labor market, in practice in most cases the pace of work cannot be stated or agreed to in advance. Rather, it emerges from the daily interaction, the day-by-day conflict, of employers and workers, as employers try to extract work from workers and workers try to defend themselves from exhausting work.

Out of this workplace conflict may emerge a prevailing or customary pace of work. Workplaces with exceptionally high or demanding work intensities may become known as "sweatshops," and workers may be reluctant to take these jobs or may attempt to find other jobs. Thus there are competitive pressures to equalize work intensities (or to compensate for differing intensities by differing wage rates). This prevailing rate, or the average of differing rates, will be higher or lower depending on the relative strengths of employers and workers.

☐ Profitability versus Efficiency

Profitability measures how much profit is derived from a labor process.

Efficiency measures how little of the productive inputs can be used to produce a given level of output.

Profitability refers to how much profit is derived from a labor process. Profit is the excess of output revenues over the cost of purchased inputs.

Efficiency refers to the relation between the inputs to production and the output. A labor process is efficient if, given the existing technology, a given amount of output is produced with the smallest possible quantity of inputs.

As we have seen, technical change can improve efficiency by reducing the amount of materials and machines used per labor hour (m), increasing the output per unit of work done (e), or reducing the capital goods needed per labor hour (cg *in use*). Each of these changes would reduce the amount of inputs needed to produce any given quantity of output.

Increased efficiency may lead to greater profitability. Other things being constant, an increase in efficiency reduces the cost of the firm's inputs without affecting its revenues from outputs; therefore, under these circumstances, an increase in efficiency will increase profits. Neoclassical economics, observing this connection, asserts that in a market economy profitability is identical with efficiency. However, this is clearly incorrect, even as a rough rule of thumb, because situations commonly arise in which a less efficient technology is a more profitable one. What is profitable does not always need to be efficient, and vice versa.

While greater efficiency may lead to greater profitability, there is no necessary connection between the two. In fact, a new technology may be profitable but still use more of some input (labor, intermediate goods, or capital) and therefore be inefficient.

How might a more inefficient technology be more profitable? The system of technical control and the process of deskilling provide us with two examples. First, suppose that a new method of production—say, an assembly line—allows the employer to speed up production without raising wages; assume, however, that it also reduces efficiency. This will raise d, leave w constant, and reduce *e*. If the rise in *d* more than offsets the fall in *e*, then this change will lower unit labor costs. But saying that *e* is reduced as a result of the new technology simply means that the new technology is less efficient than the old technology. Nonetheless, the new technology lowers unit labor costs, and for this reason it will generally be more profitable. Therefore capitalist employers will adopt the new technology. We call this an example of *inefficient technical change*.

A second example: deskilling, as we have just seen, is a technical change that permits employers to use more easily replaced workers, usually workers with less bargaining strength. This change could allow the employer to lower wages or raise work effort per hour. Even if the new job design led to a fall in output per unit of work input (*e*), unit labor costs could fall. The deskilled technology, like the one above, would be more profitable even though it was less efficient.

The principal reason why profitability differs from efficiency is that, in the case of labor, the purchased quantity (labor time) differs from the input to production (work done). Therefore, other profit-rate determinants remaining unchanged, any change that reduces the per-unit labor cost of production while increasing the actual labor input will be profitable but inefficient.

For capitalist firms, what counts is profitability, not efficiency. Therefore, firms will tend to introduce those methods of production that are most profitable, whether or not they are most efficient. And when they invest, including when they invest in research to develop new technologies, the firm will again choose what is most profitable, which may but need not be what is efficient.

Since current technology is the product of past technical changes, the idea that the technologies currently in use and being developed are the "best that modern science has to offer" is a mistake. Today's technologies—and current corporate research in new technologies—reflect the fact that to a large extent science has been harnessed to the criterion of profitability. What technologies would be possible if different criteria were used—for example, to minimize the work effort required to produce necessary goods and services—are undoubtedly quite different.

Inefficient technical change occurs when some technical changes are developed and implemented because they are profitable but other technological or technical changes, which are at least equally efficient, are unexplored and ignored because they are less profitable.

☐ Markets and Hierarchies

Markets and hierarchies are sometimes thought to be alternative ways of organizing social relations. Markets seem to establish conditions of (horizontal) equality; voluntary exchange between buyer and seller means that either party can back out of the transaction if he or she wants, and so a kind of equality exists between them.

Hierarchy, on the other hand, depends on the creation of (vertical) inequality; command relations require superiors and subordinates, and the bosses must have power over their underlings.

Hence markets have sometimes been counterposed to hierarchies, as though a social relationship must be one or the other. Selling gasoline retail is seen as a market-type transaction, whereas the U.S. Army and the Catholic Church are seen as being organized in hierarchies. Capitalism is seen as a market system, economic systems using central planning as hierarchical. Yet in this chapter we have seen that profit-making firms, in their efforts to gain a competitive advantage over their market rivals, have established huge and sophisticated hierarchies.

Whereas markets once seemed to promise relief from command relations and a kind of equality between buyer and seller, they have in fact produced a whole new system of bosses and workers, of superiors and subordinates. This capitalist need for hierarchy has called forth whole new fields of study (with their associated experts): industrial psychology, personnel management, occupational testing, industrial engineering. Corporations have reinvested substantial sums of the social surplus product to develop and refine their techniques of controlling hierarchies. For instance, large corporations in the post-World War II era, in what was sometimes praised as the "managerial revolution," developed and refined the techniques of bureaucratic control. Thus market competition has not only led to the growth of hierarchy but also to its development and refinement.

And whereas capitalism once promised to abolish (feudal) hierarchies and release people into the freedom of voluntary contracts, we now find that most people in the capitalist economic system spend virtually their entire work lives in hierarchically organized jobs. Finding work has become not so much a matter of making contracts among equals as it is choosing which hierarchy to work in and which bosses to work under—and with luck, how to get to be a boss rather than a subordinate.

In capitalist society, markets and hierarchy are not alternative and competing methods of organization. The horizontal and vertical aspects of the capitalist economy—competition and command—are mutually reinforcing and complementary.

☐ Suggested Readings

Barry Bluestone and Bennett Harrison, *The De-Industrialization of America* (New York: Basic Books, 1982)

Heidi Hartmann and Donald Treiman, *Women, Work and Wages* (Washington, D.C.: National Academy of Sciences Press, 1982).

David Noble, *The Forces of Production* (New York: Knopf, 1984).
Michael Reich, *Racial Inequality* (Princeton, N.J.: Princeton University Press, 1981).
Studs Terkel, *Working* (New York: Avon Books, 1982).

CHAPTER 10

AMERICAN CAPITALISM: THE DUAL ECONOMY AND SEGMENTED LABOR MARKETS

Competition is often depicted in textbooks as a game played by countless numbers of small, powerless, anonymous firms. For some markets this picture is perfectly accurate. There are hundreds of thousands of American farmers, for instance, who sell their grain in the international grain markets. And there are millions of Americans who buy or sell stock through their stockbrokers.

Yet it would also be possible to gather together, in one large university lecture hall, the heads of those corporations that, together, do roughly *half* of the nation's business. Just 1200 very large corporations are almost as important, economically, as the other 16 *million* American businesses combined. These 1200 firms in 1980 sold 2.7 *trillion* dollars worth of goods and services, and they employed about one out of every three American workers.

These giant firms are anything but anonymous—indeed, it is impossible to watch TV or read a magazine or drive along a highway without having them tell you about their new products. Nor are they powerless.

Yet, strangely enough, while most of the 1200 big corporations are well known, their leaders are not. The average person in the street would have to think hard to name even one of them and surely would be hard-pressed to name five. Senators, movie stars, professional athletes, astronauts, musicians, even "star" criminals—all these are much better known than the heads of major corporations. Nonetheless, their fame is no measure of their power: These are men (and a few women) who make basic, far-reaching decisions about our society and its future.

The fact that so much of the U.S. economy is run by so few people—by Big Business—does not mean, of course, that they can do whatever they want, or that they all agree, or even that they have the same interests. It does suggest, however, that when analyzing the present American economy, we should take into account this fact: American economic development has led to a situation in which a major portion of American business is organized in a few very large and powerful corporations.

Similarly, when the AFL-CIO Executive Council holds its annual winter meeting in Florida, the 30 or so union presidents sitting around the conference table carry some clout. Add another 5 or 10 presidents of independent (non-AFL-CIO) unions such as the Teamsters, and these few dozen leaders speak for more than 20 million employees, 1 of every 5 workers. (About 80 million workers, however, are not represented by unions at all. Many of these are low wage workers, often racial minorities and women.)

This chapter investigates the growth of big corporations and labor unions in the United States since the Great Depression, and examines how these institutions affect the way our economy operates.

The main idea of this chapter is that the microeconomic structure of contemporary American capitalism is characterized by *industrial dualism* and *segmented labor markets* and that these institutional features shape contemporary processes of accumulation and conflict.

This main idea is expressed in four main points:

1. The development of the American industrial structure has led to what has been termed the *dual economy*—the emergence of two relatively distinct business sectors. One sector, called the *core*, consists of a small number of large businesses with substantial market power; the other sector, called the *periphery*, includes the rest of the private economy, mainly small and middle-sized businesses with little market power.
2. The American trade union movement, particularly as a result of its successes in establishing *industrial unions* and in gaining legal protections and political influence, has become a central factor in the bargaining and conflict between employers and workers. In particular, a set of mutually agreed understandings, called the *labor accord*, came to govern relations between (most) unionized workers and (most) large employers.
3. Industrial dualism and the labor accord, combined with different systems of control in the workplace, racial and sexual discrimination, and other factors, produced a system of *segmented labor markets*.
4. This set of institutional features—industrial dualism and segmented labor markets—constituted the basic microeconomic structure of the post-1945 *social structure of accumulation*.

The institutional relationships described in this chapter provided the context within which competition among firms and conflict between employers and workers—processes analyzed in preceding chapters—occurred. In Chapters 7, 8, and 9 our concern was to define and understand these processes themselves, as they might operate in any capitalist economy; here, we consider how they have developed in the real economy of the United States in the post-1945 period.

The institutional features of contemporary American capitalism are themselves products of earlier processes of competition, accumulation, and conflict. For example, the major corporations of the core sector began to emerge from the competitive process around 1900, and industrial unions were successfully established during the intense class conflict of the 1930s. Similarly, we should expect that competition, accumulation, and conflict in the present period are working to shape, erode, and change present institutions.

☐ The Dual Economy

The **dual economy** is the industrial structure of contemporary American capitalism, consisting of core firms and periphery firms.

Core firms are giant corporations with substantial market power.

Competition and accumulation have produced a split among American businesses. Essentially two different types of firms now characterize American capitalism—*core* firms and *periphery* firms.

The core sector consists of today's giant corporations—very large firms, each having thousands of employees and billions of dollars in sales. Although no precise boundary can be drawn between core firms and other firms, we may take the largest 1200 corporations—out of over 16 million American businesses—as a reasonable definition. These 1200 corporations account for roughly half of all corporate sales in the economy, and the average sales of each big firm was in excess of $2 billion.

The names of many of these firms are familiar: IBM, Texaco, Eastman Kodak, Boeing, General Electric, Procter & Gamble. Others are known to us mostly by their products. Beatrice Foods, with $8 billion in sales in 1981, sells Dannon Yogurt, 7-Up, Charmglow Insect Control, Samsonite Luggage, and dozens of other products.

Periphery firms are firms not in the core; most of them are small and medium-sized businesses with little market power.

The periphery sector includes all firms not in the core—that is, the other 16 million or so small and middle-sized firms. These firms display an enormous diversity of circumstances and operations, and indeed, the only common characteristic they have is that they are not core firms. Some peripheral firms operate primarily in local markets, as, for example, local retailers or construction companies. Some firms are closely attached to core firms, as, for instance, suppliers of parts to the big auto companies or franchise outlets of fast-food chains. Some may directly compete with core firms, as independent petroleum refiners compete with big oil companies, for example, but most do not. Outside of their own locality or industry, these firms are largely anonymous.

The division of the American economy into core and periphery, or a large-corporation sector and a small-business sector, was produced by the competitive process. Competition, as we learned in Chapter 7, creates two opposing effects with respect to economic concentration: Dynamic competition among existing firms leads to increasing concentration, whereas the high profitability often associated with concentration attracts new firms. The outcome—whether economic concentration increases or decreases—depends on which of these effects is stronger.

The dual economy emerged because competition during the nineteenth and early twentieth centuries produced a persistent trend toward economic concentration. Out of an economy that consisted almost entirely of small business, a small number of very large corporations emerged—U.S. Steel, Standard Oil, and others—increasingly distinguishing themselves from the many small businesses that remained.

This trend toward concentration affected particular industries and the economy as a whole. Economic concentration in particular industries is shown in Figure 10.1. In these and other industries, a few firms account for much, in some cases virtually all, of the sales of the entire industry. In the breakfast cereal industry, for instance, Kellogg, General Mills, and General Foods provide 86 percent of the breakfast cereals sold. In the aircraft engine market, General Electric and United Technologies (Pratt and Whitney) sell over 90 percent of the domestic supply.

Economic concentration in particular industries measures how much of the economic activity (such as sales) of a particular industry is accounted for by the largest firms in that industry.

We may also observe the effects of economic concentration in the economy at large. Here, our interest is in the extent to which large corporations have captured an increasing share of the nation's business activity. In examining concentration in the whole economy, however, we can observe one possibility not present when we look just at individual industries. Firms may choose to reinvest in industries different from where the profits were first earned. Oil companies have recently invested heavily in the coal industry, for example. U.S. Steel has made a $6 billion investment in the oil industry and now does considerably more business in the petrochemical industry than in steel. Thus these firms may grow larger, even though their market share in their original industry does not grow. Whether they grow within their original industries or by entering different ones, large firms will increase their share of the nation's business so long as they grow faster than small firms.

Economic concentration in the whole economy may be measured in several ways. Core firms—defined as those 1200 largest nonfinancial corporations that account for roughly half of all corporate sales—also, by and large, are the biggest employers, have the biggest profits, and contribute a major portion of net output. For instance, their total assets in 1980—$2.3 trillion worth of capital goods, an average of more than $2 billion per corporation—consti-

Economic concentration in the whole economy measures how much of the economic activity of the whole economy is accounted for by the largest firms in the economy.

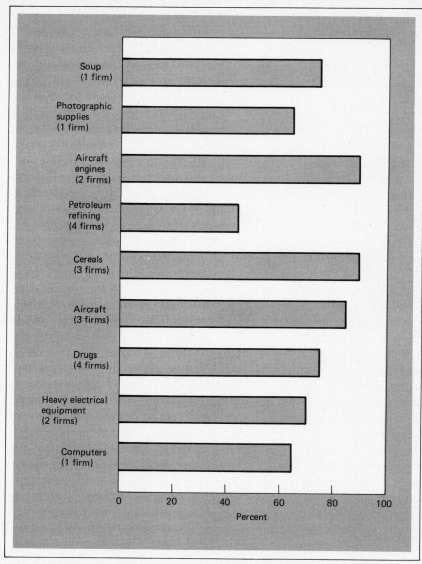

FIGURE 10.1 Economic concentration in selected markets, 1983. The degree of concentration is measured by the percent of total sales of all U.S. firms done by the largest firms in the market. For example, one firm (Kodak) accounted for 70 percent of the total output of photographic supplies sold; two firms (Pratt and Whitney and General Electric) sold over 90 percent of all aircraft engines.
Source: William D. Shepherd, *Market Power and Economic Welfare* (New York: Random House, 1970), pp. 152–154, updated by the author.

tuted about 65 percent of all nonfinancial corporate assets. And the profit of these 1200 corporations amounted to more than 70 percent of the total.

The core, then, is the province of big corporations with substantial market power. It is the product of economic concentration, both within individual industries and in the economy as a whole.

The core-periphery division of the economy would be important even if its consequences were limited to those differences between core and peripheral firms already described. For instance, the bargaining between workers and employers is quite different depending on whether workers in an industry face many small employers (as in auto repair or garment manufacture) or a few giant firms (as in automobiles or insurance). Other things being equal, large employers are likely to have much more power in bargaining than are small employers. Similarly, the concentration of much of the economy's capital goods and business in very large corporations likely increases the political power of employers (see Chapter 13).

The consequences of the dual economy, however, also extend to microeconomic performance. Core firms have changed the nature of competition; as a result, profit rates in the core tend on average to be higher than in the periphery. They have also been central in the creation of segmented labor markets. We consider next the changed nature of competition.

Competition among the giants

Giant corporations—firms like Exxon or IBM or Prudential Insurance—compete for markets in quite different ways from the small, mostly anonymous firms of the periphery. Rather than engaging solely in price competition and simply reacting to markets, these corporations are able to shape markets in important ways. Their fundamental goals are to achieve breakthroughs and monopoly positions. To understand competition among these firms, we must consider the *command* dimension of political economy, because the large firms' size and resources permit them to exercise a degree of command over their markets.

How do these firms compete? The prevailing market structure of the core is *shared monopoly*. And here we can distinguish two different situations: competition among giants in an *already* established shared-monopoly industry; and competition *during* the process of establishing a shared-monopoly market structure.

Established shared monopoly. In industries such as breakfast cereals or steel or tobacco, a few firms have dominated each industry for decades. Each of the shared-monopoly firms has learned to live within certain unwritten rules or ways of doing business that all of the shared-monopoly partners accept. Competition tends to be governed by these rules.

Each firm accepts the rules only because it judges that it will be more profitable to abide by the rules than to violate them. A firm will generally decide that it is more profitable in the long run to

Fishing for Higher Prices

Westinghouse and General Electric provide one example of collusion or price fixing in shared monopoly. These two companies sold switchgear—big pieces of heavy electrical equipment used by electric companies and in industry.

Executives from GE, Westinghouse, and two other companies met together regularly to fix prices and divide up the market. They carefully rotated their bids on contracts (first one firm being the low bidder, then another) so that GE got 45 percent of the business; Westinghouse, 35 percent; Allis-Chalmers and Federal Pacific, each 10 percent. Between 1951 and 1958 these companies divided up $650 million in sales.

The executives developed their own secret code words. The list of who attended the price-fixing meetings was called the "Christmas card list"; meetings were known as "choir practices"; companies had code numbers—GE, 1; Westinghouse, 2; Allis-Chalmers, 3; Federal Pacific, 7—so they never had to use company names.

Sometimes they met in hotels, other times on golf courses. On at least one occasion they took side-by-side fishing cabins in North Bay, Ontario. That time, a messenger kept running back and forth between cabins carrying little slips of paper until an agreement was reached. The executives returned to their companies and announced a 10 percent price increase. Quite a catch for a day of easy fishing!

In this case the conspirators got caught. The companies paid about $2 million in fines (though the fines were tax deductible, so the government, in effect, wound up paying half or so of the fines). Seven executives got 30-day jail terms. To read about the case, see "The Incredible Electrical Conspiracy," *Fortune*, April and May 1961.

We know about *this* case because the conspirators got caught. But how common are these practices? We don't know. Understandably, other price fixers who have not been caught do not brag about their success!

follow the rules, even if some short-term profits are thereby lost, because the rules protect shared-monopoly firms from some of the ravages of dynamic competition. But not always. If a firm decides that it can gain long-term advantages by acting outside the rules, it likely will abandon the rules. And if the firm faces short-run bankruptcy, then profits in the long run no longer matter. Hence, in investigating the rules we must keep in mind that there will likely be certain circumstances under which firms will violate them.

What, then, are these rules? The first rule that shared-monopoly firms try to establish is that they should avoid price competition. Because the firms have no way to stop competitive price cutting in a highly competitive market, firms will be driven to reduce the prices of their outputs (Pz) to the point where they receive merely competitive profits. But when there are only two or four or five major firms, the opportunities for cooperative rather than competitive pricing expand.

Sometimes shared-monopoly firms directly conspire to fix prices; more often, they develop informal, tacit, indirect methods to produce the same result. Tacit or informal methods for fixing prices and avoiding price competition differ from industry to industry, since each industry's system evolved out of the peculiar circumstances of its historical situations. Most commonly, these methods reflect the long experience each firm has had in dealing with the others; GE and Westinghouse, for instance, have dominated the electrical products industry for more than half a century. The pricing methods typically involve a mechanism for signaling price changes that all the major firms agree to or are forced to abide by.

In the breakfast cereal and auto industries, there has traditionally been *price leadership* by the biggest firms—Kellogg and General Motors. These firms set prices at a level that they believe would be the most profitable for themselves and for the industry. They have carefully observed other firms' behavior and occasionally have used their size to force other producers to keep their prices approximately in line.

Price leadership is an informal system for setting prices in which the biggest firm in an industry establishes an output price and the other firms in the industry tacitly agree to set the same price for their own outputs.

In petroleum and tobacco, trade institutes—supposedly independent "research" institutes funded by the major firms—have played important parts in price setting; if the American Tobacco Institute, for example, reports that its latest "research" indicates a $0.02 per pack price rise likely to occur in the next three months, the companies may take this as a signal to raise their prices. In other industries different arrangements exist. Banks sometimes act as intermediaries. In other cases, interlocking directors provide the coordinating link. In all these cases, the central point is that big corporations find it profitable to suspend the market as their pricing method and replace it with some more collusive arrangement.

Shared-monopoly pricing arrangements do not always work. Among airline companies, price wars have frequently broken out in recent years. In grocery retailing, the biggest firms—A & P, Safeway, Kroger, and others—had established by the mid-1960s an informal pricing agreement (the standard markup over wholesale prices). However, A & P, the biggest firm, consistently lost some of its market share, and its future was so bleak that, in the early 1970s, it was driven to break the pricing agreement. It began cutting prices under its WEO ("Where Economy Originates") program. Other supermarket chains retaliated, with the result that all firms earned lower profits and A & P's business still faltered. By the late 1970s, A & P rejoined the tacit agreement, proclaiming

"Price *and* Pride" as its principles, and grocery profit margins were restored (though A & P continued to have trouble).

But if price competition is avoided, other forms of competition attain a new intensity. The industry demand curve still limits what producers can sell. For instance, suppose that establishing the shared-monopoly price *Psm* in Figure 10.2 maximizes the industry's profits; this still does not resolve the question of how the sales and profits will be divided among firms in the industry. At price *Psm* consumers will buy quantity *Qsm* of the product (and no more), but from which firms? Each firm is interested only in its *own* profits, not industry profits. In the grocery retailing case discussed above, consumers kept switching from A & P to other firms until A & P decided the whole pricing arrangement was no longer worth supporting. Thus, a battle for *market shares* ensures, and each firm intensifies its efforts to sell its products—its *sales effort*.

Consider, for instance, the case of Ragu Spaghetti Sauce. Ragu used to be an independent company located in the Northeast. In 1969 it was purchased by Chesebrough-Ponds, a huge corporation

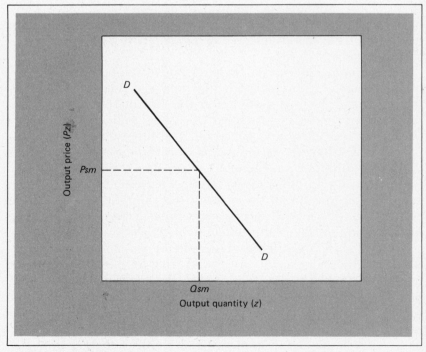

FIGURE 10.2 An industry's demand curve and the battle for market shares. *DD* is the demand curve for an entire industry. If this industry is a shared monopoly and if *Psm* is the price that maximizes the industry profits as a whole, the firms making up the industry may avoid price competition by (tacitly) agreeing not to charge less than *Psm*. Then a battle over market shares ensues, fought not through price competition but by other means.

that makes Q-Tips, Vaseline, Health-Tex baby clothes, cosmetics, and many other products. Chesebrough immediately set out to build Ragu's market share through an intensified sales effort. Advertising expenditures grew rapidly, by as much as 70 percent each year. The company adopted the slogan, "That's Italian!" and over the next several years spent $35 million to put the slogan on nationwide TV. Chesebrough also opened several new plants, in the South, the West, and Canada, so Ragu could be sold everywhere in North America; in addition to opening new markets, the new plants permitted the company to use network advertising, which is cheaper (per household) than buying commercials on local TV.

Still another element in Chesebrough's marketing strategy was creating "new" products. Originally, Ragu had only 4 varieties of sauce, but soon Chesebrough's chefs had come up with a total of 37 different products (including the new "thick and zesty" sauces, which are advertised as different from Ragu's other sauces—making the others, apparently, runny and bland). There are advantages in having 37 items. For example, if grocery stores stock all 37, Ragu will obtain a big stretch of self space, perhaps several feet; consumers walking down the aisle are more likely to notice Ragu's products, and even those who did not intend to buy any sauce may pick up a jar or two on impulse. Then, too, if much shelf space is devoted to Ragu, the retailer will have less space to devote to competitors' sauces.

Chesebrough's Ragu campaign succeeded: By 1980 Ragu produced and sold about 80 percent of all the prepared spaghetti sauces. It had largely eliminated other competitors (like Chef Boy-ar-dee) from the market. And it had achieved this huge market share without any price cuts or price competition of any sort; indeed, Ragu products often cost consumers more than competing brands.

In a mature shared monopoly, then, firms try to avoid price competition but they struggle over market shares (and profits). Prices and profits tend to be established at higher levels than would exist if no pricing agreements existed. To increase its share, each firm will intensify its sales effort, including advertising and all the other techniques of marketing.

Developing a shared monopoly. A somewhat different form of competition emerges when large corporations enter a market with the intention of establishing a shared monopoly. This situation might arise when a firm seeks to enter a new geographical area in an already existing industry, as, for example, when Procter & Gamble entered East Coast coffee markets. Or it might arise when an outside firm enters a new market, as was the case when Philip Morris, a tobacco company, entered the beer market. In these cases, no pricing agreement exists and market shares are not at all established. Firms take profits earned elsewhere and reinvest in the new markets, as did Philip Morris and Procter & Gamble in the examples cited.

These corporations are interested in long-run profits; they are even willing to suffer short-term losses if that is what is required for them to transform the industry into a shared monopoly. They are, in a sense, making an investment in market structure itself. Their goal is not so much to pick the right point on the demand curve facing their firm, but to move the entire curve outward so as to enhance their profits whatever the price is.

When big firms enter new markets, price competition can be very intense. Indeed, smaller producers often complain that the big corporations charge such low prices that they drive the small producers out of business—which may be precisely the point. The big firms can survive because they have profits from their other markets. Then, when most small producers are driven out, the few surviving firms can operate the industry like a (high-profit) mature shared monopoly.

We can see this process at work in the recent history of the roast coffee market. Coffee processors buy raw coffee beans in the international market, roast and grind the beans, and sell the cans of coffee familiar to us on store shelves. For some time the biggest processors have been Procter & Gamble (the enormous soap and household products firm that sells Folger's Coffee) and General Foods (manufacturer of breakfast cereals and Maxwell House Coffee). Maxwell House was sold nationwide, and Procter & Gamble decided that Folger's, then a brand mostly marketed west of the Mississippi, should also be a national brand. Both firms geared for battle over national market shares. This clash spelled doom for many small coffee processors who had somehow survived in local markets, firms like Breakfast Cheer Coffee in Pittsburgh (Pa.) and deLima Coffee in Syracuse (N.Y.). In Syracuse, for instance, Folger's entered the market in 1974. Procter & Gamble offered discounts to Syracuse supermarkets of up to 28 percent on the wholesale price of Folger's. Coupons giving $0.35 off per pound were mailed to homes in the area. On each can was another coupon worth another $0.10 off. In all, the real price of Folger's Coffee was then *less than $0.50 per pound*—and about half the price of deLima's coffee.

While Folger's coffee was cheap in Syracuse, its price was not reduced elsewhere. Thus, the deLima Company, whose sales mostly depended upon the Syracuse market, was competing with a company still earning high profits in San Francisco, St. Louis, and elsewhere. Procter & Gamble could afford to lose money in Syracuse for a long time, but deLima could not.

As a result of Procter & Gamble's strategy, Folger's gained a 25 percent share of the Syracuse market. Huge General Foods, whose Maxwell House had been the leading brand, poured in money to counter Folger's attack; they sent out their own coupons and maintained its 53 percent market share. Little deLima, without the financial resources to fight back, saw its share decline from 15 to 7 percent.

The giant corporations' willingness to engage in geographically limited, temporary, but ferocious price competition does not mean that they abandon the sales effort. In Syracuse, for example, Procter & Gamble unleashed a 50-person sales force to swoop down on the grocery stores and badger store managers into giving Folger's lots of shelf space in highly visible places. The company also saturated local TV with ads featuring the redoubtable "Mrs. Olson" serving her "mountain grown" coffee. General Foods sent "Cora" in with the reminder that "If anyone knows beans about coffee, Maxwell House does." DeLima tried to keep up but did not have the resources to do so.

In some cases the corporations may rely entirely on the overpowering effects of nonprice competition. Philip Morris reinvested its tobacco profits in the beer industry by purchasing the Miller Brewing Company in 1970. Then PM set off on a campaign to make the seventh-ranked Miller (with only 4 percent of the market) into the top-selling beer. But its strategy involved no price competition; instead, huge sums, upwards of $60 million a year, were poured into advertising and athletes' endorsements. PM also built up a large sales force to convince bar owners to have Miller on tap. (Other brewers, most prominently Anheuser-Busch and Schlitz, apparently countered with illegal payments—bribes—to beer retailers, but the Treasury Department caught them.) And Philip Morris introduced several new Miller products: the 7-ounce "pony" bottle, lower calorie Lite beer, Lowenbrau, and so on. In a decade, PM increased Miller's market share from 4 percent to 22 percent, ranking it just behind Anheuser-Busch. And all without once cutting its price.

In establishing a new shared monopoly, then, big corporations are able to draw upon their vast resources to invest in market structure. Profits from another industry or from sales of the same product elsewhere permit long periods of unprofitability (Philip Morris did not make a profit on Miller's for nearly 10 years), whereas small-fry competitors generally cannot last under such pressure. Once established, however, shared monopoly offers the prospect of much more than competitive profits.

The process of economic concentration is quite visible today. Safeway, Kroger, and other national grocery chains are quickly driving all local ("mom and pop") grocery stores out of business.

National beers like Miller and Budweiser replace regional beers like National Bohemian (Baltimore) or Hamm's (Minneapolis), either by driving them out of business or by buying them up. Agribusiness firms like Del Monte and Hunt crowd out small farmers. And markets with potentially fast growth, like office machinery, are captured by huge firms reinvesting their profits from oil or computer or telephone operations. Dynamic competition, over time, places more and more business in the hands of the biggest firms and simultaneously transforms the nature of competition among them.

Here we see the importance of the command or power dimension for understanding how markets work. To review: As Chapter 2 noted, power is most commonly used in the following way. Economic agent A (a firm or a boss, say) exercises his power over B by shaping the conditions under which B makes a choice (remember the choice offered by the thief: "Your money or your life!").

Shared-monopoly firms exercise power over both competitors and customers. To competitors, such firms offer market competition on unequal terms. If deLima Coffee wishes to compete with Procter & Gamble and General Foods, it must do so on terms set by the big companies: deep price discounts, a large sales force, national advertising. If National Bohemian Beer wants to compete with Budweiser and Miller's, it must try to gain customers who have been conditioned to think of Bud as the "king of beers" and to associate Miller's with successful and popular athletes. However, deLima and National Bohemian cannot really compete effectively on these terms, since they do not have the size or resources to do so.

Similarly, core corporations exercise power over their customers by using their resources to shape their customers' tastes. True, the customer is always right—no one forces consumers to choose Folger's or Maxwell House over deLima coffee or to choose Miller's or Bud over National Bohemian beer. Still, consumers make these choices in part because their perceptions of the products have been shaped by the calculated, sophisticated, and costly sales efforts of the big companies. Profits are made not only by producing commodities that meet people's tastes, but by producing people's tastes for the commodity that the firm sells. In this sense, these companies exert power over customers.

Profits in the core sector

As a result of the changed nature of competition in the core, the average profit rate of core firms tends to be higher than that of peripheral firms.

In each sector, the profit rates of individual firms vary—some

Profits in the Dual Economy

How does the dual structure of the economy affect the profit rates of companies? Core corporations—big firms with significant market power—earn substantially higher profit rates than do other (peripheral) firms. In the chart below, consider first the three groups of firms shown on the left side. These three groups of firms in the periphery had average profit rates that were quite similar, all around 8 percent.

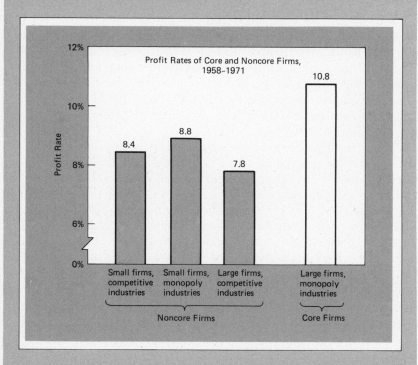

Profit Rates of Core and Noncore Firms, 1958–1971

This rate may be interpreted as the average profit rate in the periphery.

The group of firms on the right-hand side—core firms—earned nearly 11 percent on the average. The core's average profit rate was nearly 30 percent higher than that in the periphery.

Thus, a substantial premium existed (on average) for firms that can enter the core part of the economy. As we see below (p. 219), this premium is especially large for nonunionized core firms.

Source: Richard Edwards, *Contested Terrain*, Basic Books, New York, 1979, p. 83.

firms earning higher than the sector average rate, others lower than average. To say that the core-sector average is higher than the peripheral-sector average does not mean, of course, that all core-sector firms have higher profit rates than any periphery firm. But *on average* core firms have higher profit rates than periphery firms.

Indeed, profit rates in the periphery usually differ much more widely than core-sector profit rates. The highest profit rates in the economy are almost always made by small firms—those few firms, like Apple Computer and Jordache Clothes, that, having made breakthroughs, achieve huge profits (compared to their small but lucky investments). On the other side, a much higher percentage of small firms make losses and go bankrupt than do core firms. When all core-sector firms and all periphery-sector firms are considered, the core average is higher than the periphery average. Recent studies suggest that in the 1960s and 1970s the core's average after-tax profit rate was about 25 to 30 percent higher than the periphery's rate.

That core firms on average earn higher profits than peripheral firms is hardly surprising, since core firms have available to them many profitable investment opportunities not available to peripheral firms. All the advantages of size (see Chapter 7) work to favor core firms. The higher profits from monopoly power go almost entirely to core-sector firms. Core firms can undertake large investment projects that small firms, even if they recognize these projects' high profitability, cannot undertake because they lack sufficient resources (including access to sufficient credit). And large firms are likely to be more successful in seeking assistance or favored treatment from the government. For all these reasons, core firms have advantages that permit them on average to earn higher profits.

Within each sector there are forces tending to make the profit rates within the sector more equal, and other forces tending to create greater disparities. Within the periphery, these forces are similar to those described earlier (see Chapter 7): Breakthroughs (and monopoly power, to the minimal extent it exists in the periphery) tend to create unequal rates; competition and entry and exit tend to equalize rates.

In the core sector as well there are forces working in both directions. The much greater importance of monopoly power would seem to make the core sector, relative to the periphery, likely to have more unequal rates. And indeed core firms do achieve highly unequal profit rates on those investments in markets where they exercise substantial monopoly power. However, core firms typically are highly diversified—they produce many different types of products—compared to peripheral firms, and each firm's profit rate is a composite of the different rates earned on its investments in different industries. Moreover, many of the additional or new investments are made in new markets (for example, in establishing new shared monopoly) where there are strong competitive pressures pushing toward an equalized or general core-sector profit rate.

The outcome of these various pressures has been, in practice, that profit rates of core-sector firms have differed less from the core-sector average than have periphery-sector profit rates differed from the periphery-sector average.

Growth of the core

Core-sector firms emerged out of a less differentiated small-business economy through the process of competition and economic concentration. The first core firms had already appeared by the beginning of the twentieth century (or the stage of monopolistically competitive capitalism—see Chapter 5). And the core had further expanded—through the growth of existing core firms and the addition of new firms—by the 1940s, the first years of contemporary capitalism.

During the course of this century, the core sector has become more important. When the whole economy grows, firms in both the core and the periphery can grow in absolute terms—each year's sales or output can be larger than that of the previous year. However, the core sector has grown faster than the economy as a whole; that is, its relative *share* of the economy has increased. The core sector's share grows (by definition) at the expense of the periphery.

We see this process at work, in the cases described earlier, when core firms like Procter & Gamble and General Foods successfully invade the coffee markets of Breakfast Cheer and deLima Coffee, or when Chesebrough-Pond's Ragu captures the bulk of the spaghetti sauce market.

The core sector can increase its share of the American economy because, on average, core firms earn higher profit rates than do peripheral firms. And, as Chapter 7 showed, profits are the fuel for growth. A core firm's higher profit rate makes possible a greater level of reinvestment and hence a faster rate of growth.

There are, however, several factors that cause the core's growth to be slower than would be expected on the basis of its higher average profit rate alone. First, core firms are more likely to invest abroad than are peripheral firms. In investing outside the United States, the core firm's size gives it an advantage, since small firms can usually ill afford either the costs or the risks of such ventures. While investing abroad may be very profitable for the core firm, it has the effect of siphoning off investment resources that otherwise might have been used to expand at home.

Second, the core firms' monopoly power in established shared-monopoly industries may, over time, be challenged by peripheral firms. Deregulation (as in the airline industry), antitrust laws (as in telephone service), technical progress (as in office equipment), or other changes may erode monopoly power and make it impossible for core firms to maintain barriers to the entry of new firms.

Third, an even more serious challenge to core firms' monopoly power is the entry into American markets of foreign firms, especially large foreign companies. With increasing success in the 1970s and 1980s, foreign producers of automobiles, shoes, clothes, stereos, steel, and other goods captured substantial shares of American markets (see Figure 10.3).

Whether and how fast the core sector grows will depend, then, on the relative strengths of those factors that promote the core's growth (such as the core's higher average profit rate) as compared to those elements that tend to retard or reverse the core's growth (such as investment outside the United States by core firms, erosion of their domestic monopoly power, and rising international competition).

☐ Unions and the Labor Accord

Unions constitute a second prominent feature of contemporary American capitalism.

Despite their uncertain legal status, trade unions grew along with the size of the wage labor force in the nineteenth century. As more and more of the labor force ceased to be self-employed and instead found itself under the scrutiny of a boss, workers sought the protection of a union. And especially in particular trades, these unions were quite powerful. Nationally, they formed the American Federation of Labor (AFL).

A **craft union** is a labor union whose membership is restricted to workers in the same craft, skill category, or occupation.

Most unions reflected the craft nature of production and only enrolled skilled workers in a particular occupation. Furriers, railway engineers, iron molders, carpenters, and plumbers each belonged to a separate *craft union*. In the same industry or even the same workplace, each type of skilled worker would belong to a different union.

Many workers recognized that craft unions, although they unified workers within a craft, perpetuated division and disunity between the workers of different crafts. Moreover, most unskilled workers were not permitted to join these unions. Black and women workers were also usually excluded. Despite these limitations of the narrow craft unions, attempts to form broader unions open to all workers failed.

Unions were very weak during the monopolistically competitive stage of American capitalism. Just before the turn of the twentieth

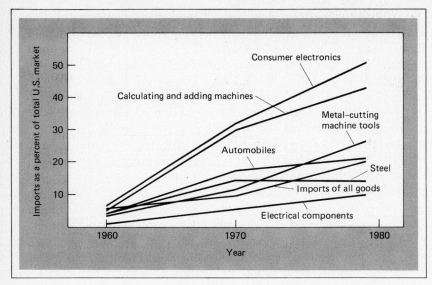

FIGURE 10.3 Imports increase their share of U.S. market. Some of the United States' demand for goods is spent on goods produced outside the United States. This percentage has increased rapidly in recent years. In 1960, for example, foreign cars made up less than 5 percent of the U.S. market; in 1979, they made up 20 percent.
Sources: "The Decline of U.S. Industry," *Business Week*, June 30, 1980, p. 60; "Economic Report of the President, 1984," tables B-6, B-99, pp. 228, 332 (Washington, D.C.: GPO, 1984).

century, the union movement suffered a major defeat and many unions were destroyed by the onset of deskilling and the increased use of unskilled labor. From the late 1890s through the 1930s, workers had great difficulty in establishing or maintaining unions. Employers' power was buoyed by the ample supply of labor resulting from rapid labor-saving technical change, the decline of employment in agriculture, and immigration from Europe. Employers used this power to press deskilling to the limit, further strengthening their position. They actively fought unionism, often aided by court injunctions, troops, and government programs to round up and deport "radicals." Most of the craft unions were destroyed or greatly weakened.

The growth of industrial unions

The next major effort to build unions occurred in the late 1930s. The Great Depression had begun in 1929. At its worst, it had thrown a quarter of the labor force out of work. By 1934 and 1935, after five or so years of this social disaster, few workers could believe that capitalism was working at all, and having a union to defend their interests seemed more important than ever. Despite the continuing high unemployment (and what would seem, therefore, to be the workers' weak position), workers successfully established the modern union movement.

In the mass-production industries (steel, autos, textiles, electrical products, rubber tires, and so on), employers had so thoroughly reorganized the labor process that the old system of craft unions was no longer possible. Deskilling had made most of the old craft distinctions irrelevant. Now workers tried to form *industrial unions*. All workers employed in an industry, whether skilled or unskilled, and without regard to craft, joined the same union.

An **industrial union** is a labor union whose membership is open to all workers in a plant or industry, regardless of which specific occupations or jobs they work at.

Unionists developed new tactics to force employers to accept the union. In San Francisco, for instance, workers organized a *general strike*; instead of workers in just one plant or one industry going on strike, workers in nearly all industries joined to support the longshoremen's strike. The general strike quickly transformed an industrial dispute into a wider political and social crisis. Throughout the city, capitalists, suffering losses because their workers were striking to support the longshoremen, put pressure on the shipowners to settle the original strike.

In the tire and auto industries, workers developed the *sit-down strike*; instead of walking off the job (and out of the factory) to go on strike, the workers simply sat down inside the factory. They refused to permit the machines to run, and their presence in the factory meant that the employers could not bring in strikebreakers to take the strikers' jobs. "Sitting down" ensured that the plant remained idle during the strike. In a famous strike in 1937 at the GM plant at Flint (Mich.), workers occupied the factory for 44 days. Wives and supporters daily brought the strikers food and mobilized political support. GM, fearing for the safety of the plant, could do little to intervene. The Governor of Michigan was asked but refused to use the national guard against the strikers. Finally, GM agreed to recognize the union.

Another important victory for workers was passage of the Wagner Act in 1935. Under pressure of the rising number and violence of strikes, Congress passed and President Roosevelt signed a bill explicitly protecting workers' efforts to form unions. It established the National Labor Relations Board to conduct elections in plants to determine if workers wanted unions and to obligate capitalists to bargain in good faith with unions so chosen.

Within a few years industrial unionism was established in law and reality. The United Auto Workers, the United Steel Workers, the Teamsters, and most other industrial unions were built during these years. Together, they formed the Congress of Industrial Organizations (CIO). By 1945 the CIO had 6 million members, and total union membership topped 13 million.

The union structure that had developed by 1945 continues to the present, with two significant changes. First, unions suffered a major defeat in the late 1940s, under the blows of McCarthyism and the anticommunist scare. The Wagner Act was amended by the Taft-Hartley Act (1947), which placed many important restrictions on what unions could do. For instance, general strikes were outlawed, anti-union state laws were permitted, secondary boycotts banned, and so forth.

The effect of the Taft-Hartley Act and the political attacks on unionists did not destroy the unions (unlike the attacks on unions at the turn of the century and after World War I), because the unions were too strong. However, they did limit and weaken the union movement; for instance, in the face of right-to-work laws designed to thwart the growth of unions, the unions were unable to organize many workers in the South. More generally, unions did not advance beyond the plateau they reached in the early 1950s (see Figure 10.4) in the percentage of American workers unionized.

The second development, concentrated in the 1960s and 1970s,

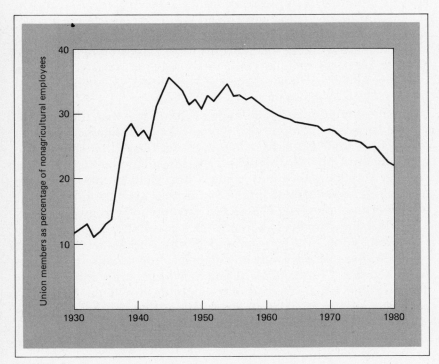

FIGURE 10.4 Union membership in the United States. The number of trade union members grew rapidly between 1935 and 1945. In recent years, there has been a decline. As a percentage of total employment, trade unions have been losing ground since the 1950s.

Source: Bureau of Labor Statistics, *Handbook of Labor Statistics*, Bulletin 2070 (Washington, D.C.: GPO, Dec. 1980), table 165.

was the increasing unionization of white-collar and service-sector workers. In the 1930s and 1940s almost all unionists were blue-collar workers. But as white-collar and service work has been increasingly subjected to more stringent employer controls, low wages, and deskilling, hospital workers, teachers, university professors, state and municipal employees, police, sanitation workers, store clerks, restaurant and hotel employees, and clerical workers began to join unions. These groups represent the only significant advance for unionism since the 1940s.

Today unions represent less than 20 percent of all American nonagricultural workers. This percentage has declined consistently since 1954, when unions represented about 35 percent of all workers (see Figure 10.4).

The labor accord

After the intense class conflict of the 1930s and 1940s, core corporations and the large unions developed an uneasy but nonetheless enduring working relationship. This accord or truce was never an explicit, formal agreement; rather, it consisted of a set of understandings and expectations that unions and corporations shared. These working relationships were expressed legally in the Wagner Act (1935) and the Taft-Hartley Act (1947) and in the union contracts or collective bargaining agreements signed by individual employers and unions.

The most important shared understanding was that, through collective bargaining, unions would obtain for their members relative job security and regularly rising real wages based on sharing the gains made available through increases in productivity. In exchange, corporations would retain a free hand to introduce new technology, to reorganize production as they saw fit, and to invest wherever they pleased. The accord was intended to give workers a fair deal and employers a free hand.

These relationships between unions and corporations are called an accord because each side was forced to compromise to achieve some benefits. Corporations in unionized industries chose to bargain with the unions instead of trying to destroy them; some corporations gave up such strategies as deskilling and heavy threats of dismissal to discipline workers; they moved from simple and technical control to bureaucratic control (see Chapter 9) as their strategy for reducing unit labor costs.

Similarly, unions lost certain rights and abandoned their sometimes radical pasts. Many militant union leaders were driven out of union office. Unions could no longer legally conduct sit-down and general strikes. Bargaining for better wages and working con-

The **labor accord** was the truce or implicit social contract between large corporations and labor unions that provided the basis for collective bargaining in contemporary American capitalism.

Unions and Profits

How do unions affect the profit rates of companies? Recent studies suggest that the answer depends on *which* companies—core corporations or companies in the periphery.

For the periphery, the data suggest that unions have little or no impact on profit rates. Unionized firms during 1958–1971 had about the same 8 percent profit rates as nonunion firms. (See box on page 211 for average profit rates.)

For the core sector, however, unions have a big impact: they reduce the profit rate. Core firms whose workers are not unionized had the highest average profits in the economy—about 12.5 percent. Core firms whose workers are unionized had average profit rates of about 9.1 percent, much closer to firms of the periphery.

Unions in the core sector, then, have evidently been successful in obtaining for their members a share of the higher core-sector profits.

Sources: Calculated from Richard Edwards, *Contested Terrain* (New York, Basic Books, 1979), p. 83; and R. B. Freeman, "Unionism, Price-Cost Margins, and the Return to Capital," N.B.E.R. paper no. 1164 (1983).

ditions was limited to contract negotiations and occasional strikes. Pressing for better social welfare measures (such as minimum wage laws) was limited to certain activities in electoral politics.

Neither side would have voluntarily chosen to have made the concessions embodied in this accord. Corporations were forced to compromise because the CIO was too strong to destroy. As the huge wave of strikes in 1946 showed, if employers were to have any sort of labor peace, they needed to come to an agreement with the unions. The unions were also forced to compromise because while powerful and growing in the 1940s, they were still no match for the economic and political clout of the business community. Businessmen united to obtain the legal curbs on union activities embodied in the Taft-Hartley law.

The result was a working relationship or accord. Corporations could regularly introduce substantial technological changes to raise productivity and reduce unit labor costs, while union members obtained substantial job security and regularly rising real wages.

The labor accord did not put an end to conflict between employers and workers, even in those cases where both union and employer subscribed to the accord. But as the example of the 1959 steel strike indicates, it did place limits on how the conflict could be fought. Some core firms ignored the accord and continued to resist unionism. The J. P. Stevens textile company, for instance, earned its reputation as the nation's "biggest labor law violator" in a decades-long and eventually unsuccessful battle to prevent unionization.

For the large segment of the labor force outside of unions (even at the peak, unions only represented about a third of all workers), there was no labor accord. Some corporations—IBM and Polaroid, for example—introduced their own form of bureaucratic control to discourage their workers from forming unions; in these cases, non-union workers obtained some rights similar to those of the accord. But for other workers, especially black, Latin, Asian, and female workers, the terms of the labor accord did not extend to them.

☐ Segmented Labor Markets

Segmented labor markets are labor markets that have been divided institutionally into distinct or separate markets (market segments); the separation of the segments is often maintained by racial, sexual, and other forms of discrimination.

The limited coverage of the labor accord reflects another important institutional feature of contemporary American capitalism—*segmented labor markets.*

Labor markets are *segmented*—divided into separate or distinct markets—when the demanders and suppliers of labor in one market do not compete with demanders and suppliers in other markets. Instead of having one large market for all jobs and all workers, there are in effect different markets—called market segments—each with its own demand for labor (employers) and supply of labor (workers).

Labor markets may be segmented either because workers (and to a lesser extent, employers) in some jobs are *shielded* from competition with other workers or because workers are *prevented* from competing for certain jobs.

The development of unions and a labor accord tended to create segmentation by shielding some workers from wider competition. Unionized workers, through strikes and collective bargaining, won increased job security for themselves; union contracts obligated employers to limit arbitrary firings, grant workers increased job security as their seniority increased, and abide by grievance procedures. Thus, although there remained substantial competition for entry-level jobs (the jobs people get when they are first hired), unionized workers in higher-level jobs or with more seniority were shielded to some extent from outside competition. Union contracts prevented employers from simply firing more experienced workers in order to replace them with people standing in the unemployment line.

Unionized workers won important protections from labor-market competition, but since only a portion, not all, of the labor force was unionized, these union protections covered only a part of the labor force. A segmentation, or division, was created between the jobs in which the workers were covered by union protections and those in which they were not covered.

The increasing use of bureaucratic control also tended to shield some workers from wider labor-market competition. Firms using bureaucratic control organize work by stratifying their work forces and establishing job ladders, seniority-based pay and promotion, and other incentives to extract work from workers (see Chapter 9). Bureaucratic control thus shares many features with the provisions that unions won in collective bargaining, and there are good reasons for this surprising similarity. In some cases, bureaucratic control emerged out of the very union contracts that collective bargaining produced. In other cases, however, core firms whose workers were *not* unionized attempted, by introducing bureaucratic control, to prevent unionization. They "voluntarily" granted many of the gains won by unionized workers, hoping thereby to convince their own workers that unions were unnecessary. The effect of the increasing use of bureaucratic control was to extend protections similar to those of the labor accord to many nonunionized workers, especially technical, professional, and lower-level managerial employees in core corporations. Still, large numbers of workers were not covered, even implicitly, by the accord.

In addition to the effects of the uneven spread of the labor accord and of bureaucratic control, *job discrimination* tended to segment labor markets by preventing some workers from competing for certain jobs. Discrimination in job hiring meant, for instance, that female job applicants were considered for clerical work but in practice not considered for many production or managerial jobs. Similarly, racial discrimination resulted in black or hispanic workers being channeled into certain jobs and barred from others.

Discrimination thus segmented labor markets by exclusion: women and black and hispanic males could not compete for some of the jobs primarily held by white males.

Three segmented markets

These various forces—the emergence of a labor accord, growth of bureaucratic control, and discrimination—eventually produced three relatively distinct labor markets. Two of these markets—the *primary markets*—incorporate the jobs of workers covered by the labor accord or otherwise organized bureaucratically. The remaining segment—the *secondary market*—encompasses all those jobs of workers neither covered by the accord nor organized bureacratically, and who therefore are not shielded at all from labor-market competition.

The **subordinate primary market** includes those jobs in workplaces organized according to the collective bargaining agreements of the labor accord; it contains mainly the jobs of the traditional, unionized, industrial working class.

The subordinate primary market. The subordinate primary market includes the jobs of the traditional, unionized, industrial working class: auto workers, truckers and railroad workers, underground coal miners, steelworkers, dockworkers, and so on. These jobs are distinguished from jobs of the secondary market mainly because these workers, or at least substantial portions of their industries, are unionized. (Some industries, steelmaking, for instance, contain both unionized and nonunion firms; what places a job in the subordinate primary market, therefore, is its market features, not its industry.)

These jobs are better paying than secondary employment, and, at least when their firms are growing, they generally involve long-term, stable work with prospects for pay raises and some job security. Indeed, seniority is usually highly rewarded. On the other hand, these jobs are distinguished from independent primary jobs in that their work tasks are repetitive, routinized, and often subject to machine pacing. The required skills are learned rather quickly and are often acquired on the job. The jobs provide little opportunity for workers to exercise much autonomy in their work.

Despite their protection from being fired, workers in subordinate primary jobs remain highly vulnerable to layoffs. *Layoff* refers to firms' temporary or permanent dismissal of workers in order to reduce their workforces because of a shortage of customers. A quarter of a million auto workers, for instance, were laid off during the slump of the early 1980s. Many will never return to their jobs.

The independent primary market. The independent primary labor market includes those bureaucratically organized jobs that offer stable employment with considerable job security, clearly defined career paths, and relatively high pay. It includes bookkeepers, technicians, scientists, engineers, lower-level supervisors and managers, commercial artists, and craftworkers such as electricians, telephone linemen, machinists, hair stylists, and skilled ironworkers.

These jobs typically require skills obtained in advanced or specialized schooling or apprenticeships. Workers may need graduate school degrees, special licenses, or other credentials to qualify for these jobs, and formal credentials are highly rewarded. Some are organized into craft unions. The jobs are likely to have occupational or professional standards (not just the employer's approval) for what constitutes good work. And they are likely to permit or even require independent initiative or self-pacing of work.

The secondary market. The secondary labor market includes most of the remaining workers. It is highly diverse, unified only in that it is the preserve of workers who have few protections from wider labor-market competition: they lack both union-achieved worker rights and elaborate employer-imposed ways of organizing work. Here the relation between boss and worker is simple and direct, and workers must continually face the threat of being replaced.

The secondary market includes the jobs of blue-collar workers in nonunion factories; nonunion janitors, waitresses, hospital orderlies, messengers, guards, retail sales clerks, typists, file clerks, and recordkeepers; seasonal or migrant farm workers; and most employees of small businesses.

What marks these as secondary-market jobs is that they lack those features that shield primary workers from full market competition. Secondary jobs are usually less secure. They also are more poorly paid and typically lack a clear career path. Workers do not progress up a job ladder, gaining more skill, pay, job security, and responsibility as they gain seniority; instead, they are more likely to reach a dead end. Neither schooling nor seniority is highly rewarded in these jobs.

The effects of discrimination

Discrimination has occurred most frequently in hiring for primary jobs, or in admission to schools, apprenticeship programs, or other institutions that qualify workers for primary jobs. Such discrimination has meant that women, blacks, hispanics, and other minority workers have been less able to gain entry to primary-market jobs.

Discrimination has thus tended to crowd women and minority

The **independent primary market** includes those jobs with highly elaborated bureaucratic or professional career patterns; it contains mainly the jobs of craft, technical, professional, and lower-level supervisory workers.

The **secondary market** includes jobs in workplaces that lack the formal organization (such as collective bargaining agreements, bureaucratic control, or professional or craft patterns) of primary markets; it contains jobs like those of service and retail workers, clerks, seasonal workers, and nonunionized employees of small businesses.

workers into the secondary market and has led to their underrepresentation in the primary markets. As a result of this factor alone, we would expect women and minorities to have, on average, lower wages. Discrimination has also, however, led to systematically lower wages and job opportunities even *within* each of the three labor markets.

The result of *racial* discrimination can be seen today in blacks' higher unemployment and, when they are employed, lower earnings.

Figure 10.5 shows that even comparing year-round, full-time workers, the earnings of blacks are substantially lower than corresponding whites' earnings. Indeed, in 1980, a black male with a college degree earned on average about as much as a white male

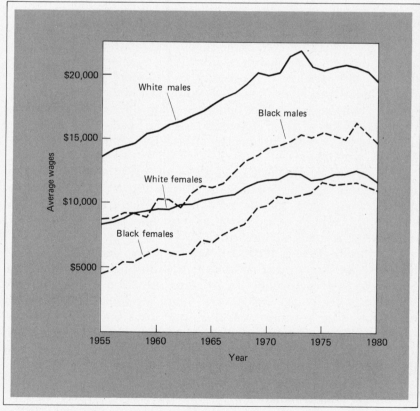

FIGURE 10.5 Black and female earnings compared to white male earnings. When comparing the annual income levels of workers, it is helpful to compare those who work roughly the same number of hours per year. The median earnings of year-round, full-time workers are shown here, corrected for inflation (by expressing all the incomes in 1980 dollars). The average earnings of people in each of the four groups rose until 1970 and then began to level off or even fall a bit. The main changes in the relative positions of the groups during this period were that black women gained ground and white women lost ground.
Source: U.S. Bureau of the Census, Series P-60, various years.

high school graduate. And, of course, the likelihood of a black worker being employed full time year round is much less than for a white worker.

During the 1960s, the civil rights movement produced antidiscrimination legislation and changes in public attitudes. It became more difficult and less acceptable for employers to discriminate openly. At the same time, the boom in the economy during the Vietnam War made jobs more plentiful. The costs of discrimination increased and employers turned away from formerly acceptable and legal overt forms of discrimination.

As a result, the racial earnings gap—the gap between black men and white men and between black women and white women—narrowed considerably in the two decades preceding the mid-1970s. Black women in particular benefited from the rapid growth in government jobs such as teaching, educational administration, and clerical work.

Since the mid-1970s, however, blacks have been able to make little further progress and in some cases have suffered reverses. The expansion of government jobs ended in the late 1970s, closing off one of the most important sources of progress for blacks. Less enforcement of antidiscrimination laws, adverse court rulings, and

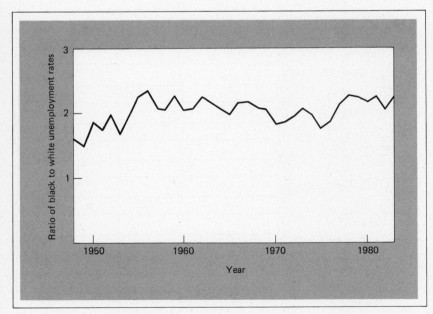

FIGURE 10.6 Unemployment of black and white men. The unemployment rate is calculated as the number unemployed (those without work who are actively seeking employment) divided by the size of the total labor force. The labor force is simply the sum of the unemployed and the employed.

The unemployment rate for black men is roughly twice that for white men; since the early 1970s, the gap has been widening.

Source: *Economic Report of the President* (Washington, D.C.: GPO, 1984), Table B-33.

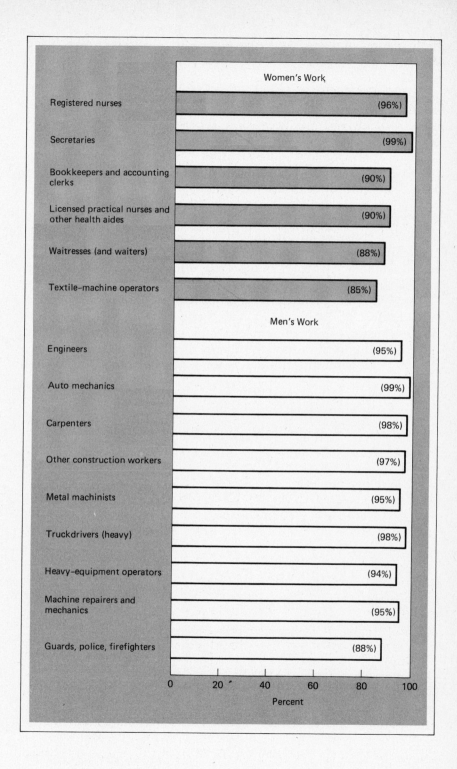

FIGURE 10.7 Women's work and men's work. Women and men tend to be employed in different kinds of jobs. For example, 96 percent of registered nurses are women, whereas 98 percent of carpenters are men.

More than 1 million people were employed in 1980 in each of the jobs listed at left. The figures in parentheses are the percentage of jobholders in "women's work" who are female and the percentage in "men's work" who are male.
Source: U.S. Census (Washington, D.C.: Government Printing Office), 1980.

the generally higher unemployment of this period seem to have signaled the end to at least the current phase of black advancement.

While blacks who are employed full time have made some progress toward earnings equality with whites, there is no corresponding tendency toward equality in finding jobs. Since 1970 the black unemployment rate has risen more rapidly than the white rate, as Figure 10.6 indicates. In 1970 the black rate was 1.8 times the white rate; in 1983 it was 2.1 times the white rate. But unemployment, as officially measured, is only part of the problem. To be counted as officially unemployed, one must be actively looking for a job. And many people—white and black—have simply given up looking. Indeed, the percentage of adult black men without jobs—either unemployed as officially defined or simply without work—rose from 22 percent in 1954 to 37 percent in 1982. This occurred because both unemployed blacks and the number of blacks no longer actively seeking work—mostly the so-called discouraged workers—rose considerably.

These trends suggest that there has been a change in the *form* of racial discrimination since passage of the antidiscrimination laws. *Pay discrimination*—paying black workers less than white workers doing the same job—has greatly declined; however, *job discrimination*—hiring nonblack workers before hiring blacks—appears to have increased. The result is a growing split among black and other minority workers between those who have jobs and those who do not.

Sexual discrimination has likewise led to a disadvantaged position for female workers. Women tend to be paid much less than men; in 1982 on average, a woman who worked full time all year earned only 63 percent of what a similarly employed man earned.

The principal reason women earn less than men is *job segregation*. Women tend to work in different kinds of jobs from men, and women's jobs pay less than men's jobs, on average. Secretaries, elementary school teachers, and nurses, for instance, are usually women, whereas carpenters, hospital technicians, and accountants are almost always men. A regular relationship exists between the percentage of an occupation that is female and the average pay. For every 1 percent more women in an occupation, the pay, on average, will be roughly $60 per year lower; the average difference between "men's work" (0 percent female) and "women's work" (100 percent female) is about $6000 per year. Figure 10.7 shows how the sex segregation of jobs results in lower pay for women workers.

Job segregation occurs even within occupations and industries. In some industries, some firms hire mostly men and other firms hire, in those *same* occupations, mostly women. Even the same firm, especially if it has plants located in different regions of the country, may hire mostly men at one plant and women at another. Pay differences, with men earning more than women, usually accompany such segregation. More prevalent is the practice of paying workers in "women's jobs" less than workers in "men's jobs" of comparable training and responsibility. Some of the differences are illustrated in Figure 10.8.

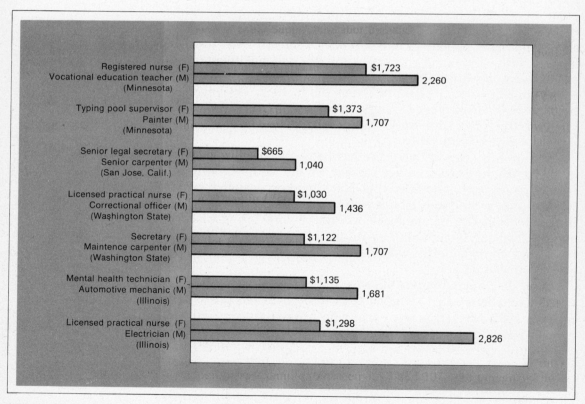

FIGURE 10.8 Women's wages, men's wages. Those jobs held predominantly by women tend to pay lower wages than those held predominantly by men, even though they require comparable levels of skill, effort, and responsibility. In the table above, government-employed registered nurses and vocational education teachers in Minnesota, for instance, are compared. The work of these two groups has been judged to be of "comparable worth," yet the (mostly female) nurses earn each month only about 76 percent of what the (mostly male) vocational education teachers earn. The dollar figures report average monthly wages.
New York Times, January 1, 1984, p. 1.

Why jobs are so sex-segregated is a matter of much dispute, but discrimination clearly contributes to it. Some women undoubtedly seek out traditionally female jobs (although the gender system—the way our culture defines what is "male" and what is "female"—heavily influences these choices). Even where an element of choice is operative, discrimination clearly increases job segregation by sex, and thereby increases the differences in average wages and other disparities between male and female workers.

In contrast to the recent progress in eliminating the racial wage gap, no progress has been made in reducing the wage gap between men and women. In 1955 full-time employed women earned 64 percent of what full-time employed men earned, almost exactly the same as today (63 percent in 1982).

☐ The Social Structure of Accumulation of Contemporary Capitalism

Profit making and accumulation always occur within a specific institutional setting. While there are some general features of *any* capitalist accumulation process—competition or the conflict between workers and employers, for example—the characteristics of the accumulation process during a *particular* historical period will be shaped by the specific institutions existing at that time. As we saw in Chapter 5, the *social structure of accumulation* is the name

---

Sex Discrimination Proven!

The exact extent of discrimination against women is said to be difficult to estimate. True, women receive much less pay than men and are often overrepresented in less desirable jobs. But some economists claim that this apparent evidence of discrimination reflects either women's lower productivity or their choices in selecting jobs; therefore low wages and undesirable jobs are not evidence of discrimination at all.

Some unusual research allows us to see which view is correct. A Stanford University researcher studied 170 people who had undergone sex-change operations. All of those who had changed from female to male earned more after the change. Most of those who had changed from male to female earned less after the change. Three males who had changed their sex decided to change back, two of them stating that they couldn't make decent livings as women. The third had had a religious experience.

Sources: *Brookings Papers on Economic Activity*, 2:1979, and *New York Times*, October 2, 1979.

given to this specific institutional setting: It is a social structure within which accumulation takes place.

We have now described the *micro*economic features of the social structure of accumulation of contemporary American capitalism. As we have seen, these features are industrial dualism (core and periphery) and segmented labor markets. The next part of this book (Chapters 11-14) is devoted to the study of the *macro*economic aspects of contemporary capitalism.

The 1970s and early 1980s were a time of *crisis* for the current social structure of accumulation (see Chapter 14). Both industrial dualism and segmented labor markets—and in particular, the labor accord—came under severe stress as a result of changing economic circumstances. As the economy's performance deteriorated, employers increasingly turned away from the labor accord and reverted to hostile anti-union attitudes more characteristic of an earlier stage of capitalism. Many employers attempted to walk away from collective bargaining entirely. Unions have been greatly weakened, have lost members, and have been put on the defensive. As a result, the relationships of the contemporary social structure of accumulation have been undermined.

The many economic problems of the years since the mid-1970s are evidence of these stresses. Times of severe stress are often also times of rapid institutional change. The two previous periods of such stress—the 1890s and the 1930s—each produced massive institutional change that, in retrospect, can be seen as the construction of a new social structure of accumulation. Perhaps something similar is happening today.

☐ Suggested Readings

Robert Averitt, *The Dual Economy* (New York: Norton, 1968).

Joseph Bowring, *Accumulation in the Dual Economy* (Princeton, N.J.: Princeton University Press, 1985).

David Gordon, Richard Edwards, and Michael Reich, *Segmented Work, Divided Workers* (New York: Cambridge University Press, 1982).

Julie Matthaei, *An Economic History of Women in America* (New York: Schocken Books, 1982).

Richard Freeman and James Medoff, *What Do Unions Do?* (New York: Basic Books, 1984).

PART FOUR

MACROECONOMICS: INSTABILITY AND GROWTH

CHAPTER 11

INVESTMENT, OUTPUT, AND EMPLOYMENT

One of the hardest things to understand—and to accept—about our economy is the fact that there are almost always factories lying idle and people looking for work at the same time that there are unmet human needs. People need the products that the unemployed workers could have produced had they been put to work in the idle factories. Yet they were not put to work. Why?

An example: Salinas County, California—a rich agricultural area—was declared an official hunger disaster area. Why? Because the unemployed workers there—many of them farm workers—did not have the money to buy food.

A more general example: In 1982, on an average day, 30 percent of the industrial capacity of the country lay idle. Had the plants that were temporarily closed down or working on short hours been working, they would have produced a quantity of goods worth something like 100 billion dollars, or $1250 worth of goods for every household in the United States. The plants were not idle for lack of help. In 1982, on an average day, 10.7 million people were looking for work and not finding it.

The fact that there are idle tools, unemployed people, and unsatisfied wants is hard to understand because it is not like our own personal experience. If you need a bookshelf, and you have the tools and lumber, and you have time on your hands, you set to work and make yourself a bookshelf. When we organize our own production—in families, small groups or on our own—we do not end up with idle tools, idle hands, and unmet needs. The reason is that when we produce for ourselves, the purpose of production is to make something that we need (or at least want). If we have unmet needs and the tools and time to do the job, we just do it.

The capitalist economy, by contrast, is organized quite differently. The purpose of producing commodities, as we saw in Chapter 4, is not to meet a need; it is to make a profit. More specifically, if the capitalists who direct the production process do not believe they will make profits, they do not initiate production; they simply leave idle the tools and factories they own, and they hire no workers. The fact that the goods that might otherwise have been produced are needed by someone is irrelevant. The system of competition with other capitalists forces them to make their decisions solely according to what is profitable.

This chapter begins our discussion of *macro*economics, meaning the economy considered as a whole. Chapters 6 through 10 focused primarily on microeconomic relations—how individual workers, firms, unions, or other economic actors act and interact, through both command relations and competitive relations. We have not asked how the countless millions of decisions and actions by each of these individuals and groups adds up for the economy as a whole.

Macroeconomics, by contrast, deals with totals, or aggregates: total demand for goods and services, total supply of labor, total investment, and the like. It also deals with averages: the average profit rate for the economy as whole, the average wage rate, the average level of prices, and the like.

The aggregates that form the basis of macroeconomics are measured in money values. Whereas the output of a firm—the number of cars produced per hour, for example—can be measured in physical units (cars), the output of the whole economy cannot be measured this way. Because the total output of the economy is a diverse collection of tons of steel, numbers of haircuts, bushels of wheat, hours of rock concerts, and so on, adding these up in physical units—adding tons of steel to numbers of haircuts to bushels of wheat—would produce a nonsense result; aggregate output can only be measured meaningfully in money terms.

To measure aggregate output, each type of output is given a money value according to its average price: The ton of steel counts as $100, the bushel of wheat as $5, and the haircut as $6.00. Thus if an additional ton of steel is produced, it counts for more in total output ($100) than an additional haircut ($6). Counting in dollars rather than physical units is far from perfect. Some things, such as farm produce consumed at home, do not have prices, so only estimates of their value can be included in the total. Other types of production, particularly the work generally done in the home (raising children, cleaning house, and so on), is counted in the official statistics only if it is paid for. Despite these shortcomings, using money terms is essential for measuring total output.

Using averages is also quite imperfect, because averages may obscure important aspects of the economy. For instance, average wages vary greatly between men and women, black and white workers, and others, and profit rates differ greatly between core and periphery. Another example: in 1982, the *average* unemployment rate was 9.7 percent, but one worker in five experienced some period of unemployment that year. However imperfect, it is only by adding up and averaging these things that we can make sense of the whole economy and its development.

As in the case of microeconomics, we are interested in how these totals and averages change over time. We will investigate how total output changes from year to year—what is called economic growth. We will also explore the changes in wages and profit rates from year to year.

The main link between the microeconomic and macroeconomic aspects of the economy is the profit rate. We have already seen that it is the principle lying behind how markets work, and the main force active in directing commodities, labor, and other inputs around the economy. The following chapters show that just as the profit rate governs the behavior of each individual firm, it also regulates the movement of most of the key economic aggregates and averages.

In this chapter we will investigate what determines how many goods and services will be produced, how many workers will be hired, and how many people will be left without work.

The main idea of this chapter is that profits determine investment; and investment determines the amount of output produced, the amount of employment, and the amount of unemployment.

This main idea is expressed in five main points:

1. The functioning of the economy as a whole is linked closely to the amount of *investment*.
2. The amount of investment that capitalists undertake depends on the *expected profit rate* that capitalists think they will make on their investment.
3. The American economy is part of a *world capitalist economy*. For this reason the levels of investment, employment, and output in the U.S. economy depend not only on domestic (U.S.) investment and profits, but also on investment and profits in other parts of the world.
4. The amount of output produced and the number of people employed is determined—in the short run—by the *total demand* for goods and services. Investment is part of total demand. Fluctuations in investment give rise to fluctuations in total demand and hence, also, to fluctuations in output and employment.

5. *Unemployment* is the difference between how many people want work (labor supply) and how many jobs are being offered by employers (labor demand). Labor demand almost always falls short of labor supply, giving rise to unemployment as a permanent feature of our economy.

We will explain these points and the interrelationships among them in this chapter using a *short-term economic model*. An *economic model*, as we saw in Chapter 3, is a simplification of economic reality designed to highlight the important aspects of some particular problem. The model used here is called a *short-term* model because one of its main simplifications is to assume that some important aspects of the economy do not change during the relatively short period of time under consideration.

In this chapter we assume that prices and wages and two key ratios do not change (are constant). The ratios are the *capital/labor ratio*, or the value of the capital goods used per labor hour *(K in use)/(Labor)*, and the *output/capital ratio*, or the ratio of net output to the value of capital goods in use *(Y/K in use)*. We also assume that the total supply of capital goods *(CG)* does not change in the short run. [However, the amount of capital goods in use *(CG in use)* and the value of capital goods in use *(K in use)* vary, even in the short run.]

We know, of course, that these magnitudes, over a longer period, *do* change. Chapters 7, 8, and 9 analyzed some of these changes; and Chapters 12 and 14 return to them. But this chapter treats them *as if* they did not change. The results of our analysis would not be very different if we considered changes in these ratios and in prices and wages. But the analysis would be much more complicated.

The structure of the short-term model is summarized in Figure 11.1. Each arrow means *influences* or *determines*. Thus an arrow from A to B (A → B) indicates that A is a main influence determining how large B will be. This influence could be either positive or negative. More A could cause more B (positive relationship), or more A could cause less B (negative relationship). The dashed arrows indicate other influences that may be important but that we are not considering for the moment.

Only the arrows that indicate the most important influences are shown here. The point of an economic model, after all, is to simplify things, not to represent every detail, whether important or not.

Figure 11.1 presents what is called a causal structure—things to the left cause (or influence) the things to the right. Later the model will become more complicated. We will see in our next chapter that some of the things on the right double back and exert an influence on the things on the left. For example, unemployment— which appears on the right of our diagram here and is therefore an

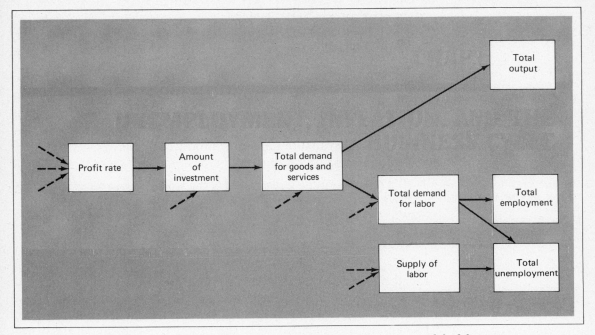

FIGURE 11.1 Basic short-run macroeconomic relationships. This is a short-term model of the macroeconomy. The arrows, representing basic causal relationships, point from causes to effects. The cause may influence the effect either by increasing or decreasing it. For example, an increase in the demand for labor will reduce the amount of unemployment, while an increase in the supply of labor will increase it. The dashed arrows indicate influences on the main variables coming from outside the model. (The model is expanded to include most of the influences discussed in later chapters.)

effect rather than a cause—is one of the things that influences the profit rate. Our first task, however, is to clarify the causal movement from left to right.

Starting at the left of Figure 11.1 we see that the profit rate influences or determines the level of investment (this is point 1 above). The arrow from *investment* to *demand for goods and services* indicates that the total demand for goods and services is influenced by the level of investment (point 4 above). In turn, the demand for goods and services is the main determinant of the demand for labor and the main determinant of total output.

The remaining arrows in Figure 11.1 show that the level of demand for labor determines the total employment, while the difference between the demand for labor and the supply of labor determines the amount of unemployment (point 5).

Tracing through these arrows, one can easily see the importance—directly or indirectly—of both the profit rate and the amount of investment (points 1 and 2) above. We will turn first to investment.

☐ Investment and Total Demand

To understand how the macroeconomy works, we must investigate investment: what it is, what effects it has, and what determines how much and what kind of it there will be.

Investment is the use of inputs (steel, computers, labor) to build factories, to construct new machines, or to expand the stocks of goods in the process of being made—or, in short, to expand the capital goods available for use in production.

Total or *gross* investment is composed of two parts:

1. *depreciation,* or the replacement of the wear and tear on capital goods used in producing last year's output;
2. *net investment,* or the construction of additional or new productive capacity (including materials inputs) above and beyond the levels existing at the beginning of the last year.

The replacement of capital goods used up is like replacing—if you recall the example of the grain-producing economy in Chapter 3—the seeds used in last year's crop and feeding the draft animals so that the same crop can be planted anew this year. Net investment, by contrast, is an expansion in the productive capacity of the economy.

| Total investment (or *"gross investment"*) | = Replacing wear and tear on capital goods used in production | + Increasing the stock of materials and capital goods |

or

| Total investment | = Depreciation | + Net investment |

In everyday language, the word *investment* has a different meaning. An individual or firm may invest money by buying stock, opening a savings account, purchasing antiques, or speculating in real estate. None of these actions *by itself* increases the productive capacity of the economy. This type of activity is sometimes called *paper investment,* but it is not really investment at all, according to the economist's definition of investment. Rather than increase the productive capacity of the economy, it simply rearranges the ownership of various parts of it. Stock certificates, titles of ownership, savings account books, and dollar bills are valuable assets and important parts of our economy. But they do not produce goods and services. Only if they are used to finance the construction of drill presses, typewriters, and the like do they contribute to production. Therefore acquiring stocks, buying U.S. Treasury bills, or similar activities are not, by themselves, investments.

Investment is the use of inputs to expand the stock of capital goods ("machines") available for use in production.

Depreciation is the cost (due to wear and tear) of restoring the capital goods used in producing last year's output.

Gross investment is depreciation plus (net) investment.

Investment, properly defined, is the key to understanding the macroeconomy's performance, and it affects the economy both through total supply and through total demand. First, as we saw in Chapters 5 and 7, investment is the central force increasing the supply of total outputs. Investment increases the stock of capital goods potentially available for use in production. Equally important, it is the means by which new technology is developed and implemented, productivity raised, new markets invaded, new products brought to market. We will not consider the·effect of investment on the supply of goods and services in this chapter, but we will return to this aspect in Chapter 14.

Second, investment adds to total demand. When investment is high, total demand for goods and services tends to be high and output is high; when investment is low, total demand for goods and services tends to fall off and output falls. Why? Remember: For capitalists to make a profit, goods must not only be produced, they must also be sold. If capitalists cannot find buyers ready to buy their output, they will make losses and cut back production. Because one firm's investment means it must buy something from other firms—the steel, computers, or whatever makes up the investment—investment is crucial in providing a demand for output.

Total demand is simply the sum of all the demands—demands for consumer goods and services, capital goods and materials, and things the government purchases. It is the total amount that all customers are willing and able to buy. (Total demand does not measure people's needs for goods and services, but rather only those wants that are backed up by dollars. A want not backed up by a dollar is not a demand.)

Total demand is the sum of all demands for goods and services in the economy, including those by consumers, businesses, governments, and foreign buyers.

To see how investment stimulates demand, consider a simple example. Suppose a company's board of directors decides to build a million dollar extension on an existing plant. It employs architects and engineers to make up the plans and workers to begin the construction. It buys the construction materials needed to build the structure as well as the machinery to be installed in it. All in all the company will spend a million dollars buying inputs (labor, engineers' plans, cement, machinery).

The companies that supply the concrete, machinery, and engineers' plans will find that the demand for their output has increased. They will hire more people to meet the demand or put their existing workforce on overtime. In this way, jobs will be created not only in building the plant, but in building or producing the things needed to build the plant.

And the new demands will not even stop here. Those who landed the new jobs or the overtime will now have more money to spend. They will head to the clothing store or the car dealer to make more purchases. Whatever they buy will mean that some company will find that the demand for *its* product—clothes, cars, or whatever—has risen. That company will employ more people to produce more to meet the demand. They in turn will go out and spend more.

Further, when the companies supplying the concrete and machinery for the extension to the factory expand their production to meet the demand, they hire more labor and buy more of other inputs too (steel and parts to make the machinery, for example). The companies supplying these inputs therefore will face increased demands and will increase their employment and other purchases.

Like the ever-widening ripples spreading out on the surface of a pond after a stone has been thrown in, the effects of an investment (building the new extension) spread out throughout the economy. Will it ever end? Yes, because some of the new money received will not be spent; people will choose to save some of it instead. Some will be spent buying goods produced in other countries, thus expanding demand and employment abroad, but not in the United States.

Unless savings and expenditures on goods produced elsewhere are very large, however, the investment's ripple effect on total demand and on employment is much larger than the direct or first-round effects. This is why the multiple effects are called the *investment multiplier*. The initial million dollar investment is multiplied into a much larger total effect on demand. If the multiplier is 2, for example, this means that the million dollar investment will end up increasing total demand by $2 million.

The **investment multiplier** is the amount (multiple) by which total demand will go up in response to an increase in investment; it counts both the direct and indirect effects.

The same reasoning holds for an increase in government expenditures. For example, the decision to build a million dollar extension to a school, if the multiplier for government spending is 2, would increase total demand by $2 million.

Investment has a central role in stimulating demand. It is not that other ways of stimulating demand do not exist; they do, but in our economy these other sources of demand—consumer purchases or government expenditures, for instance—tend to change slowly compared to investment. Because investment fluctuates and the other sources of demand remain relatively steady, the sum of these demands—aggregate or total demand—fluctuates mainly in response to changes in investment. Because total output depends on total demand, total output also fluctuates mainly in response to investment.

The inputs used for net investment come from the *surplus product*. If more is produced in the country than is consumed or used to replace the wear and tear on capital goods, then all or part of the excess—the surplus product—can be invested. The surplus product is made up of real resources, such as bricks, steel, grain, or whatever, available for investing. They may be invested by corporations, by individuals, or by the government.

Real resources for investment could come out of the surplus of other countries. If ships bring to our ports more goods than they carry out of the country, then that excess is also available for investment. Why? Because the surplus available in the United States has been increased (and some other nation's surplus decreased).

A very important conclusion follows: The amount of investment in the United States or any single country is not limited by the amount of saving done by people in the United States. *Saving* equals the difference between how much is produced (net product) and how much is consumed. It may be larger or smaller than the amount of investment. Because investments may be made anywhere in the world, a country may invest considerably more than it saves or considerably less; whether investments are greater or less than savings depends on where the surplus produced in that country is invested and where other countries' surpluses are invested.

A familiar example may make this clear. Imagine that (as in Chapter 3) our economy has only one product, grain, which is used both as a consumer good (food) and as a capital good (food for draft animals, seeds). Suppose that 100 bushels of grain are produced in one year, and 60 bushels are consumed by the producers, while 10 are used to feed the draft animals and to replace the seeds used up last year (depreciation). The surplus is then 30 bushels.

How will the surplus be used? Some of it—say 10 bushels—will be consumed by the owners of the land or perhaps used by the government to support an army and a police force. What of the other 20 bushels? Will it be used for net investment (planting more and raising a larger stock of draft animals)? It might, but some of it might also be used to plant and cultivate crops in other countries, leaving our country with less than 20 bushels of net investment. Or the surplus from other countries could be invested in our country, giving it more than 20 bushels of net investment.

Savings is the amount of resources out of the surplus product that are available for investment.

☐ Profits and Investment

Why do people invest? In the above hypothetical example, the investment (more planting) could have been controlled by the landowners, by the workers, by the government, or by some other group. Each would have had different reasons for making the investments, and each group might have chosen a different amount to invest. In every society, it matters greatly who controls investment, and why they invest.

Investment and the surplus product

In our economy, as in any capitalist economy, most investment is undertaken by capitalists and is done for the purpose of making profits. Capitalists control the investment-making process because they control (own) most of the surplus. How does this come about?

The surplus may be thought of in two ways—as a collection of things and as a sum of money. As a collection of things, it consists of tons of steel, bushels of grain, weapons, yachts, architects' plans, and the like. As a sum of money, it is profits, what is left over out of the capitalists' sales revenue after they have paid for productive inputs (labor, wear and tear on machines, materials, and so on). Some of this money surplus will, of course, be taxed away by the government. (We will consider government taxes and spending in Chapter 13.) The surplus product is purchased with the money surplus, when capitalists spend their profits.

Profits may be invested, but they need not be. Indeed, often they are not. What can capitalists do with their profits? Basically, six possible uses for profits exist, only one of which is investment in the U.S. economy:

Foreign investment is the use of some of the American surplus product to expand the capital goods used in foreign production.

1. Capitalists can invest their profits domestically, that is, in the United States.
2. They can increase their own consumption.
3. They can send the resources abroad to build factories elsewhere (foreign investment).
4. They can attempt to raise their profit rate through expenditures such as advertising or through political expenditures.
5. They can loan out their profits at interest.
6. They can use their profits to repay their existing debts, thus reducing their interest payments.

Some of these uses are summarized in Figure 11.2.

The decision to invest

How do capitalists decide how to use their profits? What influences their decision whether to invest or to consume and whether to invest in the United States or abroad? Capitalists invest for one overriding reason: the expectation of receiving a future profit. For no other reason will a business commit resources that could be consumed or used elsewhere. This is not evidence of greed or some other character defect in the capitalist. As we saw in Chapter 7, investing for profits is simply one of the rules of the game; businesses that invest for other reasons are sooner or later out of business. Because capitalists invest to make profits, the amount of

Uses of Profits by U.S. Firms	Example
1. Invest in United States	Honeywell builds a new plant in Minneapolis
2. Invest elsewhere	Atari builds an assembly plant in Asia
3. Consumption by owners of firm	Construction of 50-room homes in Palm Springs
4. Political expenditures and advertising	Mobil's public opinion advertising; lobbying to influence political leaders; TV commercials
5. Lend (at interest)	Exxon loans money in Eurodollar market
6. Repay existing debt	Chrysler pays back government-guaranteed loans

FIGURE 11.2 Investment and other uses of corporate profits. When a firm makes a profit, investing in the United States is only one of the many things it can do. Firms choose those uses of funds that they believe will yield the highest profit rate.

Political expenditures range from election campaign contributions to bribes to advertising to influence public opinion; all may have the objective of achieving more favorable treatment from the government (for example, getting lower taxes or relief from pollution-control laws). Neither advertising nor political expenditures constitute investments, because they do not increase the economy's productive capacity.

investment depends on how high businesses think the profit rate will be.

Capitalists considering making an investment must look to the *future* profit rate, because investment involves constructing new factories and purchasing machinery, materials, and other things that will be in existence for a long time. The capitalist is interested in how these new capital goods and materials will contribute to profits over the investments' entire lifetime, what the investments will cost, and what alternatives are available.

The expected profit rate. At the time that an investment is made, of course, the investor cannot know what the profit on the investment will actually turn out to be. The profit will be gained in the future, and no investor (despite the claims of many) can in fact foretell the future. So the investment is made on the basis of investors' predictions or expectations of what the (future) profit rate will be.

Summarizing the Determinants of the Expected Profit Rate

The expected profit rate, like the profit rate itself, depends on many things. The determinants of the expected profit rate can be grouped as follows:

1. the expected profit rate on utilized capital
2. the expected utilization rate

Expected profit rate = Expected profit rate on utilized capital (*expected ru*) × Expected utilization rate (*expected cu*)

Cost Conditions Affecting Investment:

expected output price (*Pz*)

expected work done per hour (*d*)

expected output per work done (*e*)

expected materials input (*m*)

expected price of materials input (*Pm*)

expected tax on profits (*tax*)

expected value of utilized capital goods per worker (*k in use*)

Demand Conditions Affecting Investment:

expected capacity utilization (*cu*)

expected output price (*Pz*)

Note: the effect of taxes is considered in Chapter 13.

What things influence investors' expectations? Here, two elements enter:

1. Capitalists' expectations of what the future profit rate will be on that portion of their capital goods that will be employed in production
2. Capitalists' expectations of what proportion of their capital goods will actually be employed

The *expected profit rate* is simply the product of these two terms. Thus:

The **expected profit rate** is the profit rate that capitalists believe will exist in the future; it is composed of two parts: the expected profit rate on that portion of the capital goods that will be in use; and the expected utilization rate.

Expected profit rate = Expected profit rate on that portion of the capital goods that will be in use × Fraction of the capital goods expected to be in use   (11.1)

or

expected r = (*expected ru*) × (*expected cu*)

Suppose for example, that a capitalist expects (predicts) that the profit rate on the capital goods in use will be 15 percent but that only two-thirds of his capital goods will be used, the remainder being idle due to insufficient demand for the product; the expected profit rate will then be 10 percent.

Here then are two quite different factors affecting the expected profit rate. The first, the expected profit rate on the capital that will be employed, takes into account all aspects, both known and only guessed, associated with buying inputs and producing the output. What will the raw materials or energy input prices be? What will the unit labor costs be? What technologies will be used? And so on. (Figure 6.2 on page 125 summarizes these determinants.) These things that influence the expected profit rate on the capital actually in use are called the *cost conditions affecting investment*.

The second factor affecting the expected profit rate is the fraction of total invested capital that investors think will actually be used in production, or the *expected capacity utilization rate (expected cu)*. Of course, investors must wonder whether the economy will be booming and there will be many buyers with a lot of income to spend when the new factory (or other productive capacity represented by the investment) opens. If so, they will probably find customers for everything they can produce, and they will fully employ their capital goods. The fraction of the total capital goods in use, or capacity utilization (*cu*), will be high, and this will tend to raise the profit rate. If not, however, and there is recession or hard times when the new factory or other investment goes into operation, there will not be enough customer dollars to buy everything that can be produced; some of the new machines may sit idle, waiting for better times and more customers for the product. As a result, *cu* will be low, and the profit rate depressed. Those things that influence how much of all capital will be utilized are called the *demand conditions affecting investment*.

While the cost conditions and the demand conditions affecting investment are distinct and refer to different aspects of the profit-making process, they influence each other. If demand conditions are good, for example, cost conditions are likely to be bad. Why? Because a high level of demand for products means a high demand for labor and low unemployment; and, as we saw in Chapter 8, when unemployment is low, we may expect workers' bargaining power to rise. This may have the effect of raising wages (*w*) or lowering the amount of work done (*d*), thus worsening the cost conditions affecting investment (by lowering *expected ru*).

Similarly, it is easy to see that some of the things that would improve the cost conditions affecting investment will have just the opposite effect on the demand conditions affecting it. For example, if all or many firms manage to lower their wages, their cost con-

The **expected profit rate on capital goods that will be in use** is the profit rate that capitalists believe will exist on that portion of their "machines" that will be utilized.

The **cost conditions affecting investment** are those things that affect the expected profit rate on capital goods that will be in use; some of the most important are the labor cost index and the prices of the inputs to production.

The **expected capacity utilization ratio** is the utilization ratio that capitalists believe will exist in the future; it is the percentage of all capital goods that capitalists believe will be in use.

The **demand conditions affecting investment** are those things that affect the expected utilization ratio; the most important of these is whether capitalists expect the economy to be booming or to experience hard times.

Pushing on a String

If the government cuts business taxes or does other things to raise the after-tax profit rate, will this stimulate investment? It might, but some economists say that trying to stimulate investment by giving money to corporations is like pushing on a string.

The automobile industry provides a striking illustration. Profits have increased greatly since the Reagan tax program cut corporate income taxes, and the United Auto Workers union made major wage concessions. It was hoped that the result would be an investment boom. The company profits that would be plowed back into investment, it was hoped, would not only help modernize the industry, but would also allow the 250,000 auto workers on layoff in the early 1980s to return to their jobs.

The *Wall Street Journal* published two articles about the auto industry on the same day in early 1984. The first was headlined: "Firm Profits soared 64% in Fourth Quarter . . . Auto Makers Had Big Swing From Red to Black Ink . . . More Strong Gains Forecast." Apparently the first part of the reinvestment game plan was working.

The second article told the bad news: "GM Weighing More Big Cuts in Work Force . . . Reduction of up to 120,000 People Possible in Next 2½ Years."

There was more bad news in the annual reports of the major companies. General Motors, for example, made record profits in 1983; but it invested so little in building new plants and in equipment that the investment did not even keep up with the wear and tear on its existing facilities. Between the beginning and the end of 1983, GM's stock of productive equipment and buildings deteriorated in value by $2.3 billion.

What went wrong?

The major companies did not lack money to invest. But they did not put their money into building new plants and modernizing old ones. During 1983, GM increased its holdings of cash and government securities by over $3 billion. A May 1984 *New York Times* article noted, "We are now witnessing one of the biggest cash buildups in corporate history." It was expected that GM would end 1984 with $15 billion worth of cash, enough to rebuild and retool every plant it owns with the most up-to-date technology available, if it were spent on new plants or modernization. But it will not be.

What the auto companies lacked was confidence in the future growth in the demand for cars and trucks. Competition from imported cars was not the only problem. A major reason for the auto companies' pessimism about the future demand for their products was the slow growth in the income of the average American family. Another *Wall Street Journal* article analyzing this problem pointed out that in 1973—a record year for car sales—it took the average production worker 28 weeks of work to earn enough wages to buy the average car sold in the United States that year. In 1983, it took 38 weeks.

People who are feeling pinched financially do not buy new cars; those who buy are often the relatively few who are feeling well-off. The average income of the family who bought a new car in 1983 was $40,000, almost twice what the average family makes. The hottest-selling car in 1983 was no longer the economical Ford Escort, but the up-market Oldsmobile Cutlass Supreme.

The wage concessions and tax cuts that helped the owners of the auto companies make record profits failed to modernize the industry and put auto workers back to work. The reason: the logic behind the tax cuts and the wage concessions paid attention to the cost conditions affecting investment, but it ignored the demand conditions affecting investment. But both must be favorable for investment to take place.

It's hard to make things happen when you are pushing on a string.

Sources: *Wall Street Journal*, February 21, 1984, and May 3, 1984; *New York Times*, May 27, 1984; General Motors Corporation, *Annual Report*.

ditions will have improved (unless d also falls), but their demand conditions will probably have worsened. Why? Because the demand for what firms produce depends on people (workers) having enough income to buy the goods, and wages are by far the largest source of people's incomes. In this case, a general reduction in wages may worsen the expected profit rate and lead to a reduction in investment.

Achieving a high level of investment requires that the economy strike a balance between favorable cost conditions and favorable demand conditions. When this is done, large amounts of investment take place (by both U.S. and non-U.S. companies). When either the demand or cost conditions are very unfavorable, little investment will take place; the profits made by firms in the United States will be spent on investment in other countries or on luxury consumption. Unfavorable demand conditions seem to be an important reason why investment was so low during the early 1980s, for example.

Let us go one step further. We have found that investment depends on the expected profit rate. That in turn depends on the expected profit rate on the utilized capital and on the expected capacity utilization rate. The next step, then, is to see how capitalists make their predictions about the capacity utilization rate and the profit rate on utilized capital.

Let us start with what affects investor expectations of future profits on utilized capital. Of course many factors may influence each individual investor, and each investor may be different. Nonetheless, one factor is without question by far the most important—*current* (and *recent*) *profits*.

Future profits, by definition, cannot be known, but potential investors do know how high the profit rate was last week or last month or last year. Not surprisingly, if capitalists last year earned big profits, they may think that next year will be the same; if last year was a poor year, they may fear that next year will be no better. So although what capitalists really want to know is what profits will be *next* year, the thing they do know is what the profit rate is *currently.* On this basis they must predict the future.

Now let us turn to the proportion of invested capital that capitalists think they will use. Again, many things may influence each individual investor, but in general we can expect one factor to dominate—the present or recent past. If times have been good and markets booming, capacity utilization (*cu*) will be high, and investors may expect the same in the future. If times have been bad and a lot of plants and equipment have been sitting idle (low *cu*), investors are likely to fear continuation of that situation.

The present capacity utilization rate (*cu*) affects investment in two important ways. First, capitalists base their expectation of future *cu* in part on present *cu*. And second, capitalists are not likely to build new capacity—that is, to invest—if they already own productive capacity that is lying idle. With low levels of capacity utilization, a capitalist realizes that even if an increase in demand occurs, production can readily be expanded without additional investment just by putting the idle machines to work.

Other factors. The amount of investment capitalists make in the U.S. economy does not depend on the expected U.S. profit rate alone. It depends as well on two other things: the expected profit rates in other parts of the world and the interest rates in the United States and elsewhere. We now take up these new determinants of investment.

☐ Accumulation in the World Capitalist System

The **expected profit rate in the United States** is the profit rate that capitalists believe will exist on investments in U.S.-based labor processes.

The **expected profit rate in the rest of the world** is the profit rate that capitalists believe will exist on investments in labor processes located outside the United States.

How much gets invested in the United States depends not only on the *expected profit rate in the United States,* but also on the *expected profit rate in the rest of the world.*

Why does investment in the United States depend on profit rates elsewhere? Because American businesses, especially the core corporations, usually have the opportunity to invest in other countries also; they will invest abroad if the expected profit rate there is higher than it is in the United States. To ensure access to the growing Mexican market, for example, in late 1982 Hewlett Packard opened a computer plant in Guadalajara, Mexico. Attracted by low-wage labor, Atari in 1983 moved its assembly of video games and home computers to Hong Kong. On a grander scale, the Ford Motor Company builds cars and car parts in plants in 28 countries on 6 continents. It makes as many automobiles outside the United States as in the United States, deciding where to produce on the basis of where the profits are higher, as determined by computers at Ford's international control center at Dearborn, Michigan. New plants are constructed and other investments made when existing plant capacity at a particular location cannot handle the levels of output dictated by Ford's global profit-maximizing plan.

Profits received from investments abroad make up an important part of most corporations' total profits. Ford made 49 percent of its profits abroad in 1978; IBM made 50 percent; General Electric, 22 percent; and ITT, 39 percent. In the early 1980s, all corporations derived about one-fifth, on average, of their total after-tax corporate profits from foreign investments.

Similarly, businesses in other countries—say, in Germany or Japan—may decide to invest in the United States rather than in their own countries if they come to the conclusion that profits will be higher in the United States than at home. For example, both Volkswagen and Honda built plants in the United States during the past decade.

Capitalists may sometimes speak as patriotic nationalists. But they invest as *inter*nationalists, with little consideration for national boundaries or national interests unless such considerations affect their expected profit rates.

Let us call expected future profits earned in the United States *U.S. profits* and expected future profits on investments made any place other than the United States *non-U.S.* The expected profit rate in the rest of the world (non-U.S.) depends on factors similar to those that affect the profit rate in the United States. For instance, the expected non-U.S. profit rate depends on the expected capacity utilization rate abroad and on the expected profit rate on foreign capital that is utilized. But the economic, political, and other influences that affect these profit-rate determinants will differ among countries. If incomes are growing rapidly in some country, demand conditions are likely to be very favorable. If another country has a severe shortage of skilled labor, cost conditions there may be very unfavorable. If labor unions are illegal in a country, unit labor costs may be lower and profits higher, and so on.

Thus investment in the United States depends on how high the expected future profit rate in the U.S. is, compared to the expected future profit rate in other parts of the world—or on what is called the *relative expected U.S. profit rate.*

Figure 11.3 summarizes this relationship. When the relative expected U.S. profit rate is high, more U.S. and non-U.S. investors will want to invest in the United States and each investor may

The **relative expected U.S. profit rate** is the profit rate that capitalists believe will exist on investments in U.S.-based labor processes *as compared to* (divided by) the profit rate that capitalists believe will exist on investments in labor processes located elsewhere.

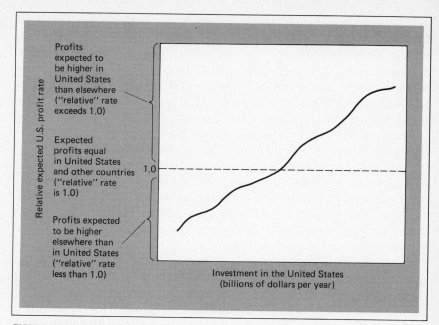

FIGURE 11.3 Domestic investment and world profit rates. The level of investment in the United States depends on the expected future profit rate in the United States as compared to the expected future profit rate in other countries. Both U.S. and foreign firms can invest in the United States, and they will watch the relative expected U.S. profit rate. The chart above shows that the higher the relative expected U.S. profit rate, the more investment will be undertaken in the United States. The level of investment in the United States will also depend on the interest rate, since it affects the cost of borrowing money to make the investments.

want to make bigger investments. When the relative expected U.S. profit rate is low, fewer capitalists will want to invest and each capitalist may want to make smaller investments. So investment in the United States rises when the relative expected U.S. profit rate rises and falls when the relative expected U.S. profit rate falls.

The level of investment also depends on the *interest rate*. As we saw in Chapter 7 the interest rate (i) is simply how much it costs to rent (borrow) money. When a business is considering making an investment, it may need to borrow money from a bank in order to finance the purchase of the new factory, materials, or other goods. The loan will be paid back after the new equipment is in place and in operation. When an investment is financed by borrowing, the interest rate will affect the total cost of buying whatever is needed to make the investment: The higher the interest rate, the more costly the investment and the less attractive it will be to an investor.

We also saw in Chapter 7 that interest rates may influence investment in another way. If the interest rate is very high—higher than the profit rate, for example—a company will decide not to borrow money to finance the investment; it may decide not to invest at all, but rather to take advantage of the high interest rates and use profits to *loan* out money to other businesses, to individuals, or to the government. This illustrates that the interest rate is not only a cost to the prospective investor; it is also an opportunity to make money without investing in real capital goods.

Just as with profit rates, it is not the U.S. interest rate alone that matters, for large corporations can borrow or lend money throughout the world with the ease that it takes a computer to record the transaction. Because the interest rate represents both a cost and a moneymaking opportunity to the potential investor, the level of investment depends on interest throughout the world.

To summarize: The level of investment in the U.S. will be *higher*

the *higher* is the expected profit rate in the United States
the *lower* are profit rates in other parts of the world
the *lower* are interest rates throughout the world

Figure 11.4 summarizes all these factors to show how the amount of investment in the United States is determined. Starting from the left, the determinants of the (current) profit rate are grouped, as in the box on page 133, into two parts—the present capacity utilization rate and the profit rate on the capital goods in use. The present (and recent past) rate of capacity utilization then determines the expected rate of utilization; and the present (and recent past) profit rate on utilized capital determines the expected profit rate on capital that will be utilized. These two—the expected capacity utilization rate and the expected profit rate on utilized capital—determine the expected future profit rate. And the expected future profit rate compared to expected profit rates and interest rates in the rest of the world determines the amount of investment in the U.S.

☐ Employment and Output

We have already seen that the level of investment is a major determinant of the level of total demand for goods and services. For this reason it is also a major determinant of the level of total output and of total employment. We will first consider how total output is determined.

Total demand determines the amount of capital goods to be used. In the short run, assuming the output/capital ratio to be constant, the amount of capital goods used determines the amount of output (goods and services) actually produced.

The first step is that the demand for goods and services deter-

What Determines the Interest Rate?

The interest rate (i) is simply the price of renting money. If the interest rate is 10 percent per year, the borrower who borrowed $100 must pay back $110 at the end of the year. $10 is the annual rent on $100.

There is no single interest rate but many, depending on the length of the loan, the purpose of it, and who the borrower is. But because all the interest rates tend to go up and down together, we will analyze an average interest rate.

Very simply put, the (average) interest rate is determined by supply and demand, as are other prices. The relevant supply is the supply of money to lend, or what is called the *supply of loanable funds*. The demand in question is the *demand for loanable funds*. The interest rate is thus determined by how much money individuals, corporations, and the government want to borrow, and how much individuals, businesses, and the government want to lend.

The graph below shows how the demand for loanable funds and supply of loanable funds interact to determine the interest rate. The demand-for-loanable-funds curve indicates for each interest rate how much money all the potential borrowers want to borrow. Thus, for example, if the interest rate is (b) borrowers want to borrow a total of *OD* dollars. The demand for loanable funds stems from many different sources: consumers wanting to buy a car on time or to buy a house (that is, get a mortgage); businesses wanting to borrow to make an investment such as building a new plant, buying land for speculative purposes, or buying another company or simply to have enough money on hand to do business; governments (state, local, and federal) wanting to borrow to be able to spend more than they take in in taxes (when they run a deficit). If the interest rate is low, the demand for loanable funds will be higher, as is indicated by the fact that the demand curve slopes downward to the right.

The supply-of-loanable-funds curve is also indicated in the graph. It should be read the same way as the demand-for-loanable-funds curve. If the interest rate is b percent, individuals, businesses (including banks), and the government will want to lend a total *OS* dollars. If the interest rate is higher, they will want to lend more, so the supply curve slopes upward to the right.

The borrowers and lenders need not be U.S. citizens, businesses, or governments; they may be from anywhere in the world. Thus the supply of loanable funds (as well as the demand) is not determined solely by what happens within the United States. For example, if the rate of interest is low in the United States, many foreign borrowers may choose to borrow money in the United States rather than in their own countries. This would increase the demand for loanable funds in the United States. On the other hand, when the interest rate is high in the United States, as it was during the early 1980s, foreign banks and other lenders from outside the country will want to lend money here, raising the supply of loanable funds in the United States.

A very important determinant of both the supply and demand of loanable funds is the monetary policy of the government. In the United States, the Federal Reserve System can make it easier or more difficult for banks and other lending institutions to loan money.

The supply and demand for loanable funds determines the interest rate in the following way. Let us say the interest rate is *b* and the demand for loanable funds is *OD*, while the supply is *OS*. Because *OD* is greater than *OS*, some borrowers will not get to borrow the amount they wanted at that rate. Noticing this unsatisfied demand, banks and other lending institutions will reason that they could have charged a higher rate. As they raise their rates, the supply of loanable funds will increase and the demand decrease. The interest rate will tend to rise to *c* percent, the level at which the amount demanded and the amount supplied are equal. At this point the market for loanable funds is said to have *cleared*, for there is neither excess supply nor excess demand.

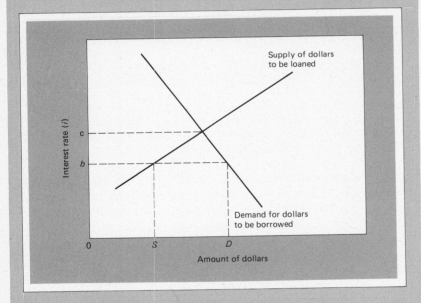

Many factors other than the interest rate will influence the supply and demand for loanable funds. Whether suppliers or demanders expect war or peace, political stability or instability, high or low inflation, or other changes will affect their willingness to loan or their eagerness to borrow money. When suppliers change their expectations about these matters, they *shift* their supply-of-loanable-funds curve; when demanders alter their expectations, they *shift* the demand curve.

In times of great uncertainty (during depressions, great political changes, wide fluctuations in foreign exchange markets, international speculation, and so forth) these factors may, by affecting expectations, play a prominent role in determining the interest rate.

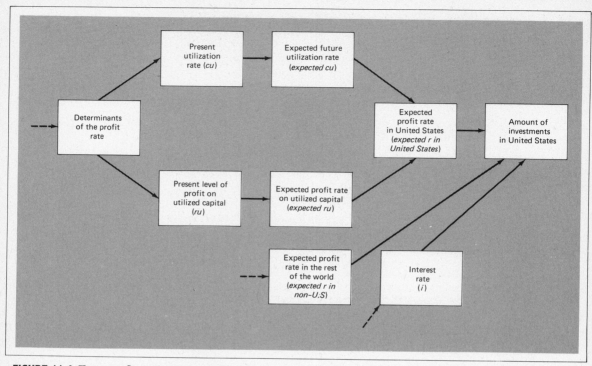

FIGURE 11.4 From profits to investment. The determinants of the profit rate set the current level of capacity utilization *(cu)* and the rate of profit on utilized capital *(ru)*. The two, *cu* and *ru*, then influence the expected future profit rate in the United States; this expected profit rate along with the expected profit rate in the rest of the world and the interest rate determine the amount of investment in the United States.

mines how much of the existing capital goods will be used. When businesses have few customers, they may find that it is most profitable to use only part of their facilities. When they have more customers and can sell a lot of goods, it may pay to utilize more of their capacity. The higher the total demand, the higher the level of capacity utilization *(cu)*, and the larger the *amount* of the capital goods *in use (CG in use)* will be. The total amount of capital goods *in existence* is *CG*—the tools, factories, offices, machines, stores, and so on already ready to use. The total available capital goods *(CG)* takes time to change. Most big investment projects, building new factories, for example, are completed years after the decision is made to invest. As a result, during any short period of time it is reasonable to assume that the amount of capital goods in existence does not change very much.

If the amount of machines and other capital goods *in existence (CG)* is assumed to be constant and if the prices of capital goods *(Pc)* can also be assumed to be constant, then the *value* of the capital goods in existence *(K)* is also given.

To see how total demand determines the extent to which available capital goods are used, note that K *in use* $= (cu)(K)$. Since K is fixed in the short run and since total demand determines cu, we can easily see that total demand also determines K *in use*.

For example, suppose the economy produces only grain and the entire capital stock consists of three fields. Each field (together with its tools, machinery, and so on) represents an investment of $1 million. However, because of the currently depressed demand conditions, only two fields are being worked and the third is idle. Then

Value of total owned capital goods (K) = $3 million
Capacity utilization rate (cu) = ⅔
Utilized capital $(K$ *in use*$)$ = $2 million

The second step is that cu determines the total output of goods and services. Total output is simply capital goods in use (K *in use*) times the average amount of goods and services produced per dollar of capital goods in use, or the output/capital ratio

$$Y = (K \text{ in use}) \left(\frac{Y}{K \text{ in use}}\right) \qquad (11.2)$$

or

$$Y = (cu)\,(K) \left(\frac{Y}{K \text{ in use}}\right)$$

Labor Hours and Jobs

In the short run, total demand for goods and services determines *Labor*, the number of labor hours that employers will seek to buy. How is *Labor* related to *jobs*?

For example, suppose the nation's employers wish to buy 200 billion labor hours this year. How many jobs does that create?

If each job were to be a full-time, year-round job—say 8 hours per day for 5 days per week for 50 weeks a year, or 2000 labor hours per year—then we could calculate jobs as follows:

$$\text{Jobs} = \frac{Labor}{2000} = \frac{200 \text{ billion labor hours}}{2000 \text{ hours per job}} = 100 \text{ million jobs}$$

This calculation would also work if *part*-time work in some jobs exactly offset *overtime* work in other jobs. (Otherwise the computation is more complex but the idea is the same.)

One strategy to create more jobs is to reduce the average work week, say to 35 hours per week instead of 40. If total hours demanded (*Labor*) remained unchanged, then a shorter work week would create (in the example above) 8 million new jobs.

$$\text{Jobs} = \frac{Labor}{1850} = \frac{200 \text{ billion labor hours}}{1850 \text{ hours per job}} = 108 \text{ million jobs}$$

In the short run, we assume that the output/capital ratio, Y/K *in use*, and the value of capital goods, K, do not change, so once *cu* is determined by the level of demand, the rest is simple. Total output is simply the output/capital ratio times the value of capital in use.

To continue the example of the three-field grain economy, suppose that each field produces 400,000 bushels of grain, each bushel sells for $1, so a total value of $400,000 per field per year is produced.

Then

$$\text{utilized capital, } K \text{ in use } = \$2,000,000$$
$$\text{output/capital ratio, } \quad = \frac{\$\ 400,000}{\$1,000,000} = .4$$
$$Y/(K \text{ in use})$$

and total output is just

$$Y = (\$2 \text{ million}) (0.4) \quad = \$\ 800,000$$

The third step is that the total amount of employment is determined in a manner similar to how output is determined. The labor/capital ratio—*Labor/K in use*—can be taken to be constant in the short run; this means that once employers have determined how many capital goods to use (K *in use*), there will be a certain number of workers needed to operate these capital goods. So once the demand for goods and services has determined the amount of capital goods in use, this will also determine the total demand (by employers) for labor.

The *demand for labor* determines how many jobs (or labor hours of employment) employers will have. Why is this? Why is the total amount of employment not also determined by the *supply of labor*? Labor demand determines employment because the supply of labor (people looking for jobs) is almost always greater than the demand, so there is always some unemployment. It is not the suppliers of labor time (workers and prospective workers), but the demanders (the employers) who determine how many jobs there will be, because of course it is employers who own the capital goods and make the decisions about how many people to hire.

We may summarize the determination of total employment by saying that total demand for labor time is equal to the utilized capital goods times the labor/capital ratio, and total employment is equal to total demand for labor time, or

$$\text{Total demand for labor } (LD) = (K \text{ in use}) (Labor/K \text{ in use}) \quad (8.3)$$
$$= \text{Total employment}$$
$$= Labor$$

Labor demand is the schedule or list showing, for each wage, the amount of labor time (total hours) that would be hired by employers in response to that wage.
Labor supply is the schedule or list showing, for each wage, the amount of labor time (total hours) that would be offered by workers in response to that wage.

For instance, in our three-field grain economy, the value of capital goods in use is $2 million. Suppose each worker uses a machine and land together worth $20,000.

Then

$$\text{Labor/Capital Ratio} = \frac{Labor}{K \text{ in use}} = \frac{1 \text{ worker}}{\$20,000 \text{ in capital goods}}$$

and

$$\text{Employment} = Labor = \left(\frac{Labor}{K \text{ in use}}\right)(K \text{ in use})$$
$$= (1 \text{ worker}/\$20,000 \text{ capital})(\$2 \text{ million})$$
$$= 100 \text{ workers}$$

So a total of 100 workers will find jobs. (The basic structure of how total employment and output are determined is summarized in Figure 11.5.)

☐ Unemployment and the Paradox of Wage Cutting

We have now seen how much employment there will be. But how much *unemployment* will there be? President Calvin Coolidge's theory of unemployment was simple (and not quite as simple-minded as some more recent official ideas on the subject). "When people are laid off," Coolidge reasoned, "the result is unemployment." More generally, unemployment results when employers hire fewer workers than there are people seeking work—labor supply exceeds labor demand. Figure 11.6 shows how unemployment is determined. Along the top of Figure 11.6 we see the determinants of labor supply—population and the labor force participation rate. The *labor force participation rate (LFPR)* is the name given to the percentage of the population that is working or trying to find work; it is the proportion of the total population willing to supply labor (to "participate" in the labor force). This percentage will be lower the longer people stay in school and the earlier workers retire, for instance, since these factors increase the number of students and retired people not looking for jobs and reduce the percentage of the population who are working or looking for work. On the other hand, as larger numbers of women seek wage jobs, the participation rate goes up. Together, the size of the population and the labor force participation rate determine the labor supply.

Let us be a bit more precise about labor supply (*LS*) and labor

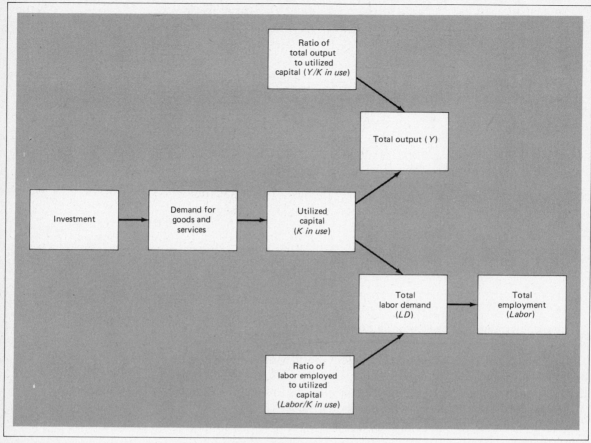

FIGURE 11.5 From investment to output and employment. Investment is a major determinant of the level of demand for goods and services. The level of demand determines how much of the existing capital goods will be utilized. The capacity utilization in turn determines both the amount of labor hired and the amount of output produced.

demand (*LD*). Labor supply is simply the population times the participation rate:

$$LS = (\text{population}) \cdot (LFPR) \qquad (11.4)$$

Labor supply will grow as population grows and/or as the participation rate increases.

Labor demanded (*LD*), as we have seen, is given by the value of capital in use (*K in use*) multiplied by the labor/capital ratio (*Labor/K in use*).

Why then do we have unemployment? Why is *LD* generally less than *LS*? Or rather, why would we ever expect to have full employment, or labor supply equal to labor demand?

The supply of labor is determined by one set of forces operating

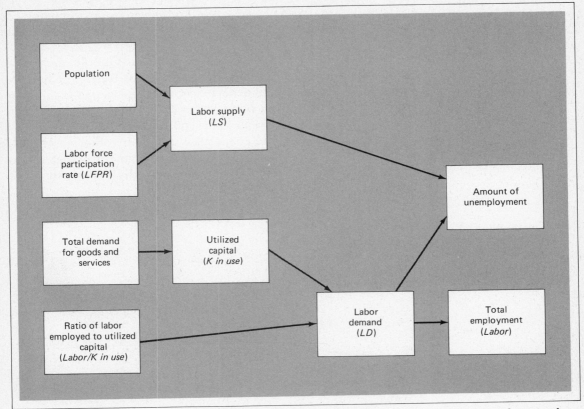

FIGURE 11.6 From employment to unemployment. Labor demand and labor supply are determined separately. Labor demand depends on the total demand for goods and services, while labor supply depends on the size of the population and the percentage of people who are seeking employment. Labor supply generally exceeds labor demand, giving rise to unemployment.

on families, workers, and potential workers, leading them to look for a certain amount of work outside the home. The demand for labor in the capitalist economy is determined by an entirely different set of forces operating upon employers and influencing their idea of the expected profit rate and their desired levels of production. It would be quite coincidental if the results of these two separate sets of determinants—one of labor supply and the other of labor demand—produced the same number of people looking for work as there were jobs being offered by employers.

Some economists have argued that when labor supply exceeds labor demand the price in this market (the wage) will fall until supply equals demand, thus eliminating unemployment. This would certainly be the case in many other markets. An excess supply of milk, for example, would lead to a fall in the price of milk, which would both increase the demand for milk and reduce the supply (by discouraging some producers from producing so much milk, and perhaps stimulating production of butter or steaks instead).

The idea that cutting the wage will increase employment and eventually eliminate unemployment also seems sensible when we consider our own personal experience. If, when you go looking for a job, you ask for $13 an hour, you may not find one; but if you were ready to settle for $3 an hour, you probably will.

For these reasons, some economists and many other people believe that the only reason we have unemployment is that wages are too high. Unions or the government or individual workers are

---

Growth of Labor Supply and Labor Demand

The rate at which labor supply (LS) grows is the sum of the growth rate of population and the labor force participation rate:

(% increase in LS) = (% increase in population)

(% increase in $LFPR$)

For example, suppose that the population is 100 and $LFPR$ is .80; then LS is 80 workers ($100 \times .80$). Now let the population grow by 2 percent and the participation rate grow by 5 percent. The labor supply will grow by 7 percent.

Similarly, the rate at which labor demand grows is the sum of the growth rates of utilized capital and the labor/capital ratio:

(% increase in LD) = (% increase in K in use)

(% increase in Labor/K in use)

(Try, for example, K in use = $1000 and Labor/K in use = .05; then let K in use increase by 5 percent and Labor/K in use grow by 1 percent. How much does LD grow?)

Now we can see the unemployment problem:

Unemployment = Labor Supply (LS) − Labor Demand (LD)

For unemployment not to grow worse, then, it must be the case that

(% increase in population) + (% increase in $LFPR$)

is less than or equal to

(% increase in K in use) + (% increase in Labor/K in use)

The private economy provides no mechanism to make sure this happens. For example, between 1973 and 1975 the percentage increase in population was 1.5; in the $LFPR$, 0.7; this led to an increase in labor supply of 2.2 percent. On the other hand, K in use declined; this produced a decline in labor demand of 1.4 percent. The result was an increase in the unemployment rate of 3.6 percent (that is, 2.2 percent plus 1.4 percent) from 4.9 percent in 1973 to 8.5 percent in 1975.

blamed for being unwilling to see wages cut, and as a result, we have unemployment. Unemployment, according to this view, is voluntary, for it could be eliminated if workers would be only willing to work for less. To investigate this idea that unemployment is voluntary, let us see what happens if we drop our earlier assumption that prices and wages are constant and let the wage rate vary.

The idea that cutting wages will necessarily eliminate unemployment is incorrect. It is based on the false notion that the labor market is just like other markets, and the false inference that what is true for a single worker looking for a job is true for all workers taken as a whole.

The idea that wage cutting will achieve full employment ignores *the paradox of wage cutting*. While being willing to work for a lower wage may help *one* worker get a job, if *all* workers get paid less the result is as likely to increase unemployment as to decrease it. This paradox exists because, as we shall see in detail shortly, a fall in the wages of all workers may well result in less consumer spending (because workers will be poorer) and hence in a worsening of the expected demand conditions facing capitalists. If demand conditions affecting investment deteriorate, there may be a reduction in investment and employment. Let us consider this reasoning in detail.

We have already seen in Chapter 8 that the labor market is quite different from other markets. To review:

1. The demand for labor depends on capitalists' expectations to make a profit.
2. Their ability to make a profit depends on their power over labor.
3. Their power over labor depends on unemployment putting workers in a weak bargaining position.

Therefore, a situation of no unemployment (no excess supply of labor) cannot be an equilibrium of the labor market. In this, the labor market is very much unlike other markets such as the milk market. In the milk market, an excess supply indicates that the market is not in equilibrium, whereas in the labor market *no* excess supply indicates that the market is not in equilibrium.

The difference between labor markets and other markets that we discussed in Chapter 8 is based on the relationship between unemployment and the power of employers over workers. But there is another difference between the labor market and other markets. It has to do with the connection between the wage rate and the total demand for goods and services.

The demand for labor time by employers is called a *derived* demand; this is because it depends on (or is derived from) the demand for the commodities produced by labor in the profit-making process. Firms buy labor time because they anticipate that they will be able to sell the commodities at a profitable price. Their ability to do so, of course, depends on the demand for these commodities by consumers, other businesses, or the government.

The demand for commodities depends on many things, but by far the most important is how much income people have to buy commodities. For most people, the wage (or salary) is the main source of income. How much income people have thus depends critically on the wage rate. So when firms are thinking of sales, they would like wages to be high; and when they are thinking about buying the inputs for the production process, they would like wages to be low. In each capitalist's dream world, all other capitalists pay their workers high wages whereas he gets his own workers to work for free!

We may summarize this by saying that the wage enters into the process of capitalist profit-making not once, but twice: first as a *cost of production* and second as a *source of demand* for the produced commodities. As a source of demand it affects both the price at which the commodities can be sold and the percentage of capital goods owned by the capitalist that will actually be in use rather than be idle. We can now see if cutting wages will reduce unemployment, using the familiar supply-and-demand graph applied to the whole labor market (see Figure 11.7). LS is the labor supply. LD_1 is the demand curve for labor. The labor demand slopes downward to the right. Like other demand curves, this one is drawn assuming that other things are "held constant." Among the other things held constant is the total demand for goods and services. Thus the downward slope of LD_1 indicates that *if* the demand for commodities in general is not altered, a lower wage will induce employers to hire more labor—a big *if*, as we shall soon see.

Suppose that to start the wage is w; the amount supplied (on the supply curve, at w) is s; and the amount demanded by employers, as we shall see from the LD_1 demand curve, is l. The level of unemployment, then, is $s - l$. Now consider what happens if the wage is cut to w'. Will this reduce the amount of unemployment? There is no reason to think that it will; the most that can be said is that it *might*. The key to understanding why is the distinction—basic to supply-and-demand analysis—between a *movement along* a demand curve, describing how a change in the price affects a change in the amount demanded when all other influences on demand are held constant; and a *shift* in the demand curve, which results from a *change* in one of these influences that had been held constant.

The lower wage will make it more attractive to hire labor so long as firms can be sure of selling their output. It will improve the cost

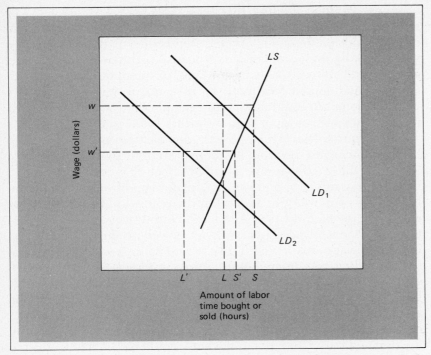

FIGURE 11.7 The market for labor time. The labor supply curve is *LS*. Its upward slope indicates that at higher wages more people will seek employment for more hours. Labor demand is originally *LD₁*. The downward slope of *LD₁* indicates that, at lower wages, employers will find it cheaper to organize production using more labor and fewer machines. Both curves are drawn on the assumption that other things are held constant. The labor demand curve is drawn assuming that the level of total demand for goods and services is at a given level.

At the wage w, unemployment (excess supply) is $s - l$. *If neither curve shifts,* a cut in wages will increase the amount of labor demanded and decrease the excess supply. But because wages are such a large element in people's income, a cut in wages, say from w to w', may well reduce total demand for goods and services, leading to a leftward shift in the demand curve to *LD₂*. Unemployment is now $s' - l'$, greater than before. If a cut in wages leads capitalists to have very favorable expectations of future profits, this expectation might stimulate investment to such an extent that the increased demand for investment goods would offset the decrease in workers' demands for consumption goods.

conditions affecting investment, encouraging capitalists to increase their investment. By lowering costs it may also increase the ability of firms to sell their products abroad. Both of these effects are described as movements *along* the demand curve and will tend to increase total demand for goods and services and hence to increase the demand for labor.

But the effect of the lower wage will also be to lower workers' incomes. Workers, finding that they now have less money, will reduce their purchases of commodities. Stores will be left with unsold goods on their shelves, and storekeepers will be compelled to cut back on their orders for new goods. As the demand for goods falls, capitalists will have to cut back on production and lay off workers. As demand conditions for investment worsen, capitalists will decide not to build new factories and other production capacity. The demand for labor will be further reduced as a result.

This negative effect on employers' demands for labor is indicated by the downward *shift* in the demand curve from LD_1 to LD_2. Which of these effects—the positive effect of lower labor cost or the negative effect of worsening demand conditions—will be the larger? We cannot say, in general. If the real world is like the quite realistic case picture in Figure 11.7, cutting wages will *increase* unemployment. It need not work out as indicated in the figure. If, when the wage was lowered, the reduction in workers' consumption spending was immediately offset by increased consumption spending of capitalists, or by their purchases of additional materials for production, or by the building of new factories, there would be a change in *which* commodities were demanded (away from necessities and toward luxuries and materials and capital goods), but the demand curve for labor as a whole would not be much affected and might even shift upward. Workers producing necessities would have been laid off and would eventually have found jobs producing luxury goods, materials, and capital goods. But there is no reason to expect that this instantaneous and fully compensating change in the decisions of capitalists will take place. It does not generally happen. Reducing wages may or may not reduce unemployment; we cannot be sure. Sometimes it will; other times it will not.

The supply curve in Figure 11.7 is very steep (or what is termed *inelastic*). A steep supply curve indicates that for all workers taken as a whole, lower wages do not much reduce the hours supplied on the labor market. A steep or inelastic labor supply curve will make it more likely that wage-cutting will not reduce unemployment; however, the paradox of wage-cutting does not depend on it.

Why might the labor supply curve be steep? If one company or industry offers lower wages for a given type of labor, those workers will certainly find employment elsewhere if they possibly can. But if wages are low everywhere, in most or all firms, workers will have to supply labor hours to *some* employer, because they depend on the sale of labor time to maintain themselves and their families. Indeed, the labor-hours supply curve might be vertical, or even backward bending, and a good case can be made that lower (real) wages force more people into the labor market, as probably happened during the 1970s and early 1980s. Since the early 1970s, after-tax real wages have *fallen*, but labor force participation rates have risen significantly, leading to a substantial increase in labor supply.

Here we see one of the ways in which the labor market is unlike other markets. If labor time were just like a commodity, offered to the market only to make a profit, and if households were companies whose survival depended on making profits, a fall in the price of labor time would encourage households to produce and sell something else instead—the labor-supply curve would be *elastic*. But this is not the case; most households have only labor to depend on for getting an adequate income; they cannot switch to something else when the price of labor (the wage) falls. So the steep labor-hours supply curve is quite realistic.

If lower wages could just as well increase as decrease unemployment, it is obviously nonsensical to argue that involuntary unemployment is caused by too-high wages. It did, however, make sense to say that an excess supply of T-shirts was caused by a too-high T-shirt price. Why are these markets—commodity markets and labor markets—so different in this respect? There is one fundamental difference, and one additional difference.

The first and most important difference is that when the wage was reduced, the demand curve shifted as a result. Now it is true that in a market for a commodity—T-shirts, or drill presses, or beer—when the price changes, the change will have effects throughout the economy, and these effects may cause the demand curve to shift. The reason that economists usually let the curves stay put when they analyze a price change is that they assume that these indirect effects are small enough to be ignored. Generally these effects are small, and changing the price of any one commodity is unlikely to shift the demand curve for that commodity.

There are exceptions, of course, even in the case of commodities. A large change in the price of oil has major reverberations throughout the economy, leading to structural changes that change the position of *all* demand curves, including that for oil. Our point is not to argue that *all* commodity markets work like the supply-and-demand model of perfect price competition but rather to point out that labor markets *do not*.

Because labor incomes (wages and salaries) provide about two-thirds of the total demand for commodities in the economy, a change in the price of labor hours (the wage) has immediate and large effects on the whole economy, far greater than the effects of a change in the price of any single commodity. This is why the demand curve for total labor hours shifts every time the price of labor changes. The reverberations back on the demand for labor are simply too great to be ignored under the practice of "holding everything else constant."

The second reason why labor markets do not work like commodity markets—that is, why wage-cutting may increase rather than decrease excess supply—depends on the distinct positions of employers and workers. Two differences are relevant here. First, capitalists, unlike workers, are not under immediate pressure to spend the income they get. When the wage is reduced, workers will get less income and capitalists more; but when workers get less income, they must reduce their spending or go into debt, whereas when capitalists get more income they do not necessarily spend more. The total amount of spending may fall, tending to cause the downward shift from LD_1 to LD_2 in Figure 11.7.

The second difference between capitalists and workers of importance here is that workers, unlike capitalists, depend on the sale of their labor time to maintain themselves. They cannot cut back on their labor supply, even when the wage is cut. Therefore, a cut in wages does not have the usual effect on market supply; that is, it generally fails to reduce supply (and so fails to reduce any excess supply).

There is no reason, therefore, to expect the labor market to clear—that is, for labor supply to equal labor demand and for unemployment to disappear. Equally important, there are many reasons to expect that of the two possibilities—too many jobs or too few jobs—we are much more likely to have too few jobs (unemployment). We will explain in detail how this occurs in the next chapter. But we have already seen that unemployment is essential for employers to maintain their control of the labor process, and this gives us a clue as to why unemployment is likely to be a permanent feature of capitalism.

Unemployment is more than a theoretical possibility or prediction. It has been an almost permanent fact of life in the United States over the past century. Figure 11.8 presents data on the unemployment rate (percentage of the workforce that cannot find work). The only periods in which unemployment was low for more than a year or so at a time have been during wars. The low unemployment during World Wars I and II, the Korean War, and the Vietnam War reflects both the reduction in labor supply (as workers become soldiers) and the dramatic increase in demand (as the government increased its purchases of military goods). The historical record is in agreement with the theoretical prediction: In the absence of a major push for full employment from the government, capitalism by itself does not come close to providing jobs for all who want work. And as we shall see in Chapter 13, even when the government adopts policies to increase employment, these policies are often thwarted by the workings of the capitalist economy.

The paradox is that not only people are unemployed: machines and other parts of our productive capacity are unemployed, too.

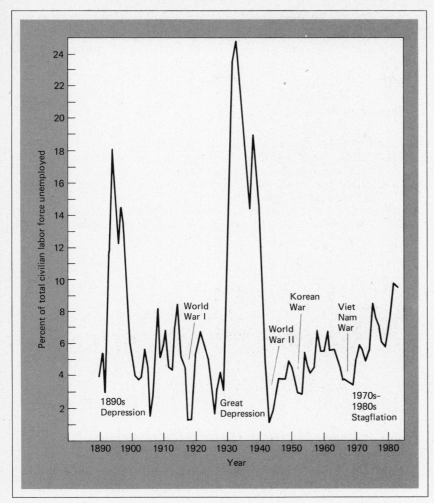

FIGURE 11.8 The unemployment rate in the United States, 1890–1983. Unemployment is a permanent feature of the capitalist economy. Its level fluctuates with the business cycle. Low points in unemployment have occurred during the two World Wars and during the Korean and Vietnam Wars. Although the rate of unemployment since the end of World War II has been low by historical standards, average unemployment rates over the decade 1974–1984 are higher than for any decades other than the depressions of the 1890s and the 1930s.

Source: U.S. Department of Commerce, *Historical Statistics of the United States* (Washington, D.C.: U.S. Government Printing Office, 1975); and *Economic Report of the President* (Washington. D.C.: U.S. Government Printing Office, 1984).

Idle hands and idle machines would make sense if there were nothing useful that they might do; if, for example, all our needs for goods and services had been met, it would make sense to lay down our tools and kick up our heels. But this, sadly, is not the reason why unemployment is an ever-present specter in capitalist society. The reason is that the motivating force for the production of commodities is not to meet people's needs but to make money. And for those who control the investment and production process, unemployment is one of the things that makes money making possible.

☐ Suggested Readings

Robert L. Heilbroner, *Beyond Boom and Crash* (New York: Norton, 1978).

John Maynard Keynes, *The General Theory of Employment, Interest, and Money* (New York: Harcourt Brace Jovanovich, 1936).

Arthur M. Okun, *Prices and Quantities: A Macroeconomic Analysis* (Washington, D.C.: The Brookings Institution, 1981).

Harry Magdoff, *The Age of Imperialism* (New York: Monthly Review Press, 1969).

Studs Terkel, *Hard Times, an Oral History of the Great Depression* (New York: Pantheon Books, 1970).

CHAPTER 12

UNEMPLOYMENT, INFLATION, AND THE BUSINESS CYCLE

Unemployment imposes two costs on society. The first is waste—the loss of goods and services that were needed and could have been produced but were not. The second cost of unemployment is the personal insecurity and hardship that it creates. Workers never know when unemployment will hit, or where; it is impossible to plan for unemployment because being laid off seems so unpredictable, so arbitrary.

It is not just those actually unemployed who suffer. Even employed workers who have never been unemployed must worry that they *might* be laid off. The most vulnerable are, of course, recently hired workers, those with few skills, workers who are especially young or old, women, and black and other minority workers. But others—auto workers with 10 years' seniority, salesmen, secretaries with seemingly safe jobs, long-term employees, professionals and technicians, and even managers—worry about being laid off as well.

They have good reason to worry. For many, the loss of a job can shatter one's life. Indeed, we know that each time unemployment increases, there will be more suicides, more child abuse, more battered wives, more people going to prison, more heart attacks and strokes.

Why must unemployment create so much insecurity? After all, as we saw in Chapter 11, unemployment is simply an excess of labor supply over demand. If there is only enough work in our society to hire 9 out of every 10 workers, why not devise some system so that the tenth worker need not suffer? For example, why not give each worker 1 week off out of every 10 weeks? Then everyone would be "unemployed" 1 week out of 10. A certain amount of belt tightening would be required, but unemployment would not create the insecurity and pain it does now. Or, unemployment could be insured against, just as other calamities—fire, storms, explosions, accidents—are now. When your home burns down, your insurance pays to replace it. Why not provide all workers with an insurance program so that if they lose their jobs, the insurance would make up their lost wages?

In fact such an insurance system—called *unemployment compensation*—does exist, but it only pays on average about one-third of the lost wage. This payment helps stave off acute hardship for as long as the unemployment benefits continue, but it hardly reduces the fear of unemployment. You would consider fire insurance to be poor insurance indeed if, after your house burned down, the insurance only paid to fix one-third of the damage.

If there are ways of eliminating the insecurity attached to unemployment, why are they not implemented? The answer is simple. Capitalism *needs* the insecurity of unemployment. As we saw in Chapter 6, if there were an authoritarian or fascist government to repress workers or if there were a social democratic government to establish a social contract, there might not have to be this kind of insecurity. But otherwise the workers' fear of being laid off is essential for maintaining the employer's control in the labor process, and in the absence of fascist or social democratic government, capitalism, cannot function without it.

In fact we will see later that if, for some reason (war, for instance), there is a sustained period of low unemployment and workers lose their fear of being laid off, capitalism works in such a way as to restore unemployment and restimulate the fear of job loss.

So we find this curious result: In the last chapter we saw that the cause of unemployment is not that all human needs have been met and there isn't enough work to go around; rather, we have unemployment (and its attendant loss of production) *despite* unmet human needs. Here we see that unemployment creates insecurity not because we cannot think of ways to separate or uncouple unemployment and insecurity, but rather because for capitalism to function it needs the insecurity, and unemployment is what creates it.

This chapter investigates the role of unemployment and the business cycle in the economy as a whole. The *business cycle* is the pattern of relatively short-term ups and downs in the economy. Typically, the economy goes through an *expansion*, or growth phase, followed by a *recession*, or contraction phase, every four years or so. One of the most important changes during the business cycle is the rise in unemployment (during recession) and later the fall in unemployment (during expansion).

The main idea of this chapter is that unless some other method is found for resolving the conflict between employers and workers on terms that allow adequate profits, unemployment will exist in a capitalist economy. However wasteful or painful it is, unemployment is something that is required to make capitalism work.

This main idea is expressed in the following three main points:

1. Unemployment regulates the expected profit rate, governing the balance between the *cost conditions* and the *demand conditions* affecting investment. Increased unemployment tends to worsen the demand conditions but improve the cost conditions.
2. The *business cycle* (recession and expansion) follows from the fluctuations in the expected profit rate and from the interaction between the level of investment and the profit rate. Unemployment rises during a recession and declines during an expansion.
3. Recessions are needed from time to time to *restore the cost conditions* for profitable investment. When the recession works to reduce costs and increase the profit rate, a *well-behaved cycle* occurs. When, for whatever reason, recession fails to reduce costs and hence fails to increase the profit rate, a *misbehaved cycle* occurs.

Even though capitalists may, from time to time, want and need a recession, that is no assurance that they will get one. Recessions do not result from a conspiracy by capitalists (though, as we see in the next chapter, they may try to get the government to cause a recession or to prolong one). Instead, recessions occur in response to changes in the expected profit rate and the uncoordinated reaction of individual capitalists to these changes. Capital*ism,* not capital*ists,* produces recession.

This chapter considers the economy over a somewhat longer period of time than the short-term model of Chapter 11. Here we consider how the economy changes during the period of a business cycle, say, a few years. The basic analysis presented here may be considered a "medium-term" model.

Over this longer period, most of the economic variables can change. Unlike in Chapter 11, here we assume that the output/capital ratio (Y/K *in use*) can change. Productivity, or $Y/Labor$ can also change. Prices of outputs and inputs also change. On the other hand, we do continue to hold the capital/labor ratio (CG *in use/Labor*) constant. What is perhaps even more important, we assume no changes in the basic institutions and social relationships within which investment and profit making take place—the social structure of accumulation. (These last assumptions will be dropped in the long-term model of Chapter 14.)

☐ Unemployment Regulates the Expected Profit Rate

To understand how unemployment regulates the expected profit rate, we must take one step backward in order to get a better view. In Chapter 11 we learned how the current determinants of the profit rate help establish an expected future profit rate, which in turn helps determine the level of investment, output, employment, and unemployment. These relationships are reproduced in the shaded portion of Figure 12.1.

But what started this whole process? How were the current determinants of the profit rate *themselves* determined? Here is

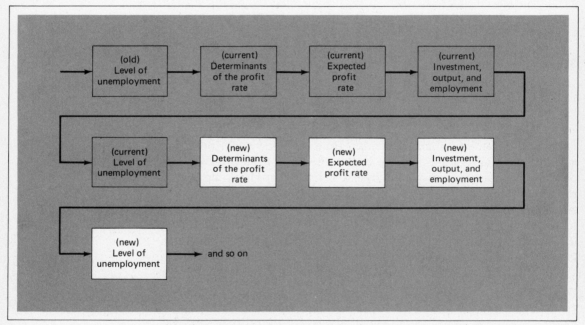

FIGURE 12.1 Unemployment regulates the expected profit rate. The level of unemployment is one of the principal factors influencing the expected rate of profit.

The determinants of the profit rate, as we saw in Chapter 11, establish an expected profit rate, a level of investment and output, and a level of unemployment. These relationships are reproduced here (the shaded portion above reproduces the relationships depicted in Figures 11.1 and 11.4). But what determines the determinants of the profit rate?

Here we take one step back to see a bigger picture. Starting in the first row of the figure above, we see that the "old" level of unemployment helps determine the "current" determinants of the profit rate, and the "current" level of unemployment (in the second row) helps determine a "new" set of determinants of the profit rate, and so on.

Unemployment in one period, then, helps regulate the expected profit rate in future periods.

where we take one step back to see that *unemployment is one of the main things determining the determinants of the profit rate.*

So we now see the bigger picture. The macroeconomy is like a continuous chain, as Figure 12.1 illustrates. The level of unemployment helps determine the determinants of the profit rate and so helps to determine the profit rate itself; and profit rate (through its effect on investment) helps determine a new level of unemployment. This new level of unemployment then helps determine a new profit rate, and so on and so on.

The idea here is that when we look at the economy over a somewhat longer period than we considered in Chapter 11, we allow for *feedback* to occur. We start with some conditions (including the current rate of unemployment) that establish the determinants of the profit rate; but these conditions will themselves be changed when investors respond to the profit rate.

Note that the level of unemployment *helps* determine the expected profit rate, and the expected profit rate *helps* determine the (new) level of unemployment. While these are the most important relationships, there are other influences as well. Think, for instance, about what affects unemployment. We saw in Chapter 11 that the expected profit rate (through its determination of the level of investment) is the main determinant of the level of employment; but labor supply (*LS*) helps determine how high *un*employment will be.

Similarly, other factors besides the level of unemployment help determine the determinants of the profit rate. Although in this section we are focusing on unemployment's effect on the profit rate, other factors are also important. Among them are the cost of imported inputs to the production process (for example, imported oil), the price at which the outputs are sold, and government policies such as tax rates and the availability of credit.

How, then, does unemployment regulate the expected profit rate? Recall that the expected profit rate has two parts, the expected capacity utilization rate and the expected profit rate on utilized capital.

$$
\begin{array}{ccc}
\text{Expected} & \text{Expected} & \text{Expected} \\
\text{profit} & \text{capacity} & \text{profit rate} \\
\text{rate} & = \text{utilization rate} & \times \text{on utilized capital} \\
(\textit{expected r}) & (\textit{expected cu}) & (\textit{expected ru}) \qquad (12.1)
\end{array}
$$

The demand conditions affecting investment determine the expected utilization rate; the cost conditions affecting investment determine the expected profit rate on utilized capital. The level of unemployment will affect both parts of the expected profit rate.

Rising unemployment, as we will see, tends to damage the demand conditions affecting investment. But, by contrast, our analysis of unemployment in Chapters 6 and 8 already suggested that rising unemployment tends to improve the cost conditions affecting investment. Increased unemployment will therefore have two *opposing* effects on the profit rate, one (the impact on demand conditions) that tends to lower the profit rate (by lowering *cu*) and the other (the effect on cost conditions) that tends to raise the profit rate (by raising *ru*).

The overall effect of rising unemployment on the expected profit rate depends on which effect is larger—the (negative) effect on demand conditions or the (positive) effect on cost conditions. Which will dominate—the fall in *expected cu* or the rise in *expected ru*?

The impact of increased unemployment on demand conditions facing investment is quite easy to understand. When people lose their jobs, they have less income to spend. They generally must cut back on their purchases—try to buy less, to purchase cheaper products when they do buy, to make more things themselves, to make do with less. Businesses will have a harder time finding customers for their products. As the laid-off workers cut back on their purchases, total demand will fall. Employers will cut back production, laying off even more workers. In this case, the *multiplier* works in reverse.

Rising unemployment is likely to affect the buying habits of a lot of people, not just the unemployed. When one person on the block gets laid off, many others will be a bit more worried about who might get laid off next. They may decide to cut back on their purchases and attempt to save a little bit more, just in case. So the effect of rising unemployment on total demand will be to reduce it even more. When a quarter of a million auto workers were laid off in the early 1980s, for example, about an equal number of workers outside the auto industry ended up losing their jobs as well, as unemployed auto workers cut back on their buying.

As businesses consider building new factories or buying additional machines, one factor to be taken into account is whether they will be able to find customers for the output from their investment. If they see rising unemployment, they will undoubtedly think of its negative impact on demand conditions, and so they will tend to predict that less of their capital stock will likely be utilized in the future (that is, *expected cu* will be lower). This is unemployment's negative effect on the demand conditions affecting investment.

Unemployment's positive effect on the cost conditions affecting investment are a bit more complicated; they are considered in the next section.

Increased unemployment reduces unit labor costs

While increased unemployment tends to make less favorable the demand conditions affecting investment, it tends to improve the cost conditions affecting it. The main improvement is a reduction in labor costs. Lower labor costs raise the expected profit rate on utilized capital (raise *expected ru*), the second term in equation 12.1

From Chapter 7 recall that

$$\begin{matrix}\text{Output} \\ \text{price}\end{matrix} = \begin{matrix}\text{Unit} \\ \text{labor costs}\end{matrix} + \begin{matrix}\text{Unit costs} \\ \text{of other inputs}\end{matrix} + \begin{matrix}\text{Unit} \\ \text{profits}\end{matrix} \quad (12.2)$$

For the economy as a whole, unit labor costs are the largest of the cost terms. So unless offset by an even larger increase in the other

---

Labor Costs—Two Measures

Labor costs may be measured in two ways. Which we use depends on the problem being considered.

The first way—that used in Chapters 8 and 9—defines unit labor costs in terms of *physical* units of output.

$$ulc = \frac{\text{Wage per hour}}{\text{Units of output per hour}} = \frac{w}{(e)\,(d)}$$

This results in *ulc* expressed as, say, "dollars per *barrel* of beer produced."

The second way—the labor cost index—is used in Chapters 12 to 14. The labor cost index is expressed in terms of each *dollar's worth* of output. In this case we have

$$\text{Labor cost index} = \frac{\text{Wage per hour}}{\text{Value of output per hour}} = \frac{w}{(Pz)(e)(d)}$$

This labor cost index would be expressed as, say, "labor cost per *dollar's worth* of beer produced."

The labor cost index takes into account not only the production aspect (labor cost in producing a unit of the output) but also the selling price (*Pz*) of the output.

Using *per hour* data calculated from the information on page 80, in the coal industry in 1979,

$$\text{Unit labor cost} = \frac{\$13.12}{1.9 \text{ tons}} = \$6.90 \text{ per ton}$$

$$\text{Labor cost index} = \frac{\$13.12}{\$(23.50)\,(1.9 \text{ tons})} = .29$$

It is easy to see that

$$\text{Labor cost index} = \frac{ulc}{Pz}$$

costs or a reduction in output price, lower unit labor costs will increase the profit.

Labor costs are measured by the *labor cost index,* which is closely related to the unit labor cost measure that we used in the earlier microeconomic chapters. The main difference is that the labor cost index takes account of the price of the output produced, while unit labor cost does not. Thus while unit labor costs measure the labor cost *per unit* of output, the labor cost index measures labor cost *per dollar* of output. Unit labor costs are measured in dollars of wages per ton (or barrel or bushel) produced, whereas the labor cost index is measured in dollars or wages per dollar of output produced.

The labor cost index may be written as:

$$\text{Labor cost index} = \frac{w}{Pz\,(e)(d)} \qquad (12.3)$$

where w = wage rate
Pz = output price
e = output per unit of effort (efficiency)
d = work done per hour (intensity of work)

The denominator, $Pz(e)(d)$, measures how many dollars worth of output is produced in an average hour of work, because ed is simply output per hour and Pz is the price of output. The numerator, w, measures the wage per hour.

From equation 12.3 we see that employers could reduce the labor cost index in the following ways:

$$\frac{w}{Pz} \text{ can be reduced}$$

d and/or e can be increased

The term w/Pz is sometimes called the *product wage* because it measures the real buying power of the wage in terms of how many units of output one hour's wages could buy. Thus if w = \$10 and Pz = \$2, product wages are 5—1 hour's work is paid enough to buy 5 units of output.

Why growing unemployment might reduce product wages (w/Pz) is clear. With more unemployment, workers are in a weaker bargaining position. Employed workers will be less able to push for big increases in wages (w), fearing unemployment themselves and competition from unemployed workers. Wage increases will be more likely to lag behind price increases. If output prices (Pz) rise by 5 percent, then wages must rise by at least 5 percent for product wages to remain even. If workers are not able to obtain wage increases at least equal to price increases, product wages will fall. Workers will have greater difficulty getting wage increases

The **labor cost index** is a measure of the unit labor costs of production *as compared to* (divided by) the price of the output; it consists of two parts, the output per labor hour and the product wage.

The **product wage** is the hourly wage rate *as compared to* (divided by) the price of the output.

equal to or greater than the increase in output prices when unemployment is high or rising.

Increasing unemployment is also likely to have an impact on the level of work effort (d). When workers are worried about losing their jobs, they will be less able to resist employers' efforts to increase the pace of work, cut corners on safety rules, and increase the effort level in other ways. The result will be that d will tend to rise with the rise in unemployment, further reducing the labor cost index.

For example, with high unemployment in the coal industry, miners have been more reluctant recently to insist on strict enforcement of safety rules. These rules save lives but reduce the amount of work done (and hence production) because miners are supposed to be out of the mines while a potential safety problem is being inspected. If unemployment is high, miners worry that when they call for a safety inspection, the employer may just shut down the mine and expand production in other mines where they can hire other (currently unemployed) miners. So miners will be less willing to insist on their rights, and this will have the effect of raising d.

The effect of rising unemployment on output per unit of work done (e) is uncertain, but it is not as important as the effects on w/Pz and d. This variable, e, measures how efficiently the work effort is used. The main determinants of e are the quality and quantity of the machines, tools, and other capital goods with which the worker works and how well management coordinates the production process. On the one hand, rising unemployment may raise e because as employers cut back on production, they will leave in use only their best machines—of the machinery *in use,* then, the average level of efficiency rises. On the other hand, rising unemployment may reduce e because as the capacity utilization rate falls, employers may be less able to take advantage of the economies of large-scale production.

The negative effect of unemployment on labor's bargaining position may not be immediate. If the unemployment rate is high but workers expect it to go down soon, they are less likely to make concessions to their employers than if they expect unemployment to remain high or even get worse. If wages are fixed in a two- or three-year contract that is not up for renegotiation soon, unemployment may have little effect on wages.

But rising unemployment is likely, sooner or later, to reduce the labor cost index, both through a reduction in w/Pz and through an increase in d. The relationship between unemployment and the labor cost index is summarized in Figure 12.2. High levels of unemployment lead to reductions in the labor cost index; low levels lead to increases.

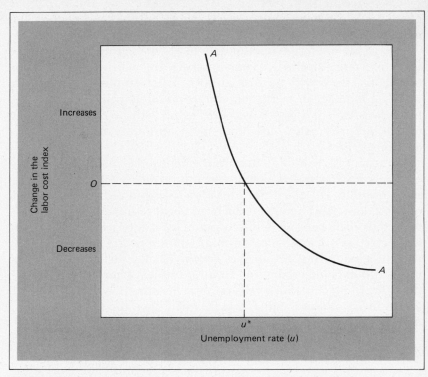

FIGURE 12.2 Changes in the labor cost index depend on the level of unemployment. The level of unemployment helps determine changes in the labor cost index. Low levels of unemployment tend to increase the labor cost index, whereas high unemployment tends to cause declines in the index.

Line *AA* shows the relationship between changes in the labor cost index and the level of unemployment. The level of unemployment is measured along the horizontal axis; the rate of change in the labor cost index is measured on the vertical axis. The graph shows that the lower the level of unemployment, the higher will be the increase in labor costs; and, conversely, the higher the level of unemployment, the greater will be the decline in labor costs.

The level of unemployment at which the labor cost index neither rises nor falls is the *neutral rate of unemployment* ("neutral" because neither employers nor workers improve their share); it is shown here as u^*.

The level of unemployment at which the labor cost index neither rises nor falls is called the *neutral rate of unemployment*, because at this level of unemployment the bargaining strengths of employers and workers are balanced. At the neutral rate of unemployment, workers' share of the total output produced remains constant.

As businesses think about whether to invest, they will consider how much they will have to pay in labor costs. If they see rising unemployment, they will undoubtedly think of its positive impact on labor costs, and so they will tend to predict that the profit rate on utilized capital will be higher (that is, *expected ru* in equation

12.1 will be higher). This is the principal positive effect of unemployment on the cost conditions affecting investment.

Recession also reduces other unit costs

Recession refers to a period in the business cycle when investment declines, demand for labor falls, and total economic output is reduced. So far we have concentrated on only one aspect of recession, rising unemployment, and its impact on unit labor costs (and thus more generally on *expected ru*). But economic recession has other effects on the cost conditions affecting investment besides those already described.

Recession may reduce costs other than the labor costs. An important example of this is the reduction in the cost of imported materials used in production. If businesses have to pay less for such inputs, this will improve their profit prospects.

We can analyze the unit costs of other inputs (see equation 12.2) in a manner similar to the way we considered unit labor costs. In the case of imported inputs such as oil, the most important factor in determining these costs will be the price (to American businesses) of such imported inputs compared to the price the U.S. businesses are paid for their products. This term is exactly analogous to what was called product wages in the previous section. This is written as:

$$\text{Real price of imported inputs} = \frac{Pim}{Pz} \qquad (12.4)$$

where Pim = price U.S. businesses must pay for imported inputs
Pz = output price (price at which U.S. businesses sell their products)

The numerator measures how much U.S. businesses pay out for each unit of the imported input; the denominator, how much they get back from selling each unit of their goods.

The real *price of imported inputs* will fall whenever the price of improted inputs (Pim) increases more slowly or declines more rapidly than do American businesses' output prices (Pz).

Recession will tend to improve this price ratio by reducing the demand for imported inputs and causing their product price to fall. As businesses cut back on production during the recession, they will also cut back on their orders for imported inputs, such as oil. Unless there is an offsetting decline in supply, this recession-induced decline in demand will have the usual effect. Buyers—in this case U.S. businesses—will find their bargaining power increased and will most likely be able to lower the real price of their inputs. And so long as Pim falls faster than Pz (or grows more

Recession is that part or phase of the business cycle in which total output falls; during recessions, investment also usually declines and the demand for labor is reduced.

The **real price of imported inputs** is the price of imported inputs *as compared to* (divided by) the price of U.S. output.

slowly than Pz), U.S. businesses will find that imported inputs are becoming cheaper. The profit rate will rise as a result.

So recession is likely to reduce the real price of imported inputs and thus improve the cost conditions affecting investment. As businesses think about whether to invest, they will consider what they must pay as the real price of imported inputs. If they see a recession occurring, they will undoubtedly think of its positive impact on the real price of imported inputs and will tend to predict that the profit rate on utilized capital (*expected ru* in equation 12.1) will be higher.

Yet another way in which recession restores the profit rate is by reducing the value of existing capital goods. Low capacity utilization implies that there is an excess supply of capital goods (more capital goods exist than are currently being used in production), and so the price of capital goods (Pc) tends to fall. Since the value of the capital goods (K) is now less, a given amount of profits (R) results in a higher profit rate.

Thus recession has many positive effects on the cost conditions affecting investment. It will most likely reduce labor costs and reduce the cost of imported inputs.

These effects will be strengthened by the survival-of-the-most-profitable rule of capitalist competition. A severe recession may drive high-cost firms out of business, for while even high-cost firms can survive during a boom, they are hard-pressed to stay in business when total demand falls off. With fewer competitors, the demand curves facing the surviving firms will shift upward; as a result, they will be able to sell more output, or raise their prices, or both. Selling more output will raise cu and hence raise r. Raising the price will increase ru and thus raise r.

Suppose, for example, that the Chrysler Corporation had been allowed to go bankrupt during the recession of 1980–1982 and that its customers had instead purchased cars from the remaining automobile producers, both domestic and foreign. Ford and GM would have experienced a substantial increase in their levels of capacity utilization and consequently a big boost in their profit rates. With these brighter prospects for profits, they might have increased their investments.

Despite all of these positive effects on investment, recession remains a double-edged sword. Even while recession is restoring better cost conditions affecting investment, and perhaps improving the demand conditions facing a few particular firms, it is damaging the general demand conditions affecting investment throughout the economy. Demand conditions deteriorate because unemployed workers are forced to cut back on their spending. This is the dilemma. Being able to produce goods very cheaply but having no customers is no better than having lots of customers but costs so high that there is no profit left.

Just because employers need a recession does not guarantee that they will *get* one. What starts a recession? To answer this question, we must investigate the business cycle.

☐ Inflation and Unemployment in the Business Cycle

The presidents of the Fortune 500 corporations could hold a meeting and decide to stop investing; this would surely produce a recession. But recessions in capitalism come about in a quite different way.

In Chapter 11, we saw how the amount of investment depended on the rate of profit. But the rate of profit depends on the level of investment as well. The influence is mutual. To see why, recall that fluctuations in the amount of investment are the main reason for fluctuations in the level of total demand for goods and services. The demand for goods and services is the main influence on the demand for labor and therefore on the unemployment rate. And we have just seen that the level of unemployment affects the profit rate. For this reason, the level of investment influences the profit rate.

This logic is summarized in Figure 12.3. All of the arrows except

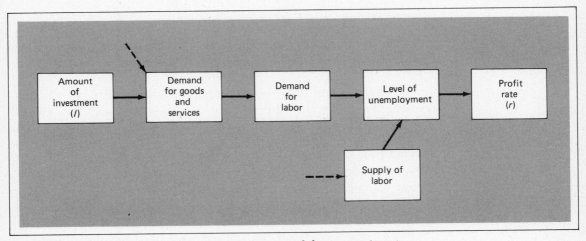

FIGURE 12.3 From investment to the profit rate. How much businesses invest helps determine what the profit rate will be. This figure reproduces part of Figure 12.1—the movement from (current) investment to the (new) expected profit rate. Current investment, along with other factors (represented by the dashed arrow) such as government spending and foreigners' purchases, determines the total demand for goods and services; total demand, in turn, sets the demand for labor. Together, the demand and supply of labor establish the level of unemployment. The level of unemployment will affect the new profit rate, but it may have either a positive or negative effect. For instance higher unemployment will tend to reduce *cu* but increase *ru*; which effect will dominate depends on circumstances.

one indicate a positive influence. The arrow farthest to the right, however, says that the rate of unemployment influences the profit rate. But the influence could go either way—more unemployment could either raise or lower the profit rate. Therefore, more investment could raise or lower the rate of profit. How do we know when one or the other influence will be the stronger?

When the capacity utilization (cu) is very low and unemployment is very high, an increase in investment will have a positive effect on the profit rate. Investment in this case will increase the level of capacity utilization (tending to raise r), whereas it will not generally have much effect yet in raising unit labor costs (thus having only a minor effect tending to reduce r). The reason rising investment does not yet trigger higher costs is that, with unemployment still quite high, workers still fear losing their jobs.

When capacity utilization (cu) is high and unemployment is low, more investment will likely have a negative effect on the profit rate. The existing level of investment is already so high that the demand for goods and services is high. With more investment, capacity utilization will rise toward the limit of 100 percent, after which it can rise further only at great cost (using costly overtime, insufficient machine maintenance time, and the like). Further increases in investment will, moreover, increase the demand for labor and continue to lower the rate of unemployment, eventually diminishing the fear of unemployment and strengthening workers' bargaining positions. At some point, then, further increases in investment will lower the profit rate.

This argument is summarized in Figure 12.4. As the amount of investment rises, the profit rate first rises; then it levels off and falls.

What will determine how much investment there will be? Because we know that the amount of investment depends on the profit rate (among other things), we can graph investment along with the profit-rate curve from Figure 12.4. Simply borrowing the graph from Figure 11.3 and combining it with Figure 12.4, we have Figure 12.5.

As we see in Figure 12.5, most combinations of I and r will not be possible. This is because the profit rate and the amount of investment depend on each other. For example, if the profit rate were r', the amount of investment (reading from the investment curve) would be I'; but if the amount of investment were I', the profit rate (reading from the profit curve) would be r'', which is different from r'. So these combinations of the profit rate and investment are inconsistent.

There is, however, one combination that is consistent. It is the point lying on *both* curves, that is, the intersection of the two curves. At this point the profit rate and the amount of investment

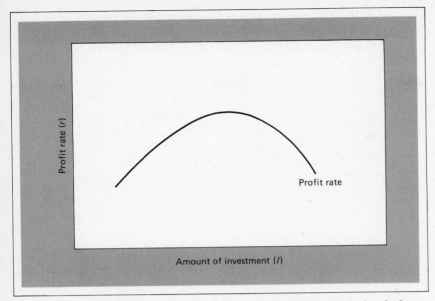

FIGURE 12.4 The profit rate depends on the level of investment. The level of investment affects the profit rate in the short run in two ways—more investment tends to raise cu and lower ru. The overall effect on r depends on how much investment is undertaken.

Consider first the situation when investment is relatively low (the left-hand side of the graph). Here, increases in investment will raise capacity utilization (cu) without seriously reducing ru (that is, without seriously worsening the cost conditions affecting investment). Greater investment increases the profit rate, as we see in the rising portion of the profit-rate line.

However, when investment is already relatively high (the right-hand side of the graph), further increases in investment reduce the profit rate by reducing the level of unemployment, increasing labor's bargaining power, and tending to increase the labor cost index. (Notice how the line AA in Figure 12.2 becomes very steep at low levels of unemployment.) Now, greater investment produces a big decline in ru, which more than offsets any further increases in cu. The profit-rate line in the graph now falls.

are compatible. (There could be more than one such point if the curves crossed many times.)

There is no assurance that the economy will settle down at point a (with investment equal to Ia and the profit rate equal to ra). Why? Investment is determined by things other than the profit rate. For example, if the profit rate is very low but businesses expect things to get better in the near future (possibly because of the election of a probusiness government or as the result of a highly profitable technological breakthrough), the amount of investment might increase, even if the profit rate had not yet changed. Figure 12.6 shows that business expectations of a favorable shift in profits would mean that they expected an upward shift of the profit curve.

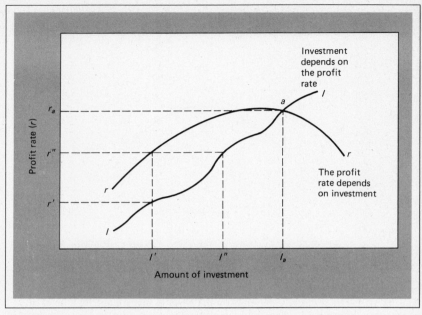

FIGURE 12.5 The determination of investment and the profit rate. The level of investment depends on the profit rate and the profit rate depends on the level of investment. Here we see how they are mutually determined. (This figure brings together the relationships shown in Figures 11.3 and 12.4.)

Imagine that the level of investment is I'. When investment is I', the profit rate (from the rr line) will be r''. But if the profit rate is r'', investors will want to change their level of investment (reading the II line) from I' to I''. But since I'' produces a profit rate different from r'', there will be further adjustments.

At point a, the current level of investment (Ia) produces a rate of profit (ra), and at profit rate ra investors want to invest Ia. Hence no further adjustments will take place until some aspect of the situation changes, leading to a shift in one of the curves.

Anticipating the change, they would increase the amount of investment, say to a level equal to Ib, hoping to gain a profit rate of rb.

Their expectations may be borne out; but there is no guarantee. They may have been overly optimistic. Suppose the profit curve does not shift. Businesses have already invested Ib. Then the profit rate will not *rise* to rb; it will *fall* to rc. When they see this happening, businesses will want to cut back their investment (reading off the investment curve) to Ic. As they cut back their investment, the demand for goods and services will fall and unemployment will rise. A recession will be underway.

Costs and profits in the business cycle

We can now see how the periodic ups and downs of the economy—the business cycle—follow from fluctuations in the expected

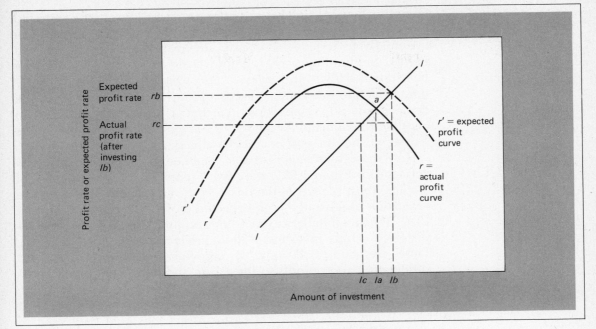

FIGURE 12.6 Investor expectations: Dreams fulfilled or hopes dashed? The relationships between the level of investment and the profit rate may be affected by many other factors. One of the most important of these is investor expectations.

The figure above reproduces the *II* and *rr* curves from Figure 12.5. (The curves in Figure 12.5 were drawn assuming that nothing else affecting the curves changed.) If investors expect the profit curve to shift upward from *rr* to *r'r'*, then they will increase their investments to *Ib*. If their expectations were *justified*, the profit rate (read off line *r'r'*) would *rise* to *rb*; but if their expectations were *not justified*, the profit rate (read off line *rr*) will *fall* to *rc*.

profit rate (*expected r*). When the expected profit rate declines, investment will fall, and the economy goes into recession. When the expected profit rate rises, businesses will want to invest more, and the economy enters the *expansion* phase.

Each business responds individually to these fluctuations in the profit rate, simply trying to earn the highest profits it can. There is no conspiracy among capitalists to cause recession. Rather, each capitalist acting alone will tend to respond like most other capitalists. They will all act in the same way, even though they have not agreed to do anything of the kind, simply because they will see the same set of signals. When the expected profit rate falls, many or most will cut back on investment. As most capitalists reduce their investment, the recession begins.

The *business cycle* draws together the relationships explained earlier in the chapter. First, there is feedback. The (current) level of unemployment helps determine the expected profit rate (and hence investments), which in turn helps determine a new level of

Expansion is that part or phase of the business cycle when total output rises; during expansions, investment also usually rises and the demand for labor increases.

The **business cycle** is the pattern of medium-term economic fluctuations in which expansion is followed by recession, which is followed by expansion, and so on.

unemployment, which helps determine a new level of the expected profit rate, and so on. Second, there is the tendency of recession eventually to reduce labor costs, to lower the cost of imported inputs, and in other ways to improve the cost conditions affecting investment. However, recession also worsens the demand conditions affecting investment. Third, expansion tends to improve the demand conditions affecting investment, to raise profits, and to increase the demand for labor, but sooner or later expansion tends also to worsen the cost conditions affecting investment.

How these relationships come together in the business cycle is depicted in Figures 12.7 and 12.8. Figure 12.7 charts the path of the labor cost aspects of the business cycle. Let us start during the expansion phase with "high expected profits" (at the left of Figure 12.7). When capitalists expect high profits they increase their investment. High investment then produces high labor demand. Times are good, with capitalists enjoying high current profits and anticipating good profits in the future and with labor demand rising.

High labor demand produces full employment as unemployment falls. Workers find that it is easier to get jobs, and they want to share in the benefits of the expansion. With a stronger bargaining position, they are able to obtain higher product wages (w/Pz) and resist speedup (lower d) in their jobs. But lower d and higher w/Pz mean lower profits on utilized capital (ru). This ends the expansion phase of the business cycle.

A lower current profit rate means that capitalists become more gloomy about the future, reducing their estimates of future profits. Expecting lower profits, they cut back on their investment plans. Reduced investment leads to a diminished demand for labor, and the economy is now in the pit of recession.

Some workers lose their jobs; and many other workers see them lose those jobs and begin to fear for their *own* jobs. As unemployment grows, workers worry more about keeping their jobs than about getting higher wages or a less fatiguing work pace. Wages rise more slowly, or even fall, and employers are successful in using the threat of unemployment to speed up the work.

The economy has now come all the way around Figure 12.7. With lower w and higher d, unit labor costs have been reduced and the expected profit rate has been raised. The stage is set for another expansion.

This process is very evident in recent history. The high levels of total demand and low levels of unemployment during the Korean War (1951-1953) eventually led to a sharp drop in the profit rate on corporate capital (from 7 percent after corporate taxes in 1950 to 5 percent after taxes in 1953). The result was a recession, which raised the unemployment level from 2.9 percent in 1953 to 5.5

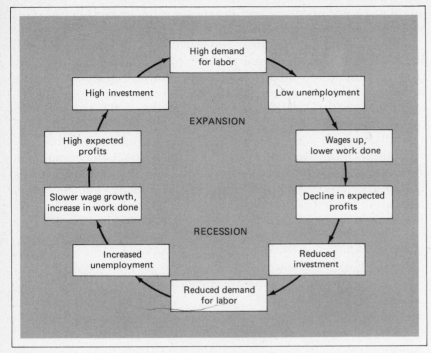

FIGURE 12.7 The path of the business cycle (labor aspects). The economy's path through a business cycle is reflected in the changing conditions in the labor market and their effect on the profit rate.

Suppose that the economy is initially in recession, at the bottom of the above circle. The reduced demand for labor during recession increases unemployment, which cuts wage growth and speeds up work. As wages *(w)* fail to rise and work done *(d)* increases, the profit rate *(r)* and expected profit rate *(expected r)* rise, causing in turn an increase in investment.

The economy now enters the expansion phase, with rising investment and growing demand for labor. As the expansion continues, unemployment may be reduced, *w* rises, and *d* falls. The expected profit rate declines, investment falls off, and the economy enters a new recession.

percent in 1954 and 4.4 percent in 1955. By 1955, the profit rate, rising because of the stronger bargaining position of business versus workers, topped its 1950 level. Investment increased and the expansion was underway. But by 1956, the profit rate had begun to fall again. The expansion ended in 1957, and another recession began.

What about costs other than labor? Figure 12.7 describes how the business cycle and recessions restore the *labor-related* determinants of the profit rate. We can also see how recession is necessary to restore other conditions for profitable investment. The expansion, as we have seen, tends to increase the demand and hence the price of imported raw material *(Pim)*; recession reduces the demand for materials and causes their price (*Pim*) to fall. This process is illustrated in Figure 12.8.

Figure 12.9 shows that this process occurred in the 1970s and 1980s. In 1973, at the peak of a business cycle expansion, the Organization of Petroleum Exporting Countries (OPEC) sensed its strong bargaining position and successfully raised the price of oil. In contrast, in the 1980s, after years of recession, they were forced to accept a price cut.

Similarly, credit and financial institutions react to good times by expanding credit. Wanting to share the high profits, they often loan out money avidly during the expansion, overextending themselves and making risky (and, in retrospect, bad) loans. The recession makes it difficult for some firms to pay back their loans, and bankers change from worrying about missing the high profits to wondering

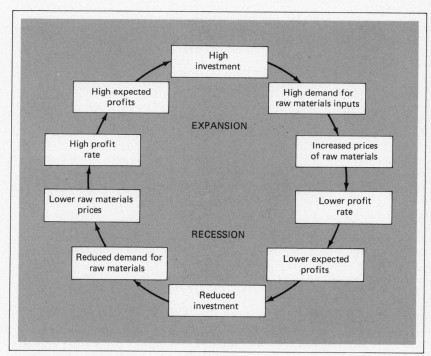

FIGURE 12.8 The path of the business cycle (imported materials aspects). The economy's path through a business cycle is also reflected in the changing price of imported materials and its effect on the profit rate.

As in Figure 12.7, imagine that the economy is initially in recession, at the bottom of the above circle. The reduced investment during recession reduces the demand for imported materials (like oil), resulting in a lower price. The lower price helps restore the profit rate; and as investment rises, the economy enters the expansion phase of the cycle.

During expansion, the demand for materials increases, raising their price and helping to reduce the profit rate. As *r* falls, investment declines and the economy enters a new recession.

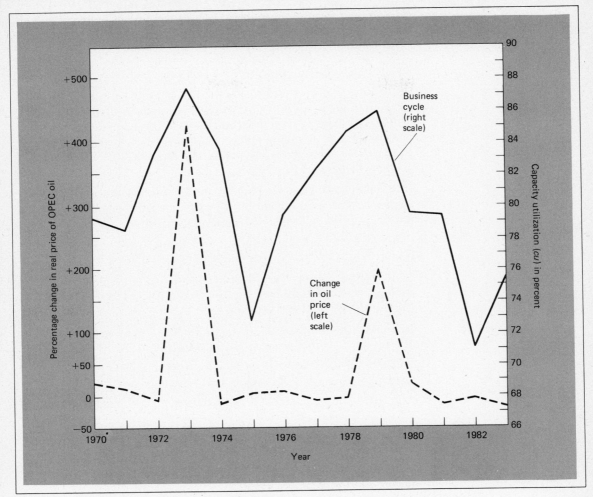

FIGURE 12.9 Oil prices and the business cycle. If the price of imported materials rises more rapidly than output prices, the profit rate will be reduced. This seems to happen in the latter part of business-cycle expansions. This relationship is especially clear in the case of imported oil, an important material (used as fuel and for the generation of electricity, which powers electrical machinery).

The oil price in the figure is the percentage change from one year to the next in the real price of oil sold to the United States by the countries of the Organization of Petroleum Exporting Countries (OPEC). The real price of OPEC oil is the price ($ per barrel) divided by the average price of outputs produced in the United States.

The business cycle is measured in the figure by the level of capacity utilization in the manufacturing sector of the economy.

The two large increases in oil prices took place in 1973 and 1979, both after periods of expansion of the economy. During the years 1980–1983, by contrast, the real price of oil fell by over a third. This decline resulted in large part from the depressed demand for oil, itself caused by the economic stagnation of the early 1980s.

Source: *Economic Report of the President,* 1984; *International Energy Annual,* various years; and OPEC Statistical Unit, *Annual Statistical Bulletin,* various years.

if they will get their loans back. The recession restores "prudence" and "probity" to their credit operation.

Inflation and the business cycle

The business cycle affects not only costs but prices as well. In this section we will see that because business cycle expansions tend to increase labor costs and materials costs, output prices also rise. Likewise, during recessions, labor and materials costs tend to rise less fast or even to fall, so the prices of goods produced do not rise as fast (and may fall) during recessions.

An increase in most prices is called *inflation*. Inflation is most often measured by the increase in the average prices paid by a typical family. This average is called the *Consumer Price Index*. When the Consumer Price Index increases from one year to the next, inflation is taking place. Inflation means simply that the buying power of a dollar has been reduced. Each dollar buys less at the grocery store, at the gas pump, or wherever families purchase the things they consume.

The *inflation rate* measures how fast this average of prices is

Inflation is a general increase in prices, often measured by an increase in the Consumer Price Index.

rising. Suppose that a typical family bought some goods last year for $100; an inflation rate of 6 percent means that the same goods will cost $106 this year. The Consumer Price Index doubled between 1973 and 1983. Each dollar was worth half as much in 1983 as it was a decade earlier. The average annual inflation rate over this period was about 7 percent.

When the Consumer Price Index *declines* from one year to the next, *deflation* is taking place. This is now a very rare occurence. The last time it happened in the United States was between 1954 and 1955. But in the past, deflation was at least as common as inflation. In 1900, for example, prices on the average were only about half as high as they were in 1864. In 1900, therefore, a dollar would buy about twice what it bought 36 years earlier.

We can distinguish two different types of inflation. One kind of inflation, *cyclical inflation,* is related to the business cycle. It regularly appears during the latter part of a business cycle expansion and is a response to the decline in the unemployment rate and the rise in capacity utilization that occurs toward the end of expansion. Cyclical inflation is often described by the inflation-unemployment trade-off.

The second kind of inflation is *structural inflation.* Structural inflation is not related to the business cycle, and it occurs during recessions as well as expansions. This type of inflation is analyzed in Chapter 14.

We can investigate how prices change over the course of the business cycle—or cyclical inflation—by returning to the analysis (in Chapter 7) of how businesses set their prices. The price is made up of costs per unit and profits per unit, or, dividing the costs into its two parts:

Price = Unit materials cost + Unit labor costs + Unit profits

or

$$\text{Price} = (\text{Unit costs})\,(1 + \text{markup})$$

where the markup is

$$\text{Markup} = \frac{\text{Profits}}{\text{Costs}} = \frac{\text{Unit profits}}{\text{Unit costs}}$$

During the expansion phase of the business cycle—particularly after the expansion has gone on for some time—unit materials costs and unit labor costs tend to rise, as we saw in the previous section. The result is an increase in prices, or inflation. During the recession phase of the cycle, costs fall or rise less fast, leading to less rapid inflation. The result is that the rate of inflation is correlated with the business cycle. The ups and downs of the economy correspond to ups and downs in the inflation rate. For the same reason,

Cyclical inflation is the general increase in prices that takes place during the expansion phase of the business cycle, in part in response to the associated decline in the unemployment rate.

Structural inflation is a general increase in prices that occurs during all phases of the business cycle (recessions as well as expansions).

A **trade-off** is a relationship between two or more things in which more of one thing can be obtained only at the cost of getting less of the other.

The **inflation-unemployment trade-off** is the relationship between the inflation rate and the unemployment rate in which less inflation may be obtained only at the cost of higher unemployment and vice versa.

there tends to be a *trade-off:* when unemployment goes down (during the business cycle expansion), the rate of inflation tends to go up; and when unemployment goes up (during recessions), the rate of inflation tends to go down.

The *inflation-unemployment trade-off* is presented in Figure 12.10. The trade-off line indicates that unemployment and inflation are negatively correlated—more of one is generally associated with less of the other.

In the 1970s and 1980s, the U.S. economy has had more of *both* unemployment *and* inflation than in earlier years. In effect, the trade-off line has shifted upward and to the right, producing worse combinations of inflation and unemployment. This shift cannot be explained by increases in costs induced by the expansion of the business cycle. (Chapter 14 explores this problem.)

Even though there was very high inflation in the 1970s (and high unemployment in the 1980s), the nature of the business cycle's effect on inflation has not changed. The business cycle peaks of 1973–1974 and 1979–1980, for example, were very inflationary years (the Consumer Price Index rose 11 percent and 13.5 percent respectively those years). By contrast, the business cycle troughs of 1975–1976 and 1982–1983 experienced relatively low rates of inflation (5.8 and 3.2 percent, respectively).

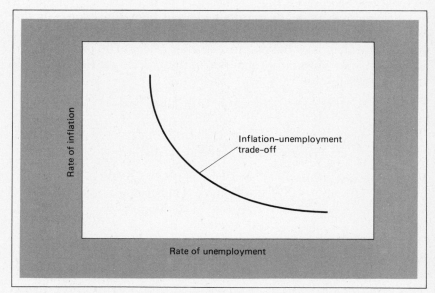

FIGURE 12.10 The inflation-unemployment trade-off. More unemployment is usually associated with less inflation, because the business-cycle recession generally reduces cost pressures on firms. Correspondingly, low levels of unemployment are generally associated with more inflation, because cost pressures build up as the economy expands and unemployment declines.

How rapidly prices rise during the business cycle expansion depends not only on the increase in costs, but also on changes in the markup. If businesses do not change the markup, prices will rise by the same amount as costs.

Businesses generally do not immediately raise prices by the full amount of the cost increase. It takes time to change prices, and businesses are often locked into longer-term contracts. Also, businesses fear that increasing prices will lower their profits by causing them to lose sales to competitors, thus reducing their levels of capacity utilization. This is particularly the case for businesses selling in competition with producers located outside the United States. These competitors may not be facing the same cost increases, because the business cycle expansion occurs at different times in different countries. The result is a decline in the markup and therefore in the profit rate toward the end of the expansionary phase of the business cycle.

☐ Recessions as a Necessary Part of Capitalism

Businesses would like to have both conditions affecting investment be positive—favorable cost conditions and favorable demand conditions. For the economy as a whole, however, improvement in one of the conditions is likely, sooner or later, to lead to a deterioration in the other condition.

The positive effects of the expansion phase of the business cycle—positive for both employers and workers—led conventional economists to think that the "right" governmental policies could produce a perpetual expansion. Why ever suffer the lost production and increased insecurity of recession, they asked, if it is possible always to have expansion?

Alas, as we are now in a position to see, in capitalism it is *not* possible to have continual expansion. True, expansion improves the demand conditions affecting investment, but at the same time it makes worse the cost conditions affecting investment. Eventually the latter will dominate the former.

Expansion works on the two components of the expected profit rate in exactly the opposite way from a recession.

	During recession	During expansion
Cost conditions affecting investment	improve	get worse
Demand conditions affecting investment	get worse	improve

The Recession Speaks

Washington—This is your Recession speaking. The Democrats blame me on Reaganomics and Mr. Reagan blames me on Jimmy Carter. Everybody agrees I am bad news and something must be done about me right away. Nobody appreciates my contribution to the general welfare.

But consider what I have done for you and be grateful.

First, I have cured the plague that was ruining the country. Who brought inflation down from 15 percent to 5 percent? Me, the Recession. . . .

Second, I rate herohood because I am making American business and labor productive and competitive again. Greed and sloth had taken over, and the only force that can stop them is pure fear. Fear of me and what I call my "discipline therapy."

. . . Workers who priced themselves and their industries out of the world market are getting laid off, and after they quit hollering for tariff protection, they'll come back to produce better products at less cost.

I'm going to hang right in there with my discipline therapy until productivity jumps. . . . That is how your Recession reallocates resources efficiently, amid all the wailing and groaning. . . .

The third reason you should embrace me and not revile me is that I've put some zip back in the stock market. . . .

Yet Prosperity has a thousand fathers and Recession is an orphan. I have saved you from inflation; I have forced your managers and workers to become productive again; I have pulled your stock market out of a 10-year depression; I have returned you to the ways of economic righteousness.

All this have I done for you, and more. So how come I get no respect?

Source: William Safire, *New York Times*, December 13, 1982.

Capitalists need recession to keep the cost conditions affecting investment from becoming too unfavorable. Too much expansion is great for demand but causes serious problems with costs.

The longer an expansion continues, the more rapidly the cost conditions are likely to deteriorate. During the early years of the long boom of the 1960s, for instance, the expansion had relatively little effect on cost conditions affecting investment. The labor costs index actually *fell* 0.5 percent per year between 1960 and 1965. But as the expansion continued, its effect on cost conditions dramatically reversed and worsened (from businesses' standpoint). The labor cost index *increased* by 1.0 percent per year between 1965 and 1970. The longer the expansion continued, the more serious the problem became.

While business needs recessions to relieve the upward pressure on unit labor costs, recessions are likely to hurt capitalists as well as workers. Not only do workers lose jobs during recession, capitalists find that profits initially fall during recession (when demand for businesses' products falls) and cu declines. During recessions, the effect first experienced is that the recession's impact on demand conditions (decline in cu) is more powerful than its impact on cost conditions (increase in ru).

Despite the fact that current profits will decline, recessions are essential in order to restore favorable cost conditions affecting investment (and hence ensure higher *future* profits). In a sense, the recession imposes a price on capitalists. The decline in profits during the recession must be accepted as the down payment on ensuring higher profits during the next expansion. Recession is needed every few years to remind workers of their vulnerability to unemployment and thereby to reestablish employers' control in the workplace.

The well-behaved cycle and the misbehaved cycle

Recessions have an important job to do—they are essential to maintaining profits. Recessions occur when thousands of firms make independent decisions not to invest because the expected future profit rate is not high enough. Recession produces unemployment, slack demand for imported materials, and other changes; these conditions then restore the expectation of higher profits in the future.

In this respect the economy works somewhat like the human body, which has its own built-in mechanisms for defending its health. Some of these mechanisms are painful but necessary, like the pain of a sprained ankle, which strongly discourages a person from walking on the foot and worsening the injury during the period of recuperation.

With the economy, however, the mechanism sometimes does not work. The conditions for profitable investment may not be restored if there is a fall in the profit rate but for some reason the expansion continues and the recession does not occur. This is what happened during the 1960s when the economy missed the recession it "should" have had in 1966, following the decline in the profit rate of 1965. The fall in the profit rate should have signalled an oncoming recession. But partly because of the increase in military production for the Vietnam War, the expansion stretched from 1961 to 1969, well over twice the usual length of an expansion, with very low unemployment rates from 1964 to 1968. The result, as we shall see in Chapter 14, was a continuing fall in the profit rate from 1965 to 1970.

The second failure of the capitalist economy to right itself occurs when a recession happens—but it does not do its job. Recession may fail to restore the expected profit rate if (1) the worsening of the demand conditions for investment outweighs the improvements in the cost conditions; or (2) the cost conditions do not improve during the recession. In either case the recession may make things worse rather than better; this is like when the immunization system of the human body goes awry, so that instead of combating an infection, it feeds and spreads it.

One way that recession may fail to improve the cost conditions is if it fails to reduce the labor cost index. How could recession fail to reduce the labor cost index? Recall that the labor cost index has the wage (w) in the numerator; and in the denominator, it has the output price (Pz), work effort (d), and efficiency (e). Suppose that during recession the decline in demand for their products forces capitalists to cut their own output prices—Pz would fall. If, at the same time, they cannot increase the amount of work done per hour (d), raise efficiency (e), or lower wages (w) by enough to offset the price cuts, then the labor cost index will not fall but instead will rise. In effect, the change in Pz is so big that it swamps changes in all the other variables.

When the recession fails to do its job or does it weakly and slowly—as it did during the years 1892–1899, 1926–1933, and 1969 to the present—the economy enters a period of instability. Like a ship without a rudder or a human body without an immunization system, it does not right itself—the capitalist economy is in crisis.

Resolving the crisis is not automatic. It requires changes in basic economic institutions, that is, changes in the social structure of accumulation. Crises, then, are quite different from the usual ups and downs of the business cycle. Crisis periods are often marked by sharp political conflicts and by debate on new ways of organizing the economy. The 1890s, the 1930s, and the 1970s and first half of the 1980s were such periods. To understand this process of fundamental institutional change, as well as other important aspects of the capitalist economy, we must first explore the relationship between the government and the economy.

☐ Suggested Readings

John Kenneth Galbraith, *The Great Crash, 1929* (London: Hamish Hamilton, 1955).

Andrew Glyn and Robert Sutcliffe, *British Capitalism, Workers, and the Profit Squeeze* (Baltimore: Penguin Books, 1972).

Robert Aaron Gordon, *Economic Instability and Growth: The American Record* (New York: Harper & Row, 1974).

Michel Kalecki, *Selected Essays on the Dynamics of the Capitalist Economy 1933–1970* (New York: Cambridge University Press, 1971).

Wesley Clair Mitchell, *Business Cycles and their Causes* (Berkeley, Calif.: University of California Press, 1941).

CHAPTER 13

GOVERNMENT AND THE ECONOMY

Ronald Reagan was elected President of the United States in 1980 on a pledge to "Get the government off the backs of the people." Yet over the next few years, federal spending increased dramatically. In 1980 the federal government spent $577 billion; President Reagan's budget for 1985 called for $925 billion worth of expenditures. About half of this increase resulted from the fact that prices rose—so to perform the same activities, the government had to spend more. But even taking account of this, the federal government planned to spend 30 percent more in 1985 than it did in 1980.

State and local government spending also increased. In 1980, total government spending—federal, state, and local—amounted to 33 percent of total output (Gross National Product). By 1983, total government expenditures had climbed to 38 percent.

Why did government expenditures continue to grow under President Reagan, the self-proclaimed foe of "big government"?

In part, the growing role of the government under President Reagan simply continued a long historical trend. When George Washington formed the first cabinet under the new Constitution, there were only four departments (those of State, War, Navy, and the Treasury); the annual budget was a little over $4 million (in today's dollars the figure would be about $24 million or about one-tenth of the budget of the city of Tulsa, Oklahoma, for example). When Abraham Lincoln took office, the cabinet had grown to seven departments and federal expenditures that year came to $66 million (about $700 million in today's dollars). Franklin D. Roosevelt named nine cabinet secretaries when he took office in 1933; that year, federal spending topped $4 billion ($40 billion in today's dollars), which represented about 8 percent of total output (GNP).

The long-term trend is only part of the answer, however, because there has also been a great speeding up in the growth of government expenditures in contemporary capitalism. In 1948, for instance, *federal* expenditures still amounted to only 12.8 percent of GNP. But by 1983 this figure had nearly doubled to 24.6 percent; federal government expenditures totaled $826 billion.

This chapter explores the relation between government and the capitalist economy. The capitalist economy is organized according to one set of principles, one set of the "rules of the game"— commodity production for profit using wage labor and privately owned capital goods. Governments are organized according to different principles, a different set of game rules. These rules facilitate collective action and impose a compulsory relationship between citizens and government. Governments—or government leaders— are capable of taking collective action. They can act on behalf of all of us and enforce their actions on all of us.

The main idea of this chapter is that government, especially democratic government, operates on different principles from those of a capitalist economy, and each shapes how the other functions.

This main idea is expressed in five main points.

1. Government is organized according to a *different set of rules* (collective action, compulsory relationships, democratic government) from the rules of the capitalist economy.
2. The government, both because of its power and its size, has *important effects on how the economy works.* Government alters the horizontal or market relations among buyers and sellers; it affects the vertical relations of employers and workers, and it influences the time or change dimension of the economy.
3. The *government has grown* and become more important as part of the economy. The capitalist economy itself produced many of the tensions and pressures that led to the growing economic importance of the government.
4. Government activities have diverse effects on the profit rate, and these effects explain much of the conflict over government economic policy. They explain why government economic policies are so often contradictory and hotly debated. We will illustrate these conflicts by an analysis of what is called the *political business cycle.*
5. The *capitalist economy places certain limits on what the government can do.* We will see that some of the political power of the owners of large businesses derives from their ability to set political agendas and to make lavish contributions to electoral campaign finances. Equally important, they have political power because they control the process of investment, which in turn determines which states or even which nations will have jobs and economic growth and which ones will be faced with rising unemployment and economic stagnation.

☐ The Rules of Government Organization

Activities or relationships organized through the government tend to be compulsory, collective, and (in the United States and some other countries) democratically determined.

In using compulsion, a government is quite different from the other economic actors we have seen: firms, workers, families, and unions. Some of these actors do, of course, have the power to structure the choices and limit the options facing the others. An employer, as we have seen, has power over workers because he can impose an uninviting menu of choices on each worker. An early twentieth-century employer in the garment industry expressed this power succinctly in a notice to his employees: *If You Don't Come in on Sunday, Don't Come in on Monday.*

However narrow the choices are, a worker's relationship to his or her employer is voluntary in the limited but important sense that other employers exist and, even if it is difficult, other jobs may be found. The same goes for the consumer's relationship to a particular seller. These relationships, and the others we have introduced, involve exchanges and contracts (written or not). An exchange always involves a choice—even when the choice is very uninviting, as when the alternative to one's job is a long period of unemployment, financial headaches, family disruption, and job search involving uncertain prospects.

The citizen's relationship to the government, by contrast, is not voluntary; it is *compulsory.* One is born into it and can escape from it only by changing one's nationality.

Consider taxes. Taxes are not paid in exchange for something, in the sense that one might exchange $10 for a shirt. They are sometimes paid willingly because people support the educational services, police protection, or whatever the government will use the taxes for. But they are not paid voluntarily—the "choice" is to pay or have the government seize your property. Only the government can legally take your money or your property without obtaining your agreement. Only the government can legally lock you up, draft you, or take your life.

Government activities are usually *collective,* in the sense that government generally acts on behalf of all citizens. Taxes are supposed to be paid by all citizens. Goods and services provided by or distributed through the government are made available to all citizens, or to all citizens eligible for the particular service. In the capitalist economy, money is paid in each particular transaction and a product of service received by the buyer. In contrast, government monies are usually collected from all (as taxes) and the benefits (potentially, at least) distributed to all.

A corollary of the compulsary and collective nature of govern-

A **compulsory relationship** exists when a person cannot choose whether to enter the relationship but rather becomes subject to the relationship because of his or her status (such as citizenship).

Collective activities are activities whose benefits or burdens extend, potentially at least, to all citizens.

Citizen rights are the basis for a claim to share (some of) the benefits of society; this claim is based on one's citizenship instead of, for example, on possessing sufficient money to buy the benefits.

Democratic government is a way of organizing a government based on (1) accountability of officials through elections with widespread and equal voting rights and (2) civil liberties and personal freedoms.

ment is that a citizen obtains whatever benefits are due to citizens by *right*. The citizen does not have to purchase police protection or the right to vote, nor do his or her children have to buy a place at the public school. When benefits are available to only part of the citizenry (such as food stamps for the poor), any citizen who meets the criterion (being poor) gets the benefit by right. In contrast, benefits are available in the capitalist economy only in the form of commodities that must be purchased—no commodities can be claimed as a right.

Fortunately, the rules of the game by which the government operates are not limited to the government's possession of life or death powers. The government of the United States (and perhaps of 30 or so other countries) is organized according to the principles of what is called *democratic government:* popular accountability of government officials through elections with widespread and equal voting rights; and civil liberties, such as freedom of the press, of speech, of assembly, and so on.

The democratic rules have often, of course, been violated, even by democratic governments. In U.S. history, for example, some citizens were legally denied the vote because they did not own enough property, were not white, or were not male. Until the 1970s the principle of "one person, one vote" was widely (if illegally) disregarded in those states that effectively excluded blacks from voting. Groups unpopular with the government, or with business or other powerful institutions, have often been harassed by the FBI or otherwise deprived of their civil liberties.

But the basic idea of democratic government—that government leaders will be selected by the principle of voting, with each per-

Democratic Government: Fair Game or Stacked Deck?

The rules of democratic government are a set of procedures to govern how and by whom public decisions are made. Democratic procedures are like the rules of baseball or tennis—they determine only how the game of democratic government is to be played, not who wins.

The rules of democratic government do not ensure that each citizen will have a more or less equal say in the outcome of the governmental process. Whether the actual decisions made by a democratic government benefit all citizens equally or favor some special group, whether they are fair or biased, depends on more than the rules: it also depends on how much political influence each group has. Those people with more money or other resources to lobby, advertise, support candidates, and so on are likely to have more political influence, even when the democratic rules are faithfully followed.

son having one vote, after an open competition among competing candidates and ideas—is very different from the rules that govern the capitalist economy.

The heads of a corporation—the management—are not elected by the people who work there, nor by the community in which the firm is located. In fact, they are not elected at all in the sense that we usually use the word election, for they are selected by those who own the corporation, with each owner having as many votes as the number of shares of stock he or she owns. Similarly, freedom of speech and other civil liberties are very limited in the workplace. The majority of businesses place restrictions on workers' freedom to post information concerning unions, for example.

These two sets of rules—the rules of democratic government and the rules of capitalist economy—exist side by side in our society. Both affect the economy. They represent different ways of coordinating labor processes and distributing the product. For example, a person may buy a ticket to a rock concert arranged by a company (a commodity) or may go to a free rock concert sponsored by the city and paid for with taxes. In one case, the concert is held because someone—the promoter—is hoping to make a profit; in the other, it is held because the mayor or city councillors thought it would be a good idea or possibly a vote-getting thing to do. Another example: how much income a worker has to spend is determined *both* by how much labor time he or she has to sell (and at what price it sells) and by how much tax the worker must pay.

☐ The Economic Activities of the Government

The government *enforces the rules* that regulate our social lives—the rules of the capitalist economy, the rules of democratic government, and other rules (for example, rules concerning relations among family members). The government *changes the rules* as well. And the government is one of the *major actors in the economy.* We will consider each—the government as rule enforcer, as rule maker, and as economic actor.

Rule enforcer

As the enforcer of rules, the government has the power to impose penalties on those who violate the rules. Important activities of the government in this respect are the protection of civil rights through prevention of assault, rape, and homicide and the defense of property rights by the prevention of theft and the enforcement of contracts. National defense (when it is truly defense) may be included as part of the enforcement of the rules, as it attempts to prevent other governments from enforcing new sets of rules on us.

The enforcement of rules sometimes appears to be an aspect of government activities that works to the benefit of all. Except possibly for kleptomaniacs and the pathologically violent, we all benefit from the prevention of the theft of our personal property and of assaults on our person.

But appearances can be deceptive. The fair enforcement of some rules works to the advantage of some people and to the cost of others. Consider, for instance, the laws that once made it illegal for women to inherit property or for blacks to hold public offices; fair enforcement of these rules did not make the outcome fair. Or consider the laws that make it illegal for people to steal—even if they are on the verge of starvation and the person from whom they would steal makes a million dollars a year. It is often illegal for both a rich person and a pauper to sleep overnight in the park; but the rich person owns a house to sleep in and the pauper does not, so the law in effect prevents only the pauper from sleeping in the park. Thus there are winners and losers in the enforcement of the rules, even when that enforcement is scrupulously fair.

Classes and other groups that benefit from the present rules often seek to get the government to enforce rules in ways that are particularly advantageous to them. Over the years, the capitalist class in the United States (and in other countries as well) has benefited

---

Voting with Your Dollars?

It is sometimes said that markets are like elections, in which consumers "vote" for the commodities they want with their dollars. The more dollars that are "voted" for yellow shirts, the more yellow shirts will be produced—competition for profits will take care of that.

But it is an unusual kind of election, because some people vote more times than others. If every dollar of income counts as a vote, the average family among the richest 400 families in the United States had at least 65 million votes in 1982 (according to *Fortune* magazine, these families averaged $65 million in capital gains income alone that year). In contrast, the average American family received $22,000 in 1983.

Thus the rich voted 3,000 times for every vote cast by the average American family. Even taking account of income and other taxes, the rich voted about 2,000 times the average. Rather than the one-person, one-vote principle of democracy, this may seem more like an economic version of ballot box stuffing.

Sources: *Fortune*, Fall 1983; *Statistical Abstract of the U.S.* (Washington: U.S. Government Printing Office, 1983).

substantially from the governmental enforcement of a set of rules that worked disproportionately to their advantage, maintaining their economic privilege and relative freedom of action.

Rule maker

The government also changes the rules, making new rules or altering old ones. The existing rules of markets and private property have never been accepted as eternal—there are always groups seeking to change the rules in ways more advantageous to themselves. For example, in the 1780s some people—Alexander Hamilton was the most famous—wanted the government to *prevent* some markets from working. Hamilton wanted to have the government tax imports of manufactured goods into what would become the United States, because he believed that preventing or discouraging this type of exchange would stimulate the domestic development of industry.

Later, the new factory owners wanted the law of property rights changed so that they could divert the flow of rivers to power the new textile machinery in their mills. The existing property rights of farmers and others along the river banks—for access to water and protections against others inundating their land with water—were sacrificed so the textile mills could be more profitable. Still later, just before the Civil War, others pressed for yet another change in property rights, the abolition of slavery, making it illegal to own, buy, and sell people.

In 1935 the Wagner Act defined new rights for workers to bargain collectively in unions—that is, to collude rather than to compete individually—on the labor market. This process of continual change, redefining property rights and altering the rules of markets, has continued through the present century. In 1964 the public accommodations section of the Civil Rights Act restricted the way owners of restaurants and hotels could use their property; this law made certain forms of racial discrimination illegal. More recently, companies manufacturing and operating nuclear power plants obtained special laws limiting how much they could be forced to pay out in damages in case of a nuclear accident; like the earlier changes in laws governing water rights, this law effectively limits the property rights of others whose property might be damaged by the plants. All of these changes in the rules of the capitalist economic game altered the way the economy works.

Economic actor

The government—or more accurately, the decision makers in the various governments (state, local, and national)—is also an economic actor in its own right. The major governmental economic activities may be considered under the headings of government as *producer, microeconomic regulator, distributor,* and *macroeconomic regulator.*

As *producer,* the government employs people to produce goods or services, the most important of which are health, schooling, postal, police, fire, and military. With the exception of the military and the post office, most government production takes place in state and local governments.

As a *microeconomic regulator,* the government influences what the private economy will produce, how goods and services will be produced, and where they will be produced. To do so, it uses a combination of means. Taxes on cigarettes discourage the consumption and hence production of this product (as does the health warning on the package). Subsidies and other government payments encourage certain kinds of production—nuclear power has received government subsidies amounting to over $40 billion, a substantial percent of the operating costs of the industry over the past 20 years. Direct regulation of production includes limitations on product design (auto safety standards); production methods (mine safety regulation); and location (zoning and environmental protection). As a regulator of markets, the government may set limits on prices, such as the minimum wage or public utility rates; it may stockpile agricultural and other goods to control prices and for other reasons; it may foster competition through antitrust activities or inhibit competition, for example, by buying military goods primarily from large firms or by requiring licenses—as in health care—of persons practicing a particular occupation.

As a *distributor,* the government affects the distribution of income—between rich and poor; between one region and another; and between people of different ages, sexes, or races. It does this in part by maintaining a set of rules of the game that benefit one group over another, as we have seen. It acts as a distributor in part through its activities as producer, as when it provides more adequate schooling to one group than to another. As microeconomic regulator, the government also acts as distributor. When, for example, the government keeps agricultural prices high by buying up farm produce whose sale to consumers would have kept prices down, it distributes income away from the less well-to-do— who spend a large fraction of their income on food—and toward those who produce, process, and sell agricultural commodities.

The government also engages in distribution more directly. It taxes some people at higher rates than others, and it provides for government payments (or transfers) to those who, because of physical handicaps, old age, unemployment, child-care responsibility, or other reasons, have low incomes from other sources.

As *macroeconomic regulator,* the government uses various

methods to affect the business cycle and to control the instability of prices, profits, and employment that result from its alternating rhythm of boom and recession. It may raise taxes on families or businesses, thus discouraging spending for consumer goods or investment and causing production cutbacks and increased unemployment. It may expand its own employment, thus reducing unemployment. It may (through the Federal Reserve System) make it easier or more difficult for businesses to borrow money to build new factories, thus encouraging investment and expanding job opportunities. In its activities as macroeconomic regulator, the government has major effects on the distribution of income, forcing wages down through higher levels of unemployment or squeezing profits by providing more job opportunities.

☐ The Expansion of Government Economic Activity

Over the past half-century, the economic importance of the government has grown. There is no single adequate measure by which its growth could be gauged, in part because not all government activities are equally important from an economic standpoint. For this reason, measures of the size of the government—its total expenditures, total employment, or other measures—can only roughly capture the economic impact of the government. But there is little doubt that the growth has been substantial. Though the economic importance of the government has grown in the United States, it is still considerably less than in most other advanced capitalist economies, as Figure 13.1 indicates.

The largest growth in government *employment* has taken place in state and local rather than federal employment. Federal *expenditures*, by contrast, have grown quite rapidly, in part due to the rapid growth of military, Social Security, and health-related expenditures.

The reasons for this growth in the economic importance of the government are much debated. Some see it as a triumph by the ordinary citizen over the self-serving interests of business. Others see it as a carefully orchestrated strategy of business to provide itself with ever-greater opportunities for profit. Still others see it as a triumph of the bureaucratic mentality, which thinks that if there is a problem, there must be or should be some government office to deal with it.

But there is a more persuasive explanation. The survival and workability of capitalism as a system required the government to grow. The ceaseless search for extra profits and the ensuing social, technical, and other changes outlined in previous chapters created conditions that provoked demands for a more economically in-

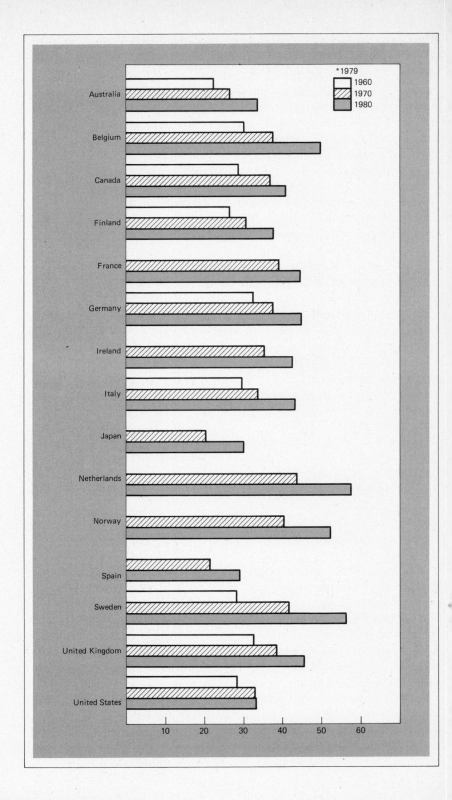

FIGURE 13.1 Government expenditures as a percentage of total output. Government expenditures as a percentage of total output increased between 1960 and 1980 in all of these advanced capitalist countries.

Among 15 leading capitalist countries (including some not shown here), the United States ranked fourth from the bottom in 1980 in the percentage of its total output used by government. Between 1960 and 1980 it also experienced very slow growth, compared to other countries, in the government share of total output.

Sources: Organization for Economic Cooperation and Development; *National Income Accounts* (Paris: OECD, 1983).

---

volved government. These demands, as we will see, have come as often from businessmen as from workers, as often from the Chamber of Commerce as from the AFL-CIO, as often from Republicans as from Democrats. The growth of the government is not something that happened in *opposition* to capitalism, but rather something that happened in very large measure *because* of capitalism.

Why did the government grow?

Economic concentration. Much of the growth of governmental economic activity can be explained by the growth of large corporations and the decline of small competitive producers. The enormous power of modern corporations has allowed its owners to engage more effectively in lobbying and in the formation of public opinion. Partly for this reason, big businessmen have become more confident that they can put the government to work to raise their profits. The government involvement in the nuclear power industry and in the production of military goods are good examples of this. Corporate leaders have also supported the expansion of government regulation in those many cases in which they wanted protection from competitive pressures that might lower profits. Examples include regulation of airline ticket prices and routes and milk price supports. Consumers and workers have supported an expansion of the economic activities of the government, in part to protect themselves from the power of the giant corporations. Passage of the Sherman Antitrust Act (1890) and the Consumer Product Safety Act (1973) are examples of this.

International expansion. The increasing international involvement of the large corporations and of the U.S. economy generally contributed to the development of a worldwide conception of "U.S. interests." As corporations expanded from national to international businesses, they changed from wanting the government to impose tariffs to keep out goods made abroad to insisting that the government protect "American" (their) investments around the world. This required an increasingly expensive military system to promote and defend these interests. The preparation for war and the payment for past wars have accounted for much of the economic expansion of the government. Capitalism did not invent war, but the degree of international economic interdependence and rivalry produced by the expansion of capitalism did make *world* wars more likely. After World War II, high levels of military expenditure became a permanent feature of the U.S. economy. In 1983 military expenditures were about 7 percent of net output, an amount equal to the agriculture, forestry, fisheries, and mining sectors of the economy combined.

Economic instability. The increasing instability of the economy, marked by periods of severe unemployment and dramatized by the Great Depression of the 1930s, has provided another impetus for the growing economic importance of the government. The stabilization of the economy was a major objective of the businessmen who promoted the formation of the Federal Reserve System in 1913 and the Securities and Exchange Commission in 1935. Much more important was the inability of the economy to revive from the Great Depression without the stimulus of massive World War II military expenditures. During the depressed 1930s, political instability and radical political movements spread as people came face to face with the failure of the capitalist system to provide for even a minimal livelihood.

A broad coalition of employers and workers, including such elite business groups as the Committee on Economic Development, concluded that the government would have to take greater responsibility for maintaining profits and employment through its activities as macroeconomic regulator. Immediately following World War II, this coalition was successful in gaining congressional passage of the Employment Act of 1946. This committed the federal government to at least the principle of maintaining adequate job opportunities.

The post–World War II growth of total government expenditures has contributed to the ability of the government to regulate employment. Some government expenditures (like unemployment insurance) act as *built-in stabilizers* that automatically increase when the economy slows down, thus helping to maintain enough total demand to avoid severe recessions. Other, more deliberate macroeconomic regulation of the economy may also counteract the economy's tendency to provide too few jobs. But these means have never managed to achieve anything approaching the elimination of unemployment, except during the Korean War and the Vietnam War (see Figure 11.8). In part this is because, despite the commitment apparently made in the Employment Act, the elimination of unemployment has never really been the objective of the government's macroeconomic regulation. Alben Barkley, a U.S. senator critical of the inadequacy of the act (and later Vice President), quipped that the new law "promised anyone needing a job the right to go out and look for one."*

Income support. During the Great Depression, large majorities of Americans became convinced that those unable to make a living should be supported, at least at some minimal level, by the government. Government programs to support poor people replaced informal support systems and private charity, both because people who fell on hard times could no longer count on their families or neighbors to tide them over and because private charity (church and private philanthropy) did not have the funds necessary to do the job. When most Americans were self-employed and families and neighborhoods formed tight communities, the families and communities provided most of the support for the handicapped, the elderly, and others unable to work or unable to find work. But as families and communities became less tightly woven, this system of support began to leave increasing numbers of people with little place to turn for help during hard times.

More recently, unemployment has inflicted a form of economic hardship for which even hard work is no remedy, and it has greatly increased the need for income supports. During the Great Depression, for instance, sources of private charity were simply overrun with people needing help. Only the government could provide income support on the scale needed.

Ironically, workers' constant moving around in search of work played a major part in undermining the ability (or perhaps the inclination) of families and neighborhoods to take care of those who did not find paying work. Equally important was that the capitalist accumulation process spelled the doom of the family farm and the small family business. For earlier generations, going home to the family farm or business had been a way of making it through a period of unemployment, but now there was no family farm or business to go home to.

The new vulnerability to unemployment became quite clear during the Great Depression, and people demanded a more adequate system of income support for the needy. In the 1930s unemployment compensation, general relief, and Social Security were established. With the numerical growth and political mobilization of the aged population and of single-parent families during the 1960s and early 1970s, benefits and beneficiaries expanded,

Public safety. Many groups have demanded that government regulate the conflict between profitability and public safety. While competition pushed firms to develop technology in the most prof-

---

* Quoted in Anthony Woodiwiss, "The Struggles of Capital," unpublished manuscript, 1979.

itable directions, advances in these developments have not always benefited society. The pharmaceutical industry dramatizes the danger of leaving economic decision making solely up to the profitability criterion—drugs dangerous to people's health may be very profitable. For example, drugs that earn big profits for drug companies may have effects that are complicated, long delayed, and potentially lethal for individual consumers. The chemical industry illustrates another conflict between profits and public safety. Some production processes, developed because they are highly profitable, may ultimately inflict brain damage, sterility, and cancer on workers; their effects often become known only after many years of exposure.

These conflicts created new demands for government action. Consumers organized for product-safety legislation. Workers—in mining, in textiles, in chemicals, and elsewhere—organized for occupational health and safety regulation. As a result, particularly in the last twenty years, a series of protective legislative acts have been passed, the most important of which are the Mine Safety Act (1969), the Occupational Safety and Health Act (1970), and the Consumer Products Safety Act (1973).

Environmental protection. Many people pressed government to protect the natural environment from capitalist development. Our natural surroundings—our land, fresh water, air, and oceans—were not only being used, they were being used up. Part of the reason was that no one was charged a price for using most of these things. In many cases, the most profitable way of disposing of wastes—even very hazardous ones—was simply to throw them away, using our natural environment as a free dumping ground. Incidents like the burning of the Cuyahoga River in 1969 and the poisoning of the Love Canal residential area in the 1970s dramatized the need for controls. The formation of the Environmental Protection Agency in 1970 and the passage of the Clean Air and Water Act were important steps in this direction.

Discrimination. Over the last three decades people have come to realize that the unrestricted exercise of rights in private property and in capital goods often results in racial and sexual discrimination against both customers and workers. The lunch counter sit-ins that began the civil rights movement of the 1960s posed the issue sharply—the right of owners of the restaurants and lunch counters to do what they pleased with their property, including the exclusion of black customers, versus the rights of black people to be treated equally in public places. Since 1964 the U.S. Civil Rights Commission has brought suits against companies, unions, and other institutions, seeking to force them to eliminate discriminatory practices.

Many of these seven sources of expanded government economic activity may be understood as responses to particular aspects of the accumulation process of the capitalist economy. The growth of the government is as much a part of the capitalist economic growth process as is the growth of investment or the growth of technology.

But if government has had to grow to repair the problems and hardships caused by capitalist development, it does not follow that this has been an adequate response. It is quite debatable whether people are today more secure economically than they were a hundred years ago, or less susceptible to environmental or natural disaster, or less likely to encounter health hazards in their workplace or in their food, or better protected from the unaccountable power of the giant corporations. It seems highly unlikely, in fact, that bigger government programs have managed to keep pace with the escalating challenges posed by the pattern of capitalist economic growth.

Just as we should not overrate the effectiveness of the expansion of the government's economic activities, we also should not exaggerate its extent. Government employment is still a small fraction of the total labor force—15 percent, including the armed forces. The crucial determinant of the future course of the economy—investment—is still almost entirely in private hands.

☐ Conflicts over Government Economic Activity

In recent years there has been substantial controversy over the amount of government participation in the economy. To understand this debate, one must understand the effects of government economic activity on the profit rate and how these effects give rise to a complex pattern of conflict and coalition among government leaders, business, labor, and other citizens. We will begin with the effect of the government's economic activities on the profit rate.

After-tax profits

The discussion of the profit rate thus far has—for simplicity—left the question of taxes aside. But businesses are concerned with the profits left *after* a firm has paid its taxes, or what is termed the *after-tax profit rate (atr)*.

To keep things simple (and not too unrealistic), we will assume that businesses pay a tax to the government that is a given fraction of their total before-tax profit. In 1983 this average corporate profits tax was about 25 percent. The after-tax profit rate, then, is some fraction of the before-tax rate. Suppose the tax rate is 25 percent and the before-tax profit rate is 16 percent; then the after-tax profit

The **after-tax profit rate** is the profit rate capitalists receive, having taken into account (subtracted) any taxes they must pay.

rate is three-quarters of the before-tax rate, or 12 percent. If r is the before-tax profit rate, and *tax* is the tax rate, the after-tax profit rate (*atr*) is simply:

$$atr = (1 - tax)r \qquad (13.1)$$

where   *atr* = after-tax profit rate
             tax = tax rate on profits
               r = before-tax profit rate

We can now turn to our complete list of the determinants of the after-tax profit rate. (It may be helpful at this point to review the box on page 120 in Chapter 6.)

The government may affect the after-tax profit rate of a company, an entire industry, or the economy as a whole. It does this by affecting one or more of the things that determine what the after-tax profit rate will be. The number of ways that the government might raise or lower the profit rate is, of course, practically endless. But to illustrate some of the major effects, the accompanying box lists some examples. A number of important conclusions may be made even on the basis of this limited list.

Government Policies and the After-Tax Profit Rate

Profit Rate Determinant	How Government Policies Might Raise the Profit Rate
1. Hourly wages (*w*)	Maintain enough unemployment to depress wages
2. Prices of output (*Pz*)	Use U.S. military and political power to obtain adequate foreign markets for the output
3. Output per unit of work done (*e*)	Subsidize research in applied science, promote job training
4. Amount of work done per hour of labor (*d*)	Fail to enforce occupational safety standards
5. Amount of materials used and wear and tear on capital goods per labor hour (*m*)	Support research in improved technology
6. Price of materials and capital goods used in production (*Pm*)	Allow businesses bigger tax reductions (depreciation allowances) when they purchase equipment; use U.S. power to gain access to cheap raw materials
7. Capital goods in use per hour of labor employed (*cg in use*)	Repeal regulations requiring waste treatment equipment
8. Capacity utilization ratio (*cu*)	Maintain growing and predictable level of demand for goods through macroeconomic management
9. Price of capital goods (*Pc*)	Grant tax credits for investment
10. Profits tax rate (*tax*)	Reduce the tax rate

First, there will be conflict between employers and workers over many of the government's economic activities. While some activities—like promoting research—may be in the economic interest of most U.S. citizens, many other activities will benefit some groups and harm others. In these cases, what is good for employers is bad for workers. Consider the government policies listed in lines 1 and 4 of the box. These governmental policies make possible a higher profit rate by cutting corners with safety and by providing higher levels of job insecurity, thus permitting employers to reduce wages, speed up work, and obtain other concessions from workers. As we have seen, these are all contrary to what workers want—higher wages, safer and less strenuous working conditions, and more job opportunities (less unemployment).

Second, many of the ways in which the government might help to raise the profit rate are likely to work at cross purposes:

> Maintaining high levels of unemployment (line 1) is also likely to cause many of the capital goods owned by business to be idle, thus lowering the capacity utilization ratio (contrary to line 8).

> Reducing the tax rate (lines 6 and 9) may make it more difficult to pay for the military (lines 2 and 6), research and training (lines 3 and 5), and other activities that business favors.

> Using military power (lines 2 and 6), as in the Korean and Vietnam Wars, may drive down the rate of unemployment (contrary to line 1).

Thus even if there were no conflicts with workers, business attempts to shape government policies to raise the profit rate might be contradictory and ineffective.

Third, businesses themselves may have contradictory goals for government. Each firm is not so concerned about the average profit rate as it is about its *own* profit rate. For this reason businesses are often ready to urge the government to adopt policies that will raise their (own) profit rates at the expense of other businesses. Individual firms lobby government to reduce their taxes, to give them subsidies, or to set the prices of their output at a high level. Big oil companies benefit enormously from tax credits for foreign royalties paid. Boeing Corporation regularly obtained a substantial subsidy through government-subsidized cheap credit for the company's foreign customers. Companies in the oil industry were quite happy to see the government decontrol oil, permitting the price of their output (a raw material input for most other companies) to go up, not down. The oil companies' support of decontrol seemed unaffected by the fact that this policy inflicted big losses on the auto industry, whose high-profit gas guzzlers fell from favor among consumers as gasoline prices rose. Most businesses (as we saw in Chapter 12) would be happy to promote government policies that would allow them to pay their own workers less while forcing other firms to pay more. In all these ways, businesses lobby for special benefits that are often in conflict with policies to raise the general profit rate.

Workers, too, have divided interests concerning what the government should do, although often for quite different reasons. Workers in the automobile industry, for example, may want government policies to limit imports of cars produced elsewhere; other workers may want to save money by purchasing a Honda Civic. Those unions that have mainly white male members, to take another example, may be less enthusiastic about governmental affirmative action programs for minority workers than unions with substantial minority and female memberships.

Our understanding of government policy is further complicated by the fact that employers and workers are not the only players in the game. Government leaders have their own objectives and face their own constraints. Most of all, they must find ways of being reelected or reappointed. This requires appealing to a large number of voters, which may be done by a combination of two things: enacting policies that are in the interest of a majority of voters; and enacting policies that are favored by individuals who can make substantial contributions to election campaign funds. Both types of policies appear to be necessary, because politicians who faithfully serve the interests of the majority but cannot finance electoral campaigns are just as surely losers as the ones who too blatantly favor the few at the expense of the many.

Government leaders, like businessmen, may find that their objectives work at cross purposes. To gain favor with business, government leaders may want to cut taxes on profits. But it may then be difficult to raise other taxes without incurring the wrath of the electorate. And with lower taxes all around, it may be impossible for the government leaders to offer needed public services favored by the majority of voters.

This three-way tug of war among government leaders, workers, and business is illustrated, in the following section, by the problem of macroeconomic regulation of the unemployment rate.

The political business cycle

Imagine that the economy is in the midst of a strong expansion. Output is increasing rapidly, businesses find that new orders are rolling in, and the demand for labor is high. Unemployment is at quite low levels. The economy is in the expansion phase of Figure 12.7.

As the expansion continues, workers realize that they have little to fear should they lose their jobs. They can usually go across the street and find other work. For this reason they are willing to run some risks. They begin to ask for big raises or improvements in working conditions. They are not quite as concerned about refusing overtime or missing a couple of days of work. They worry less about working hard enough to secure favor with the boss.

Capitalists begin to worry. While growing markets will raise the capacity utilization ratio (cu) and thus tend to raise the profit rate, a long expansion may be too much of a good thing from their point of view. Why? Because with the low unemployment that a long expansion brings, the profit rate will be reduced by rising wages (w) and falling work effort per hour (d).

They appeal to the government leaders. In private they tell the politicians that a recession is needed to restore a little more unemployment and thereby discipline workers. No capitalist single-handedly can create a recession, but the government can; and so business lobby groups, the business-oriented press, and others approach government leaders. Of course no one can publicly call for more unemployment, but the policies that produce it can be sold as "fighting inflation" or "fiscal responsibility" or "keeping the money supply under control."

Government leaders may go along with business. If they do, they can use a number of strategies, all of which will reduce total demand for output. They can

Cut back on government expenditures (reducing government demand);

Restrict credit and adopt other policies that make it more difficult or more costly for businesses to borrow money to finance their investment expenditures (reducing demand for new capital goods) or for families to borrow in order to buy cars, houses, or other goods on credit (reducing the demand for consumer durable goods and housing);

Raise personal or business taxes, cutting into people's consumption expenditures or leaving businesses with less to spend (reducing demand for both consumer goods and capital goods).

With total demand down, new orders for goods and services start to dry up, production is cut back, and workers are laid off. Workers begin to hear about friends who got laid off or plants that closed, and they begin to worry about keeping their jobs. Discipline becomes stricter in the workplace. If the contraction is short and is effective in lowering labor costs, businesses may consider the temporarily low capacity utilization ratio a price worth paying in order to regain the upper hand over labor. And when the economy begins expanding again, capacity utilization will rise and the profit rate will recover.

Thus, the recession may be a success story from the employers' standpoint. But the politician knows there is an election around the corner. Unemployed workers and their families often (correctly) blame political leaders for at least part of their distress, and they may vote for the opposition at the first available moment.

The result of these complicated interactions and reactions is what has been termed the *political business cycle*. The word "political"

A **political business cycle** occurs when recession and/or expansion are in part intentionally created by governmental economic policy, as officials attempt to generate a business cycle for their own or others' interests.

is added to the usual term "business cycle" to indicate that something has been added to the usual ups and downs of employment, output, and other macroeconomic measures. These are no longer determined solely by the millions of relatively uncoordinated spending decisions of investors and consumers; now the business cycle is also determined in part by a political process whereby government leaders juggle the interests of workers, employers, and their own reelection in the process of macroeconomic regulation.

We will see in the next chapter that the political business cycle is not only a theoretical possibility. It is a repeated occurrence in the U.S. economy.

☐ The Limits of Democratic Control of the Capitalist Economy

Can the government control the economy? If recessions can be initiated by public policy, is it not possible to use the power of the government for more beneficial purposes? Can the citizens of a democratic government control the economy? As we will see, in a capitalist economy there are definite limits to what even a determined majority can do.

In the previous section, because of the often conflicting effects of government economic activity on the profit rate, we saw that conflict and inconsistency are built into government economic policy in our economy. In this section, we see that the ability of the voters—even large majorities of them—to alter the course of economic events in our economy is quite limited as long as the economy remains capitalist.

The **power of capital** refers to the ability of employers, especially the largest corporations, to influence governmental policy or otherwise create conditions favorable to their own interests; this power grows out of their position in the capitalist economy.

The **power of the citizenry** refers to the ability of citizens to influence governmental policy or otherwise create conditions favorable to their own interests; this power grows out of their position in democratic government.

To understand the limits on government, recall that our economy may be considered to be like a game in which there are two different sets of rules. One set of rules—the rules of the capitalist economy—confers power and privilege on those who own the capital goods used in production, particularly on the owners and managers of the largest corporations. The other set of rules—the rules of the democratic government—confers substantial power on the electorate, that is, on the great majority of adult citizens. Thus our social system gives rise to two types of power: the *power of capital* and the *power of the citizenry*.

Those powers are often at loggerheads, as when the citizens want to restrict the power of capital to sell dangerous or environmentally destructive products. In most of these conflicts, capitalists have immense and often overwhelming advantages, despite the fact that the owners of businesses (and particularly large businesses) are greatly outnumbered. There are three sources of their power—one obvious, the others not so obvious.

One reason capitalists have great political power is that economic resources can often be translated directly into political power. This happens when businesses or wealthy individuals contribute to political campaigns; advertise to alter public opinion; hire lawyers, expert witnesses, and others to influence the detailed drafting and implementation of legislation; and otherwise apply their economic resources to the political system. Corporate control of economic resources implies substantial corporate political influence over government officials.

There is a second, more indirect reason for the disproportionate political power of business leaders. It is that mass communications are run by businesses: capitalists in this industry own the TV stations, newspapers, publishing houses, and other capital goods used in production. Even "public" radio and TV depend heavily

---

The Power of Business: Here Comes the Judge

"Money is power." This is one of the oldest political truisms. But how *exactly* does money become power? One example is the reeducation of Federal judges.

Many cases brought to Federal court involve economic issues. An enterprising academic at the University of Miami and several dozen large corporations decided to make sure that judges learned the *right* economics. The corporations, including Exxon, GE, IBM, and more than 100 others, have contributed millions of dollars to finance special training institutes to teach their brand of economics to judges. The Law and Economics Center at the University of Miami runs the program.

Judges are invited to spend two weeks in Florida, all expenses paid (including golf and tennis fees); all they need to do is sit and listen to the economic principles taught by the corporate-financed economists.

And what kind of economics do they teach? They focus on such topics as the importance of property rights, criticism of current antitrust laws, and government interference in the private economy.

Do these seminars really reeducate judges to be more sympathetic to corporations, or are the judges just getting a nice paid vacation and a tan? Several recent graduates indicated that the seminars have had an effect. One Court of Appeals judge wrote, for instance, "I have no doubt whatsoever that I have been influenced subjectively in my understanding and approach to regulatory matters."

Perhaps other groups in society could gain the judges' ears if these groups opened "training seminars" in Hawaii, Aspen, or the Bahamas and paid all of the judges' expenses. But then, most other groups do not have the money.

Source: G.C. Staple, "Free Market Cram Course for Judges," *The Nation*, January 26, 1980, pp. 78–81.

on corporate contributions. Freedom of speech and of the press (which includes TV and radio) guarantees that people can say, and journalists can write, whatever they please. On the other hand, the private ownership of the capital goods used in the TV industry, for example, guarantees that what is broadcast is in the end controlled by capitalists—either by the owners of the station or by owners of the major corporations that buy the advertising for the shows. These are people who understandably have little interest in seeing the idea of citizen power applied in ways that limit the freedom or profits of those who own the capital goods used in production, whether in the TV industry or elsewhere.

There is a third way in which money brings power—capitalists control investment, and so they determine the fate of the economy. Think back to the political business cycle. Why were the government leaders initially willing to go along with businesses' demands to bring on a recession that would increase the unemployment rate? Because they knew that a long-term reduction in the profit rate would have disastrous consequences for their chances of getting elected. And why was this? In part, because they might lose the support of businessmen and their contributions. But as important, because if profits are low, businessmen will complain of a bad *investment climate*. They will not invest, or they will choose to invest in some other country. The result will be unemployment, economic stagnation, and perhaps a decline in living standards of the majority of the people, who will lose no time expressing their disappointment on election day.

Since capitalists control investment and hence the key to a healthy economy, political leaders often must do what capitalists want, in order to create the right investment climate. They know that in the end it is capitalists who make the decisions whether to invest and where to invest. Business thus holds a kind of blackmail over democratically elected political leaders.

This form of blackmail is called a *capital strike,* because it involves capital going on strike. When workers strike they refuse to do their part in the economy—they do not work. When capitalists strike they also refuse to do their part—they do not invest. But here the similarity ends. When workers strike they must organize themselves so that they all strike together. A single worker cannot go on strike (that is called quitting). By contrast, when capital goes on strike, no coordination is needed. As we saw in Chapters 7 and 11, each corporation routinely studies the economic and other conditions relevant to its decision to invest. If they do not like what they see, they will simply not invest or will invest elsewhere. *Nobody* organizes a capital strike. It happens through the independent decisions of corporate leaders. If things look bad to a large number of corporations, the effect of their combined withholding

The **investment climate** is the business community's general mood or level of confidence with respect to future conditions for the profit rate; individual investors are likely to be more willing to invest when capitalists as a group are in a more favorable or optimistic mood than when the business community is more gloomy about investment prospects.

A **capital strike** occurs when, as a result of a negative investment climate, many individual capitalists decide to reduce their investments or not to invest at all.

of investment will be large enough to alter the course of the economy.

Capital strike severely limits what citizen power can accomplish when citizen power conflicts with the power of capital. An example may make this clear. Usually, unemployed workers get unemployment insurance checks for, at most, 39 weeks. Let us imagine that the voters of a particular state—we will call it Wisconsin—decide that they want to provide more generous unemployment benefits, so that the checks will keep coming in as long as the worker is unemployed. These payments are to be financed by a heavy tax on the profits of firms that pollute the environment. Because a majority of the citizens support the idea, the government of the state of Wisconsin enacts the needed taxes and other programs and enforces them. So far, so good.

Now imagine that you are the chief executive officer of General Motors, or of General Electric, or of any other corporation that employs large numbers of workers in Wisconsin. Assume you are considering investing in Wisconsin (say, opening a new plant). Not only will you worry about the taxes, you will wonder how hard workers will work if they know they have permanent unemployment insurance. You may ask yourself what the citizenry will vote for next. You obviously will think twice before investing in Wisconsin, not necessarily because you do not like the new laws personally, but because your profit rate, both before and after taxes, will most likely be lower in Wisconsin as a result of the new laws. You will probably put your new plant someplace else, perhaps in a state that actively advertises its favorable investment climate.

Quite independently, other businessmen will no doubt come to the same conclusion. Some may even close down plants or offices in Wisconsin and move elsewhere. The result will be increasing unemployment and lower incomes for the people of Wisconsin.

The hard times may bring on a state financial crisis. As unemployment increases, state expenditures on unemployment insurance will rise, as will other costs of maintaining minimum living standards. As income falls, the state's tax revenues will decline. Rising costs and falling revenues create a soaring deficit in the state budget.

But the problems have just begun. In order to spend more money than the taxes are currently bringing in, the state government will be forced to raise taxes again or borrow more from the banks and from others with money to lend. Because of the declining state of the Wisconsin economy, the banks will be unsure that their loans will be paid back promptly or even at all. If they agree to loan the money, they will do so only at high interest rates. If the loans are granted, the problem will be put off, but it will return with greater intensity when the high interest charges must be paid, in addition to the other demands on state revenues. The resulting vicious circle, now common in the government sector, is called a state fiscal crisis.

The Power of Business: Free to Move

High Tech Leader Issues Warning to State

The president of the Massachusetts High Technology Council said yesterday that about 75 member companies are planning expansions in the next few months, but many of them—at least 40—are holding off deciding where until the Legislature resolves two issues: unitary taxation and so-called plant closing legislation. Howard P. Foley . . . stressed high tech's opposition to both proposals and said the way they are resolved will indicate the (Governor's) and the Legislature's "commitment or lack thereof to continued direct high tech job creation."

Unitary taxation . . . prevents a corporation from using bookkeeping methods to shift profits to subsidiaries located in other states or countries that are low tax areas.

Plant closing legislation . . . would require a company to notify the state in advance of a layoff or plant closing. Foley said the legislation would arbitrarily restrict a company's ability to adjust to changing conditions.

Representative Thomas Gallagher, cosponsor of the plant-closing legislation criticized high tech's use of plant expansions as political leverage. Gallagher added that the same type of do-it-our-way-or-we-walk arguments have been used time and time again by industry even dating back to opposition to child labor and minimum wage laws.*

[*Update:* The High Technology council's threats proved effective. Despite the fact that 97 of Massachusetts's 200 state legislators had cosponsored the mandatory plant-closing notification legislation and, according to a poll, 81 percent of the voters favored it—only 14 percent opposed—the proposed law was withdrawn and replaced by a bill that would make the companies' notification of future plant closings voluntary. Even the *Wall Street Journal*, which is no supporter of plant-closing legislation, termed the resulting bill a "toothless compact."

Only two states, Maine and Wisconsin, have plant-closing laws on the books, but bills mandating prior notification and benefits to displaced workers have been introduced in 38 other states.]†

* Bruce Mohl, *Boston Globe*, March 1, 1984, p. 11.
† Eugene Carlson, "Massachusetts Deftly Handles Volatile Issue of Plant Closings," *Wall Street Journal*, June 26, 1984, p. 37, and Rosemary Hamilton, "Bay Staters More Worried about Taxes than Jobs, New Poll Reveals, *Boston Business Journal*, March 19, 1984, p. 1.

There are two likely outcomes. First, with repayment increasingly uncertain, the banks may refuse further loans until the state government changes its policy. If the state government is on the verge of bankruptcy—which means breaking contracts with state employees and not paying wages or bills—the banks' advice may be quite persuasive. Second, the sovereign citizens of Wisconsin may decide to elect a new government, in order to revoke the laws. In either case the new laws will be repealed.

The example is hypothetical; Wisconsin has avoided these problems. But in recent years—in Cleveland and New York City in the 1970s—the above example was acted out in real life.

Our example was for a single state. But what is true for one state is true for all states, and more important, it is also true for the nation as a whole. As we have seen, General Motors and General Electric do not have to locate in the United States at all. Increasingly these firms and others have located new plants in other parts of the world, often in dictatorships—South Korea, Haiti, South Africa, and Taiwan are examples—where the investment climate is better because capitalists do not have to deal with problems of citizen power.

Let's go back over our Wisconsin example. Were the citizens' voting rights or civil liberties violated? No. Did capitalists collude and deliberately undermine citizen power? No, they acted independently and in competition with each other. Did they use lobbyists to influence the government officials or campaign contributions to influence elections? Maybe they did, but they did not need to.

Did the citizens exercise control over the economy? That is a much harder question. The capitalist economy certainly imposed limits on what they could do. The citizens could vote for any policy they wanted, but they could not force businesses to invest in Wisconsin, and that severely limited what citizens could get.

Henry Ford, who was famous for his cheap, single-design, no-frills Model T, once said, "You can have any color car you want as long as it's black." In many respects, the voters of our hypothetical state of Wisconsin had a similar choice.

Where did they go wrong? The example could have turned out very differently.

One course the citizens of Wisconsin could have followed would have been to limit their expectations; they could have instructed their government to concentrate only on those programs that would benefit citizens but would at the same time *increase* the profit rate in the state or at least not lower it. In other words, they might have accepted from the outset that they were not "sovereign" in economic matters, and made the best of a less than ideal situation.

Thus, for example, they might have concentrated on eliminating

Sovereignty refers to the ability and right of a person or group to make a decision; democratic government confers sovereignty on the citizenry, whereas capitalist economy confers sovereignty, especially with respect to investment, on the owners of capital goods.

those forms of pollution that reduce profits in the recreation business and lower property values. They might have designed programs to give economic security to old people but not to current workers. They might have tried to increase equality of opportunity by giving all children more business-oriented schooling. And they might have voted to finance these programs by taxes that did not fall on profits. If they had done this, many Wisconsin citizens would have benefited, and the losers might not have been in a position to disrupt the program. Specifically, capitalists might have looked favorably, or at worst indifferently, on these events and might not have brought about the economic decline of the state by leaving.

Again, this is just a hypothetical example, but it is similar to what actually happened in real life Wisconsin. Wisconsin was a leader early in this century in trying out programs to make the most of citizen power while operating within the confines of the capitalist economy. The federal government and other state and local governments now engage in many beneficial economic activities that also fit this description. Making the best of the limits of the capitalist economy is most fully developed in some European nations such as Sweden and Austria, where social democratic governments have been in power over much of the post–World War II period. However beneficial, these programs are severely limited, since many of the ways to improve living standards and the quality of life sooner or later also threaten the rate of profit or the idea of profits.

There is a second course that Wisconsin citizens could have followed, which, if not likely, is at least conceivable. When General Motors and General Electric decided to close their operations in Wisconsin, the plants could have been taken over by the communities in which they are located, by those who work in them, or by the state government. When a business leaves a community, what it takes, usually, is its money. Most of the plant, the machines, and the workers stay. There is no reason—other than the private ownership of the capital goods used in production—why the workers could not continue working at their old jobs. They could do this as part of a community-owned enterprise, a worker-owned firm, or some other organization.

But for this to happen and for the example to work out differently, the citizens of Wisconsin would have had to have been ready and willing to use their rights as citizens to change the rules of capitalism—in this case, to change the rights of ownership and control of the capital goods used in production. They would have needed to claim citizen power not only over the government, but also over the production process.

What can we conclude from this example? That citizen power is severely limited in its ability to alter fundamental economic events, unless citizens are willing to change the rules that govern the workings of the capitalist economy. Thus a democratic *government* is not the same thing as a democratic *society,* for in a democratic *society* decision making in the economy as well as in the government would be accountable to the majority.

☐ Suggested Readings

Samuel Bowles and Herbert Gintis, *Schooling in Capitalist America: Educational Reform and the Contradictions of Economic Life* (New York: Basic Books, 1976).

Thomas Ferguson and Joel Rogers, *The Political Economy: Readings in the Politics and Economics of American Public Policy* (Armonk, N.Y.: M. E. Sharpe, 1984).

Charles E. Lindblom, *Politics and Markets: The World's Political-Economic Systems* (New York: Basic Books, 1977).

James O'Connor, *The Fiscal Crisis of the State* (New York: St. Martin's Press, 1973).

Frances Fox Piven and Richard Cloward, *The New Class War: Reagan's Attack on the Welfare State and Its Consequences* (New York: Pantheon Books, 1982).

CHAPTER 14

LONG-TERM GROWTH AND STAGNATION IN THE AMERICAN ECONOMY

When you think of the 1920s, prosperity and optimism come to mind—"the Roaring Twenties." Mention the 1930s, and one immediately thinks of bread lines, soup kitchens, the song "Buddy Can You Spare a Dime," and the Great Depression. The 1950s and 1960s were prosperous years of economic growth and promise. *The Affluent Society* was a best-selling book; *High Society* a box office hit. Since 1973, however, everyone has worried about the hard times: inflation, unemployment, and *stagflation,* a new entry in the English dictionary meaning inflation and unemployment together.

In "good times," like the 1950s and 1960s, productivity and living standards grow rapidly and people are generally more optimistic about the future, expecting it to be bigger and better than the present. Neither inflation nor unemployment seems to be such a serious problem. Attention turns to solving the "remaining" problems. In the midst of the 1960s boom, for instance, President Lyndon Johnson proclaimed his War on Poverty to eradicate poverty in America. Simultaneously, the United States fought the war in Vietnam, doubled university enrollments, and sent a man to the moon. Everything seemed possible.

In "hard times," like the 1970s and early 1980s, the economy seems to be a perpetual source of problems. Inflation, high unemployment, factories closing their doors, loan defaults, cuts in needed government services, and government deficits seem to compete with one another for attention. People are more worried about the present and pessimistic about the future. Hit songs feature lines like "We're living here in Allentown and they're closing all the factories down." Holding on to what you have replaces great hopes for more, and public discussion focuses on limits, constraints, sacrifices, and "trade-offs."

During hard times people begin to feel that the system is not working as well as they would like. Thoughts frequently turn to basic changes in structure of the capitalist economy and its relationship to the government. The Great Depression, as we have seen, brought on the New Deal, the recognition of trade unions, and the expansion of government responsibility for regulating unemployment and guaranteeing a minimum of economic security.

The hard times of the 1970s and early 1980s, though very different from the Great Depression, have also stimulated proposals for radical changes. Conservatives like Ronald Reagan have proposed and partially achieved a fundamental change in the relationship of the government to the economy, in effect attempting to reverse some of the innovations of the New Deal period. Others, including some important business leaders, have proposed equally radical changes in the other direction, toward greater government involvement in planning and implementing economic priorities.

By almost anyone's standards, the economy has performed poorly in the 1970s and early 1980s. The term *crisis*, meaning an acute rather than a lingering problem, has been regularly attached to our recent economic performance (financial crisis or deficit crisis or unemployment crisis).

Why has this period produced such hard times? What are the sources of our current economic problems?

One thing *has* been produced in abundance—explanations for our problems. Some blame high wages; others point to insufficient investment; still others talk of a capital shortage, a productivity crisis, OPEC, bad government policy, too much government, declining research budgets, or unfair trade policies by Japan and Europe. One leading economist spoke of the economy "suffering a thousand cuts and needing a thousand Band-Aids." Ronald Reagan spoke of 30 (sometimes 40) years of "bad habits" and "misguided policy," including, evidently, the years of the great post–World War II boom.

Why does the economy go through this alternating pattern of good times and hard times? We have already discussed the business cycle, and this is surely part of the answer. Yet the business cycle explains relatively short-run fluctuations. A recession of a couple of years' length is followed by an expansion for a few years.

In contrast, the difference between the prosperity of, say, 1948 to 1973 and the hard times since 1973 represents what economists call a *long swing* in economic performance—periods of 15 to 25 years of prosperity are followed by long periods of economic dif-

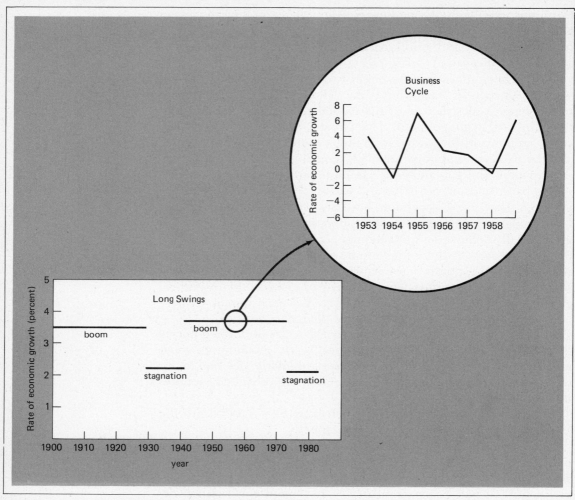

FIGURE 14.1 Long swings and business cycles. Long swings are long-term fluctuations between booms and hard times; business cycles are shorter ups and downs experienced by the economy during a few years.

The figure shows that the U.S. economy has passed through two long swings in this century. Between 1900 and 1929, during a boom, the economy grew by an average of 3.5 percent per year. But between 1929 and 1941, during the Great Depression, the economy averaged only 2.2 percent growth annually. The second long swing began with a boom period—between 1941 and 1973, the economy averaged 3.7 percent annual growth. But between 1973 and 1983, average annual growth slumped to 2.1 percent.

Business cycles occur during both long-swing booms and stagnations. For example, between 1953 and 1956, in the middle of postwar boom, the economy went through a business cycle, with a recession in 1953–1954 followed by an expansion in 1954–1955.

Sources: Calculated from *Historical Statistics of the U.S.*, series F-3; and *Economic Report of the President, 1984*, table B-2 (Washington: Government Printing Office).

ficulty. Figure 14.1 illustrates the relationship of long swings to the business cycle.

This chapter focuses on the long-term pattern of alternating economic growth and stagnation to explain the recent poor performance of the economy. Because long swings in a capitalist economy are related to profits and investment, we can build upon the analysis of the previous chapters to explain long swings and the crisis of the U.S. economy in the 1970s and early 1980s.

The main idea of this chapter is that capitalism is a system of power that works well (on its own terms) when the power of the capitalist class is secure and not too costly to maintain. When that power is undermined—either by other groups or by the contradictory nature of capitalists' own objectives—or when it becomes very costly to maintain, the capitalist economy is likely to falter.

This main idea is expressed in six main points:

1. The American economy has developed in a pattern of *alternating booms and hard times,* or *long swings* in economic activity. The post–World War II long swing consisted of a long-swing boom from the end of the war until the late 1960s, followed by long-swing hard times from the late 1960s to the present.
2. The post–World War II boom took place within an institutional environment—a social structure of accumulation—that we have described in Chapter 5 as *contemporary capitalism.*
3. The postwar *boom* turned to *hard times* when these institutional arrangements were eroded. Erosion of the social structure of accumulation caused the U.S. profit rate to decline, starting in the mid-1960s. As the profit rate fell, investment began to decline.
4. Slow productivity growth combined with conditions of political stalemate in the 1970s to produce *rapid inflation.* Unlike earlier periods of inflation, during the 1970s prices increased rapidly not only during the expansion phases of the business cycle but during the business cycle downturns as well.
5. While the economic stagnation continued into the early 1980s, the *political stalemate was broken* in 1980. The results were a long recession, increasing economic hardship, and high levels of *unemployment.*
6. The crisis in economic institutions and economic performance is likely to be resolved only with *major economic reform.* Such fundamental changes in the past have required both a powerful political movement and a successful economic program.

☐ From Boom to Hard Times: Anatomy of a Long Swing

When the United States emerged victorious from World War II, many people's thoughts returned to the Great Depression.

True, the military buildup for the war had finally ended the crushing unemployment of the 1930s by increasing the demand for goods and services. But would this war-induced prosperity prove to be just temporary? Could the capitalist economy survive a return to peace? And if it did, would the bitter struggles between employers and workers and the ominous international rivalries of the 1930s return as well, promoting economic instability and insecurity?

The success of the capitalist system, indeed even its ability to survive, was very much in question. A prominent group of economists wrote a book titled *Saving American Capitalism*, and while the authors thought that it could be done, many believed that the task would not be an easy one.

The immediate postwar years seemed to confirm these fears. A massive strike wave erupted in 1946, appearing to end the temporary government-imposed wartime cooperation between large corporations and unions. The Cold War between the United States and the Soviet Union menaced the prospects for international stability and security.

Two decades later, in the mid-1960s, the doubters had been proved wrong. The U.S. economy had experienced a long period of more or less trouble-free growth. Open conflict between employers and workers had fallen to levels reminiscent of the days before the establishment of unions. And the U.S. government and multinational corporations had extended their operations and interests over a major part of the globe.

In fact, there was now such confidence that people spoke of 1945 as the beginning of an "American Century," much like the British domination of the nineteenth century. Economists proclaimed that advances in economic science now made possible virtually uninterrupted economic growth, and debate turned to the question of how to use the fruits of growth.

After two additional decades, in the mid-1980s, some of the earlier pessimism has returned. We now know what was not apparent in the mid-1960s. The record-setting expansion of the economy from 1960 through 1968 was not the beginning of a future of uninterrupted good times but quite the opposite; the late 1960s were a turning point, bringing to an end the postwar boom and ushering in a period of hard times that has persisted through the mid-1980s. The economy had moved from the boom phase of the long swing to the hard-times phase.

The basic differences between the two periods may be described in any number of ways, each showing the U.S. economy as first robust and then in ailing health. But the economic fact that most accurately reveals this pattern is the after-tax profit rate.

The after-tax profit rate is a measure of the health of the capitalist economy seen from the perspective of the owners of the capital goods used in production—the capitalist class. Because the after-

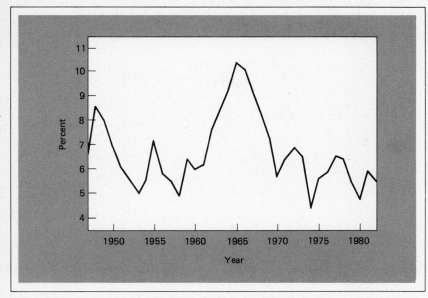

FIGURE 14.2 After-tax corporate profit rate, 1947–1983. After an early decline, the profit rate rose to peak in the mid-1960s, after which it has declined through the early 1980s. The series shows the expected cyclical ups and downs, generally turning down toward the end of a business-cycle expansion (e.g., 1955, 1959, 1965, 1973).

The profit-rate data presented here are for the nonfinancial corporate business sector of the economy and refer to profits after corporate profits taxes *(ATR)* divided by the value of the capital goods owned *(K)*.

Source: U.S. Department of Commerce, Bureau of Economic Analysis (Washington: Government Printing Office).

tax profit rate is also a main determinant of the level of investment, and therefore of the growth of the economy as a whole, the profit rate serves as a barometer of general economic conditions as well. Figure 14.2 presents data on the after-tax profit rate for the corporate sector of the economy, excluding banks and other financial institutions. (This rate is a close approximation for after-tax *r*; while there are many measures of profitability, the rate shown in Figure 14.2 accurately measures the overall profitability of the economy.)

The cyclical pattern of profitability suggested by Chapter 12 is evident in Figure 14.2—profits declining during the latter part of expansions (1955, 1959, 1966, 1973, 1978–1979) and then rebounding after the following recessions.

But a long swing pattern is clear as well—profits rising steadily until the mid-1960s and then falling thereafter. This long swing in the rate of profit is one of the most important factors lying behind the long swing of the economy as a whole.

Wages represent another indicator of deteriorating economic performance. Real (inflation-corrected) after-tax wages grew rapidly

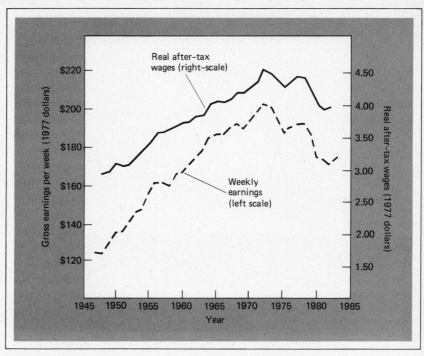

FIGURE 14.3 Real after-tax wages and weekly earnings of production workers: 1948–1983. Workers' earnings in real (or inflation-adjusted) terms generally rose over the postwar period until the early 1970s; they have fallen since then.

Average real gross weekly earnings of production workers measures the total weekly pay before taxes have been deducted, corrected to take account of the effects of inflation. The figures reflect not only the hourly wage rate, but the number of hours worked per week. (Farm workers, supervisory, workers, and government workers are not included.) In 1983, gross weekly earnings were at the same level as in 1962.

The real after-tax wage is the hourly wage rate, after taxes have been deducted, corrected for the effects of inflation, for the same group of workers.

Sources: *Economic Report of the President*, 1984, table B-39; and U.S. Department of Labor, *Monthly Labor Review* (Washington: Government Printing Office), November, 1984.

from the late 1940s through the mid-1960s, but in recent years this growth slowed down and then was reversed. Figure 14.3 shows that since 1973, after taking account of inflation, wages have fallen considerably. In order to avoid a decreased living standard, people have had to work more jobs or longer hours (if they could find the work).

This chapter explains why the U.S. economy did so well for so long and then faltered, apparently resisting all efforts to set the engines of growth back on the tracks of steady expansion. As with most important questions there are no simple answers and few answers at all upon which most economists agree. We will see, however, that the now familiar concepts—the profit rate, the labor accord, investment, the political business cycle, and most of all, the social structure of accumulation—can help us develop a factually based account of the curious rise and fall of American prosperity in the post–World War II period.

☐ The Social Structure of Accumulation in Contemporary Capitalism

The success or failure of the social structure of accumulation is the key to understanding the long-swing pattern of alternating hard times and boom. The *social structure of accumulation,* as we saw in Chapter 5, is the institutional environment, political and ideological as well as economic, that regulates the profit-making and investment process known as *accumulation.*

During the long boom periods, the social structure of accumulation provides favorable conditions for capitalists. These conditions produce a high and rising level of profits, leading to very favorable expected future profit rates for business and therefore (as we saw in Chapter 11) high levels of investment. During crisis periods the social structure of accumulation fails—in one way or another—to provide these conditions for high levels of profits, expected profits, and investment.

Investment clearly plays a central role in this process, since insufficient investment (and high unemployment) is associated with hard times, whereas plentiful investment (and low unemployment) characterizes good times. As we saw in Chapter 11, investment is determined principally by the profit rate that capitalists expect for the next few years. But what causes investment (and the expected future profit rate) to be "insufficient" or "plentiful" for long periods?

Whether the expected future profit rate is high or low, and hence the level of investment is insufficient or plentiful, depends on what capitalists expect the determinants of the profit rate to be. The determinants of the profit rate, in turn, depend on the *social structure of accumulation,* for it is the laws, institutions, power relationships, and social customs making up this social structure that provide the context within which the profit rate determinants are set.

A long-swing boom results when the social structure of accumulation is favorable to capitalists. The institutional setting within which the profit-rate determinants are set facilitates capitalists' efforts to obtain a high profit rate and stimulates rapid investment. Hard times result when the social structure is unfavorable to capitalists; it tends to provide an adverse setting for the determinants of the profit rate, making it difficult for employers to reduce unit labor costs, acquire imported materials cheaply, and achieve a high profit rate.

The most recent social structure of accumulation was created during the period 1935 to 1950. It served as the basis for the postwar boom. This social structure of accumulation was based on four crucial aspects of the U.S. economy, the first two primarily microeconomic, the second two macroeconomic:

The dual economy
Segmented labor markets
Expansion of governmental activities to carry out certain key activities in the economy
A dominant position for U.S. businesses in the world capitalist system

Chapter 10 discussed the microeconomic aspects of the accord. Here we turn to its macroeconomic aspects.

Expansion of government activities. A central part of the postwar social structure of accumulation was an expansion of the federal, state, and local governments' domestic economic activities.

Chapter 13 outlined how governmental activity grew to encompass not only rule enforcing and rule changing but microeconomic regulation, regulation of the macroeconomy, distribution, and the production of services. These activities ensured growing demand for goods, helped reduce social conflict, and indirectly supported the profit rate. They were rooted in such legislation as the Social Security Act (1935) and the Employment Act (1946).

Undoubtedly the main contribution of government activities during this period was maintaining a reasonably high level of total demand, thereby ensuring strong markets for goods. Military spending contributed to this goal, because the federal government directly purchased the output of defense contractors. Throughout this period, military spending has provided a significant portion of all demand (GNP), and virtually all of the large corporations and many thousands of smaller ones have profited from military contracts or subcontracts.

Another way that government stimulated economic activity was through monetary and fiscal policies, such as credit and tax programs. In part, these programs had an automatic effect. The income tax rate that a family pays declines when its income falls, and unemployment payments rise when unemployment goes up. The effect of these automatic stabilizers, as we saw in Chapter 13, is to cool off expansion and to soften the fall during recessions. Other policies were more deliberate—President John F. Kennedy's tax cut (proposed in 1963 and passed after his death) was designed specifically to favor corporations that invest and thus to stimulate investment.

Government activities extended far beyond regulation of the macroeconomy to include activities like Social Security, support of education and job training, financing of research activities, and subsidizing industries such as nuclear power.

These various government activities helped establish a favorable context in which the determinants of the profit rate were themselves determined. The success—particularly in the 1960s—in maintaining a high proportion of capital goods actually in use (cu) depended, for instance, on regulation of the macroeconomy and on military spending. When the government stimulated the economy by increasing military spending and lowering taxes, these policies raised cu and thus raised the profit rate.

Military Spending—Everyone's Dream Turned Nightmare

Despite President Eisenhower's warning that a powerful "military-industrial complex" was growing out of control, military purchases remained exceptionally high during the peace years between the Korean and Vietnam Wars.

One reason is that military spending helped maintain the postwar social structure of accumulation:

It strengthened the labor accord, because it provided jobs in key industries. Moreover, any labor leader who protested could be labeled a "Red."

It was an ideal way to increase aggregate demand, because no matter how much the government spent on arms, some military expert could say it was not enough. Unlike roads or other spending, there was no natural limit.

It also was thought to strengthen U.S. hegemony in the world capitalist system, since the U.S. position appeared to rest in large part on military power. More arms seemed to mean more power.

Of course the buildup of military hardware *did* use resources that might have gone to produce other goods and services. But in an age that remembered the Great Depression, it was natural for business leaders to worry most about their ability to sell what they produced and thus to welcome the added stimulus of government demand for military goods. Many labor leaders, too, concluded that the alternative to more tanks was not more cars but more unemployment.

It was hardly a bargain in the long run:

The military got to use its arms in a series of unpopular and largely unsuccessful interventions in the Third World: the Bay of Pigs invasion of Cuba in 1961 and the Vietnam War (1964–1973) among them.

Equally important, during these same years those countries that had devoted their surplus product to productive investments rather than military goods production (notably Japan and Germany) outpaced the United States in competition for world markets.

Not all government activities necessarily contribute to sustaining the profit rate and a boom. Pollution controls or occupational safety regulations, for instance, no matter how socially desirable, are likely to reduce, not raise, the profit rate.

What was characteristic of government activities during the 1950s and early 1960s, however, was that virtually all activities directly or indirectly helped to raise profits. Government support of research or education, for instance, meant that critical shortages of professional labor (such as engineers) were relieved and technological bottlenecks broken. The public, rather than capitalists, paid for these contributions to the production process. Even Social Security, especially during the 1950s and 1960s when there were many people paying in and few getting benefits, served to reduce conflict and promote social harmony.

While a generally probusiness policy was adopted by Republican and Democratic administrations alike, there was much conflict about how best to stimulate investment and growth. A slogan on which John F. Kennedy was elected in 1960, for instance, was "Let's get the country moving again." This referred to the fact that the more conservative Eisenhower administration had kept unemployment quite high and had refused to stimulate the economy. Kennedy then proposed his proinvestment tax cut.

Hegemony is the power to define, interpret, and enforce the rules of the game and thus to determine the range of possible alternatives for all of the players.

U.S. hegemony. The power that the United States exercised in the world economy is called *hegemony*. It means having the power to define the rules of the game and thus to determine the range of relevant alternatives for all the "players." (In a high school, for example, the school administration may be said to exercise hegemony in the selection of elective courses, for even though the student has a choice, it is the administration that determines which electives will be offered to the students.)

U.S. international hegemony had several effects on the determinants of the profit rate.

1. It provided the conditions for getting raw materials from other parts of the world at very low (and declining) prices. *Result:* lower *Pim.*
2. It gave U.S. corporations a stable international political and economic situation in which they could move their plants wherever the profits would be highest (sometimes using the threat to gain concessions from workers and governments in the United States as well). *Result:* lower *w*, higher *d.*
3. It established a situation in which U.S. corporations, particularly during the early postwar period, faced very little competition from other companies, thus strengthening their monopoly position. *Result:* higher *Pz.*

U.S. dominance or hegemony resulted in part from the fact that during World War II all of the other major powers suffered extensive war destruction, whereas the United States emerged intact. And, of course, during the immediate postwar years two of the major capitalist countries, Germany and Japan, were under U.S. military occupation.

United States hegemony manifested itself in many ways. One was military. Throughout the capitalist world, U.S. military might, or the support of U.S. allies, prevented any serious interference with American investments. For instance, in 1953 the nationalist government in Iran had nationalized a Western oil company's holdings; it was promptly overthrown by the U.S. Central Intelligence Agency (CIA). In 1954, when the democratically elected Arbenz government in Guatemala sought to redistribute United Fruit Company land to landless peasants, the U.S. government instigated the overthrow of Arbenz, providing arms and pilots to do the job.

A second important manifestation of U.S. hegemony was the Bretton Woods agreement for the international monetary system (named after the New Hampshire resort where the agreement was hammered out). This agreement made the U.S. dollar "as good as gold" in international payments and provided for fixed exchange rates between all the major currencies. Bretton Woods permitted rapid expansion of U.S. investments overseas, made Wall Street the banking center of the world, and facilitated the growth of world trade.

A third aspect of U.S. hegemony was the successful insistence by the U.S. government that in those countries with which the United States traded, taxes on imports (tariffs) and other obstacles to the sale of American-made goods be lowered or eliminated. The United States reciprocated by lowering or eliminating most of our tariffs. The result was that tariffs and other obstacles to international trade were gradually eliminated in the 1950s and early 1960s, and international exchange of commodities grew rapidly. Initially the development of what is called *free trade* or the *open world economy* mainly benefited the United States, because it gave U.S. producers access to other countries' markets. Later, however, the absence of substantial barriers to international trade was essential to the ability of other countries' corporations—Volkswagen, Sony, Toyota—to gain access to U.S. markets.

U.S. hegemony did not end international conflict; like the labor accord between U.S. corporations and unions, it simply set the terms of the conflict in ways favorable to U.S. corporations. Conflict was apparent in Third World countries like Guatemala, Iran, Cuba, and the Dominican Republic, where nationalist groups struggled to gain control over their own economies. Conflict existed even between the major countries—President Charles de Gaulle's long effort to have an independent French nuclear force and to resist American investment and political leadership in France was per-

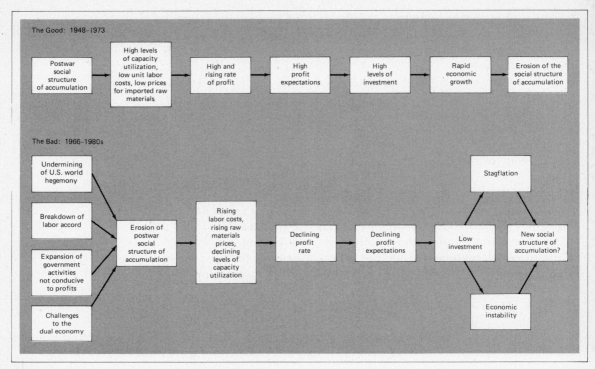

FIGURE 14.4 The good times and the bad. The economy's performance is strongly influenced by the success or failure of the social structure of accumulation to provide favorable conditions for accumulation.

During good times—like the period from 1948 to 1973—the social structure of accumulation results in a favorable set of profit rate determinants, high and rising profit rates, high levels of investment, and rapid economic growth.

During bad times—like the period from 1966 to the mid-1980s—the social structure of accumulation no longer provides such a favorable context for accumulation. The profit rate determinants are less favorable, profit rates fall, investment declines, and economic growth slows.

The years from 1966 to 1973 represent a transition period—profit rates fell and investment began to decline). The basis for future problems was laid, but economic performance remained reasonably strong.

haps the most strident and open case. But in similar ways other countries also fought against U.S. hegemony, even as many of them participated in the American-led boom.

The way in which the four aspects of the postwar social structure of accumulation facilitated the boom is summarized in the top panel of Figure 14.4. From the bottom panel of Figure 14.4, however, we can see that the boom did not last forever. By the mid-1960s, the social structure of accumulation had weakened and could no longer assure high levels of profits. The next section shows how this process of erosion of the social structure of accumulation took place.

The Postwar Social Structure of Accumulation and the Profit Rate Determinants		
Element of the social structure of accumulation	**Example**	**Example of an effect on profit-rate determinants**
1. Segmented labor markets (labor accord)	1950 agreement in coal industry: labor shares in productivity gains, employers gain a free hand in running the mines; the growth of the low-wage sector of the economy.	Permitted steady growth of output per unit of work done (e rises); employers cut corners on safety issues (d rises) labor cost index does not rise
2. Dual economy	Three major firms share domestic auto market	Higher profits in core due to monopoly power (Pz, cu higher)
3. Extension of government economic activity	Regulation of macroeconomy—for example, 1964 (Kennedy) tax cut to stimulate investment	Provides continuing high demand for products (cu remains high)
4. U.S. hegemony in world capitalist system	1953 CIA overthrow of Iranian government	Kept raw materials prices low (Pim remains low)

☐ The Erosion of the Social Structure of Accumulation: 1966–1973

The postwar boom ended in the early 1970s. It ended because in the late 1960s and early 1970s the four central elements of the social structure of accumulation eroded or were altered in such a way as to cause a long-term decline in the profit rate. Reduced profit rates subsequently produced lower investment levels and slower economic growth.

The hard times of the 1970s and 1980s can therefore be traced to the demise of the postwar social structure of accumulation (and the failure to create new conditions favorable to accumulation). The demise of the social structure of accumulation took place in large measure in response to what it itself had produced: social movements, conflict, and new economic realities that grew out of the social structure of accumulation itself. In a sense, its success was its own undoing. We consider each of the four principal elements in turn.

The conditions underlying *segmented labor markets* changed because the *labor accord* was eroded. The labor accord failed because both partners, in pressing their rights within the accord for their own advantage, undermined the bargain of higher productivity in exchange for higher wages. Recall that the labor cost index (see equation 12.3 on page 276) can fall with rising wages

Productivity and the Growth of Productivity

Many commentators blame the recent troubles of the U.S. economy on the decline in productivity growth. There is little doubt that the productivity slowdown *has* had serious unfavorable consequences for the U.S. economy, but it is not the underlying cause of our difficulties. Rather, the productivity slowdown is a consequence of the erosion of the social structure of accumulation.

Between 1948 and 1966, productivity in the private business economy grew by 3.1 percent per year. This means that for every hour worked, an additional 3.1 percent of goods and services was available each year for someone—workers, capitalists, government, whomever—to use. By contrast, productivity growth fell to 2.3 percent between 1966 and 1973 and fell again to 0.8 percent between 1973 and 1983.

Productivity is generally measured as

$$\overline{y} = \frac{\overline{Y}}{Labor}$$

where
$\overline{y}$ = productivity (the real—inflation-corrected—value of net output per labor hour)

$\overline{Y}$ = real value of (net) output (also known as value added)

$Labor$ = total number of labor hours worked

Net output in *money* terms (from Chapter 6) is

$$y = Pz\,(ed) - Pm\,m$$

where
d = work done per hour

e = output per unit of work done

m = amount of materials used and machines used up in production per labor hour

Pz = price of output

Pm = price of materials and machines

To correct for inflation we simply divide by Pz, so that an increase in output price does not increase our measure of productivity, as

$$\overline{y} = y/Pz = (ed) - (Pm/Pz)m$$

As long as prices (Pm and Pz) do not change, for productivity to grow, work done per hour (d) must increase, the output per unit of work done (e) must increase, or the use of nonlabor inputs (m) must be reduced (or some combination of these).

Productivity growth may have declined because e or d failed to grow as fast as before or because m increased more rapidly than before. Note, also, that an increase in Pm (for example, in oil prices) will lower productivity.

Productivity is often thought of as identical to *efficiency*—but we can see that it involves much more than that. An increase in e or a decrease in m would certainly be called an improvement in efficiency, but an increase in d may come about through a "speedup" of the labor process, while a decrease in Pm may be the result of U.S. military power securing access to inexpensive raw materials in the Third World.

Source: The data on productivity growth refer to the U.S. business economy and are reported in the *Economic Report of the President, 1984* (Washington: Government Printing Office, 1984), p. 266.

only if productivity (the denominator, or ed of equation 12.3) rises even faster than product wages (w/Pz). Rising productivity—a growing ed—was thus an essential accompaniment (as well as a consequence) of the labor accord. But rapid productivity growth came to an end in the mid-1960s.

Corporations helped undermine the accord by choosing to concentrate new investment outside of unionized areas (that is, in places or in industries not covered by the accord). This left their facilities operated under the accord underutilized and rapidly becoming obsolete. Coal companies, for instance, made huge new investments in (nonunion) western and Australian strip-mining operations. Rather than building new auto plants in the United States, GM and Ford built plants abroad. Mines and factories in the industrial Midwest and Northeast, the heartland of the accord, became dilapidated and increasingly uncompetitive as productivity failed to grow rapidly.

Corporations began to step up the pressure on their workers. Feeling the pinch of increased competition from foreign firms and hoping to reverse the decline in the profit rate that began in the mid-1960s, the corporations hoped that an increase in d, the amount of work done in an hour, would restore the failing profitability of U.S. business. Partly as a result of the attempted speedup of production, workplace safety suffered. Industrial accidents, which had declined over the post–World War II era, began to increase in the 1960s, reaching World War II levels by the end of the 1970s. Workers' resentment mounted. For other reasons as well, workers became less satisfied with their jobs. Many came to desire not only well-paying jobs but also interesting work and more autonomy and respect on the job.

Workers also contributed to the erosion of the labor accord. Reacting to the relative job security provided by their employers (under the accord) and to the low overall rate of unemployment (due in part to government macroeconomic policies), workers organized to establish safer working conditions and lower effort levels. As workers, especially in the period 1966–1973, became confident of finding other jobs if they were fired, they became stronger in resisting their employers' efforts to maintain or accelerate the pace of production. Recall the example of GM's ill-fated speedup of its Lordstown plant.

These forces made the terms of the accord less profitable. As a result of a continuation of unproductive business investment policies and labor's increasing ability to resist speedup, both the efficiency with which the economy used labor (e) and the amount of work done per hour (d) fell or stopped rising as rapidly. For this reason, the rate of growth of output per worker hour in the private sector of the U.S. economy (y) grew more slowly or even fell. Between 1948 and 1966 productivity grew at an average rate that would double productivity every 22 years. Between 1966 and 1973 productivity growth slowed down to a rate that would double productivity every 30 years, and between 1973 and 1983 it fell to a rate that would take 77 years to double.

Lower levels of productivity growth undermined the labor accord, for the economy no longer provided a big enough productivity bonus to provide workers with rising real wages and still support high profit rates.

The deterioration of the accord may be seen in coal mining. Here, the 1950 collective bargaining agreement had symbolized the new accord. But during the 1960s, coal miners became increasingly effective in protesting against the rising number of mine fatalities. Through strikes and union pressure for the passage of safety legislation, they achieved dramatic reductions in the number of miners killed between the late 1960s and the mid-1970s. But as a result of changing investment patterns and increased worker militance over job conditions, as mine safety improved, output per miner per day fell from 19.3 tons in 1968 to 14.3 tons in 1979.

In the economy as a whole, capitalists experienced declining profit rates during the 1970s and early 1980s. Output per unit of work done (e) failed to grow, work effort levels (d) fell, and wages (w) continued to rise. These all tended to reduce the profit rate. Workers, however, found that their higher wages would not buy much more. Because the income taxes paid by workers (and others) rose rapidly during these years, the real value of workers' *after-tax* hourly wages rose less rapidly after 1966 than before. After 1973 the real value of workers' take-home pay (after-tax hourly wage) fell considerably, as we saw in Figure 14.3.

The *dual economy* (described in Chapter 10) was based on significant advantages enjoyed by the large corporations of the core sector. The dual structure of the U.S. economy had, in effect, channeled higher profits into the hands of the largest and in many cases the most dynamic businesses. But international competition began to intensify, in part because of the "open world economy" approach that the United States had insisted on under the Bretton Woods agreement. The profits of some core corporations in the steel and auto industries and elsewhere were hit particularly hard. Many peripheral firms produce services or goods that are not imported—a Laundromat does not have to worry about foreign competition; U.S. Steel and the Ford Motor Company do. As a result, though the core corporations remained dominant in the U.S. economy, their advantage relative to the rest of the economy eroded.

Government activities also changed in such a way as to be less favorable for profits and investment. Many government programs (Social Security, welfare, other social programs) had provided *promises* of benefits, at little real cost, at the beginning of the boom; now they began to impose heavier costs as beneficiary rolls expanded. Unions, which had initially given up politically motivated industrial actions for the *promise* of political influence through electoral politics, were increasingly able to make their bargain pay off. They obtained minimum wage laws, occupational health and safety rules, the expansion of unemployment insurance, and other legislation that directly or indirectly imposed costs on capitalists. Groups left out of the labor accord—primarily blacks, women, the elderly, consumer activists, and environmentalists—were successful in obtaining further government programs that imposed direct or indirect costs on business.

U.S. hegemony also eroded under the twin pressures of rising international competition and the defeat of the U.S. military in Vietnam. The rapid development of Japanese and Western European industry ended the highly favorable conditions under which corporations had earlier entered world markets (see Figure 10.3). Whereas in the early years of the boom U.S. products had flooded foreign markets, more and more goods produced outside the United States now entered U.S. markets. Moreover, growing investment abroad by U.S. corporations meant that, increasingly, "American" products for foreign markets were made abroad.

The automobile industry provides an illustration. In 1955 sales of imported cars were 0.25 percent of the U.S. auto market. Enter the VW bug, followed by Toyota and others. By 1970, imports had risen to 15 percent of the market, and by 1982, to 28 percent of this market. During this same period, U.S. car companies had established assembly plants and other production installations throughout the world.

Moreover, unlike in the early boom years, U.S. power no longer commanded deference. American leaders, now in a situation of growing economic weakness, were increasingly unable to obtain economic policies favorable to the United States from the other important capitalist countries. This changing balance had many effects, one of which was the collapse in 1971 of the Bretton Woods monetary system. This system had depended for its workability on the dominant position of the United States in the world economy. The inability of U.S. armed forces to win in Vietnam also provided an immense blow to U.S. hegemony. What was important was not so much what happened in Vietnam as the signal that this defeat gave to the world—it advertised the limits of U.S. power. The oil-exporting countries (OPEC) were able, within a few years, to raise the price of oil to roughly 15 times its pre-1973 price.

The erosion of U.S. hegemony meant rapidly rising prices for imported raw materials (*Pim*); reduced markets for U.S. goods (more idle capacity, that is, lower *cu*); and increased competition in its markets, thus reducing the prices at which U.S.-produced goods could be sold (*Pz*). These all tended to reduce the profit rate.

The erosion of the four parts of the postwar social structure of accumulation—segmented markets based on the labor accord, the dual economy, pro-profit government activities, and international hegemony—accelerated during the late 1960s. A brief account of what happened during these years will illustrate the way in which the four aspects of the social structure of accumulation were interrelated.

During the mid-1960s total demand in the economy was expanding rapidly and the economy booming. This was the result of a high level of investment stimulated by a high level of after-tax profits; the expansion of government social expenditures; and the beginning of the buildup of military production for the Vietnam War.

By 1965 unemployment had been quite low for a number of years—the unemployment rate was 4.5 percent in that year and falling. President Lyndon Johnson's economic advisors knew that a continuation of such low levels of unemployment would sooner or later improve labor's bargaining position enough to cause a decline in the profit rate. It was time, many in government and business thought, to have a recession.

Johnson could have caused a recession by changing government policy so as to reduce the growth of total demand. This would have required at least one of the following:

1. Cutting government expenditures without cutting taxes
2. Raising taxes without raising government expenditures
3. Restricting credit and raising interest rates (so as to discourage businesses from borrowing money to finance new investment)

Johnson could not risk cutting domestic social expenditures, because he was faced with large, well-organized movements of welfare recipients, the elderly, civil rights workers, and others for an *increase* in the social programs. He had just declared the War on

Poverty a year earlier in an attempt to address the concerns of these movements. Similarly, he could not cut military expenditures, as he was just gearing up for his second war, the one in Vietnam. In the end he did not cut government expenditure; he raised it.

His reasons for not wanting to raise taxes were similar. Already an antiwar movement was emerging. Johnson feared that people who otherwise might support the war would turn against it once they had to pay its cost in higher taxes, so he wanted to obscure as much as possible the cost of the war. Raising taxes in 1965 or 1966 would have drawn attention to the costs of the war and further fueled antiwar sentiment.

Johnson's third option was to raise interest rates. Raising interest rates might well have induced a recession and brought on the increase in unemployment needed to restore business's bargaining power over labor. However, in the heady atmosphere of the 1960s boom many corporations had borrowed heavily and were substantially in debt. Raising the interest rate would have dealt them a serious blow, as it would have greatly increased their costs. They protested loudly at the thought of a tightening of credit.

Hemmed in on all sides, Johnson had little choice but to ignore the danger signals. The economy barreled on. Very low unemployment persisted until 1969. The effect was to alter considerably the balance of power between employers and workers during these years. Wages grew more rapidly than productivity (output produced per labor hour), leading to an increase in the labor cost index. In the late 1960s the after-tax profit rate began to decline.

Why did Johnson's program not do better for the profit rate? The failure was closely connected to the erosion of U.S. power in the world (the high cost of the Vietnam War) and to the successful challenge by grass-roots movements (civil rights, environmental, occupational health and safety, and others) to those government priorities that previously had been heavily tilted toward helping business.

In Figure 14.2 we saw that aside from the ups and downs associated with the business cycle, the average corporate profit rate had risen steadily from 1953 until the middle of the 1960s. But as the postwar social structure of accumulation provided an increasingly unfavorable context for profit making, the after-tax profit rate peaked and then began to fall.

The profit rate continued to decline during the late 1960s and early 1970s. Evidence began to accumulate that the economy was in serious trouble. Capitalists lowered their expectations of future profits. As a result they cut back on investment (see Figure 14.5).

To summarize, the period from 1966 to 1973 was a time of declining profit rates. It resulted in declining investment as well. The

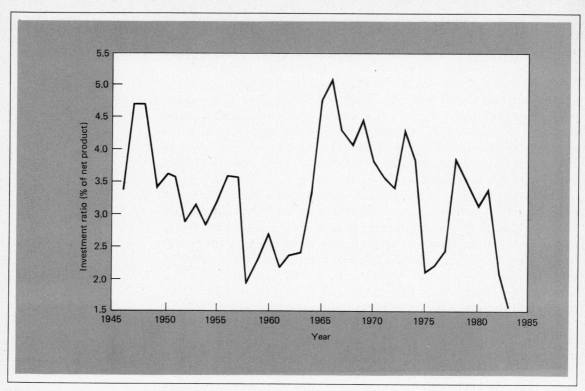

FIGURE 14.5 Investment in the U.S. economy, 1948–1983. Investment slowly declined between 1948 and the early 1960s; then it rose rapidly until the late 1960s. After a slight decline until 1973, investment fell precipitously until 1983. Investment was lower in 1983 than in any year since World War II.

Like the profit rate, the level of investment shows both long-term movements and short-term cyclical ups and downs. Investment generally peaks at or near the top of a business cycle. e.g., 1955, 1959, 1966, 1973, 1979.

Investment is the expansion of the supply of capital goods used in production. It is measured here by the net fixed private investment expressed as a percentage of net output (net domestic product). Investment in housing and investment outside the United States are excluded.

Source: *Economic Report of the President, 1984*, tables B-19 and B-15 (Washington: G.P.O.).

decline in investment in the 1970s contributed further to a slowing down of productivity growth. A period of hard times had arrived.

☐ The Inflationary Economy: 1973–1980

The continuing decline in the profit rate after 1973 and the associated decline in investment were both given a considerable helping hand by government policy. Ironically the government policies most responsible for the decline in profits and investment after 1973 were designed to *raise* the profit rate. They did not work. We shall see why not.

By 1973 many business and political leaders had recognized that the U.S. economy had entered a crisis and was suffering from more than the usual ups and downs of the business cycle. Many attributed the problem to increasing costs of imported materials, especially oil, and to rising international competition.

Businesses could not make up for higher costs of imported materials by pushing down labor costs—for example, by reducing the wage (w) or raising the amount of work done per hour (d). Workers

Is Unemployment Caused by Imports?

When American consumers, businesses, or governments decide to buy foreign-produced goods in place of U.S.-produced goods, they lower the demand for U.S.-produced goods. This in turn reduces the demand for labor in the United States. It is easy to conclude that the rapidly rising U.S. demand for Japanese steel, German cars, and other imports is a major cause of unemployment. Many workers who have lost their jobs producing steel or cars have come to this conclusion.

They are partly right. If imports of steel and autos had not increased as a share of the U.S. market (see Figure 10.3) and if all the other relevant facts had remained unaffected by this hypothetical change, employment in the auto and steel industries would not have declined by as much as it did.

But the auto and steel industries are among the most extreme cases of losing jobs to imports. And even in these industries, most of the job loss was due to the slow growth of consumer incomes (cars) and investment (steel) rather than to imports.

On the other hand, international trade in such goods as computers, aircraft, and farm products has created jobs in the United States. Exports of U.S. goods mean more employment in the United States.

Which effect has been stronger? At least one study suggests that for the United States, jobs generated by exports normally offset jobs lost to imports. However, when the United States imports much more than it exports—as it has recently—jobs lost through imports outnumber jobs gained through exports.

Imports may affect the relative strengths of workers (especially unionized workers) and employers. Suppose that imported goods compete mainly with goods (like autos and steel) made by unionized workers and that exported goods (like computers and farm products) use mainly nonunion workers. An increasing share of imports, even if it is matched by enough additional exports so no net unemployment is created, still would tend to undermine unions and weaken workers.

Where imports have caused major job losses, it often makes sense to limit the destructive effects on the affected people and communities through government assistance for job retraining, retooling the impacted industry, and even temporary restrictions of imports.

could not be made to bear the cost of the deterioration of the U.S. international position unless their bargaining power was significantly weakened. The most obvious way to weaken workers was to increase the unemployment rate.

Starting in 1973 the federal government, under Presidents Nixon, Ford, and Carter, used its control over fiscal policy (taxes and expenditures) to maintain fairly high levels of unemployment. While the unemployment rate was below 4 percent in half of the years from 1966–1973 and averaged 4.5 percent, it *never* fell below 5.5 percent from 1974 to 1978 (see Figure 14.9). This part of the strategy to restore the profit rate worked—product wages (w/Pz), which had grown at an average annual rate of 2.7 percent from 1963 to 1973, slowed to an average annual rate of growth of 1.1 percent from 1973 to 1983.

But there was a hitch. The dampening effect of restrictive fiscal policies left a substantial fraction of capital goods unutilized. *After-tax* wages actually fell during this period, further reducing demand. Thus the policies reduced *both* product wages and the utilized

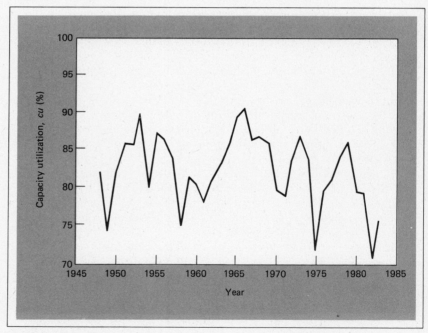

FIGURE 14.6 Capacity utilization in the U.S. economy, 1948–1983. Capacity utilization *(cu)* tends to rise during expansions and fall during recessions. For example, *cu* in manufacturing rose during the expansion of 1975–1979 from 83 to 86 percent; during the succeeding recession, it fell to nearly 71 percent.

Capacity utilization measures how much of the stock of capital goods already in existence and available for production is actually used. The figures here are for the manufacturing sector alone.

Source: *Economic Report of the President, 1984,* table B-45 (Washington: Government Printing Office).

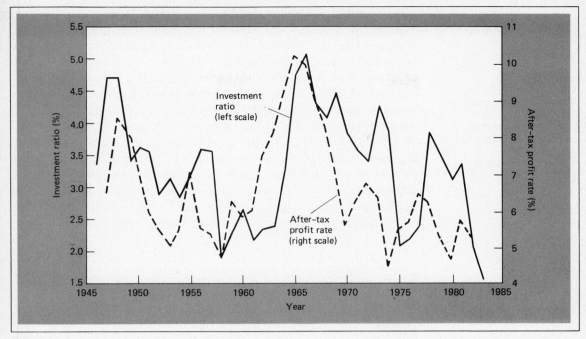

FIGURE 14.7 Profits and investment, 1948–1983. Profits and investment moved very closely together, suggesting a strong relationship between the two. Moreover, movements in the profit rate generally come before movements in investment, suggesting, as in Figure 11.5, that the profit rate is a major determinant of the level of investment.

The profit rate and investment curves shown here are taken directly from Figures 14.2 and 14.5.

Sources: *Economic Report of the President, 1984,* and U.S. Department of Commerce, Bureau of Economic Analysis (Washington: Government Printing Office).

percentage of the capital stock (*cu*). Figure 14.6 shows the resulting decline in capacity utilization. Because the profit rate (*r*) is simply the rate of profit on utilized capital goods (*ru*) times capacity utilization (*cu*), the decrease in *cu* had the effect of lowering the profit rate.

The policy aimed at improving the *cost conditions for investment* had the effect of worsening the *demand conditions for investment.* The net result: The two effects influenced the profit rate in opposite directions, and the second proved the stronger. As we saw in Figure 14.2, the decline in the profit rate continued.

The continued decline in the profit rate promoted a further decline in investment. With the profits low, and especially with existing productive capacity underutilized, it did not make much sense for capitalists to invest. Why should they continue spending money to build new productive facilities when they were not using all the facilities they already owned?

As investment fell and total demand fell with it and as productivity growth slowed, the rate of growth of output in the economy fell and unemployment increased. As the economy slowed down,

Stagflation refers to the combination of slower economic growth (*stag*nation) and generally rising prices (in*flation*) that characterized the hard times of the 1970s.

Stagnation refers to the hard-times phase of a long swing; it is characterized by slower economic growth or even economic decline.

Inflation is a general rise in prices.

prices started to increase rapidly. Economists termed this unusual situation of high unemployment and rapid inflation *stagflation*. *Economic stagnation*, the first part of *stag*flation, refers to slow economic growth, which is generally associated with unemployment. *Inflation* is the second part of stag*flation*.

The 1973–1980 phase of stagflation was characterized by slow economic growth, generally poor economic performance, and inflation rates considerably higher than the unemployment rate.

Figure 14.8 shows that for most of the postwar boom, inflation remained quite low—it averaged about 2 percent from the early 1950s through 1965. Starting in 1965, inflation steadily increased, making new post-1949 records of, at first, more than 4 percent (1970), then going over 10 percent (1974), then exceeding 12 percent (1980). A decade-and-a-half-long bout of inflation of this mag-

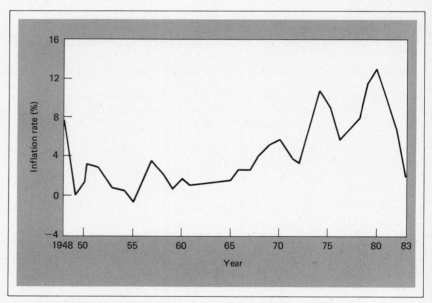

FIGURE 14.8 Inflation in the U.S. economy, 1948–1983. American inflation experience during the postwar years can be divided into two quite different periods, reflecting the long-swing boom and stagnation. From 1951 to 1968, inflation was low and rose only slowly; between 1968 and 1980, inflation was high and rose quickly. During the first period, inflation *never* exceeded 4 percent; during the second period, it exceeded 4 percent in *every* year except 1972. Since 1980, the inflation rate has declined.

Changes in the inflation rate also reflect the movement of the business cycle. For example, inflation increased during the expansion of 1955–1957 and declined during the recession of 1957–1958. The recession of 1980–1982 is the main reason for the reduction in inflation since the late 1970s.

Inflation is here measured as the average annual percentage change in the Consumer Price Index. It measures changes in the prices of goods purchased by a "typical" consumer.

Source: *Economic Report of the President, 1984*, table B-56 (Washington: Government Printing Office).

nitude is unprecedented in U.S. history. Just how unusual this period from the late 1960s through the early 1980s has been may be suggested by the fact that prices *fell* throughout most of the nineteenth century. The average price level in 1900 was half the price level of 1800, so the buying power of the dollar doubled over this 100-year period. During most of the twentieth century, prices have risen, but slowly; it took the first 67 years of the present century for prices to quadruple, cutting the buying power of the dollar to one-fourth of its 1900 level. But in just 16 years, from 1967 to 1983, prices tripled; if *this* rate had continued for 67 years, a dollar at the end of the period would have been worth less than a dime in 1967.

Inflation was far from the only problem during these years, however. As Figure 14.9 indicates, unemployment was also high during the latter part of the 1970s.

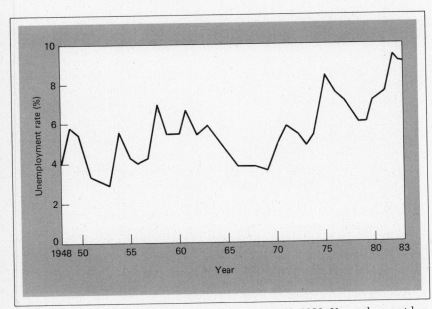

FIGURE 14.9 Unemployment in the U.S. economy, 1948–1983. Unemployment has been at the "full-employment" level (4 percent or less) only during the Korean War (1951–1953) and Vietnam War (1966–1969).

Between 1948 and 1969, during the long-swing boom, unemployment averaged less than 4.7 percent; between 1970 and 1983, during the long-swing hard times, unemployment averaged nearly 6.9 percent—nearly 1.5 times the earlier rate.

Fluctuations in the unemployment rate also reflect the movement of the business cycle. For example, the unemployment rate declined during the expansion of 1975–1979 from 8.5 to 5.8 percent, then increased during the 1979–1982 cyclical downturn from 5.8 to 9.7 percent.

Unemployment measures the number of people who are without work and actively seeking jobs, expressed as a percentage of all those both working and looking for work. The figures here are for the civilian labor force.

Source: *Economic Report of the President, 1984*, table B-29 (Washington: Government Printing Office).

Is Unemployment Caused by Technical Change?

General Motors over the past few years has begun to use robots to weld auto bodies. Suppose that a bank of these new robot welders can be operated by a single worker, who now can do as much welding as previously was done by eight workers. If GM now lays off the eight welders, technical change (the new robots) has created unemployment for these eight workers.

The relationship between technical change and unemployment in the economy as a whole is, however, considerably more complicated. Technical change may create new jobs as well as destroy old ones. The eight unemployed workers *may* eventually find work making robots. If the robots greatly reduce the cost of building cars, the number of U.S.-built cars sold both in the domestic market and abroad *may* increase enough so that some of the eight workers can get jobs as robot operators.

Even laborsaving technical change may create new jobs. Laborsaving technical change, as we have seen in Chapter 3, increases the amount of output that can be produced with the same amount of labor.

How could laborsaving technical change increase the number of people employed? Remember that the demand for labor (LD) is simply the total demand for goods and services divided by the average output per worker hour (ed). Laborsaving technical change has two effects on LD:

(1) a *labor-replacing effect* caused by the rise in average output per labor hour. A given total demand for goods and services will result in a smaller amount of labor demanded when the average output per labor hour rises: this will tend to reduce the number of jobs.

(2) a *total-demand effect* caused by the increase in the demand for goods and services. Technical change tends to reduce costs, making possible lower prices and thereby raising the amount of goods and services demanded.

A laborsaving technical change such as the robots will increase average output per labor hour (ed) by using labor more efficiently, that is, by raising e. But it may also increase total demand. Which effect is larger cannot be told in advance; it depends on whether the cost reductions made possible by the technical change increase the amount of goods and services demanded by enough to offset the labor-replacing effects of the increase in labor productivity.

Technical change may produce major cost reductions—either through increasing e; through deskilling, which allows a reduction in wages (w); or through an increase in work intensity (d). If it does, the profit rate on capital goods in use (ru) may rise. If ru rises, it will stimulate investment and the total demand for goods and services.

Technical change, when we consider both its effects, *may* but *need not* create unemployment. Even so, of course, it may have negative consequences for workers. As we saw in Chapter 9, technical change is often a powerful weapon in the hands of employers attempting to raise work intensity (d) or reduce wages (w). And for those who lose their jobs to robots, the "total-demand effect" does not mean much. For *they* are unemployed, and most studies suggest that they remain so for quite some time, often ending up with jobs paying much less.

The 1970s' inflation was *structural inflation* or *long-term inflation*, as distinct from the *cyclical inflation* or *unemployment-inflation trade-off* that usually characterizes the movement of prices over the business cycle. In Chapter 12 we saw that the rate of inflation tends to be high during business cycle expansions and low during recessions. The result, we saw, is the *inflation-unemployment trade-off*—high unemployment is generally associated with low inflation, and vice versa. During the 1970s, however, the rate of inflation remained high in most years, even when the unemployment rate was quite high. Thus the movement of the business cycle does not explain the inflation of the 1970s—more fundamental structural problems are involved.

The structural inflation of the 1970s was caused by the combination of economic stagnation and political stalemate. By *political stalemate* we mean a situation in which none of the major economic actors—the business community (including banks), labor, and the government—has the power to impose its will on the others.

The result of political stalemate was that while growth in the output of goods had slowed to a crawl, people kept demanding goods at a rapidly increasing rate. Despite the fact that output was increasing slowly, demand was increasing rapidly because businesses, the government, and families were borrowing and buying on credit. Given the political stalemate, neither business, nor workers, nor the government could be forced to demand less. None of the three had sufficient power to make the others cut back. It was this interaction of economic and political developments that led to the unusual combination of inflation and high levels of unemployment.

We may summarize the reasons for the structural unemployment of the 1970s as follows:

Economic stagnation + Political stalemate = Structural inflation

Inflation occurs when, at the current or prevailing prices, demanders want to purchase more goods than suppliers have or

A **political stalemate** occurs when each of the major political actors—employers, bankers, workers, and others—is able to prevent a solution to general economic problems harmful to its own interests, and so no group is able to impose a general solution on the others.

are willing to sell at those prices. This is the grain of truth behind the popular explanation of inflation as "Too much money chasing too few goods." A dollar bill (or a credit card) in the hands of a potential spender represents a claim on some goods or services. Whether that dollar is in the hands of a family about to purchase groceries, a businessman considering building a new plant, or a public school superintendent planning to buy additional textbooks makes no difference. In each case the person with the dollar is in a position to claim (by buying) the goods in question.

On the demand side, whether demanders want to purchase more or less than suppliers have to sell at the current prices depends upon two factors: demanders' spending decisions and the availability of money and credit to carry out their decisions.

The first factor concerns how much demanders desire to spend, given their present incomes, savings or wealth, and other circumstances. Demanders—consumers, businesses, government at all levels, and foreign customers—may decide to spend either less or more than their current income. One way demanders can spend more than their current income is to borrow or, what is the same thing, to buy on credit.

The second factor concerns whether demanders will be able to obtain sufficient money or credit to carry out their spending plans. If they decide to borrow, for instance, they may not be able to obtain sufficient loans from banks or other lenders to make the purchases they planned, or the terms on which credit is available may be prohibitively expensive.

When Unemployment Fails to Do Its Job

Unemployment is a key to the self-correcting nature of the business cycle. When the profit rate falls, investment falls, unemployment increases, and workers are put on the defensive in their dealings with employers. This tends to increase the profit rate and to restimulate investment, turning the cyclical downturn into a cyclical expansion.

Or, at least, that is the way it is supposed to work. As the figure indicates, higher levels of unemployment *did* tend to reduce labor costs during the period of 1949–1972, the era of the postwar long-wave expansion.

But unemployment may not do its job. If the recession has the effect of slowing down prices (Pz) faster than wages (w) and if it does not allow an acceleration of labor productivity (y) through speeding up the pace of work, the labor cost index may actually increase rather than decrease during the recession, thus tending to *lower* the rate of profit and worsen the recession rather than ending it.

As we can see from the illustration, since 1973 higher levels of

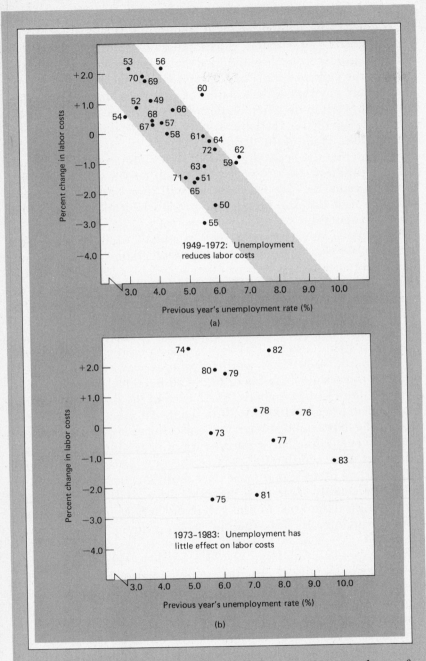

(a)

(b)

unemployment have not led to lower labor costs. The neutral rate of unemployment shifted upward from around 5 percent to around 8 percent. The "self-correcting" aspect of the business cycle has thus been impaired, and as a result recessions have been deeper and longer than during the 1960s.

There is nothing to guarantee that when all the claims are added up, there will be enough goods to go around. When there are not enough goods to go around, inflation may result.

The reason is that when the total claims exceed the total market value of the current supply of goods (valued at their current prices), there is no way that all the claims can be met. However if prices rise, as they often do when claims (demands) exceed supplies, the *market value* of the available supply will rise until it equals the money value of all of the claims.

Imagine that the economy consists of ten farmers, each of whom grows a different kind of vegetable. Each farmer's crop is sold to the farm stand for $10. Each farmer will then have an income of $10. The next day, the farmers all go back to market to buy other kinds of vegetables.

But suppose now that on the way to market, each farmer remembers that last year he grew $12 worth of vegetables, sold them, and was able to buy $12 worth of other vegetables. Hoping that this year's disappointing crop will not be repeated next year and determined to maintain his customary $12 standard of living, he stops at the bank to get a $2 loan, which along with his $10 income will allow him to buy $12 worth of vegetables. So the ten farmers now will try to spend a total of $120 (each has a crop worth $10 plus a $2 loan); but, only $100 worth of output was grown this year. Because the farmers' claims are now 20 percent larger than their incomes, the claims on goods ($120) exceed the goods available at the current prices ($100) by 20 percent. To meet all the money claims, the farm-stand owner will raise the prices of the various kinds of vegetables. The same amount of vegetables, which at the old prices were worth $100, now at the new prices sell for $120. If demanders try to spend more than their incomes and if supplies cannot be readily increased, then the prices will rise until their spending (in dollars) is, in real goods and services, equal the total output available. In the example above, prices must rise by 20 percent.

What happens when there are not enough goods is that there are too many money claims chasing too few goods. The result is that the competition among the spenders to claim the limited amount of goods creates a situation in which those who own the goods can raise their prices.

We have already seen why in the 1970s there were "too few goods." With productivity growth slowing down, the growth in total output of the economy also slowed. True, the decline in productivity growth was partially offset by an increase in the total number of hours worked. More married women began working outside the home as families struggled to make ends meet; as these women entered the labor force, total labor hours increased. Still, the growth in output slowed.

Why was there "too much money"? Why did credit expand so that government, families, and businesses could live beyond their means? How did money claims in excess of the existing supply of goods get into the hands of consumers, businesses, and the government? The answer is that under conditions of political stalemate, increasing the supply of credit was a way of papering over unresolved economic conflicts. We shall see how.

The Return of the Business Cycle

Not so long ago Keynesian economists thought that the alternating pattern of expansion and recession known as the business cycle was on its way to extinction. Through its control over interest rates and the money supply (monetary policy) and taxation and expenditure (fiscal policy), they thought the government could encourage investment (capital formation) and keep the economy on a smooth course of stable economic growth.

MIT Professor Paul Samuelson, the first Nobel prize winner in economics, is among the most distinguished of the early Keynesians and was an early exponent of this theory. In 1955 he told the Joint Economic Committee of the U.S. Congress, "With proper fiscal and monetary policies, our economy can have full employment and whatever rate of capital formation it wants."

The hopes of the Keynesians were to be fulfilled briefly during the 1960s when the economy experienced the longest period in U.S. history without a recession. Celebrating the end of the business cycle, Samuelson declared: "Business cycle theorists have done themselves out of a job."

He even rewrote the section on business cycles in his famous textbook. In the third edition (1955) he had described the business cycle in the present tense: "Such, in brief, *is* the so-called business cycle that has characterized the industrial nations of the world."* The 1967 edition, however, read: "Such, in brief, *was* the so-called 'business cycle' that *used to characterize* the industrial nations of the world . . . ."*

But during the 1970s and 1980s the business cycle returned with a vengeance. The recession of 1974–1975 drove the unemployment rate to 8.5 percent, at the time a post–Great Depression record; the recession of 1980–1982, called by some the "great recession," pushed the unemployment rate to 10.7 percent in the fall of 1982.

Professor Samuelson rewrote his business cycle chapter again. The 1980 edition reads: "Such, in brief, *is* the so-called 'business cycle' that has characterized the industrial nations of the world . . . ."*

* Paul Samuelson, *Economics* (New York: McGraw-Hill, 1955, 1967, 1980).

Low rates of productivity growth and even productivity declines meant that it was no longer possible to maintain rising real wages, high profit rates, and an expanding government sector all at once. Something had to go.

The Nixon, Ford, and Carter administrations were not able to command sufficient political support (despite continual exhortations about inflation as Public Enemy Number One) to obtain agreement on whether profits, wages, or the government itself should suffer. All groups—families, businesses, and the government—attempted to meet their objectives by spending beyond their means, that is, by borrowing. The government permitted this to happen—the Federal Reserve System facilitated the expansion of credit—because no single group or coalition was strong enough to force the others to shoulder all of the burden.

As a result the total amount of borrowing in the economy rose rapidly in the 1970s. In 1979, the year of record-setting inflation rates, net new borrowing in the whole economy had risen to a level of 20 percent of total output. Governments at all levels borrowed $58 billion, businesses (other than banks) borrowed $152 billion, and families borrowed $176 billion.

With families, governments, and businesses all attempting to live beyond their means, it was not possible for all simultaneously to do so. For as long as the total claims exceeded total supply, somebody was going to be dissappointed.

As a result of political stalemate, inflation allocated the shortage. Real profits and real wages were eroded by rising prices, setting off a scramble to raise (money) profits or (money) wages enough to compensate for inflation. This paper chase was bound to be futile, however, because the slowdown in productivity growth ensured a slowdown in the growth rate of real wages or a decline in real profits. In fact, as we have seen, both real wages and the profit rate declined.

☐ The Price of Stopping Inflation: 1980–1984

The inflation-ridden first phase of stagflation was followed after 1979 by a new development—the more intensive use of restrictive fiscal and monetary policy in a deliberate attempt to further slow the growth of demand in the economy. The logic of this policy was that given the *unemployment-inflation trade-off*, inflation could be stopped, but the price to be paid would be more unemployment.

The new policy pushed the unemployment rate up from an already high 5.8 percent in 1979 to 10.7 percent by the end of 1982. This second phase of the post-1960s hard times has been marked

Down the Roller Coaster

Since the late 1960s, the economy has continued a usual business cycle pattern. Expansions peak and turn into recessions: the recessions bottom out in a trough and turn into another expansion. There have been several cycles since the 1960s, with peaks in 1969, 1973, 1979 and troughs in 1971, 1975, and 1982.

But there is also something unusual about these cycles. Each successive cycle has been worse than the last. In fact, one of the signs that the U.S. economy is in the stagnation-and-crisis phase of the long swing is that while the economy has continued its roller coaster ride, the ride has been on the down side of the tracks:

The level of unemployment at the bottom of the cycle has been higher.

The rate of inflation at the peak has been higher.

The amount of output lost during the recession—the difference between the output the economy could have produced and what it did produce—has increased.

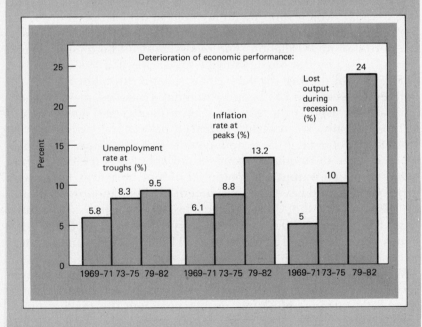

The left set of bars is the unemployment rate at the trough of the recession; the middle set is the inflation rate at the peak of the expansion; and the right set is the amount of output lost during the recession, expressed as a percentage of the output actually produced during the peak year.

by much less inflation and much more unemployment. It occurred because of the deliberate use of government policy. (See Figures 14.8 and 14.9.)

The conservative turn in economic policy was made possible because political stalemate was broken by the Republican victories of 1980. Businesses, and especially banks, got the upper hand. The economic policies of the early 1980s—hostile policies toward labor unions; large cuts in social service programs; lax enforcement of environmental, consumer protection, and workplace safety laws; large tax cuts for high-income families and businesses; and a massive increase in military spending—all signified the end of political stalemate. However, the policies of the early 1980s ended double-digit inflation by instigating almost depression-level unemployment.

How was this done? Most important, the Federal Reserve System restricted the supply of credit (or loanable funds), driving interest rates up. Banks and others with sizable amounts of money to lend benefited handsomely. These policies—particularly the policy of high interest rates—induced a severe business-cycle recession (1981–1982), which sent unemployment to over 10 percent for the first time since the Great Depression. This severe recession ended the period of high inflation. The recession itself bottomed out and was followed by the business-cycle expansion of 1983–1985.

The cost of ending the late 1970s inflation through a policy of deliberate recession has been substantial. One measure that economists have used is the gap between potential and actual output of the economy. We measure *potential output* by the output that would be produced if the economy were operating near full capacity, and with an unemployment rate of about 5 percent. The gap between actual output and potential output measures how much extra output could have been produced. By this standard (measured in 1983 prices), the U.S. economy lost $908 billion of potential output between 1980 and 1983; every household in the United States could have had an additional $11,000 in goods and services to consume.

Why were the costs so high? Economic policymakers and conservative economists in the early 1980s had hoped that they could reduce the amount of claims on the economy (by making credit harder to get and more expensive) without also reducing the amount of goods. But the restrictive monetary policies had the effect of stopping the economy in its tracks. Both the output produced per hour and the total number of hours worked (in the private business economy) *fell* between late 1979 and late 1982. Thus while restrictive monetary policy attacked the inflation problem of "too much money," it worsened the problem of "too few goods."

Whether the conservative economic policies of the early 1980s

Trickle-Down and Trickle-Up Economics

Part I: Disagreement on investment

Recent economic policy debates have pitted conservative economists, often called monetarists, against liberal economists, often called Keynesians (after John Maynard Keynes). The debate has covered a wide range of subjects; two of the most important are (1) the determinants of the level of investment and (2) the role that government should play in the economy.

Both monetarists and Keynesians agree that investment plays a crucial role in maintaining the health of a capitalist economy. But they disagree on what determines the level of investment and how investment can be stimulated. As we shall see, the monetarists focus on the *cost conditions* affecting the profit rate while the Keynesians focus on the *demand conditions* affecting the profit rate.

Monetarists believe that the amount of investment is determined by the amount of saving in the economy. (In making this assumption they ignore the international nature of lending and borrowing as well as international investment.) If the amount of saving is low, they argue, the supply of loanable funds will be small, giving rise to a high interest rate. And a high interest rate, as we have seen, will discourage investment. Monetarists go on to argue that the amount of saving is determined by how much income is received by those people who tend to save a high proportion of what they receive. Because rich people tend to save more than other people, policies that favor the rich, such as reducing taxes on profits, will encourage saving and hence stimulate investment. And increased investment will increase employment and output. The monetarist theory is sometimes called *trickle-down economics*, because it argues that giving more income to the rich will result in some trickling down to everyone else.

Keynesians hold the opposite view. According to them, investment is determined by the total demand for goods and services in the economy. The amount of demand for goods and services depends on how much income is received by people who tend to spend (rather than save) most of their income. The lower- and middle-income groups tend to spend most of their incomes and to save little. Keynesians argue that policies that put money in the hands of the less well-to-do, such as reducing taxes on low and moderate incomes, will increase the demand for goods and services and thus stimulate investment. Keynesian economics is trickle-down economics turned upside down, or *trickle-up economics*.

The simple Keynesian model, like that of the monetarists, tends to ignore the international nature of the economy. For example, higher wages will, as the Keynesians say, increase demand from domestic consumers; but it may also result in higher unit labor costs for goods produced in the United States. Higher unit labor costs make it more difficult for U.S.-produced goods to compete in world markets, thus reducing export demand (and jobs in the export sector).

have ended the underlying stagnation by stimulating investment and productivity growth is not yet clear. The tax cuts passed in 1981 gave very favorable treatment to business investment, hoping to raise the after-tax profit rate and thereby to increase business's incentive to invest. Although a substantial amount of money was thus put in the hands of business and some industries— automobile corporations, for example—made record profits, the hoped-for increase in investment did not materialize. (See the box on page 246)

As Figure 14.5 indicates, investment continued to decline in both 1982 and 1983. At least until 1984, these policies seem to have fostered business fears that expected demand conditions would not be adequate to justify building new productive capacity (due to the very low levels of utilization of existing capacity and depressed levels of consumers' incomes). This depressing effect on investment appears to have swamped the improvements in the labor cost index and materials costs associated with the high levels of unemployment and the enhanced bargaining power of business.

Investment is notoriously difficult to predict. On the basis of past experience, the expected profit rate must rise substantially to produce an investment boom sufficient to begin a new long-swing expansion. In 1983 investment finally bottomed out; in 1984 it turned upward, but whether this upturn will be short-lived or long-lived remains to be seen.

☐ **Economic Crisis and Reform**

The 1970s and early 1980s were a time of stagnation and deepening challenges to economic institutions. Many proposals for recovery have been put forward for public discussion.

In past long-swing stagnations—the 1890s and the 1930s, for instance—recovery has required two conditions, one economic and one political. First, fundamental changes in basic economic and other social institutions had to take place; a successful new social structure of accumulation was required. Second, there also had to be a new dominant political coalition of sufficient strength to over-

---

Trickle-Down and Trickle-Up Economics

Part II: Disagreement on government

Monetarists and Keynesians disagree on the proper role for government in the economy. Monetarists generally favor limited government involvement, whereas Keynesians favor more active policies.

Government spending contributes to total demand. When the government spends more than it takes in in taxes (when it runs a deficit), it expands total demand. This is applauded by Keynesians, for according to them it will stimulate investment as long as the economy is not operating at full capacity. It is criticized by monetarists, for in order to be able to run a deficit the government borrows money, thus increasing the demand for loanable funds and tending to increase the interest rate. According to the monetarists, this will discourage investment.

Both are half right. As we have seen, the level of investment is determined by the expected profit rate compared to the cost of borrowing. The expected profit rate is influenced by the percentage utilization of existing capital goods and the profit rate on the capital goods currently utilized. Keynesians focus on the *utilization rate* and the way that an increase in demand improves it. Monetarists focus on the *cost of borrowing* and the way that an increase in savings improves (lowers) it.

Why do they differ? To some extent they differ because they have different values: Keynesians place a higher value on equality, and monetarists fear that more government involvement may reduce personal liberty. But their economic assumptions differ, too. Keynesians use a short-term model (similar to that which we developed in Chapters 11 and 12) and assume that the economy always operates below capacity, with enough unemployment and unutilized capital goods so that an increase in demand will readily increase output. Monetarists tend to adopt a longer-term perspective (as we do in this chapter) and, further, to assume that the economy always operates at full capacity, that is, with no unemployment. This leads them to conclude that an increase in demand cannot increase output and will simply result in an increase in prices.

The monetarist assumption that the economy tends to operate at full capacity is inconsistent with how the labor market tends to produce unemployment. It is also strikingly contradicted by the historical record of the U.S. economy (see Figure 11.8). But the Keynesian assumption that the economy always has unutilized capacity is dubious as well. For as we have seen in this chapter, the current period of slow growth and instability in the U.S. economy began during the late 1960s, a period during which the economy operated at or near full capacity for almost half a decade. During this period, increases in demand led to a lower profit rate, inflation, and eventually slower growth of output.

A more complete analysis (such as that developed in Chapters 11 and 12) takes account of both the cost and the demand conditions affecting the profit rate and investment. Both are important, but which is *more* important depends on the state of the economy and therefore varies over time. For example, the cost conditions were more important in the late 1960s, while the demand conditions were more important in the early 1980s.

come institutional, legal, and social inertia and support or facilitate the construction of the new social structure of accumulation.

In the 1890s, the first condition was met by the defeat of the unions and the agrarian populists and the rise of both monopoly and tariffs. The second condition was met by the victory of William McKinley and the Republicans over William Jennings ("Cross of Gold") Bryan in the watershed election of 1896.

The defeat of the unions meant that employers could go full speed ahead with technical control, deskilling, and the increasing use of low-wage workers. Monopoly and tariffs against imported goods meant a reduction in competition facing capitalists. The victory of the Republicans (who remained dominant until the Great Depression) ensured that the government would support (by omission or commission) capitalist operations, since, as Calvin Coolidge was later to affirm, "The business of America is business." Thus were established the essential conditions for the first twentieth-century boom.

In the 1930s, the economic program provided by the New Deal inspired expansion of government social expenditures and the buildup of military goods production during World War II. The political coalition consisted of the New Deal Democrats, a coalition of labor unions, large corporations, and ethnic voters organized by the Democratic party and led by Franklin Delano Roosevelt. As we have seen, the New Deal ushered in the main domestic dimensions of the postwar social structure of accumulation: the legalization of trade unions and collective bargaining, Social Security, and the governmental commitment to macroeconomic regulation. These early institutional innovations were completed during and shortly after World War II, with the Bretton Woods agreement and the passage of the Taft-Hartley Act.

The expansion of total demand necessary to make the New Deal program an economic success was provided by the buildup of military production beginning around 1940. Thus were set the conditions for the long boom of the mid-twentieth century. The New Deal political coalition remained the dominant party until the election of Richard Nixon in 1968.

In 1980 the Reagan victory seemed to provide the new political coalition that, in the past, was one of the two conditions needed for a recovery of the capitalist economy. But political victory by itself was never enough. FDR won a tremendous victory in 1932, yet his "first" New Deal—the National Industrial Recovery Act and other early Roosevelt programs—was an unsuccessful economic program. It was not until the "second" New Deal and the electoral victory of 1936 that the outlines of the postwar social structure of accumulation even began to emerge. And the economy did not actually revive until the outbreak of World War II.

For the 1980s and 1990s, then, the question remains: What will provide both a successful economic program and a powerful enough political coalition? Does the conservative solution—an expansion of military production and a reduction in the other economic roles of the government—fit these standards? If not, will another emerge? And if no such combination emerges, will the stagflation continue?

These are important questions. The answers to them, to be discovered in the next decade, will determine much about how our economy performs, how our society develops, and how our own lives are led.

☐ Suggested Readings

Philip Armstrong, Andrew Glyn, and John Harrison, *Capitalism Since World War II: The Making and Breakup of the Great Boom* (London: Fontana, 1984).

Fred Block, *The Origins of International Economic Disorder* (Berkeley, Calif.: University of California Press, 1977).

Samuel Bowles, David Gordon, and Thomas Weisskopf, *Beyond the Waste Land: A Democratic Alternative to Economic Decline* (New York: Doubleday, 1973).

Robert DeGrasse, *Military Expansion, Economic Decline* (New York: Council on Economic Priorities, 1983).

Alan Wolfe, *America's Impasse: The Rise and Fall of the Politics of Growth* (New York: Pantheon Books, 1981).

PART FIVE

CAPITALISM: PROMISE AND PERFORMANCE

CHAPTER 15

AMERICAN CAPITALISM: PROMISE AND PERFORMANCE

Chapter 2 outlined three values essential for assessing an economic system: efficiency, fairness, and democracy. How efficient, fair, or democratic is U.S. capitalism? An economy is *efficient* if it requires as little of the time and energy we spend in producing things as is necessary and if it does as little damage as necessary to our natural surroundings. An economy is *fair* if the burdens and benefits of work are shared in an equitable manner. An economy is *democratic* if important economic choices—what is to be produced, where, how, when, by whom, and for whom—are subject to deliberation and control by the people affected by these choices.

Values are always debatable, and these three are no exception. What seems to one person a sensible use of our environment may not appear sensible to another. What seems fair to you may seem unfair to someone else. What is democratic in one situation may seem dictatorial in another. For example, it would be democratic if employees had the right to vote on major decisions concerning production in their firm; it would be undemocratic if they had the right to vote on what color shoes each has to wear to work.

While values always have an important personal element, they are nonetheless essential if we are to evaluate our economic system. Moreover, some values are quite common. For instance, most people believe in the values of efficiency, fairness, and democracy. Any attempt to improve aspects of U.S. capitalism must be made on the basis of an evaluation of its good and bad aspects, which requires that we be able to say what we think is good or bad.

This chapter evaluates how U.S. capitalism measures up against the values of efficiency, fairness, and democracy. To evaluate something, however, one must first have a *standard of comparison.* How efficient, fair, or democratic is U.S. capitalism, compared to what? This chapter uses three such standards: (1) compared to what came before; (2) compared to widely shared ideals of efficiency, fairness, and democracy; and (3) compared to possible or workable alternative systems.

The main idea of the chapter is that compared to what came before, capitalism has brought substantial benefits in all three areas of efficiency, fairness, and democracy. However, compared to either widely shared ideals or to available alternatives, the U.S. economy falls far short of being as efficient, as fair, or as democratic as it could be.

This main idea is expressed in four main points:

1. Capitalism and democratic government were originally seen as solutions to the twin age-old social evils of *mass poverty* and *despotism.* In eradicating these evils, capitalism (in the United States as well as in all the advanced countries) has been quite successful. It has been much less successful in the less developed nations of Africa, Asia, and Latin America.
2. Efficiency, fairness, and democracy reflect *ideal standards* against which to measure our economy. Defenders of capitalism often argue that capitalism does indeed meet these standards. Critics of capitalism believe that the way capitalism works requires that it systematically violate each of these three standards.
3. There is good reason to believe that *superior alternatives* to the current structure of U.S. capitalism exist. In particular, it does not appear that the United States must trade off one goal (such as efficiency) for the others (fairness or democracy); through changing the rules of the game of U.S. capitalism, it may be possible to have more of all three.
4. Capitalism and democratic government may have come to a *parting of the ways.* Our society may have to become less democratic for capitalism to work well, or the economy may have to become less capitalist and more democratic for democratic government to be maintained. There are increasing signs of conflict between the capitalist and the democratic "rules of the game," suggesting that the positive connection in the past between capitalism and democratic government may be a poor guide to their future compatibility.

In the United States, the economy is capitalist and the government is democratic. To review: *capitalism* is a system of production of commodities for profit using wage labor; and *democratic government* is a way of organizing and controlling the government characterized by the accountability—through democratic elections—of decision makers to those affected by their decisions, and civil liberties for citizens (the Bill of Rights freedoms such as freedom of the press, of assembly, and of speech).

We saw in Chapter 13 that the system of government in the United States today, though democratic in form, does not allow all citizens equal access to political decision making or equal political influence. The capitalist economy places often quite narrow limits on what even a large majority of the electorate can do. Nonetheless, while democratic government in the United States is far from ideal, it is still much more democratic than capitalism.

U.S. society therefore involves two quite different sets of rules of the game or principles for organizing society—capitalism and democratic government. These principles are not necessarily consistent or in harmony with each other.

☐ The Promise of Democracy and Capitalism

What was the original promise people saw in democracy and capitalism? What did people 200 years ago think these two systems would do for society? Mainly, taken together, capitalism and democracy were seen as solutions to what many then saw as the twin evils of the day, *mass poverty* and *despotism*. Some of the philosophers, economists, publicists, and politicians who first developed and promoted these ideas two centuries ago were mainly interested in capitalism; they saw it as a way of ending mass poverty. Others were mainly interested in democratic government, which they hoped would eliminate despotism.

Adam Smith, a Scottish economist and philosopher, was one of the main proponents of capitalism. In the 1760s and 1770s, in the booming factories and thriving commerce of Glasgow, his hometown, he glimpsed the possibility that poverty—which for thousands of years had been the lot of the vast majority of people—could be replaced by abundance through a process of economic development. In *The Wealth of Nations,* a best-seller on both sides of the Atlantic, Smith argued that capitalism provided a way to harness individual self-interest and modern science to increase the productivity of human labor.

Capitalism, Smith hoped, would foster both rapid technical progress and a rational use of labor and other resources. Even if each producer only wanted more for himself, each would be driven by competition, as if led by "an invisible hand," to produce more for all. The result of private greed regulated by competitive markets would be an unprecedented outpouring of goods and services to the benefit of all.

Thomas Paine was mainly interested in democracy. His pamphlet, *Common Sense,* was published the same year as Adam Smith's great book and the U.S. Declaration of Independence. It

Mass poverty is a situation in which a large portion of a society lives at or near the minimal level of physical subsistence.

Despotism is any form of governmental rule in which the rulers are largely or entirely unaccountable to those being ruled.

outsold *The Wealth of Nations* and even the *Bible* during the late 1770s. Paine had started out in England as a maker of whalebone stays for corsets, and had moved to America in the 1770s. While Smith's message was that capitalism could end poverty, Paine's was that democracy could end despotism.

While most of his contemporaries still endorsed the divine right of kings, Paine advocated an extension of the right to vote to all freeborn males (voting rights for slaves and women were still beyond the limits of even Paine's imagination), as well as those freedoms later to be enshrined in the U.S. Bill of Rights. Paine's ideas not only played an important role in persuading Americans to take up arms against the British crown; they were soon translated into French and into rallying cries—Liberty, Equality, Fraternity—that were to topple the monarchy in the French Revolution little more than a decade after the United States won its independence from George III.

Many among the wealthy had second thoughts about the combination of capitalism and democracy that they saw emerging during this Age of Revolution. Some feared that the many would eventually combine against the few and use their democratic rights to tax or even confiscate the property of the well-to-do.

But others were more optimistic, believing that economic privilege and political equality could indeed be reconciled. The potential conflicts between the economic inequality on which capitalism is based and the formal political equality guaranteed by democratic government could be avoided, they thought, by limiting government to a few classical rule-making and rule-enforcing functions. These included making war, preserving domestic peace, guaranteeing civil liberties, and enforcing contracts. All other activities were to be left within the realm of capitalism or reserved to the family. Although the two sets of rules of the game—capitalism and democratic government—were potentially contradictory, they were to be kept apart by this great barrier of *limited government*, or laissez faire, as the widely used French term described it.

With the writings of Smith, Paine, and many others before and since, the ideas that we now call *classical liberalism* were born. Classical liberalism advocated combining a limited and representative government with a capitalist economy. Most early classical liberals wanted government to be representative of the people but did not support the idea of all adults having the right to vote. Later classical liberals advocated extending the vote to all adults. The promise of the resulting combination—democracy and capitalism— was that it could put an end to *both* mass poverty and despotism.

In the two centuries since Smith and Paine, the two systems in tandem indeed compiled an impressive track record. While it is perhaps too much to hope that in this short time poverty could have been totally eliminated, capitalism did produce the outpour-

Limited government or **laissez faire** is a relationship between the government and economy in which government enforces the rules of capitalist economy but otherwise does not intervene in the operation of the economy.

Classical liberalism is a set of ideas born in the late eighteenth and nineteenth centuries advocating limited representative government and a capitalist economy.

ing of goods and services that Smith had hoped for (see Figure 15.1 for data on the U.S. record).

At the same time, democratic government spread among the capitalist countries. By a slow process—marked by conflict and disappointment as well as by democratic victories—the right to vote was extended first to all adult white male propertyholders, then to nonpropertyholders, then to nonwhites and to women in many of the capitalist countries. Whereas in 1900 no country could be said to have a truly democratic form of government (in the United States, for example, most black people, many recent immigrants, and women were excluded from voting), by the mid-1960s there were something like 30 democratic governments in the world. All of them were in countries with capitalist economies.

It is important not to claim too much for the marriage of demo-

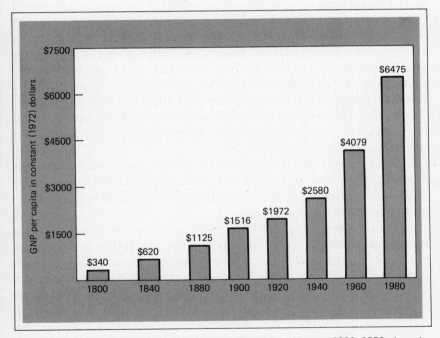

FIGURE 15.1 Growth of per capita output in the U.S. economy, 1800–1980. American capitalism has produced very rapid economic growth, both in total output and in output per person (shown here).

Total output per person probably doubled between 1800 and the Civil War, roughly doubled again by 1900, doubled again by the 1940s, and doubled yet again by the 1980s. The result is that total output per person today is probably between 15 and 18 *times* what was produced in 1800.

Total output is here measured as GNP per capita in real terms (corrected for the effects of inflation). Data for the nineteenth century are estimates subject to substantial error.

Sources: *Economic Report of the President* (Washington: GPO, 1984), tables B-2 and B-28; and U.S. Department of Commerce, *Historical Statistics of the U.S.* (Washington: GPO, 1975).

cratic government and capitalist economy. First, for most of capitalism's history, capitalist economies have coexisted not with democratic forms of government but rather with various *un*democratic forms. These governments have been ruled by emperors, oligarchies, generals, kings, dictators, and outright despots (as in Nazi Germany and Fascist Italy and Spain) and in dictatorships today (in Chile, South Korea, the Philippines, and much of the rest of the capitalist countries of Asia, Africa, and Latin America). By far the majority of the 90 or so capitalist countries in the world today are governed by undemocratic governments. So in both its history and present life, capitalism has been most commonly linked with undemocratic, not democratic, government.

Second, poverty remains a scourge throughout the capitalist world. In part, this is because any economic system that depends as much as capitalism does on material insecurity to motivate hard work finds it difficult to eliminate poverty, for the specter of poverty is what gives economic insecurity its bite. In part, the persistence of poverty in the capitalist world results from the way that the advanced capitalist nations have used their power to dominate poorer and less powerful nations. Although this book has not explored the linkages between advanced capitalist economies and the persistence of hunger, illiteracy, and other forms of deprivation in the Third World, any complete assessment of the performance of capitalism would necessarily encompass its global consequences.

Still, in the developed regions of capitalism—roughly Western Europe, North America, Australia, New Zealand, and Japan—capitalism and democracy have gone far toward eradicating mass poverty and despotic government.

The successes achieved thus far in eliminating these negative features of human society have raised the possibility of achieving more positive goals. These include efficiency, fairness, and democracy.

For instance, economists often claim for capitalism not only that it promotes rapid economic growth (a limited claim) but also that it is efficient (a more ambitious claim). At other times it is claimed that not only can capitalist economy coexist with democratic government (a limited claim) but also that capitalism itself is democratic (a stronger claim).

☐ Is Capitalism Efficient, Fair, and Democratic?

Efficiency. Efficiency means that the economy, for a given level of inputs used, produces the maximum output possible; or, what is the same thing, that to produce a given level of output, the minimum amount of input is used. The essential idea is that no inputs—our time, our energy, our natural surroundings—are wasted.

Efficiency differs from the original promise of capitalism—rapid economic growth—and it is a stricter and more demanding standard. Rapid growth focuses only on the economy's *output* (how fast does output grow?), whereas efficiency takes account of the inputs used. For example, imagine building houses quickly versus building houses efficiently. In the first case, all that is measured is how quickly the houses go up. There may be wasted inputs (boards cut the wrong way and so thrown on the scrap pile and not used, workers injured, and so on), but none of these count in calculating how quickly the work gets done. In the second case, however, efficiency measures whether, given the inputs used (boards, labor, and so on), the greatest number of houses possible to build were in fact built.

The argument from neoclassical economics that capitalism is efficient is extremely simple. The price of an input, according to

The Argument of Neoclassical Economics that Capitalism Is Efficient

Prices measure scarcity. Scarcity is the balance between what is available and what people want.

The cost of production of a commodity measures the amount of scarce resources used up in its production. In perfectly competitive equilibrium the cost of producing an additional unit (the marginal cost) is equal to the price.

The price that consumers will pay for the commodity measures how much an additional unit of the commodity is worth to the consumer. When one more unit is no longer judged to be worth the price, consumers stop buying.

Prices are thus said to be signals, indicating to consumers and producers the costs and usefulness of inputs and outputs.

The competition for profits forces producers to pay attention to these signals. Competition among capitalists forces each to minimize the costs of production and hence to minimize the amount of society's scarce resources used up in producing each good. Profit-maximizing capitalists, according to this view, will try to design products and to distribute them so as to sell for the highest price and hence to deliver as much as possible of what the consumers want. However, competition will force capitalists to sell these products at the lowest profitable price.

Competition will, by this reasoning, lead to the full employment of labor and other available inputs, for if there are unemployed workers (for example), the pressure of the excess supply in labor markets will force the wage down and lead to an increase in employment.

this argument, measures how scarce it is. Since profit-maximizing capitalists will try to achieve the lowest possible costs, they will use as little as possible of those inputs that have the highest prices (and are most scarce). Competition will drive capitalists to provide society with the maximum amount of goods and services possible, given the available inputs.

But economists have pointed out many serious problems with this argument; three of the most important involve unemployment, the environment, and the intensity of work.

Unemployment means that there is an input—labor time—that is being wasted. Today's lost production is lost forever, because the workers' lost work time can never be regained. For instance, no matter how hard we work now, we can never recover the potential production lost in the Great Depression.

We have already seen (Chapters 8 and 11) that competition among workers and among capitalists does not eliminate unemployment. And we have seen (Chapters 13 and 14) that the government, responding to employers' need to restore their power over workers, often adopts policies that result in unemployment. Other inputs—the capital goods that make up our industrial capacity, for example—are also often idled by recessions that may be the result of either government policy or the course of the normal business cycle.

The resulting nonuse of available inputs is a major source of inefficiency. The amount of wasted potential output from 1979 through 1983 amounted to a sum sufficient to pay every family more than the average family makes working from January to September.

How capitalism uses our natural environment is a second source of inefficiency. Capitalists will minimize the use of scarce inputs into production only if those inputs have a price; if they are scarce but free, capitalists will have no incentive not to use as much as they like. An example of such an input is clean river water. If used freely for waste disposal by chemical plants, paper mills, and other factories, the result would be polluted rivers and lakes and a loss of recreational, fishing, or other productive uses of the water. Another example is air, which is used by capitalists as if it were free because to them it *is* free—it has no price. But clean air is also scarce. Polluting it imposes costs on others, who cannot charge capitalists for either their pains (discomfort, annoyance, and illness) or the costs of avoiding these (air conditioners and the expense of travel in order to enjoy outdoor recreation).

The point is not that pollution should be *totally* eliminated. The costs of this might far outweigh the benefits. The point is that in making decisions about how and where and what to produce, it makes sense to take into account *all* the costs and to minimize these, rather than to obey the rule of profitability that forces capitalists to take account only of the costs which they must pay for. When business does not have to pay the full cost of inputs used in production, the resulting production is not efficient.

Thus one major flaw in the argument that capitalism is efficient is that it assumes that all inputs and outputs are commodities—are produced to be exchanged for a profit and therefore have a price. Whenever any major inputs or outputs of a labor process are not themselves a commodity, capitalism is likely to be inefficient. The clean river water used in a production process was not produced in order to make a profit—it is not a commodity. The smoke produced is also not a commodity. Our natural environment, other than land, is usually not a commodity. For this reason capitalism does not deal sensibly with our natural environment.

Capitalism not only wastes labor time through nonuse (unemployment), it wastes labor through misuse, a third important inefficiency. Both our *time* and our *effort* are scarce, and they are not the same thing. Our time, when sold as labor hours, has a price. Capitalists attempt to use as little as possible in production. Our effort—our sweat, creativity, and intelligence—when it takes the form of actual work done, has no price. Actual work done, like the environment, is not a commodity. And like the natural environment, it tends to be used wastefully in a capitalist society.

Capitalists have no interest in minimizing the intensity of work— how much effort workers put out per hour on the job—unless this lowers the price of labor time. Capitalists' interests are in fact to maximize the amount of effort expended for each hour of labor time purchased. In order to do this, capitalists hire large numbers of people, as we saw in Chapter 9, who produce nothing at all; they simply control the labor of others. If capitalists pay for labor time but not for work itself, there is no more reason to expect that they will make sensible use of work effort than there is to think that they will make sensible use of clean air or water. As we have seen in Chapter 9, the organization of production and choice of technology that results from applying the profitability criterion (minimizing the costs that capitalists must pay for) does not make efficient use of work.

As a result of the problems of unemployment, the environment, and work intensity, capitalism departs from the standard of efficiency.

Fairness. The ideal of fairness encompasses two related notions, fair processes and fair outcomes. A *fair process* is a way of doing something—hiring people for jobs, for instance—in which people are treated equally. For instance, refusing to hire a qualified person because of the person's race violates the concept of fair treatment.

A **fair process** is a way of doing things in which people are treated equally; it refers to the rules, not the outcome, of the game.

A *fair outcome* is an equitable result or consequence of some social process. A fair outcome refers not to the way in which something (such as hiring) is done but rather to the actual distribution of benefits and/or burdens. For instance, when the income of an employer is 10 or 20 times the income of his workers and when the employer works no harder or longer than the worker, this disparity violates the concept of fair outcomes. Fair process refers to the *rules* of the game, how the game is played. Fair outcome refers to the *stakes* of the game, how much the winners get and what happens to the losers.

The idea that capitalism and democratic government could promote fairness has been part of the intellectual tradition of the capitalist countries since the days of Smith and Paine. The French Revolution eliminated aristocratic and noble titles such as *Lord, Lady,* and even *Sir,* and replaced them with a title which *all* French people could bear, *Citizen.* The American Declaration of Independence proclaimed that all people "are created equal, that they are endowed by their Creator with certain inalienable Rights, that among these are Life, Liberty, and the Pursuit of Happiness . . . ." The main ideas of the French and the American Revolutions did not say that people should *be* equal but only that they should have equal rights, that they should be *treated* equally.

But what does treating people equally mean? What is it about people that should be treated equally? There are many possible answers to this question. The basic idea of fairness in democratic government is that people's *votes* should be treated equally; the basic idea of fairness in capitalism is that people's *dollars* should be treated equally.

Do Fair Processes Produce Fair Outcomes?

One surprising feature of fair processes is that they do *not* necessarily produce fair outcomes.

A fair process simply requires that everyone (every qualified person, at least) be treated equally. Imagine the following situation.

There is to be a lottery in society. Each person's name is written on a piece of paper and put in a big drum. One piece of paper will be drawn out, and that person (the winner) wins title to all the property in society. Everyone else (each nonwinner) loses all his or her property.

This is a fair *process,* since every person in society has an equal chance to win. Yet few would consider the result (one person owning all the property) to be a fair *outcome,* no matter how it was arrived at.

Each person has one vote, and each vote should count equally when they are added up. This may seem an obvious point, but it has often been violated. In Great Britain during the nineteenth century, for example, university professors had two votes, while women and most workers had none.

Likewise, a dollar is a dollar. It makes no difference if its owner is black or white, male or female, the president of the United States or the president's bodyguard. What it can buy is the same.

The idea that all dollars are equal is more radical than it may seem at first glance. In Europe during the feudal era, for example, ordinary people—those without noble titles—often could not buy land, no matter how much money they had. Until the 1960s in the United States, a dollar could buy a meal at Woolworth's lunch counters in the southern states only if the buyer were white. If he or she were black, it did not buy anything there, because the buyer was excluded on the grounds of race. Dollars, and their owners, were subject to racial discrimination. In this respect, the commodity—something produced with the intention of making money—may be considered a contribution to fairness, for it treats dollars equally.

Both capitalism and democratic government have notions of fair processes, but they are different. Sometimes it is said that in a capitalist economy we vote with our dollars. Our demands—our wants backed up by dollars—are what ultimately direct the economy, according to this view. But how many "dollars votes" we can cast in the capitalist economy depends on how many dollars we have to spend.

Thus the fact that capitalism (at least ideally) treats dollars equally does not make it fair. We must ask why some have more dollars than others. Is the process determining the distribution of income fair? And is the resulting distribution of income fair? Only then will the results of "voting with dollars" be fair.

How might we judge the process that determines the distribution of income as either fair or unfair? Two principles seem essential. First, it is not fair for some people to start out in life—from birth—with a head start or with a penalty. Being born a member of the duPont family confers millions of dollars of inherited wealth on a person, giving that person the resources and the freedom to live a life closed to most others. On the other hand, being born female or black is to inherit an economic situation that on the average will be characterized by lower incomes and obstacles to getting ahead in certain desirable occupations. When people are rich or poor as the result of inherited wealth or because of racial, sexual, or other discrimination, the results of voting with dollars are not fair.

Second, the time people spend at work should be treated more or less equally and rewarded more or less equally (of course, if some jobs are more unpleasant or difficult or dangerous than others, it may be fair to reward them more highly). There are really two ideas here: work time should be the basis of economic reward (except for those unable to work), and work time should be rewarded roughly equally. Thus it is not fair that (as we saw in Chapter 4) most capitalists receive the bulk of their income not in return for time they have spent at work, but simply as the result of their ownership of the capital goods used in production. Moreover, it is not fair that managers of the major corporations pay themselves salaries that amount to over $500 per hour when the average hourly wages is about one-fiftieth of the amount.

As we have seen in previous chapters, these are basic aspects of capitalism: profits as a return on ownership of capital goods rather than as a reward for work; the private ownership and hence inheritance of capital goods used in production; substantial wage and salary differences among those who do work; and various forms of discrimination. These elements are not the *imperfections* of an otherwise fair system. They are its *basic structure*. In this sense, capitalism departs from the standard of fairness.

Democracy. Democracy provides a third ideal standard against which to evaluate the performance of U.S. capitalism.

The fundamental idea of democracy is that basic decisions affecting the lives of substantial numbers of people should be considered and voted upon by those who are affected. Of course, people may vote directly on major decisions—as in referenda—or they may elect representatives with whom they agree or in whom they have confidence. But the basic idea is that those affected by decisions have the right to control, directly or indirectly, these decisions.

Democracy as a criterion is most commonly applied to government, not to the capitalist economy itself. Here the question becomes, Does capitalism as an economic system support and reinforce democracy in government?

Democracy is also, however, a criterion that can be applied to all ways of making social decisions, including decisions in the economy. So we should also ask, Does capitalism promote democratic decision making in the economy and in other social relationships?

While most capitalist countries have not been and are not now democratic, the strongest case for capitalism from the point of view of democratic government is that, where democratic government has developed, it has *always* been in capitalist countries.

The kinds of democracy existing before capitalism hardly measure up to our current standards. The "democracy" of ancient Athens and the other Greek city-states, for example, would not today be considered democratic. It was based on the exclusion from political life of both slaves and women. Except where an exploitative class structure did not exist, as in some Native American communities, other societies before the dawn of capitalism were at least as undemocratic as ancient Greece.

Capitalism contributed to the growth of democratic government in a curious way. Capitalism provided the context in which largely noncapitalist, sometimes overtly anticapitalist, groups of farmers, workers, abolitionists, suffragists, and others successfully fought to achieve democratic government. Businessmen and the wealthy have often had mixed feelings, at best, about democracy. Their fears, quite naturally, resulted from the fact that the wealthy are few and the nonwealthy are many. They worried that the many— the poor, workers, small farmers, the middle class—would combine against the wealthy few and impose heavy taxes on the rich; perhaps they would even confiscate their wealth and redistribute it more equally. In this sense there has always been a possible tension between the rules of democratic government and the rules of capitalism, between the rights of citizens and the rights of property, between voting power and buying power.

Some examples: in the 1780s, in the writing of the U.S. Constitution, large property owners took great pains to see that the Constitution would not be "too democratic." The Articles of Confederation, which had served as an interim constitution for the country between the American Revolution and the adoption of the Constitution, were definitely too democratic for many of them. James Madison, one of the principal drafters of the Constitution, assured readers of his *Federalist Papers* that the new political system would make it highly unlikely that the "have-nots" would be able to unite against the "haves."

In the early nineteenth century, pressure developed to allow all adult males to vote. The movement for the extension of the suffrage, as it was called, was composed in large part of small farmers and workers. It was opposed by many of the well-to-do. Slaveowners then and later (during the Civil War), for example, opposed the extension of rights to slaves.

In the late nineteenth century, after the emancipation of the slaves, a compromise between northern capitalists and southern capitalists and landowners resulted in the elimination of the voting rights of virtually all southern black people—a denial of democratic rights that survived right up to the 1960s. Throughout the nineteenth and twentieth centuries, many businessmen supported the denial or limitation of the political rights of radical political groups and trade unions.

But at least since the 1840s, large groups of capitalists made their peace with some form of democratic government, realizing that to oppose it was increasingly unpopular. Moreover, they were confident that, as Madison had written, the danger of the "have-nots" outvoting the "haves" was in any case very small.

One of the main reasons for this confidence was that mid-nineteenth-century American society still consisted largely of small property owners. Excepting slaves, the majority of families owned at least some of the tools or land with which they worked. The wealthy, of course, owned much more, but the society was not so sharply divided into those who owned the capital goods and those who did not. Moreover, the "have-nots" *were* deeply divided—they spoke a dozen different languages, prayed in different churches, and enjoyed sharply different social statuses—slave and freedom, master craftsman and apprentice, male and female.

Another comforting thought for those nineteenth-century capitalists who contemplated the spread of democracy was the idea of limited government. In fact, the government in those days played a very minor role in the functioning of the economy. As long as the government kept out of the economy, it did not matter so much if the government was a little more responsive to ordinary people.

Thus the marriage of capitalism and democracy was consummated. The couple was never really in love, but like many well-arranged marriages of convenience, this one prospered, or at least survived to this day. Do the conditions that have permitted this uneasy partnership to last still hold true today? We will return to this topic in the next section.

When we turn to the second question about democracy, that of democratic control over the economy, we find that capitalism is not democratic at all. As we saw in Chapter 13, democratic government and the capitalist economy are organized by entirely different sets of rules. Important decisions, affecting the life and death of whole communities, the health and safety of workers and consumers, and the livelihood of millions of families are taken by the owners and managers of firms.

The chief executive officers and major owners of the largest 500 corporations in the United States may well have considerably more power over peoples' lives and over the destiny of the nation than do the 535 members of the U.S. Senate and House of Representatives. Corporate leaders are a select group. They wield their power not by democratic election of those affected by corporate decisions but by being selected by people who own the capital goods (with owners casting votes in proportion to how much they own). And their decisions—to build big cars rather than small cars, to build nuclear power plants rather than solar collectors, to spend millions of dollars manipulating public opinion or pressuring elected representatives, to move their plants to Haiti or South Korea—are made behind closed doors, far beyond the reaches of public and open discussion by those immediately affected by their decisions.

Whatever desirable characteristics may be claimed for an economic system in which so few people make decisions affecting the lives of so many, democracy is not among them.

Few economists would disagree. Indeed, as we have seen in Chapter 8, the standard definition of the capitalist enterprise—the firm—is that it is a command economy in which decisions are made and resources are allocated according to some form of top-down authority. In this sense the firm is sharply contrasted with competitive markets, in which voluntary exchange—not command—is the rule.

In defense of this admittedly undemocratic system of command, it is often said that the economy—and specifically the capitalist enterprise—is private, not public, and democratic rule should only apply to public decisions. This reasoning is often based on the idea that the economy is made up of small businesses and self-employed people. But today's corporations each command the labor of thousands of people and wield power over the lives of many more. It is difficult to deny that these are public institutions, making decisions of general concern to all.

Many economists would nonetheless defend the undemocratic structure of capitalist enterprise on two grounds—that centralized and top-down command is the only efficient way to run a modern system of production and that undemocratic control is necessary for efficient investment. We are said to be confronted with a trade-off: If we want a more democratic way of organizing the production process, we will have to "pay" by having less efficiency.

Is undemocratic control of work necessary for efficient production? Chapter 9 showed that the top-down command of the modern corporation was adopted not to maximize efficiency but to minimize costs and maximize profits. Profits are often maximized by adapting inefficient but cost-reducing methods of organizing and carrying out the production process. Moreover, there is no evidence that more democratic workplaces are less efficient; indeed, there is quite a bit of evidence—from worker-owned and worker-run cooperatives—that the reverse is true.

Is undemocratic control of work necessary for efficient investment? Chapter 7 showed that the amount, type, and location of investment is determined by capitalists' expectations of where the profit rate will be highest. Are corporations likely to make investment decisions leading to the most efficient use of our labor and resources? The previous section showed that there are many reasons—including unemployment, the misuse of labor, and environmental destruction—for doubting that this will be the case. What

Undemocratic control of work occurs when the decisions about work that affect many people (workers, consumers, residents near the workplace, and so on) are made solely by the owners of the capital goods used in production.

is profitable is often not efficient; therefore, investments guided by the lure of profits are not likely to be efficient. The argument that undemocratic control over investment is the price we must pay for efficiency thus is no more plausible than the defense of the undemocratic nature of the workplace.

Capitalist organization departs substantially, then, from the standard of democracy. Historically capitalism has provided a context in which prodemocratic movements could successfully achieve greater democracy in government, but capitalism has been a powerful force opposing greater democratic control over the economy.

In conclusion, we see that U.S. capitalism (and capitalism in general) departs substantially from all three of the ideal standards of efficiency, fairness, and democracy. These failures to be efficient, fair, and democratic are not inadvertent lapses or the results of misguided policies or simply imperfections in the system. Rather, they are the consequences of capitalism's most central and basic institutions and the results of the way capitalism as a system is organized.

Some economists would object at this point, saying that we should not consider each criterion (efficiency, fairness, and democracy) separately, because there are trade-offs among them. For instance, they argue that whether fair or not, the inequality of income in the U.S. economic system is necessary, for without it the economy would not work and we all would be poorer as a result. Why would we be poorer? In previous chapters we saw that for employers to obtain profits, they must be able to exercise power over their workers; this power derives, in part, from the employer's ability to place the worker in a good job with a high income, in a bad job with a low income, or in no job at all with no income. From this observation many have concluded that a more equal distribution of income and greater job security would undercut the employers' ability to extract work from workers—that greater equality would reduce the level of profits, lower the rate of investment, reduce output, and discourage economic growth.

On the basis of these ideas many economists have come to see the amount of inequality in a capitalist society as simply a choice based on a trade-off between more equality and more output. Their reasoning is as follows: *If the government is democratic*, then the voters can simply decide how much equality they want. But *if the capitalist economy is efficient*, voters will have to "pay" for more equality, because there will be a trade-off; the more equality they vote for, the less output or economic growth they will get.

Both "ifs" are open to serious question. We saw in the last section that there are many reasons to believe that the capitalist economy is *not* efficient. We also saw in Chapter 13 that there are serious limits to the democratic choices that the voters may make, because in a capitalist system capitalists are free to invest elsewhere (or not at all) if they do not like what the voters do.

The conclusion—that there is necessarily a trade-off between equality and growth—is equally open to question. *If the capitalist economy is not efficient there is no trade-off. It is possible to have more of both output and equality,* simply by reducing the amount of inefficiency and making more sensible use of labor and other

---

A Trade-Off between Growth and Equality?

The trade-off that some economists believe exists between growth and equality (or between equality and efficiency, as the late Arthur Okun put it in his *Equality and Efficiency: The Big Trade-off*) is often represented as in the accompanying figure. Suppose there is now an amount of equality, indicated by *E*, and an amount of economic growth, indicated by *G*. The trade-off line indicates that an increase in the amount of equality, say from *E* to *E'*, will necessarily lower the rate of growth, from *G* to *G'*.

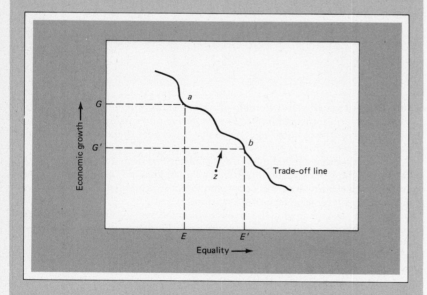

But how do we know that the economy is at point *a*, or at any other point on the trade-off line? If the economy were at point *z*, it would be possible to have more of both economic growth and equality. An example of being at point *z* would be if a large number of people were unemployed. Employing them productively would increase the rate of economic growth and reduce inequality at the same time.

inputs. Of course, reducing the amount of inefficiency may require changing some of the capitalist rules of the game, and many of those who benefit from the way the game is now played do not want to see this happen.

There are other reasons for doubting that the U.S. economy faces a trade-off between efficiency, fairness, and democracy. A number

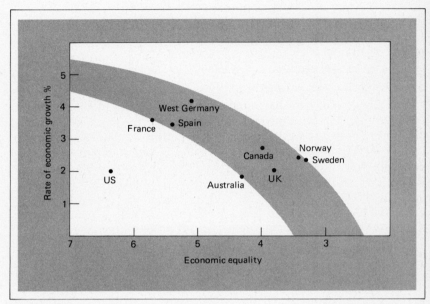

FIGURE 15.2 An equality-growth trade-off? Many economists believe that the United States faces a trade-off between more economic equality and more growth. If we try to have a more equal society we may succeed, but the price we will pay is slower economic growth, they say.

However, others have noted that many countries that have more economic equality than the United States also have had more growth. These countries have registered higher rates of growth in output per person and higher rates of growth of productivity in the manufacturing industries.

In the figure, economic growth is measured by the average annual percentage increase in real gross domestic product per capita for the years 1951–1980 (except Norway, about which data exist only from 1956–1980).

Economic equality is measured by the average income (after the payment of taxes and receipt of government transfers such as welfare) of a person in the richest 10 percent of the population compared to the average income of a person in the poorest half of the population. (The inequality figures are from the early 1970s.)

The figure shows that while there might indeed be a trade-off for the other countries shown—the broad (shaded) band may be the trade-off curve—the United States has failed to reach the trade-off curve. If the United States is like the other countries shown, it should be possible to have *both* more growth *and* more equality.

Sources: Organization for Economic Cooperation and Development (OECD), *National Accounts;* U.S. Bureau of Labor Statistics, unpublished data; and M. Sawyer, *Income Distribution in OECD Countries* (OECD Occasional Study, July 1976).

of countries that are at least as democratic as the United States have been able to achieve *both* more rapid economic growth *and* more equality in the distribution of income. The information in Figure 15.2 shows that Sweden, for example, in the post–World War II period had a more rapid rate of economic growth than the United States, eventually surpassing the United States in per capita income. (The rate of growth of productivity in manufacturing, another measure of economic efficiency, was also considerably higher than in the United States.) At the same time, the Swedish economy seems to distribute its rewards considerably more equally than the U.S. economy. And not only is the Swedish government democratic, but some progress has been made toward making control over the economy more democratic as well.

The examples of Sweden and the other countries in Figure 15.2 indicate that for the United States there is not necessarily a trade-off between the objectives of efficiency, fairness, and democracy. It may be possible to have more of each. But how could this be done? Are there practical alternatives to the current structure of U.S. capitalism that would allow us to have a society that was at once more efficient, fairer, and more democratic?

☐ Beyond Lemonade-Stand Capitalism and Lemon Socialism

We saw in Chapter 14 that long periods of economic crisis and instability—such as the 1890s and 1930s—tend to be periods of important institutional and political changes. The present period of economic stagnation may well repeat this pattern. We are likely to see—in the remainder of the 1980s and into the 1990s—proposals for basic change in how our economy is organized. It is no longer only the critics of capitalism who are calling for basic structural changes in our economy. Equally radical proposals are now voiced from the White House and in the pages of *Business Week* magazine.

Debates on alternatives to the present structure often generate more heat than light. One of the reasons is that the debaters often assume a limited menu of possibilities. The only alternative to our present system, it is often claimed, is centralized government control over all economic activity, along the lines of the economy of the Soviet Union. Others assume that the alternative to contemporary American capitalism is a government takeover of firms that are losing out in the competitive struggle for profits. Both versions merit the name *lemon socialism*.

Lemon socialism is often contrasted with an idealized view of our present economy—*lemonade-stand capitalism*. According to this view, our economy is now (or could be) composed of tens of

Lemon socialism refers to both (1) an economic system in which there is centralized control by an undemocratic government over all economic activities and (2) the takeover by a democratic government in a capitalist economy of losing or bankrupt firms; both alternatives are unattractive ("lemons").

Lemonade-stand capitalism is an idealized view of capitalism in which the economy is depicted as either potentially or now composed entirely of small businesses ("lemonade stands") operating in perfectly competitive markets; in lemonade-stand capitalism, everyone could open a business and be his or her own boss.

millions of uniformly small firms all interacting through perfectly competitive markets and providing ample opportunity for all who so wish to go into business for themselves. As we showed in Chapter 10, the idea of lemonade-stand capitalism is a fiction. The economy is, and will be for some time to come, organized in large monopolistically competitive units of production.

The age-old dispute between the perfectly competitive market and centralized planning as methods of resource allocation and economic decision making may have outlived its usefulness. There are two reasons for this. First, neither markets nor centralized planning alone could ever function as an efficient system of economic decision making. Pure cases of either system are hard to imagine and even harder to find. Capitalism, as we have seen, is a system of highly centralized decision making (firms), operating in a market environment. The economic system of Hungary, to take an example of centralized planning, is a system that makes extensive use of world and internal markets.

Second, highly centralized economic planning systems place democracy at risk. Systems such as that in the Soviet Union tend to concentrate economic power in a way that is prone to abuse by arbitrary or dictatorial authority. As a result, the centralized planning model is unlikely to be appealing to people committed to a democratic society.

For this reason, neither lemon socialism nor lemonade-stand capitalism is likely to be a practical or desirable alternative for the United States. They will not be on the menu simply because they will not be seriously advocated by any important group.

The real choices we will be facing in the years to come are considerably more down to earth and more closely related to the actual functioning of our economy and government today. The real choices are between more capitalism and more democracy, and if both, how they are to be combined or made compatible. There are four principal possibilities for the future evolution of the U.S. economy and government.

The first possible future course is that both economy and government will continue more or less as they are, with the different rules of the two overlapping games—capitalism and democratic government—continuing to raise problems but with no decisive change. This course would mean that no new social structure of accumulation would be constructed, and hard times—episodically interrupted by business cycle expansions—would continue.

The second possibility—that pursued by Ronald Reagan and supported by very conservative business groups—is to find a way of *separating* the two games, to restore the boundaries between the capitalist economy and democratic government. Let profits rule

Conservative economics or **Reaganomics** is one strategy for ending the hard times of the 1970s and early 1980s by reinstituting limited government, rebuilding American military dominance, reducing the power of unions and other noncapitalist groups to defend their interests, and using government policy to create a more favorable investment climate.

in the economy and let votes rule in the government, they say, and never the twain shall meet! The deregulation of industry, the reduction in environmental controls, the cuts in unemployment insurance and income maintenance payments of the early 1980s are all part of the attempt to get the government out of the economy and to prevent the rules of voting from interfering with the process of profit making. Defenders of Reaganomics often look with favor on the similar economic policies of Prime Minister Margaret Thatcher in Great Britain. The economic accomplishments of Thatcher's first term of office (1979–1983) included a significant reduction in the rate of inflation. But the price paid was record high levels of unemployment and a generally stagnant economy.

A third possibility, popular with *Business Week* magazine and some other business groups, is to accept the capitalist economy as it is and to limit democratic control over government. Those who favor this solution would accept the overlap between the government and the economy as necessary and irreversible and attempt to make the government serve the interests of business by limiting the democratic control of government. They would reduce the ability of the average voter to participate in or control major government decisions affecting the economy. This amounts to changing the rules of the democratic game so as to be able to preserve the rules of the capitalist game. Advocates of this alternative would like to see more economic decisions made by powerful government bodies like the Federal Reserve Board, whose deliberations are effectively shielded from public participation or electoral accountability. This third alternative is sometimes called *corporatism*, as it advocates less reliance on the market as the allocator of resources and more reliance on organizing the economy as today's corporations are organized—from the top down.

Corporatism is one strategy for ending the hard times of the 1970s and early 1980s by limiting democratic control over the government and instituting necessary planning in the economy by means of agencies or institutions more easily controlled from the top down; the Federal Reserve Board is often cited as a model.

Corporatists often take the Japanese economy as their model. There, large corporations in cooperation with one another and with the government make most of the important economic decisions. In both the corporations and the government, power is highly centralized and is rarely subject to democratic discussion and accountability. The Japanese economy in the post–World War II period has been a great success in terms of economic growth and productivity increase. Critics of the application of the Japanese model to the United States point out that its success may be due to aspects of Japanese society and culture that are absent in the United States. They also object to the centralized and undemocratic structure of decision making in the Japanese model.

This suggests a fourth possibility, one that finds most of its support among workers and other nonbusiness groups. Instead of watering down democracy to ensure the profitability of capitalist enterprise, we could extend democracy and modify the economic system instead. This would involve the reorganization of the production process within firms, replacing top-down management with committees elected by employees and consumers of the output. These committees could then hire specialists, technicians, even managers, as needed. A model for this already exists in small and medium-sized cities' school committees, which are elected democratically by those adults most immediately affected (the voters of the town) and who then hire teachers, principals, and specialists. A second part of a more democratic economy would be the democratic control over investment so that the electorate as a whole could have a say in economic priorities.

Too Much Democracy?

". . . while the critics of business worry about the atrophy of American democracy, the concern in the nation's boardrooms is precisely the opposite. For an executive, democracy in America is working too well—that is the problem." [1]

". . . some of the problems of governance in the United States stem from an excess of democracy . . . . Needed, instead, is a greater degree of moderation of democracy." [2]

"There is, of course, the risk that the democratic political process . . . may not be able to look far enough into the future to adopt appropriate policies. . . . a demand for instant solutions to difficult problems causes excessive attempts to use government intervention without a proper regard for its adverse long-term consequences." [3]

"We are in serious trouble. We need to question the system: one man, one vote." [4]

Sources: [1] Leonard Silk and David Vogel, reporting on the views expressed by top managers, in *Ethics and Profits: The Crisis of Confidence in American Business* (New York: Simon and Schuster, 1976).
[2] From a task force report on democracy for the Trilateral Commission (whose members included Jimmy Carter, Walter Mondale, and David Rockefeller), 1975, in Samuel Huntington et al., *The Crisis of Democracy: Report on the Governability of Democracies to the Trilateral Commission* (New York: New York University Press, 1975), p. 113.
[3] Martin Feldstein, chairman of the President's Council of Economic Advisors, 1982–1984, in "The Retreat from Keynesian Economics," *The Public Interest*, Summer 1981, p. 104.
[4] A business leader, quoted in Silk and Vogel, *op. cit.*

This alternative may be called *economic democracy,* as it involves extending the use of democratic decision making to the economy. Advocates of economic democracy often use the Swedish, Norwegian, and Yugoslav economies as models. In Norway, for example, the direction of technical change is determined by bargaining among workers, businessmen, and the government. A significant portion of total investment is done by the government, rather than by private corporations. In Sweden, the location of industry and the determination of wage increases are influenced less by the workings of markets and more by nationwide collective bargaining and democratically determined government policy. Most large firms in Yugoslavia are governed by a "workers' council" elected by the people who work in the plant.

All three economies have been quite successful in the post–World War II period, with rates of increase of per capita income exceeding that of the United States. Critics of these models point out that what is possible in these small countries may not be possible in the United States. In Norway and Sweden, for example, labor unions play a major role in the governing of the economy; in the United States, where the vast majority of workers are not members of labor unions, this would be impossible. Others observe that the elected Yugoslav workers' councils coexist with an undemocratic national government and that the stronger groups of workers often take advantage of less organized or less politically connected workers. Nonetheless, these countries' experiences suggest that it may be possible to significantly extend democratic rule and at the same time organize labor processes efficiently and fairly.

Economic democracy is a strategy for ending the hard times of the 1970s and early 1980s by extending democratic rules (now more characteristic of the government) into the economy; democratic control over labor processes and over investment decisions would be most important.

☐ Have Capitalism and Democracy Reached a Parting of the Ways?

The strongest democracy argument in favor of capitalism, as was noted on page 378, is that all of the present democratic governments are linked with capitalist economies. But does this mean that capitalism and democratic government will continue to live together in the future?

There are reasons for skepticism. The conditions that originally gave businessmen confidence that democracy would not threaten their interests have changed over the years. Three conditions altered. First, as we saw in Chapters 4 and 5, our society is no longer one in which a large number of families own the capital goods with which they work. Most families own a car, many own a house, but very few own any substantial part of the assets of the companies that make up the U.S. economy. The process of accumulation—and particularly the process of concentration—has greatly reduced the number of small businessmen, owners of mom-and-pop stores, small farmers, and others who could have been expected to side with the owners of capital goods.

Second, the potential conflict between capitalism and democratic government has increased as the government's economic role has grown. The concept of limited government has eroded now that the government has become a crucial macro- and microeconomic regulator, distributor, and producer (in part as the result of the urgings and needs of capitalists themselves). The government is now in a position to make a considerable difference in the fortunes of capitalists. The importance to capitalists of not letting the government fall into "unfriendly" hands has thus increased.

Third, the collapse of the notion of limited government occurred at the same time as (and partly as a consequence of) a major extension in the exercise of democracy. In the twentieth century, women and blacks achieved effective entry to voting, and working-class groups (such as unions) became major factors in the electoral process. Partly as a result of the gradual extension of democracy, some of the barriers that once politically divided the have-nots have eroded; women, black people, and other minorities have gained greater civil rights, and differences in language and religion have become less important.

Thus far, the policies adopted by the U.S. government have been anything but unfriendly to business. Whether openly allied with employers (like Grover Cleveland in the nineteenth century or Ronald Reagan in the 1980s) or more inclined toward egalitarian or populist rhetoric (like Franklin Delano Roosevelt during the 1930s or John F. Kennedy during the 1960s), the leading figures in U.S. politics have tried to give capitalists what they asked for. Part of this probusiness stance is explained by the importance of business as a source of political finance and direct political influence through lobbying and the like. At least as important, as we saw in Chapter 13, is the indirect power capitalists hold over governments, power deriving from their control over investment and their ability to move their plants elsewhere.

But the possibility exists today for a division among the voters in which business could end up on the short end. Consider a concrete possibility. Virtually all capitalists support the idea that there should be no limitations on their ability to invest wherever they please, whether within the United States or in some other country. Both their profits and their power depend on this unrestricted mobility of capital. But the benefits that other people, the majority of voters, gain from unrestricted capital mobility are dubious at best. Workers see their plants closing and their jobs being moved to some other country. Members of communities see their cities threatened with economic decline, to be averted only if tax giveaways can entice the businesses to stay. Others see the total level of investment in the United States reduced. Thus the possibility exists for major conflict between capitalist rules and democratic rules.

An open political debate on the freedom of the major corporations to invest wherever they please might be a hard one for businessmen to win. But it would also be a tough one to lose. Other examples include legislation that limits employers' ability to destroy the environment or to put workers' and consumers' health and safety in jeopardy.

In recent years representatives of business interests have increasingly raised their voices about the danger of an "excess of democracy" in the United States. Those taking this position have ranged from David Rockefeller's Trilateral Commission to the chairman of the President's Council of Economic Advisors under Ronald Reagan during the early 1980s. In this situation, many commentators have raised the possibility that the marriage of capitalism and democracy may be on the rocks; that the two systems have reached a parting of the ways.

If they are right, Americans will be faced with a choice and with some demanding tasks—either to accept the erosion of democracy as the price of making capitalism work or to defend democratic government and to democratize our economy.

☐ Suggested Readings

Martin Carnoy and Derek Shearer, *Economic Democracy* (Armonk, N.Y.: M.E. Sharpe, 1980).

Joshua Cohen and Joel Rogers, *On Democracy: Toward a Transformation of American Society* (New York: Penguin Books, 1983).

Milton Friedman, *Capitalism and Freedom* (Chicago: University of Chicago Press, 1962).

Branko Horvat, *The Political Economy of Socialism* (Armonk, N.Y., M. E. Sharpe, 1982.

Howard Sherman and Andrew Zimbalist, *Comparing Economic Systems: A Political Economic Approach* (New York: Academic Press, 1984).

Appendix   List of Variables

Note: The following system for choosing symbols to represent variables has been used. A single upper-case letter (example: *R*) always refers to a variable measured in *money*. Lower-case letters, whether single (example: *r*) or compound (example: *ulc*) always refer to a *ratio*. All other variables are upper-case compound symbols (*Labor, Amt. of M, Pm,* and so on).

☐ Totals:

Flows

These are physical or money totals for a firm or for the economy as a whole, for a given period of time (such as per year).

Z	= Dollar value of total output produced during a year = $Pz \cdot (Amt.\ of\ Z)$
Amt. of Z	= Amount of total output produced during a year
M	= Dollar value of materials used and machines used up in production in a year = $Pm \cdot (Amt.\ of\ M)$
Amt. of M	= Amount of materials used and machines used up in production in a year
Y	= Dollar value of net output produced in a year = $Z - M = R + W$; for a firm this is called *value added*; for the economy as a whole this is called *net national product*
W	= Wages and salaries (in dollars) paid during a year = $w \cdot Labor$
R	= Profits (in dollars) per year = $Y - W = Z - M - W$
T	= Taxes (in dollars) on profits per year
ATR	= After-tax profits = $R - T$
S	= Dollar value of total sales during a year
I	= Dollar value of investment during a year
Labor	= Total labor hours employed during a year
LD	= Total labor demanded by employers during a year
LS	= Total labor supplied by workers during a year

Stocks

These are physical or money totals for a firm or for the economy as a whole that are in existence at some given moment in time (such as January 1, 1985).

CG	= Amount (stock) of capital goods ("machines") owned
K	= Dollar value of stock of capital goods ("machines") owned = $Pc \cdot CG$
CG in use	= Amount (stock) of capital goods ("machines") in use
K in use	= Dollar value of the stock of capital goods ("machines") in use

Prices

These are averages, often referred to as *price indexes*.

Pz	= Price per unit of total output
Py	= Price per unit of net output
Pm	= Price per unit of materials used and machines used up in production
Pc	= Price of capital goods (per "machine")
w	= Wage rate = price per hour of labor = $W/Labor$
Pim	= Price per unit of imported inputs
i	= Rate of interest (in percent per year), which is the cost of borrowing for the purpose of investment = (interest paid)/principal

☐ Ratios

These are totals divided by other totals; they can always be interpreted as "amount of one thing per unit of something else" (for example, the ratio X/Y means "amount of X per unit of Y").

z	= Dollar value of total output per hour of labor employed = $Z/Labor$
y	= Dollar value of net output per hour of labor employed = $Y/Labor$
k	= Dollar value of capital goods ("machines") owned per hour of labor employed = $K/Labor$
r	= Rate of profit = profits in dollars per dollar of capital goods ("machines") owned = $R/K = (Y - W)/K = (y - w)/k$
d	= Amount of *work done* per hour, or intensity of work
e	= *Efficiency*, or amount of total output produced per unit of work done
m	= Amount of materials used and machines used up per labor hour = $(Amt.\ of\ M)/labor$
cu	= Capacity utilization ratio = percentage of owned capital goods actually in use = $K\ in\ use/K = (CG\ in\ use/CG)\ Pc/Pc = CG\ in\ use/CG$
$k\ in\ use$	= Value of capital goods in use per labor hour = dollar value of capital goods ("machines") in use per hour of labor employed = $K\ in\ use/Labor = (cu \cdot K)/Labor$
ulc	= Unit labor costs = wage cost per unit of total output = $W/Z = w/(d \cdot e)$
product wage	= The wage rate corrected for inflation = $\dfrac{w}{Pz}$
labor cost index	= Labor cost expressed in terms of labor cost per dollar of output = $ulc/Pz = w/(Pz \cdot d \cdot e)$
cg in use	= Amount of capital goods in use per labor hour = $CG/Labor$

Glossary

Accumulation is the process of mobilizing, transforming, and exploiting the inputs required in capitalist production and then selling the output; profit making and investment lie at the heart of the capitalist accumulation process.

The **after-tax profit rate** is the profit rate capitalists receive, having taken into account (subtracted) any taxes they must pay.

The **amount of capital goods in use per hour of labor** is the number of machines actually used in production divided by the total number of hours worked.

The **amount of materials used up and wear and tear on machines per hour worked** is the quantity of the inputs of materials and machines used in production divided by the total number of hours worked.

Barriers to entry are obstacles that make it more difficult or costly for new firms to enter a market; examples include technical secrets, initial investments that are very large, and exclusive marketing arrangements.

A **breakthrough** occurs when a firm discovers or develops a new method of doing business such as a new way of organizing work, a new product, or a new market.

Bureaucratic control is a system of control that uses job ladders, seniority rewards, and other organizational incentives in order to extract work done.

The **business cycle** is the pattern of medium-term economic fluctuations in which expansion is followed by recession, which is followed by expansion, and so on.

The **capacity utilization ratio** measures the percentage of all capital goods that are currently being used in production.

Capital goods (see **Machines**)

Capital-goods-saving technical progress is a reduction in the gap between gross and net product, permitting producers to obtain the same net output using fewer capital goods.

A **capital strike** occurs when, as a result of a negative investment climate, many individual capitalists decide to reduce their investments or not to invest at all.

Capitalism is an economic system in which commodities are produced for profit using privately owned capital goods and wage labor; capitalists obtain the surplus product in the form of profits. Capitalism is the main economic system in the United States, Western Europe, Japan, and some 80 other countries.

The **capitalist class** or **capitalists** are those who own capital goods used in production and exercise control over the labor of others; they receive their income in the form of profits or other payments (like interest and rent) for the use of their capital goods.

The **capitalist epoch** began in some parts of Europe around A.D. 1500 when capitalist organization of labor processes first appeared. It continues to the present in much of the world.

Capitalist profits are profits that result from a labor process.

Change, or the time dimension in economics, refers to the historical evolution of economic systems.

Citizen rights are the basis for a claim to share (some of) the benefits of society; this claim is based on one's citizenship instead of, for example, on possessing sufficient money to buy the benefits.

A **class** is a group of people who share a common position in the economy with respect to the production and control of the surplus product.

A **class relationship** exists between the producers of the total product, including the surplus product, and those who command the use of the surplus product.

Classical liberalism is a set of ideas born in the late eighteenth and nineteenth centuries advocating limited representative government and a capitalist economy.

Collective activities are activities whose benefits or burdens extend, potentially at least, to all citizens.

Collective bargaining occurs when, in negotiating wages and other employment conditions, all workers in a firm or occupation are represented collectively by a union; employers may also be collectively represented by an employers' association.

Command, or the vertical dimension in economics, refers to aspects of economic relationships in which power plays the predominant role.

Command relations are relationships between superiors and subordinates in which the superior exercises substantial power over the subordinate.

Commercial profits result from selling something for more than it cost to purchase ("buying cheap and selling dear"); no labor process is involved.

A **commodity** is any good or service that is produced with the intention of selling it in order to make a profit.

Competition, or the horizontal dimension in economics, refers to aspects of economic relationships in which voluntary exchange and choice play the predominant role.

Competition for profits is the scramble among capitalists and firms seeking new ways of doing business, new markets, new products, and other possibilities for profitable investment.

Competitive capitalism was the first stage of American capitalism, from the 1840s through the 1890s.

A **compulsory relationship** exists when a person cannot choose whether to enter the relationship but rather becomes subject to the relationship because of his or her status (such as citizenship).

Conservative economics or Reaganomics is one strategy for ending the hard times of the 1970s and early 1980s by reinstituting limited government, rebuilding American military dominance, reducing the power of unions and other non-capitalist groups to defend their interests, and using government policy to create a more favorable investment climate.

Contemporary capitalism is the current stage of American capitalism, from the 1940s to the present.

A **contract specifying work done** is an agreement between an employer and a worker that specifies payment for actual work activities instead of for work time.

Core firms are giant corporations with substantial market power.

Corporatism is one strategy for ending the hard times of the 1970s and early 1980s by limiting democratic control over the government and instituting necessary planning in the economy by means of agencies or institutions more easily controlled from the top down; the Federal Reserve Board is often cited as a model.

The **cost conditions affecting investment** are

those things that affect the expected profit rate on capital goods that will be in use; some of the most important are the labor cost index and the prices of the inputs to production.

A **craft union** is a labor union whose membership is restricted to workers in the same craft, skill category, or occupation.

Cyclical inflation is the general increase in prices that takes place during the expansion phase of the business cycle, in part in response to the associated decline in unemployment rate.

Decreasing costs refers to a situation in which the average cost of producing something declines as the volume (scale) of production increases.

The **demand conditions affecting investment** are those things that affect capacity utilization; the most important of these is whether the economy is booming or experiencing hard times.

A **demand curve** indicates, for each possible price, how much of the good or service demanders are willing and able to buy.

Democracy is a process with three characteristics: power is accountable to those affected; guarantees of civil rights and personal liberties exist; and citizens have relatively equal access to political resources and influence.

Democratic government is a way of organizing a government based on (1) accountability of officials through elections with widespread and equal voting rights and (2) civil liberties and personal freedoms.

Depreciation is the cost (due to wear and tear) of restoring the capital goods used in producing last year's output.

Deskilling means changing a production process in such a way as to make it possible to employ workers with fewer skills.

Despotism is any form of governmental rule in which the rulers are largely or entirely unaccountable to those being ruled.

The **determinants of the profit rate** are the things upon which the profit rate depends; they determine how high the profit rate will be.

Discrimination means treating someone differ-ently simply because that person belongs to a certain group when membership in the group is irrelevant.

The **dual economy** is the industrial structure of contemporary American capitalism, consisting of core firms and periphery firms.

Economic concentration is the extent to which the economic activity of an industry or the whole economy is conducted in the largest firms.

Economic concentration in particular industries measures how much of the economic activity (such as sales) of a particular industry is accounted for by the largest firms in that industry.

Economic concentration in the whole economy measures how much of the economic activity of the whole economy is accounted for by the largest firms in the economy.

Economic democracy is a strategy for ending the hard times of the 1970s and early 1980s by extending democratic rules (now more characteristic of the government) into the economy; democratic control over labor processes and over investment decisions would be most important.

An **economic system** is a set of relationships among people organizing the labor processes that all societies need to sustain life.

An **economy** is a collection of labor processes.

Efficiency means that for a given amount of productive inputs used in an economic system, the maximum output of useful goods and services is produced; or, equivalently, the minimum of the productive inputs is used to produce a given level of output.

The **efficiency of labor** or **amount of total output per unit or work done** is the total amount produced for a specified or given amount of work effort (intensity of work).

Equalization of profit rates refers to the competitive pressures on firms in different industries, different geographical regions, or different markets that push their profit rates toward a common or average level.

Excess demand exists when at a particular price more of some good or service is demanded than is supplied.

Excess supply exists when at a particular price more of some good or service is supplied than is demanded.

Expansion is that part or phase of the business cycle when total output rises; during expansions, investment also usually rises and the demand for labor increases.

The **expected capacity utilization** ratio is the utilization ratio that capitalists believe will exist in the future; it is the percentage of all capital goods that capitalists believe will be in use.

The **expected profit rate** is the profit rate that capitalists believe will exist in the future; it is composed of two parts: the expected profit rate on that portion of the capital goods that will be in use; and the expected utilization rate.

The **expected profit rate in the rest of the world** is the profit rate that capitalists believe will exist on investments in labor processes located outside the United States.

The **expected profit rate in the United States** is the profit rate that capitalists believe will exist on investments in U.S.-based labor processes.

The **expected profit rate on capital goods in use** is the profit rate that capitalists believe will exist on that portion of their "machines" that will be utilized.

The **expected profit rate on investment** is a firm's estimate of the future profit rate that it thinks will be earned on its investment.

The **extraction of work from workers** is the process of transforming the labor time that an employer has purchased into work done.

A **fair outcome** is an equitable result or consequence of some social process; it refers to the outcome, not the rules, of the game.

Fairness means that people in an economic system suffer the burdens and enjoy the benefits of that economic system equitably.

A **fair process** is a way of doing things in which people are treated equally; it refers to the rules, not the outcome, of the game.

Fascism is a form of government intervention in the economy in which an authoritarian government uses its power to limit workers' demands.

Feudalism was the dominant economic system in Europe in the Middle Ages; lords obtained the surplus product through rents and other customary obligations owed by the serfs.

Foreign investment is the use of some of the American surplus product to expand the capital goods used in foreign production.

Frictional and search unemployment are voluntary forms of unemployment that result from people moving between or searching for jobs; even at "full employment" there will usually be some frictional and search unemployment.

Full employment is a situation in which there is no excess supply of labor time being offered in the labor market.

Gross investment is depreciation plus (net) investment.

Hegemony is the power to define, interpret, and enforce the rules of the game and thus to determine the range of possible alternatives for all of the players.

A **hierarchy** is an organization of power in which superiors have command over subordinates.

Idle capacity consists of machines and other capital goods that are currently not being used in production.

Increasing costs refers to a situation in which the average cost of producing something increases as the volume (scale) of production increases.

The **independent primary labor market** includes those jobs with highly elaborate bureaucratic or professional career patterns; it contains mainly the jobs of craft, technical, professional, and lower-level supervisory workers.

Independent production of commodities is an economic system in which the producers own the capital goods needed in production and use (primarily) their own labor.

An **industrial union** is a labor union whose membership is open to all workers in a plant or industry, regardless of which specific occupations or jobs they work at.

Inefficient technical change occurs when some technical changes are developed and implemented because they are profitable but other technologies or technical changes, which are at least equally efficient, are unexplored and ignored because they are less profitable.

Inflation is a general increase in prices, often measured by an increase in the Consumer Price Index.

The **inflation-unemployment trade-off** is the relationship between the inflation rate and the unemployment rate in which less inflation may be obtained only at the cost of higher unemployment and vice versa.

The **intensity of labor** is how much work effort producers must expend per hour of work.

The **interest rate** is the cost of renting money; for a firm that borrows money, it is the percentage of the amount borrowed that must be repaid in addition to the amount borrowed.

Investment is any use of the surplus product which is intended to increase the stocks of materials or capital goods available for use in future production processes.

The **investment climate** is the business community's general mood or level of confidence with respect to future conditions for the profit rate; individual investors are likely to be more willing to invest when capitalists as a group are in a more favorable or optimistic mood than when the business community is more gloomy about investment prospects.

The **investment multiplier** is the amount (multiple) by which total demand will go up in response to an increase in investment; it counts both the direct and indirect effects.

Involuntary unemployment results when there are not enough jobs for all of those who seek jobs (an excess supply of labor time exists).

Job ladders link together a series of related jobs, in which a worker over the years climbs from one job to another and gains access to jobs higher on the ladder only by first succeeding in the lower job.

Labor is any activity performed by people that is needed for production or reproduction.

The **labor accord** was the truce or implicit social contract between large corporations and labor unions that provided the basis for collective bargaining in contemporary American capitalism.

The **labor cost index** is a measure of the labor costs of production *as compared to* (divided by) the price of the output; it consists of two parts, the total output per labor hour and the product wage.

Labor demand is the schedule or list showing, for each wage, the amount of labor time (total hours) that would be hired by employers in response to that wage.

A **labor market** is a market in which workers sell their labor time (not work itself) in return for a wage; employers are the demanders and workers are the suppliers of labor time.

A **labor process** is a transformation of our natural surroundings using human labor with the intention of producing something useful.

Labor-saving technical progress is an increase in the efficiency of labor, permitting producers to produce more output for every hour of labor input without working any harder.

Labor supply is the schedule or list showing, for each wage, the amount of labor time (total hours) that would be offered by workers in response to that wage.

Labor time measures the number of hours worked; it does not measure how much work gets done, since there are many different levels of work effort (intensities of work) possible.

Lemonade-stand capitalism is an idealized view of capitalism in which the economy is depicted as either potentially or now composed entirely of small businesses ("lemonade stands") operating in perfectly competitive markets; in lemonade-stand capitalism, everyone could open a business and be his or her own boss.

Lemon socialism refers to both (1) an economic system in which there is centralized control by an undemocratic government over all economic activities and (2) the takeover by a democratic government in a capitalist economy of losing or bankrupt firms; both alternatives are unattractive ("lemons").

Limited government or **laissez faire** is a relationship between the government and economy in which government enforces the rules of capitalist economy but otherwise does not intervene in the operation of the economy.

A **lockout** occurs when an employer locks the

workers out of the workplace and closes down production in order to force workers to accept the employer's terms for wages, work pace, or other working conditions.

Machines or **capital goods** are goods which are needed in production, but which are durable, and will be used up only over the course of years.

A **market** refers to all the buying and selling activities of those persons wishing to trade a good or service; a market consists of suppliers wanting to sell and demanders wanting to buy.

Market clearing occurs when, at the given price, buyers want to purchase exactly the quantity that sellers want to sell.

Market exchanges are relationships between buyers and sellers in which each party exercises substantial voluntary agreement to the particular exchange.

A **market share** is one firm's sales as a percentage of the total sales in an industry.

Mass poverty is a situation in which a large portion of a society lives at or near the minimal level of physical subsistence.

Materials are goods needed in production and used up during the process of production.

The **materials and machines price** is the average price of the materials used up and the cost of wear and tear on the machines used in production.

Middle classes in capitalist society possess one but not both of the attributes of capitalists; they therefore stand between capitalists and workers.

Monopolistically competitive capitalism was the second stage of American capitalism, from the 1900s through the 1930s.

Monopoly power is the ability of one or a few firms in an industry to exercise substantial control over the market price and other aspects of competition, usually by excluding other firms.

The **necessary product** is the amount of goods and services needed to maintain the inputs in the labor process—both workers and tools—at a given level.

Neoclassical or **conventional economics** is a theory of capitalism emphasizing the horizontal dimension of markets and voluntary exchange.

Net product is the total product minus materials and capital goods used up in the course of producing the total product.

The **new middle class** consists of those who do not own the capital goods used in their own labor processes but who do regularly control the labor of others; it includes managers and supervisers.

The **old middle class** consists of those who do own the capital goods used in their own labor processes but who do not regularly control the labor of others; they are self-employed.

Oligopoly or **shared monopoly** is a market situation in which several firms together, but no one firm by itself, can exercise substantial monopoly power.

An **opportunity cost** is the value of the best opportunity given up (foregone) in order that whatever was chosen could be undertaken.

The **output price** is the price at which sellers sell and buyers buy one unit of the output.

Parallel plants are plants owned by the same employer and producing the same product but located in different geographical regions in order to weaken the workers' ability to bargain collectively.

Periphery firms are firms not in the core; most of them are small and medium-sized businesses with little market power.

A **piece-rate** is a form of wage payment in which the worker is paid for each unit of output produced instead of for work time.

A **political business cycle** occurs when recession and/or expansion are in part intentionally created by governmental economic policy, as officials attempt to generate a business cycle for their own or others' interests.

Political economy is a theory that analyzes capitalism in terms of the three dimensions of competition, command, and change.

A **political stalemate** occurs when each of the major political actors—employers, bankers, workers, and others—is able to prevent a solution to general economic problems harmful to its own interests, and so no group is able to impose a general solution on the others.

The **power of capital** refers to the ability of employers, especially the largest corporations, to influence governmental policy or otherwise create conditions favorable to their own interests; this power grows out of their position as owners of capital goods.

The **power of the citizenry** refers to the ability of citizens to influence governmental policy or otherwise create conditions favorable to their own interests; this power grows out of their position in democratic government.

Price competition is a form of or strategy for competition in which firms attempt to attract customers primarily by offering lower prices.

Price leadership is an informal system for setting prices in which the biggest firm in an industry establishes an output price and the other firms in the industry tacitly agree to set the same price for their own outputs.

The **price of capital goods** is the average price of a new machine or capital good.

Privately owned capital goods are machines, buildings, offices, tools, and other durable things needed in production and whose owner, because of a property right, determines how the property will be used.

Production is a labor process whose output is a good or a service.

A **production possibility frontier** shows all the possible combinations of outputs available using a given technology and a fixed amount of inputs.

The **product wage** is the hourly wage rate *as compared to* (divided by) the price of the output.

Profitability measures how much profit is derived from a labor process.

Profits are the form of the surplus product in a capitalist economic system; they are what is left over, out of sales revenues, after wages, the costs of materials used up, and wear and tear on machines have been paid.

Property rights are a legal expression for the combination of class relationships and associated arrangements for using and controlling the surplus product.

The **rate of profit** is the amount of profit divided by the value of the capital goods invested.

The **real price of imported inputs** is the price of imported inputs *as compared to* (divided by) the price of U.S. output.

Recession is that part or phase of the business cycle in which total output falls; during recessions, investment also usually declines and the demand for labor is reduced.

The **relative expected U.S. profit rate** is the profit rate that capitalists believe will exist on investments in U.S.-based labor processes *as compared to* (divided by) the profit rate that capitalists believe will exist on investments in labor processes located elsewhere.

Reproduction is a labor process whose output is people; it includes not only biological reproduction but also such activities as child rearing, training, feeding, and care giving.

A **runaway shop** is a workplace that an employer has moved from an area where workers are strong to an area where workers are weak in order to escape having to meet workers' demands.

The **sales effort** consists of all those activities by a firm that relate to the selling of the firm's product.

Savings is the amount of resources out of the surplus product that are available for investment.

The **secondary market** includes jobs in workplaces that lack the formal organization (such as collective bargaining agreements, bureaucratic control, or professional or craft patterns) of primary markets; it contains jobs like those of service and retail workers, clerks, seasonal workers, and nonunionized employees of small businesses.

Segmented labor markets are labor markets that have been divided institutionally into distinct or separate markets (market segments); the separation of the segments is often maintained by racial, sexual, and other forms of discrimination.

Shared monopoly   (see **Oligopoly**)

The **separation of conception from execution** is one method for deskilling work in which the workers who plan production are different from those who carry it out.

Simple control is a system of control that focuses on the supervisors' personal exercise of workplace rewards and sanctions to maintain the work pace.

Slavery was the dominant economic system in the U.S. South before the Civil War; slaveholders obtained the surplus product by owning all of the inputs (including slaves) and the output of slave production.

Social democracy is a form of government intervention in the economy in which a democratic government obtains agreement between at least the most powerful groups of employers and workers on a "social contract."

The **social organization of work** refers to the way in which jobs are defined, work tasks assigned, supervisory power delegated, and other social aspects of the workplace organized.

A **social structure of accumulation** is the institutional setting within which profit-making and accumulation occur; it structures relations among capitalists, between capitalists and workers, among workers, and between government and the economy.

Sovereignty refers to the ability and right of a person or group to make a decision; democratic government confers sovereignty on the citizenry, whereas capitalist economy confers sovereignty, especially with respect to investment, on the owners of capital goods.

Speed up is an effort by an employer to increase the pace of work.

The **stages of American capitalism** are distinct phases in the development of U.S. capitalism; each is defined by a separate social structure of accumulation.

Stagflation refers to the combination of slower economic growth (*stag*nation) and generally rising prices (*in*flation) that characterized the hard times of the 1970s.

Stagnation refers to the hard-times phase of a long swing; it is characterized by slower economic growth or even economic decline.

Structural inflation is a general increase in prices that occurs during all phases of the business cycle (recessions as well as expansions).

The **subordinate primary market** includes those jobs in workplaces organized according to the collective bargaining agreements of the labor accord; it contains mainly the jobs of the traditional, unionized, industrial working class.

A **supply curve** indicates, for each possible price, how much of the good or service suppliers wish to sell.

Surplus labor time is that part of the year's total work time which was devoted to producing the surplus product.

The **surplus product** is what remains out of the total product after the necessary product has been deleted.

A **system of control** is an employer's strategy or method for governing the workplace to facilitate the extraction of work from the workers.

Technical control is a system of control that incorporates a work pace designed into the machinery of production.

Technical progress is a change in the relationship between inputs and outputs which permits the same output to be produced with less of one or more of the inputs.

Technology is the relationship between inputs and outputs in a labor process.

The **total cost of investment** consists of two parts, the cost of the capital goods purchased and the opportunity cost of the money used to purchase them.

Total demand is the sum of all demands for goods and services in the U.S. economy, including those by consumers, businesses, governments, and foreign buyers.

The **total product** is the total amont of goods and services produced in an economy during a year.

The **total return from an investment** consists of two parts, the repayment of the investment and the profit (or loss) earned.

A **trade-off** is a relationship between two or more things in which more of one thing can be obtained only at the cost of getting less of the other.

Undemocratic control of work occurs when the decisions about work that affect many people (workers, consumers, residents near the workplace, and so on) are made solely by the owners of the capital goods used in production.

Unemployment occurs when there are not enough jobs for all those who want jobs (an excess supply in the labor market).

A **union** is an organization of workers established with the intention of providing a unified and stronger voice on behalf of the members' interests.

Unit labor cost is the labor portion of the average cost of producing each unit of output.

The **value of capital goods owned per hour of labor** is the employer's total investment divided by the total number of hours worked by employees.

The **value of net output per hour of labor** is the dollar value of the total output minus materials and machine costs divided by the total number of hours worked.

Wage labor is work performed under the direction of an employer in return for a wage or salary.

The **wage rate** is the amount paid on average to a worker for each hour worked.

Work done is the amount of work effort expended per hour of labor.

The **working class** or **workers** are those who perform wage labor; they neither own the capital goods used in their labor processes nor command control over the labor of others.

INDEX

Blacks (*Continued*)
  unemployment, 225–226
  women, 225
  workers, 214, 220, 222–223
Boeing Corporation, 153, 200, 204, 313
Breakfast Cheer Coffee, 208, 213
Breakthroughs, 27, 129, 137–140, 142, 151–152
  and capitalist development, 3
  defined, 132
Bretton Woods agreement, 341–342, 362
Bryan, William Jennings, 362
Built-in stabilizers, 308. *See also* Automatic stabilizers
Bureaucratic control, 181, 221
  defined, 108
Business, 313
Business cycles, 269–270, 293–296, 352, 354, 357
  costs and profits in, 284–290
  defined, 285
  and expected profit rate, 271, 284–285
  imported materials aspects of, 288–289
  and inflation, 290–293
  labor cost aspects of, 286–287
  and long swings, 326
  political, 314–316
  and unemployment, 281–288
  well-behaved and misbehaved, 265–266, 271
Business Week, 385–387

C

Capacity utilization ratio, 120, 124–126, 130, 133–137, 393
  defined, 123
  expected, 244–245
  and investment, 145, 248
  in the United States, 346

Capital (Marx), 25
Capital, 138, 239. *See also* Capital goods
  power of, 316–318
  strike, 318–321
  in use, 258–259, 393
Capital goods, 51. *See also* Privately owned capital goods
  concentration of ownership of, 76
  defined, 38
  in existence, 254
  owned, 392–393
  price of, 122, 125
  and the profit rate, 107–108, 115–126
  -saving technical progress, 57
  stock of, 392
  in use, 123, 125, 130, 254, 258–259, 392–393
  in use, expected profit rate on, 244–245
  used in commodity production, 81–82
  value of, owned per hour of labor, 119
  value of, and recession, 280
Capitalism, 15–16, 64, 69–76, 159, 192–193, 196, 327. *See also* the various stages of capitalism, as Competitive capitalism
  American, 84–89, 97–99, 214, 367–391
  becomes dominant in the United States, 89–94
  and change, 18–19
  defined, 3, 68
  and democracy, 369–372, 378–382, 389–391
  and democratic government, 368–375
  development of, 3–13
  and efficiency, 372–375
  and fairness, 375–378
  and the form of government, 80–81
  lemonade-stand, 385–386

in neoclassical economics, 16–17
and population. *See* Population
profits and surplus product, 76–83
and recessions, 293–295
stages of, 94–99
and unemployment, 266, 270–271
Capitalist class, 92–93, 303–304
defined, 79
and profit, 110–113
Capitalist economy, 234
limits of democratic control, 316–323
world, 235
Capitalist enterprise, 380. *See also*
Firm
Capitalist epoch
defined, 3
history of, 3–13
and population growth, 6
Capitalist profits, 106. *See also*
Profit
Capitalists, 16, 76–77, 87–88, 161–162, 172, 175, 177, 188, 266. *See
also* Capitalist class; Employers
competition among, 128, 154
conflict between workers and, 110–113
and investment, 242–244
and profit, 103–105
relationships among, 144
richest American, 82–83
Capital/labor ratio, 236
Carter, Jimmy, 346, 356
Catholic Church, 196
Centralized planning, 386
Chamber of Commerce, 307
Change, 15, 17, 20, 128, 129
and American capitalism, 76–83
defined, 18
Chesebrough-Pond, 206–207, 213
Chile, 118
Chrysler Corporation, 103
Citizen power, 321–322. *See also*
Citizenry
Citizenry, power of, 316
Citizen's rights, 300

Civil Rights Act, 303
Civil rights movement, 225, 310, 342
Civil War, 5
Claiborne, Craig, 71
Class, 26, 160. *See also* type of class, as capitalist
defined, 64
and economic systems, 66–68
relations, 63–64
society, 63
structure in the United States, 92–94
Classical liberalism, 370
Class relationships, 114, 156
in the United States, 77
Clean Air and Water Act, 310
Cleveland, Grover, 390
Coal industry, 275, 337, 340
class relations in, 78–79
Coal miners, 174–175
Cold War, 328
Collective activities, 299
Collective bargaining, 162
Command, 15–16, 19–20, 128, 156–157, 210
defined, 17
relations, 159
Committee on Economic Development, 308
Commodity, 68–73, 375
Commons, John R., 24
Common Sense (Paine), 369
Communism, 26
Communist Manifesto, The (Marx and Engels), 25
Competition, 15, 20, 105, 169, 198, 201
among capitalists, 86
among the core firms, 203–210
defined, 17
in developing a shared monopoly, 207–210
dynamics of, 145–148
and equalization of the profit rate, 148–150

General Electric Company, 141, 178, 200–202, 204, 249, 317
General Foods, 201, 208–209, 213
General Mills, 201
General Motors Corporation, 153, 163, 167, 180, 204, 216, 246, 339, 350
  profit rate of, 108
  profits, 117
General Theory of Employment, Interest and Money, The (Keynes), 29–30
George III, 370
Germany, 118, 333, 335
Government, 27, 29, 97–99, 110
  and after-tax profits, 311–314
  and capitalist development, 12
  defined, 361
  democratic, 300–301, 323
  democratic, and capitalism, 368–372
  economic activities of, 301–305, 337
  economic activity, conflicts of, 311–316
  economic activity and concentration, 307
  economic activity and economic instability, 308–309
  economic activity and environmental protection, 310
  economic activity and income support, 309
  economic activity and international expansion, 307–308
  economic activity and public safety, 309–310
  economic policy, 316. *See also* type of policy, as Fiscal policy
  and the economy, 297–323
  employment, 303
  expansion of, 332–333
  expansion of economic activity, 305–311
  expenditures, 306–307
  leaders, 314
  limited, 370, 380, 390
  as macroeconomic regulator, 304–305
  as microeconomic regulator, 304
  monetarist and Keynesian disagreement on, 360–361
  policies and the after-tax profit rate, 312
  and the political business cycle, 314–316
  as rule enforcer, 301–303
  as rule maker, 303
  rules of organization, 299–301
  and unemployment, 266
Great Britain, 377
Great Depression, 30, 96, 215, 308–309, 325–326, 374
Greece, 379
Growth, 114
  and equality, 382–384
  long-term, and stagnation in the U.S. economy, 324–363
Guatemala, 335

H

Hamilton, Alexander, 85, 303
Hegemony, 334. *See also* United States, hegemony
Hewlett Packard, 248
Hierarchy, 17, 178
  markets and, 175, 195–196
  in the workplace, 178
High tech industries, 320
Hispanic workers, 222–223. *See also* Discrimination; Latin workers; Racial discrimination
Hitler, Adolf, 118
Hosbawm, Eric, 24
Honda, 249
Horizontal relations, 298
Humphreys, General, 85
Hungary, 386
Hunt, 210

I

Idle capacity, 122–123
Imported inputs
  costs of, and recession, 279–280
  real price of, 279–280
Imported materials, costs and the business cycles, 288–289
Income
  distribution of, 377–378
  and the growth of general economic activity, 308
Independent primary labor market, 223. *See also* Segmented labor markets
Independent production of commodities, 90–91, 94
Indians, of North America, 6–7. *See also* Native Americans
Industrial dualism, 199
Industrial unions, 214–218
Industrial Workers of the World, 185
Inflation, 352–354
  and the business cycle, 290–293
  cyclical, 291, 351
  defined, 290, 348
  long-term, 351
  in the 1970s, 327
  price of stopping in 1980–1984, 356–360
  rate, 290–291
  structural, 291, 351
  in the United States, 344–358
Inflation-unemployment trade-off, 292, 351, 356
Innovation, 152. *See also* Technical change
Intensity of labor, 59. *See also* Intensity of work
Intensity of work, 165, 193–194, 393
  and the inefficiency of capitalism, 375
Interest, 106, 108
Interest rate, 144–145, 393
  determination of, 252–253

and the level of investment, 250–251
International Business Machines Corporation (IBM), 152–153, 200, 203, 220, 249, 317
International expansion, and the expansion of government economic activity, 307–308
International Telephone and Telegraph (ITT), 249
Investment, 30, 61, 129, 142–145, 235, 237, 258, 352. *See also* Accumulation
  climate, 318
  and core firms, 213
  cost conditions affecting. *See* Cost conditions affecting investment
  and costs, 145–148
  the decision to invest, 242–248
  defined, 53, 238
  demand conditions affecting. *See* Demand conditions affecting investment
  determinants of, 251–254
  disagreement between monetarists and Keynesians on, 359
  domestic, and world profit rates, 250
  and employment, 258
  expected return from, 143
  foreign, 242
  gross, 238
  investor expectations and, 289
  multiplier, 240
  net, 238
  paper, 238
  and the profit rate, 281–285
  profits and, 241–248
  profits and, in the United States, 347
  and surplus product, 51, 53, 242
  total cost of, 144
  and total demand, 238–241
  total return from, 143
  in the United States, 244
Involuntary unemployment, 27, 171

President's Council of Economic Advisors, The, 391
Price
  of capital goods, 122, 130, 393
  of a machine, 139
  market clearing, 46–47, 49
  materials and machines, 121
  of materials and machines used up per hour of labor, 393
  output, 121, 137–138, 141
  shared monopoly, 206
  per unit of gross output, 393
  per unit of imported goods, 393
  per unit of materials used and machines used up in production, 393
  per unit of net output, 393
  variables, 393
Price competition, 27, 133–137, 142, 208–209
  and the profit rate, 134–135
Price fixing, 304
Price leadership, 205
Price setter, 205
Primary labor market, 222–223. *See also* Segmented labor markets
Privately owned capital goods, 68, 73–75
Private property, among the Arapesh, 74. *See also* Privately owned capital goods
Procter & Gamble, 85, 200, 207–210, 213
Production, 37–38
  for profit, 11
Production possibility frontier, 57–58
Productivity
  growth and the postwar social structure of accumulation, 338–340
  and the growth of productivity, 338–339
Profit, 3, 16, 63, 76–79, 86, 103–107, 143, 242, 392
  and accumulation, 86–89

after-tax, 311–314, 392
commercial, 105–106
core sector, 210–213
defined, 76
in a dual economy, 211
from investing, 144
and investment, 241–248
and the investment in the United States, 347
and the power of employers over workers, 108, 110–113
and the profit rate, 105–108
tax rate on, 312
total, 108–109
total, per employed person, 109
and unions, 219
in the United States, 109
per unit of output, 138
uses of, by U.S. firms, 242
Profitability
  defined, 194
  versus efficiency, 194–195
Profit rate, 104–109, 160, 235, 237, 293. *See also* Expected profit rate
  after-tax, 311–314, 328–329
  after-tax corporate, in the United States, 329
  average, 133
  and breakthroughs, 139–148
  on capital goods in use, 133–137
  defined, 106
  determinants of. *See* Determinants of the profit rate
  equalization of, 129, 148–151
  equation, 116–117, 148–151
  on investment, 143, 281–285
  and price competition, 133–136
  and technical change, 182
Property rights, 68, 73, 303
  defined, 67
Prudential Insurance, 203
Public safety, and the growth of government economic activity, 309–310

workers, 214, 222–224, 227
work of, and men's work, 226–227
Work, 16, 155–173
  effort, 160–161, 163. *See also* Work done
  effort and unemployment, 277
  extraction of, from workers, 162–169
  intensity of, 175. *See also* Work, effort; Work done
  social organization of, 178
  undemocratic control of, 381
  women's, and men's work, 226–227
Work done, 120, 125–126, 130, 164–165, 172. *See also* Work, effort; Work, intensity of
  contract specifying, 167–168
  defined, 122
  determination of, 192–194
  expected, per hours, 244
  per hour, 393
Workers, 3, 16, 26, 75, 105, 175, 184, 266, 314. *See also* Wage labor; Working class
  auto, 222
  blue-collar, 218
  and capitalist development, 10
  capitalists and, 184
  conflict between employers and, 114, 159–162
  defined, 79

and employers, 192, 194
extraction of work from, 157, 162–169
health of, 21
profits and the power of employers over, 108, 110–113
service sector, 218
skilled, 10, 214
and unions, 189. *See also* Unions
white-collar, 218
Working class, 92–93
  defined, 79
Workplace, 113, 153, 174–175, 185–197
  conflict in, 184–185
  safety in, 339
  social organization of, 176–182
World Bank, 71
World capitalist system, 235
  accumulation in, 248–251
World War II, 308, 327, 362

X

Xerox, 153

Y

Yugoslavia, 389